# THE
# Adirondack Guideboat

THE

# Adirondack Guideboat

ITS ORIGINS
ITS BUILDERS
AND THEIR BOATS

Stephen B. Sulavik

*with revisions and additions by*

Edward Comstock, Jr., and Christopher H. Woodward

BAUHAN PUBLISHING • PETERBOROUGH • NEW HAMPSHIRE

2018

**Second printing, June 2024**

Library of Congress Cataloging-in-Publication Data
Names: Sulavik, Stephen B., author. | Comstock, Jr., Edward, 1943, Adirondack historian. | Woodward, Christopher H., guideboat builder.
Title: The Adirondack guideboat : its origins, its builders, and their boats / Stephen B. Sulavik ; with revisions and additions by Edward Comstock, Jr, and Christopher H. Woodward.
Identifiers: LCCN 2018027600 | ISBN 9780872332607 (alk. paper)
Subjects: LCSH: Adirondack guideboats—History. | Adirondack guideboats—Design and construction.
Classification: LCC VM355 .S85 2018 | DDC 623.82/9—dc23
Remaining LOC information and LC record available at https://lccn.loc.gov/2018027600

Book design by Henry James and Sarah Bauhan
Cover design by Henry James
Front cover photograph by Christopher H. Woodward, used by permission
Frontispiece photograph by Seneca Ray Stoddard: "Haystack Mountain from Upper Ausable Pond, 1880," Courtesy of Adirondack Museum
Back cover photograph "On the beach across from the Island House," Long Lake, circa 1900, Courtesy of Adirondack Museum

*The Adirondack Guideboat* is co-published by the Adirondack Experience and Bauhan Publishing.

ADIRONDACK EXPERIENCE™
The Museum on Blue Mountain Lake
(Formerly the Adirondack Museum)
9097 NY-30,
Blue Mountain Lake, NY 12812
www.theadkx.org

BAUHAN PUBLISHING LLC
PO BOX 117 PETERBOROUGH NEW HAMPSHIRE 03458
WWW.BAUHANPUBLISHING.COM

Printed in the United States of America by Versa Press

## DEDICATION FOR SECOND PRINTING

Readying this encyclopedic monograph for publication was a collective effort as the Acknowledgments in the first printing of this book (2018) made clear. This year, with the arrival of a second printing, the book's two major supporters—Robert R. Worth and Sidney S. Whelan, Jr.—deserve a special salute. For years both had been involved one way *and* another with the Adirondack Experience (formerly the Adirondack Museum). Plus each was a longstanding admirer of that unique regional craft—the Adirondack guideboat. Sadly, neither of them is with us today. But without their steadfast support, this book would never have seen the light of an Adirondack day.

Many thanks to Bob and Sid.

—Ted Comstock and Chris Woodward, 2024

## ADDITIONAL ACKNOWLEDGMENT

This second printing of *The Adirondack Guideboat* was made possible by the Robert R. Worth Fund of the Adirondack Experience, The Museum on Blue Mountain Lake. The Fund was established by family, friends, and colleagues as a memorial to Robert R. Worth, a long-time supporter, trustee, and chairman of the Museum's board. The book itself is the product of endless skilled editorial efforts by Bob together with his collaborators to produce this definitive history of the iconic watercraft of the Adirondacks.

A Saranac boat is one of the finest things that the skill of man has ever produced under the inspiration of the wilderness. It is a frail shell, so light that a guide can carry it on his shoulders with ease, but so dexterously fashioned that it rides the heaviest waves like a duck, and slips through the water as if by magic. You can travel in it along the shallowest rivers and across the broadest lakes, and make forty or fifty miles a day, if you have a good guide.

—Henry Van Dyke, "Ampersand" in *Little Rivers,* 1895

## DEDICATION

The traditional art of building guideboats is being preserved. It survives, and thrives, in the work of the four present-day builders—Jim Cameron, Fuat Latif, Rob Frenette, and Christopher Woodward— to whom this book is dedicated. Three are local sons who grew up with the heritage and tradition of using and repairing guideboats, each in their respective locales. They represent a continuum of the craft, not a revival. Each has learned the time-honored way, by working at the side of their elders, or from direct observation of their craft. All four have chosen this line of work—not only to save the guideboat for future generations—but because it provided a modest income (one that needed supplement from other sources) from work that satisfied their passion for creating a wooden boat that could be completed by a single craftsman in a small shop. They stand with any of the builders of the nineteenth and twentieth centuries as to their authenticity.

—Stephen B. Sulavik

2013

Guide carrying his boat, Blue Mountain Lake, circa 1884. Photograph by Edward Bierstadt. (Courtesy of Adirondack Museum)

# CONTENTS

# ACKNOWLEDGMENTS

During the decades-long research that culminated in this book, many individuals aided Stephen Sulavik. At the author's death in 2015, the manuscript remained a rough draft without, among other components, proper acknowledgments. To those who helped bolster this encyclopedic history, it is insufficient to note that you know who you are, but unfortunately that will have to suffice. You are guideboat enthusiasts and collectors, camp owners and caretakers, relatives and descendants of builders profiled in these pages, as well as authors and historians with an interest in traditional small craft and in the Adirondack past. You are also past and present stewards of public collections—including curators, librarians, and archivists—at museums and historical societies across New York State and beyond. Thanks to each of you for your information, insights, and support. You made a difference.

Over a period of almost twenty years, friends of the Adirondack Museum have provided financial support for this project, initially to assist the author and then to bring the book to publication. They are:

Daniel Catlin, Jr.
John Colston
Christopher W. Covert, Jr.
Joan K. Davidson and Furthermore, a program of the J. M. Kaplan Fund
The late Richard J. Fay
John G. Fritzinger, Jr.
Beatrice Garvan
Lee and Nancy Keet
Allan P. Newell
William J. Nolan III
Mark and Victoria Oliva
David F. Remington
Craig R. Smith
The Stephen B. Sulavik Family
Anne H. Van Ingen
Sidney S. Whelan, Jr.
James H. Worth
Robert R. Worth
The late William A. Worth, Jr.

Finally, we would like to thank David Kahn and everyone at the Adirondack Museum (now the Adirondack Experience). We have been extraordinarily lucky to have so much help from all the staff as well as access to all the archives.

Indian Head, Lower Ausable Lake, Adirondacks, 1889, by Seneca Ray Stoddard. (Courtesy of Adirondack Museum)

# FOREWORD BY BOB WORTH

I FIRST BEGAN ROWING guideboats up and down the Lower Ausable Lake in the early 1960s. The vast quiet, oars the only sound, silvery water dripping off the blades; all around the steep sides of mountains, dark pines, blue distances—a spellbinding experience. Soon thereafter I got deeply involved with the Adirondack Museum. Sidney Whelan, whom I met through the museum, knew of my career in textbook publishing and thought of me when Dr. Sulavik asked to whom he might turn for help with a book he was writing.

The book was *Adirondack: Of Indians and Mountains, 1535–1838*. Steve and I were a good team. He did all the work, the extensive research, and the writing; I tidied up and helped to get the book published. So it was natural that he asked me to help with the more ambitious project he had been working on for many years, the story of the Adirondack guideboat, the region that made it possible, and the men who built it.

Dr. Sulavik came to his passion for guideboats through fishing and camping trips to the Adirondacks with his family in the 1960s and 1970s. In September 1991 he visited the Adirondack Museum to examine its boatbuilders files and its large collection of guideboats. This work was facilitated by the museum's librarian, Jerry Pepper, and its curator, Caroline Welsh. He also relied on the few living guideboat experts and builders, not only for their understanding of guideboat construction but for their knowledge of where he could find existing boats and who the past builders were. The writings of John Gardner, Kenneth Durant, Hallie Bond, and others were important sources. His own contributions were his industry, his intelligence, his stick-to-it-iveness, and his quest to come up with a procedure for determining the identity of a particular boat's builder. Not only was he a thorough researcher, he took photographs of a great many guideboats, particularly of the components that are helpful in their identification: deck caps, stem posts, scribe ribs, and so forth.

In preparing the manuscript Steve was greatly assisted by his son-in-law, Klaus Peters, a professor of computer science at Southern Connecticut State University, who made it possible for the manuscript to be illustrated with color photographs. Steve would send portions of the manuscript to me, I would edit them and send them back with questions, he would fix my editing and answer the questions. Sometimes the manuscript would go back and forth many times.

I would then send it to Sally Anderson, an editor I greatly respect. She not only copy-edited and prepared a style sheet, but also raised insightful questions about clarity and flow.

When that draft was complete, I had copies made and sent for review to Adirondack historians, guideboat builders, and wooden boat historians, namely: Hallie Bond, Maynard Bray, Sharon Brown, Jim Cameron, Ted Comstock, Rob Frenette, Ben Fuller, Fuat Latif, Ed Lynch, Peter Vermilya, Sidney Whelan, and Chris Woodward.

It was obvious from the reviews that the project was too ambitious. Precursors of the guideboat going back to the Thames River wherry, the captain's gig, the New York Whitehall, and the birchbark canoe were all included, plus the guideboat's antecedents: the bateau and the dory—also quite a few tidbits of Adirondack history. All interesting but too tangential for a book centered on guideboats.

Also, what I had assumed to be the complete manuscript turned out to be missing some essential components. A unique contribution of Steve's work, for example, was the protocol he had been devising for discerning which builder was most likely to have built a particular boat—what is now, with the input of Chris Woodward, Part Three of this book. Several reviewers knew of this work and its absence was noted.

Steve was naturally discouraged by the reviews, especially as he was in poor health and had great difficulty getting about. It was questionable whether he would be up to making full use of the reviewers' criticisms and suggestions. Some assistance would clearly be helpful, so I sent the first part of the manuscript to Anne MacKinnon, a birthright Adirondacker who I had been told was a brilliant editor. I asked her to pare it down to the essentials and reorganize it. She more than lived up to her reputation by doing so and explaining her work so persuasively that Steve accepted it wholeheartedly.

Sadly, soon after being encouraged by Anne's work but before he could take up her advice on what to attend to next, Steve died unexpectedly. It was April of 2015. The manuscript was not ready for publication, but it would have been a terrible shame to abandon the important contribution his work represented.

The entire manuscript had to be gone through, line by line, for accuracy. All the hundreds of references included in parentheses that made reading difficult had to be corrected and converted into footnotes. Who could do all that? Not only who would be able, who would be willing? It was clear that no single person had the required expertise about guideboats and their construction, and also the broad historical knowledge of the Adirondacks. It had to be a team. I decided to approach Ted Comstock and Chris Woodward, both living and working in Saranac Lake. Each had provided crucial assistance to Steve over the many years he had been learning about guideboats. What's more, they both respected what he had accomplished.

At considerable sacrifice, Ted and Chris committed themselves to the project. Their goal throughout has been to realize the potential of what Steve was cut short from finishing. Throughout this long process, we have relied on the enthusiastic support and guidance of Caroline Welsh, former curator and director of the Adirondack Museum. How fortunate we have been to have found in Bauhan Publishing the perfect publisher for this book. Sarah Bauhan, Henry James, and Mary Ann Faughnan, have been more than up to every curve we have thrown at them. Their good spirits, their responsiveness, their brilliant design sense, the long hours they have uncomplainingly spent in placing and, where possible, enhancing the many photos essential to tell this story—working with them has been a pleasure throughout.

More than once in the three years since Steve's death, we have wondered whether the job could ever be done to our satisfaction. It is with tremendous relief that I now believe Ted and Chris have succeeded. Steve would, I feel confident, be pleased with the result.

—Robert R. Worth
August 2018

The Sagamore Hotel on Long Lake, from the north. Photograph by Seneca Ray Stoddard, circa 1880. (Courtesy of Adirondack Museum)

## SULAVIK FAMILY PREFACE

STEPHEN B. SULAVIK was raised in New Haven, Connecticut, an industrial city located some 250 miles southeast of the unspoiled beauty of the Adirondack High Peaks. His love of the Adirondacks and of fishing, in particular, did not develop until his time at Georgetown Medical School, where he met our mother Jeanne, a native of Tupper Lake, New York. Our father's first contact with the Adirondack Park was during the mid-1950s when he visited our mother's parents, Charles and Mary Abdallah. Our grandparents owned and operated the Northland Hotel from 1935 until 1960, which was located in downtown Tupper Lake, and named after the surveyor, Ansel Tupper (who drowned there while fishing). One of the great pleasures our father enjoyed most in "Tupper" was fly-fishing. He would hike nearly five miles into Horseshoe Pond, fish all day, catching and releasing creel after creel of native brook trout (and no doubt displaying his preternatural oblivion to swarms of mosquitos and blackflies).

During the 1960s and early 1970s, our family summered at the Sagamore Hotel in Long Lake. The Sagamore was owned and operated by our grandfather's brother, Abbot J. Abdallah. When the hotel was demolished in the 1960s, our family stayed in the boathouse that still stands on the causeway side of the lake not far from the Adirondack Hotel. This afforded all of us the chance to indulge in our father's passion for the Adirondacks—boating, swimming, fishing—and garnet-gathering. It was during these years that he first saw—and fished from—guideboats, despite their fading use as motorized boats became the convention. His love of the outdoors also took him on fishing trips throughout the Adirondacks, New England, and beyond, to Labrador for Arctic char; to the Miramichi, the famed salmon river in New Brunswick; and even into the wilds of the Amazon for piranha, while on a medical mission in Brazil. Yet, the Adirondacks were home.

Our father was the right person for this book. He possessed an intense desire to teach others. He had an acute mind, an infallible memory, an effervescent intellectual curiosity, a lucid articulation of complex histories, and a firm resolve to see a mystery fully and thoroughly revealed and understood. These attributes shone in so many ways during his life. A clinical professor of medicine at Yale University by profession, he followed a near-daily regimen of waking up early every morning (well before his eight children got up) and spent hours "reading" slides of lung tissue and X-ray images. This was a different sort of reading—a search for visual clues, patterns, a divining of signs to inform diagnoses. In this language, he was fluent, and he was one of the best. One of his most profound contributions to medicine was to impart to legions of medical students and colleagues the incontrovertible and unerring ways to read X-rays that would lead to a proper conclusion. Similarly, far from the clinic, he taught his children how to "read" a river to suss out trout, or to assess which feeding channels would most likely reveal a lurking northern pike or largemouth bass. Indeed, he had quite a gift of seeing, literally and figuratively, beneath the surface of things.

Those same diagnostic skills—whether used as physician or fisherman—were fully brought to bear when he was faced with the task of understanding and discovering the signature marks on a guideboat that correctly revealed its builder. At the end of his medical career and during his retirement, he poured his energies into researching the history of the Adirondacks, culminating in his first non-medical book, *Adirondack: Of Indians and Mountains, 1535–1838* (Purple Mountain Press, 2007), an early history of the region. Along the way, he also became an expert on identifying guideboats, and had long planned that his next project would be to focus on the indigenous craft that helped shape the development of the region. Those efforts, many years in the making, resulted in this book.

Boat by boat, builder by builder, he started exerting an order upon what had been a balkanized yet connected history. He had taken thousands of photographs, of hundreds of Adirondack guideboats, repeating the same approach he used in collecting and cataloguing medical imagery. He systematically studied the slides until they slowly gave up their secrets and that is what he most relished. As a professor and teacher, he was aware that his work was for the benefit of posterity. But, more important, he appreciated that it might offer a sheer pleasure of learning. "This is a book," he once said, "I would have enjoyed reading had it already been written."

Our father spent the best years of his retirement and leisure on this book. His commitment can best be summed up in the paraphrased words of Cicero: "When a man commits his thoughts to paper, arranges them well, writes them agreeably, and furnishes pleasure to the reader, he wisely uses both his leisure and his paper."

Our father passed away peacefully at his home in Canton Center, Connecticut, on April 9, 2015. The completion of this book and its publication was entrusted to people who have labored to finish the good work that my father began more than thirty years ago. Bob Worth, founder of Worth Publishers, corresponded with my father for many years, kindly offering insightful advice and editing suggestions that improved the quality, clarity, and structure of this work, and who personally underwrote editing and publishing costs over many years. Our father always had in Bob a friend, an editor, and a tireless cheerleader. Caroline M. Welsh, former director of the Adirondack Museum, long supported my father's research by giving him access to the collection of Adirondack boats housed at the museum. The completion of the manuscript was entrusted to Ted Comstock and Chris Woodward, both of whom have encyclopedic knowledge of Adirondack history and guideboat building and who each supported the author's efforts for over twenty years. Their fact-checking this book and meticulously combing through it to remove any imperfections have helped to achieve our father's dream.

—Andrew T. Sulavik
August 2018

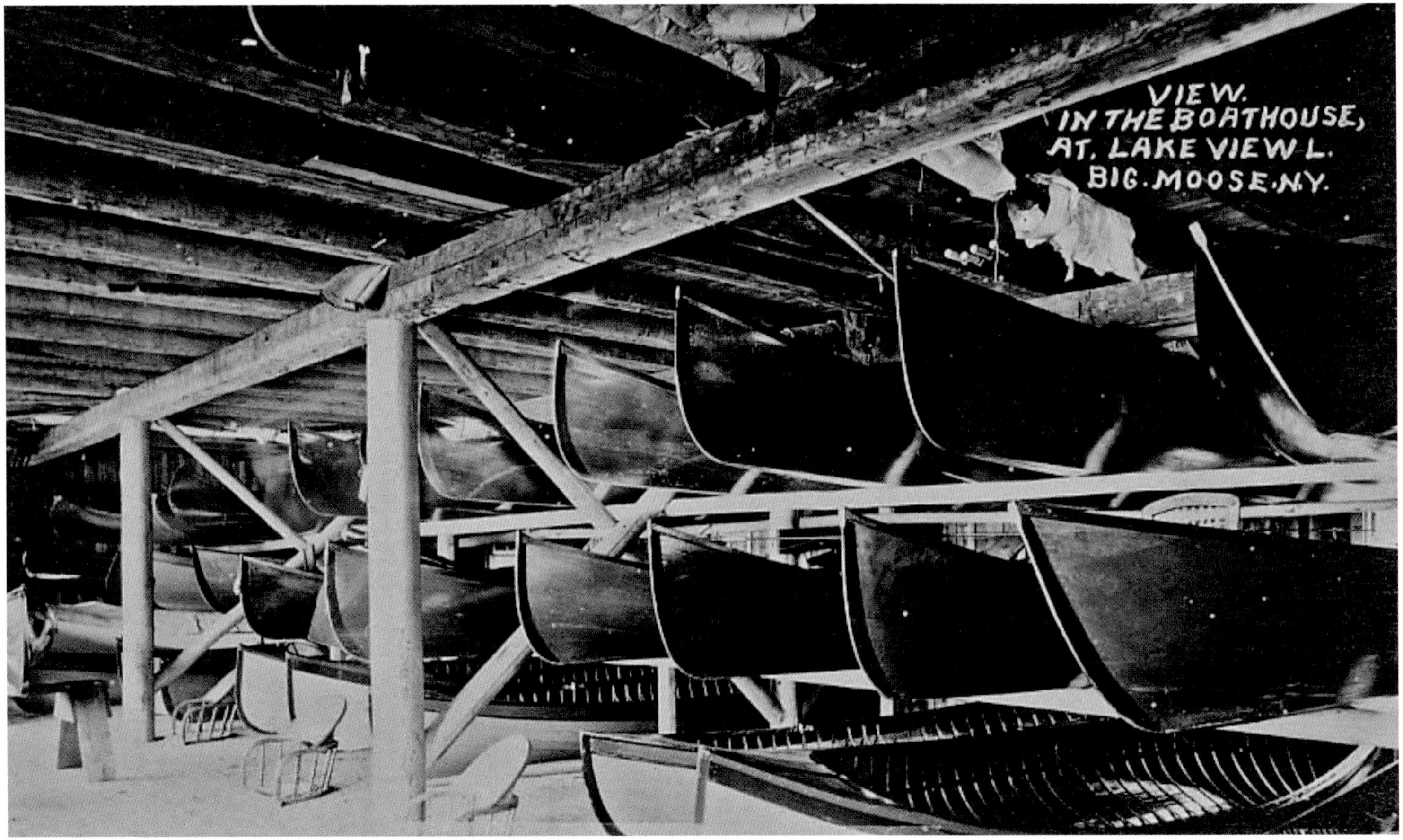


Boathouse at Lake View Lodge, Big Moose, NY. Photograph by H. M. Beach, circa 1915. (Courtesy of Adirondack Museum)

# PREFACE BY TED COMSTOCK

I FIRST MET Stephen Sulavik in June 1996 at the annual No-Octane Regatta organized by the Adirondack Museum on the shore of Blue Mountain Lake. I recall that he and I were soon comparing notes about our mutual fascination with the Adirondack guideboat. A few weeks later, Stephen wrote to ask me for "any help, advice, etc." regarding his research on the history of the boat and its builders. By that time, I had had a stint as a curator at the Adirondack Museum followed by a decade as co-owner of a store in Old Forge that specialized in items representing the best of the Adirondack past, which naturally included vintage wooden pulling and paddling boats.

That spring day, I told Stephen I was at present an independent historian and editorial consultant who also brokered and appraised antique guideboats. I said I was ready and willing to help and offered him access to my boat research files, sales records, and appraisal reports (totaling more than 200 guideboats).

Thus began two decades of my support for what I felt was exciting new research. As we got to know one another, we developed a sometimes-challenging push-me–pull-you relationship. He was the close-focus diagnostician, and I, the student of Adirondack material culture with a longstanding admiration for the unique regional carry boat.

In 2001, the museum's boat committee offered me a stipend to work with Stephen to determine the feasibility of publishing his research and, more important, whether it warranted publishing at all. In my report to the committee, I included an unqualified "yes" to both of the above. As Stephen's onsite researcher and go-fer, I continued to track down fresh examples of old boats and now and then uncovered new bits about relationships among builders and their boats. I also introduced the author to a number of my contacts, such as collectors and camp owners; plus, I visited historical societies, libraries, and village archives across the North Country on his behalf.

At the time of his death in April 2015, Stephen had completed a rough draft of the present book. Since then, thanks to the commitment of Robert R. Worth and Sidney S. Whelan, Jr., the manuscript has been able to be given the additional attention it so clearly deserved. It was Bob Worth who convinced Christopher Woodward, builder and restorer of traditional guideboats in Saranac Lake, and me to work together on the project. Chris and I, with umpteen editorial consultations with Bob, each tallied many hundreds of hours reviewing and reshaping the draft manuscript Stephen left us. While most are not enumerated, our "revisions and additions" have bolstered the author's work in ways we believe he would have approved. The result is this expansive monograph, a worthy companion to Kenneth and Helen Durant's *The Adirondack Guide-Boat.*

—Edward Comstock, Jr.
August 2018

# PREFACE BY CHRIS WOODWARD

DR. STEPHEN SULAVIK first visited my shop one day in the early 1990s, inquiring about the maker of a particular guideboat that he had rowed. Stephen explained how he had undertaken a project to identify every major builder and their boats. The boys in the shop "politely" laughed and wished him good luck. I gave him our standard line at that time, that unless the boat had a tag (builder's plate) on it, it was impossible to tell exactly who the builder was. However, I pointed out that there were boats with certain similarities that appeared to have been built by the same builders. Bloomingdale boats were easy to identify by the stem profiles. Each builder "signed" their work with the different cuts and shaping of components like the stem post, the stem foot, and the deck designs. Some builders were more readily identifiable than others. Willard Hanmer, for example, was easily identifiable by his decks, especially those with a handhold cut into them.

Over the next twenty-five years, Stephen would stop in and ask questions about guideboats and whether I had ever seen a boat built by this builder, if I had heard of that one, or had any information about another. The questions that he asked were always pointed and showed a true interest and respect for the boats and for the locals that built them, along with the desire to learn anything he could about the subject. I was always willing to take the time to teach him about the construction of these boats, and to show him the components that were critical for identifying a particular builder. Reciprocally, he was always forthcoming with information and taught me what I was looking at in regards to which builders used which specific details.

When Stephen finished his first draft, I was one of the reviewers who critiqued his effort. With our suggestions, he started his second revision, but, unfortunately, passed away before he could complete a final draft.

His biographies of the many boatbuilders, and the compilation of the characteristics and details of their extant boats are invaluable contributions to the history and culture of the Adirondacks. I was honored to be asked to help revise Stephen's work to put the information into a publishable product.

I have tried to remain true to Dr. Sulavik's vision, using his words as much as possible, so as to keep his voice in the forefront as he detailed the builders and catalogued their works.

—Christopher H. Woodward
August 2018

Among the many people who have provided help with this project, we would like, in particular, to thank Ivy Gocker, library director, and Angela Snye, former assistant curator, both at the Adirondack Museum, and Michele A.Tucker, curator, Adirondack Research Room, Saranac Lake Free Library.

—Edward Comstock, Jr.
—Christopher H. Woodward
August 2018

## INTRODUCTION BY STEPHEN B. SULAVIK

> Light, tough, and durable, the guide boat is the finest woodsman's boat ever built. . . . a work boat with the finish of a violin and the delicacy of a watch . . . unexcelled by any small-craft type anywhere.
>
> —John Gardner, *Outdoor Maine,* August 1960

KNOWLEDGE OF THE Adirondack guideboat's superb craftsmanship—its beauty, grace, lightness, durability, and speed—has existed for a century and a half. As this book will show, the guideboat, skillfully built by early guides and boatbuilders, is a uniquely American boat whose beauty has been captured in paintings by Winslow Homer, among others. This national icon has represented the United States in many exhibitions, both at home and abroad.[1]

The rich history surrounding the boat must not be lost; it forms the basis of this work—an attempt to tell this important story from a new perspective. Here you will find a wealth of information about the guideboat's origins, the personal lives and milieu of its builders, and the distinctive characteristics of their boats.

In the 1950s, as metal and plastic began to replace wood on most waters, knowledge of the history and importance of the guideboat was becoming all but obsolete. Fortunately, however, in the 1950s and 1960s, a series of events brought about a vigorous revival of interest in these unique boats.

On August 4, 1957, the Adirondack Museum in Blue Mountain Lake, New York, opened to the public. The museum was founded and supported by Harold K. Hochschild, chairman of the board of the American Metal Company and author of *Township 34*, a history of the area surrounding Blue Mountain Lake. With guidance

1 Examples include the 1876 Centennial Exposition in Philadelphia; the 1880 International Fisheries Exhibition in Berlin; the 1899 and 1900 Sportsman's Show in Madison Square Garden, New York; the 1904 Louisiana Purchase Exposition in St. Louis; and the 1967 International and Universal Exposition (Expo 67) in Montreal.

from Hochschild and the museum's first director, Robert Bruce Inverarity, the Adirondack guideboat became the centerpiece of one of the principal collections around which the new museum was organized "in view of the contribution this remarkable craft had made to the culture and development of the Adirondack region."[2]

The revival of enthusiasm for small wooden craft had been set in motion in 1951 with the publication of *American Small Sailing Craft* by Howard I. Chapelle, who was the curator of maritime history at the Smithsonian Institution in Washington. Most important, however, for the rekindling of interest in the traditional Adirondack guideboat were two articles in the fall of 1960 by John Gardner in the magazine *Outdoor Maine*. The articles described the guideboat's historical significance and extolled, with the help of drawings, its lines and beauty. In 1968, Gardner joined the staff at the Mystic Seaport Museum in Mystic, Connecticut, as associate curator and became a leader in the revival of interest in traditional small wooden craft.

Gardner's 1960 pieces had been preceded and were followed by numerous articles on other types of small wooden boats in *Maine Coast Fisherman*, *Outdoor Maine*, *National Fisherman*, *The Log of Mystic Seaport*—and finally, in the first issue of *WoodenBoat* in September 1974. These articles demonstrated clearly, step-by-step, the technical procedures used in the building of traditional small wooden craft—with details and directions complete enough to be followed by an amateur builder. Efforts to keep this craftsmanship alive came to fruition in 1969, when Edmund Lynch, curator at Mystic, asked Gardner to develop a wooden boatbuilding program at the museum. This curriculum, the first of its kind, began in the winter of 1969–1970.

On January 24 and 25 of 1975, at the suggestion of Sidney S. Whelan, Jr., with the support of Harold Hochschild and museum director Craig Gilborn, a meeting of Adirondack guideboat builders, among them Carl Hathaway and Ralph Morrow; and enthusiasts, including John Gardner, Helen Durant, and Atwood Manley, was held at the Adirondack Museum. The main consideration was the future of the traditionally built guideboat in the context of the growing use of other boatbuilding materials

2 John Gardner, "A Brief Look at Small Craft and Maritime Museums: Past, Present And Future," Museum Small Craft Association Annual Meeting, Mystic Seaport Museum, Mystic, CT, October 9, 1993.

An exhibit of guideboats in the Callahan Memorial Boat Building of the Adirondack Museum. The centerpiece represents Adirondack guide Albert "Ab" Hall of Indian Lake, New York, carrying a guideboat (posed for in the 1960s). The museum's original logo also depicts an Adirondack guide carrying a guideboat. (Courtesy of Adirondack Museum)

and methods. Wisely, the participants unanimously favored the continued use of traditional materials and methods "to keep the old traditions alive."

The publication of two scholarly works on the subject, classics in their own right—Kenneth Durant's *Guide-Boat Days and Ways* in 1963 and, particularly, Kenneth and Helen Durant's *The Adirondack Guide-Boat* in 1980—provided national recognition of the guideboat's existence and excellence.

During the winters of 1980–1988, North Country Community College of Saranac Lake offered the Adirondack Guideboat Apprenticeship Program, conceived by Dr. Murray Heller, assisted by Robert Klein, and supported by the National Endowment for the Arts. This proved to be one of the most significant contributions to preserving the craft of building Adirondack guideboats. Carl Hathaway and Ralph Morrow, both Saranac Lake master guideboat builders, taught students to reproduce an early builder's boat using traditional wooden patterns, methods, and materials. Fortunately, graduates of this program are still building and restoring finely crafted guideboats in the traditional manner today.

Of late, there has been a striking increase in the marketing of small pleasure and sporting craft. Some are described as guideboats, but although their hull shape is similar, their basic structure bears little or no resemblance to traditionally built craft. As a result, the materials, techniques, and craftsmanship involved in the construction of the classic guideboat, along with its cultural history, are again in danger of fading away. As a consequence, this "gallant craft" has become all the more highly prized by its aficionados, who have been eager to extend and broaden knowledge of its appeal. In particular, the continuing work of the Adirondack Museum under the leadership of former director, Caroline Welsh, and former curator of boats, Hallie Bond, has been an important factor, exemplified by its unequaled guideboat collection and its Boatbuilder-in-Residence program. Every summer, a guideboat is constructed in a workshop at the museum using the same tools and methods as those used a century ago, and the boatbuilder is available to answer questions and explain what she (in recent years, Allison Warner), or he, is doing.

And, of course, there is the commitment and skill of current builders and restorers, as well as the pride in and use of the craft by owners and collectors.

All of the above keep alive the legacy of the Adirondack guideboat, its craftsmanship, and its culture. It is important that the dedication of these groups continue so that traditionally built guideboats may continue to be seen on the lakes and rivers of the Adirondacks.

Also important is the preservation of the many guideboats—some a century old or older—in too poor a condition to be waterborne. These aged boats reveal minute details of their construction and also bear the scars of wounds endured during their active lives—poignant reminders of a vanishing culture.

Articles in magazines and books that mention Adirondack camps are primarily concerned with the architecture of the buildings and the design of their furnishings, both of which reflect what their affluent nonresident owners thought a "wilderness" camp should be. Other than rustic furniture and/or mounted trophies of wildlife, little is found in their great rooms that exemplifies actual Adirondack culture or the creativity of its people. The hallmark of Adirondack ingenuity—the guideboat—is often hidden from view in a distant boathouse or barn loft. It is a pleasure to see a guideboat, old and unusable as it may be, gracing a wall or ceiling in the great room of an Adirondack camp.

This book has been written not only to tell the story of this unique and admirable boat, but also to recognize and celebrate the inventiveness of its original builders and the singular culture of their time and place.

—Stephen B. Sulavik
2013

# ILLUSTRATED INTRODUCTION

What follows is an introduction to the traditional Adirondack guideboat by way of illustrations. The intention is that readers unfamiliar with the names of various boat parts will not be left in the dark when these terms are used in the text. A glossary of terms follows.

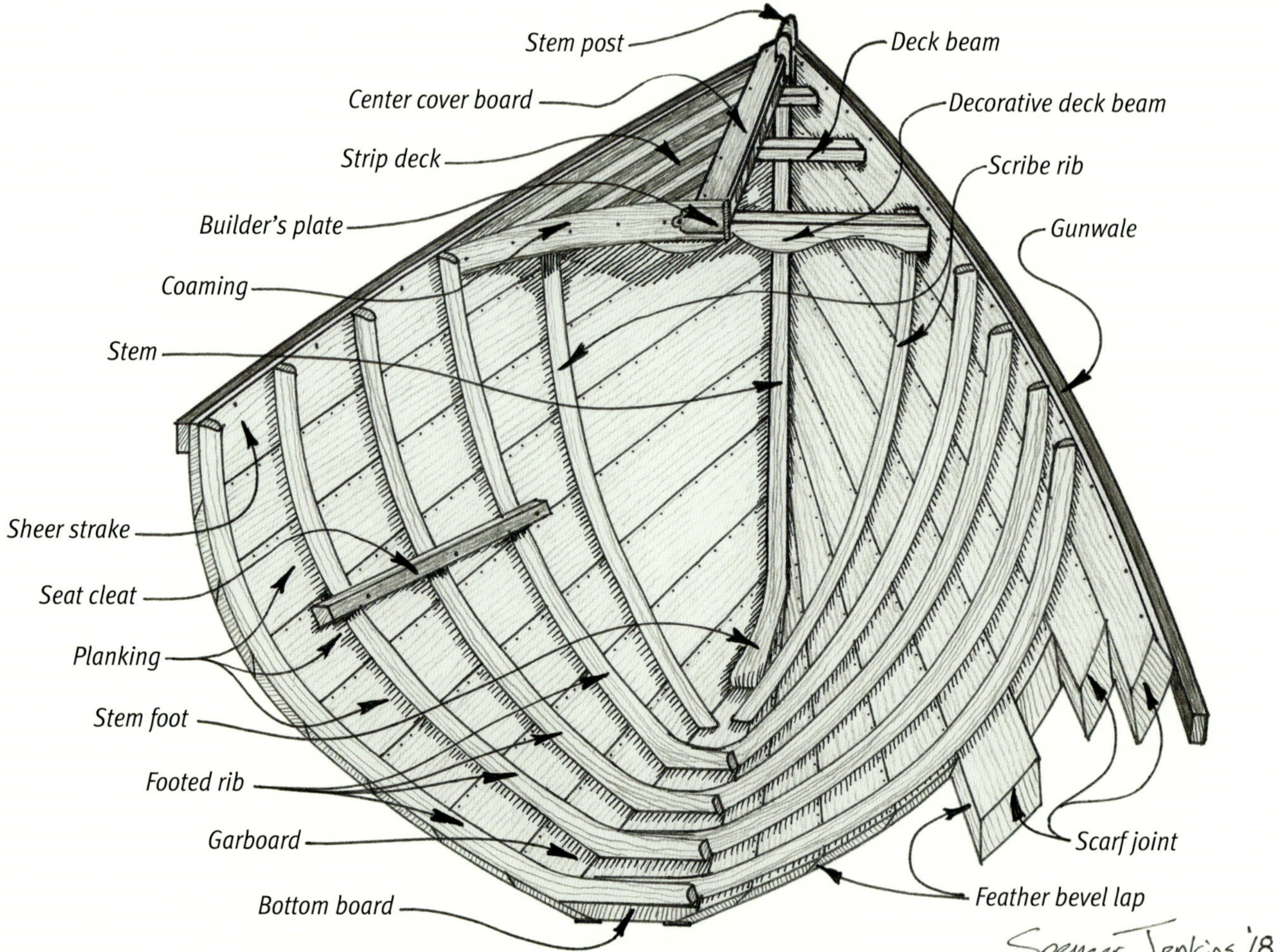

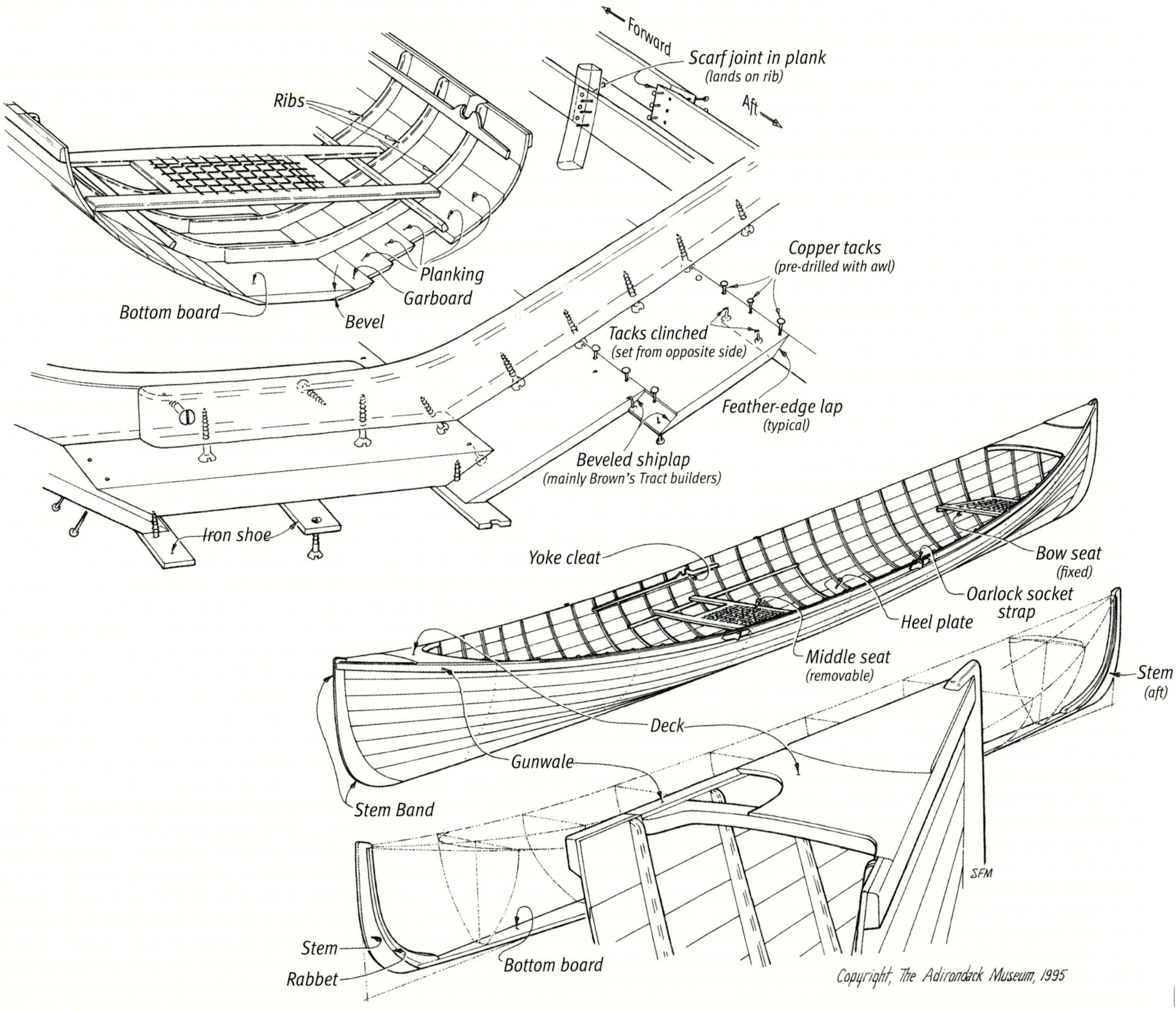
Forward
Aft
Scarf joint in plank
(lands on rib)
Ribs
Planking
Garboard
Bottom board
Bevel
Copper tacks
(pre-drilled with awl)
Tacks clinched
(set from opposite side)
Feather-edge lap
(typical)
Beveled shiplap
(mainly Brown's Tract builders)
Iron shoe
Yoke cleat
Bow seat
(fixed)
Oarlock socket
strap
Heel plate
Middle seat
(removable)
Stem
(aft)
Deck
Gunwale
Stem Band
SFM
Stem
Rabbet
Bottom board
Copyright, The Adirondack Museum, 1995

# Glossary

**backrest**
A wooden frame filled with woven rattan cane, used by a passenger for support. (see also **seat**)

**bateau** (plural, **bateaux**)
A flat-bottomed boat with raked bow and stern and flaring sides.

**bead**
A narrow, half-round molding, or an incised line, located on the gunwales and also on the carlins of some guideboats.

**beam**
The greatest width between the sheer planks of a boat.

**bearding line** (see **rabbet line**)

**bevel**
To cut at an angle that is not a right angle.

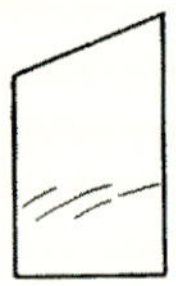

Figure G-1 Bevel

**bilge**
The internal part of a boat below the water line.

**board seats**
Seats made from a single flat board.

**bottom board**
The elliptical-shaped, flat board that is the bottom of the boat, to which the ribs and stems are attached.

**bow seat** (see **seat**)

**camber (crown)**
The slightly arched surface of the deck.

**carlin**
The curved transverse piece attached to a deck beam that supports the inboard edge of the deck. It may be one piece bent to shape, or two pieces sawn to shape.

Figure G-2 Carlin, attached to a deck beam

**carry**
A trail between two bodies of water over which a boat is transported. Also, the act of transporting a guideboat, using a yoke. The term "portage" was not used in the Adirondacks.

**carvel built**
Hull construction method with the planks lying edge-to-edge along their lengths resulting in a smooth surface, rather than overlapping as in the lapstrake method.

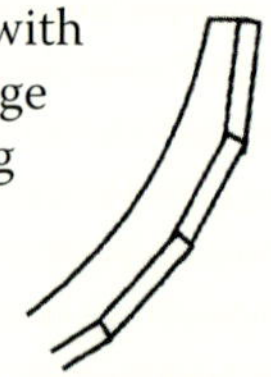

Figure G-3 Carvel planking

**center cover board**
A thin, longitudinal strip covering the middle seam of a two-piece or strip-built deck.

**chamfer**
To bevel part of the edge of a seat, rib, gunwale, cover board, or deck. On a strip deck, two adjacent chamfers create a V-groove.

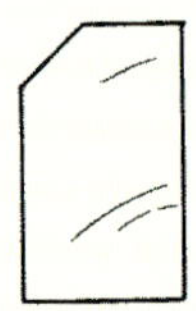

Figure G-4 Chamfer

**clapboard lapstrake**
(see **lapstrake built**)

**cleats**
Short pieces of wood that run lengthwise inside the hull, attached to the ribs, to support the seats and the yoke. (see **seat cleats** and **yoke cleats**)

**coaming**
A thin facing piece, bent and attached to the carlin or deck. It rises slightly above the deck to cover and protect the end grain of the deck pieces, and to help shed water.

**crook**
The portion of a tree where the vertical trunk curves into the horizontal root. Also the slab taken from this section, that the ribs and stems are sawn from. Also referred to as a knee.

**deadrise**
The angle of rise of the boat's hull from the bottom board.

**decks**
Horizontal wooden structures at the ends of a boat, flush with the gunwales. They may be one piece, two pieces, or more. When a deck is made up of a series of thin, parallel pieces, it is a strip deck. Decks may have a design characteristic of a particular builder.

A deck can be:

(a) let into the gunwales.
(b) mitered into the gunwales
(c) set between the gunwales
(d) set between the sheer strakes

Decks are commonly referred to as having either a straight or an arced (circle) inboard edge. A straight deck was typical of early guideboats.

(5a)
(5b)
(5c)
(5d)

Figure G-5 Deck placement (for more information on deck placement, see page 317)

(6a)
(6b)
(6c)

(6d)
(6e)

Figure G-6 Decks and deck caps. (a) A straight, one-piece deck with a straight deck cap. (b) A one-piece deck with a shield-shaped deck cap. (c) A multi-piece arced deck with a pie-piece-shaped deck cap. (d) A strip deck. (e) A V-grooved strip deck.

**deck beam**
A transverse piece spanning the boat, attached to the hull or gunwales, that supports the deck.

**deck cap**
A piece covering the stem end of the deck and resting upon it. Most surround the stem post on three sides while a few butt up to it. Deck caps may be straight across, pie-piece shaped, shield shaped, or, on some two-piece or strip decks, a center cover board. A few were heart or diamond shaped. Deck cap designs may be a characteristic of a particular builder.

**decorative deck beam**
A deck beam embellished along its lower edge with a distinctive design.

**double ender**
A boat having sharp and nearly symmetrical stems at both bow and stern.

**fair lines**
The curves and contours of a boat's hull and lines are uninterrupted by bumps or hollows.

**feather lap** (see **lapstrake built**)

**freeboard**
That portion of the boat above the waterline to the top of the gunwale, which varies with the load.

**garboard**, or **garboard strake**
The first, or bottom strake, attached to the ribs and the bottom board.

**gunwales (wales, rails)**
The exterior longitudinal pieces, flush with the top plank, that run the length of the boat at the sheer. They provide stiffness and strength to the hull and serve as a mounting piece for the oarlock socket straps.

**heel plates (wear plates)**
Protective pieces of sheet brass or copper attached to the inside of the boat on the bottom board and ribs where the rowers' feet land. They are used to prevent wear on the hull.

**hull**
The body of the guideboat, consisting of bottom board, ribs, stems, and planking.

**inboard**
Within the hull or toward the center of a boat.

**keel**
The longitudinal structure along the centerline at the bottom of a vessel's hull on which the rest of the hull is built, in some vessels extended downward as a blade or ridge to increase stability. A guideboat, however, does not have a keel; it has a bottom board. (see **bottom board**)

**knee**
A thick slice of the natural crook root (usually red spruce) from which the ribs and stems of a guideboat are sawn. (see **crook**.)

**lapstrake built**
Hull construction method with each strake overlapping the one below it. Also referred to as "clinker built." There are two variations of lapstrake construction:

**clapboard lapstrake:** The lower edge of each strake visibly overlaps the upper edge of the one below like the clapboard siding on a house. This is the most typical method.

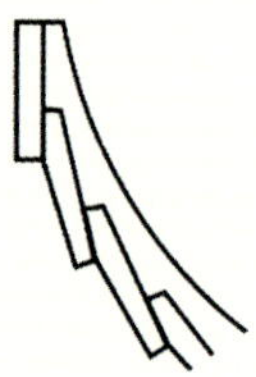

Figure G-7 Lapstrake (clapboard) planking

**smooth-skin lapstrake:** Both edges are shaped so that the planks lie flush. The following are types of smooth-skin lapstrake, depending on the construction method used:

(a) **feather-edged or bevel-lap:** The lower edge of each strake is finely beveled and overlaps the finely beveled upper edge of the one below, resulting in a smooth hull surface inside and out. This is the most commonly used method for guideboats. (see **planking bevel**)

(b) **shiplap, or half-lap:** Each plank has a square cut in the edge and a corresponding square cut in the edge of the plank below it. A method of joinery known for centuries; not used for guideboat hulls.

(c) **modified-bevel**, or **Grant lap:** The lap of each plank is not beveled to a feather edge but is left with a square shoulder. This is the method used by the Brown's Tract guideboat builders.

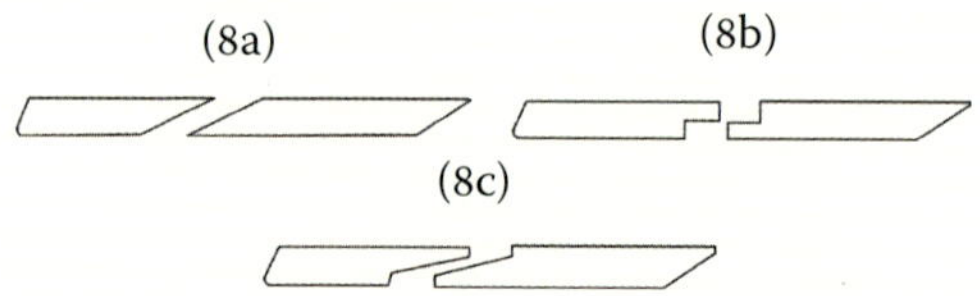


Figure G-8 Smooth-skin lapstrake planking

**length overall (LOA)**
The length of a guideboat measured from the farthest ends of the bow and stern stems.

**limber hole**
A hole through the deck ends at the bow and stern to facilitate the drainage of water from beneath the decks when the boat is overturned.

**miter**
A beveled joint where both pieces are angled.

**oarlock (rowlock)**
A two-part set made of cast iron, brass, or bronze, used to hold the oar. It consists of:

**oarlock socket strap:** The part attached to the gunwale, usually with ten screws. About 10 inches long by 1¼ inches wide, with a 2-inch high vertical barrel in the middle that has a ½-inch hole bored through it to accept the **oarlock yoke.**

**oarlock yoke:** The part attached to the oar. It has a yoke with two circular side plates that surround the flat sides of the oar, and it is fastened in place with a copper or iron pin, peened on both ends, riveting the oarlock to the oar. There is a ½-inch diameter shaft, about 2 inches long, extending below the yoke, that fits into the socket of the oarlock strap.

**oars**
Guideboat oars are designed to be light but strong, made from red maple or spruce, and are sawn, or carved, not turned on a lathe. The blades are about 5 inches wide and 21 inches long. The neck is narrow and there is a short, rounded shaft transitioning into a square loom that has been chamfered into eight sides. About two-thirds of the way up, the chamfer ends and there is a four-sided land where the oarlock is attached. Beyond that the upper loom is chamfered again to eight sides, until it transitions into the grip. The oar is tapered its whole length, with the extra mass of the upper loom counter-balancing

the longer lower loom and blade. For a 16-foot guideboat, oars are usually 8 feet in length.

**paddle**
Narrow shafted, with a long, thin, narrow blade, usually squared off on the end. Guideboats were typically supplied with a paddle, a pair of oars, and a carry yoke.

**painter**
A rope attached to the bow of a boat. A bow line.

**painter ring**
A ring attached to the stem band to which a painter is tied.

**planking (siding)**
The individual pieces that make up the "skin" of the hull. (see **strake**)

**planking bevel**
The lengthwise bevel on the edges of the planks where they overlap. The adjoining piece has a corresponding bevel so that the two overlapping planks lie flush, resulting in a smooth-skinned hull. (see **lapstrake built**)

**rabbet**
A groove cut into the stem that receives the ends of the planking.

**rabbet line**
The line of intersection of the planking with the stem. Also known as the **bearding line**.

**ram bow**
A curved stem with extreme tumblehome.

**reverse-curved rib**
The rib is S-shaped; concave from the bottom board up to the middle, convex from the middle to the sheer.

(9a)

(9b)

(9c)

Figure G-9 Ribs (a) scribe ribs have no feet. (b) footed ribs have feet that extend across the bottom board. (c) reverse-curved ribs are S-shaped. Note that along the hull, scribe or footed ribs may be: (a) relatively straight, (b) rounded, or (c) reverse curved.

**ribs (frames)**
The crosswise pieces running laterally or transversely across the bottom board, rising up to the sheer. They form the internal skeleton of the hull. For guideboats they are usually made from natural crooks (**knees**) of red spruce and are sawn to shape, not steam bent. The curve of the rib follows the grain of a natural crook, maximizing its strength. Two ribs constitute a pair, a right and a left, attached to the bottom board with their feet overlapping side by side. A 16-foot guideboat usually has 24 to 30 pairs of ribs.

**rib foot**
The part of the rib that lies across, and is attached to, the bottom board.

**rib spacing**
The distance between ribs along the bottom board measured from the centers of the rib foot pairs. Usually 5 to 6 inches on center.

**rocker**
The curvature of the bottom of the boat from end to end.

**rowlock** (see **oarlock**)

**scarf**, or **scarf joint**
The crosswise bevels made at the ends of two planks when they are joined together to make a longer plank. In hull construction, planks are scarfed together at their ends to form a strake. Each overlapping plank has a corresponding bevel cut into it so that the two planks are flush and the same thickness throughout the joint.

**scribe rib**
A pair of ribs located at the bow and the stern without feet (due to the narrowing of the bottom board). They follow the standard spacing and are scribed into place after the hull is completed, and before the decks are put on.

**seam**
The lengthwise joint of the overlapping planking. The seam is tacked together to keep it watertight.

**seat**
A wooden frame made by attaching four rails together by mortice-and-tenon or dowel joints, to form a trapezoidal or rectangular frame. The open frame is filled with woven rattan caning, forming the seat. Early seats were a solid wooden board. A guideboat typically has three seats: bow, center, and stern. The bow and stern seats are fixed in place and the center seat is removable. When alone, the rower sits in the center; with two people, the rower sits in the bow and the passenger sits in the stern. With three people, or a large load, the rower sits in either the center or the bow, whichever trims the boat the best.

**bow seat:** The trapezoid-shaped seat at the bow of the boat where the rower sits with two people in the boat. A passenger might sit there with three people in the boat. Its frame has fore and aft cross pieces that rest on, and are attached to, the seat cleats.

**center seat:** The rectangular, removable seat in the middle of the boat, where the rower sits when rowing alone, or where a passenger might sit. Its frame has fore and aft cross pieces that rest on the seat cleats.

**center seat backrest:** A wooden frame filled with woven rattan cane. It is hinged to the center seat, but is removable, and is supported by leather straps.

**stern seat:** The trapezoid-shaped seat at the stern of the boat, where a passenger sits. It is made up of a forward cross piece that rests on and attaches to the stern seat cleats, with the two side pieces extending beyond the aft cross piece. These extensions hold the backrest in place.

**stern seat backrest:** A removable wooden frame, filled with woven rattan cane, that fits into the stern seat. Its upper section rests upon the deck edge or coaming.

**seat cleats**
Short pieces that run lengthwise inside the hull, attached to the ribs 5 to 6 inches above the bottom board. The seats rest on these cleats and in the case of the bow and stern seat, are screwed to them. The bow and stern seat cleats span 3 to 4 ribs, the center seat cleats span 8 to 10 ribs.

**seat cleat ledge**
A projecting shelf on the stern scribe rib that supports the aft end of the stern seat cleat.

**sheer**
The curvature of the boat at the gunwale, as seen in profile.

**sheer strake**
The top plank of the hull.

**shoes**
Two thin metal bands attached along the edges of the bottom board to protect it from damage. A third shoe was sometimes added along the center of the board. After the 1940s, the few remaining builders substituted hardwood.

**smooth lapstrake** (see **lapstrake built**)

**square stern**
Having a small high-tucked transom. Typical of the earliest guides' boats. Also called a square-transom stern. (see **transom**)

**steam bent**
Ribs made by steaming and forcing them into the shape of the hull.

**stem**
The upright piece at the end of the boat, attached to the bottom board and rising above the surface of the decks, to which the ends of the planks are attached. Usually each stem is one piece, rabbeted to receive the planking. Occasionally it is made from two pieces, an inner and an outer stem. Stems are made from the natural **crooks** (**knees**) of red spruce or tamarack.

**stem band (bang iron)**
A brass, bronze, or iron strip running the length of the stem, from the gunwale to the bottom board. The lower end of stem band typically flares to correspond with the shape of the bottom. In some guideboats the upper end of the stem band extends to cover the stem post.

**stem foot**
The lower section of the stem that is visible inside the boat, which has been notched out to receive the end of the bottom board. Its shape is part of the overall signature of the builder.

**stem post**
The part of the stem that rises above the deck. It protects the deck from being damaged on carries. Its shape is part of the overall signature of the builder.

10(a)

10(b)

10(c)

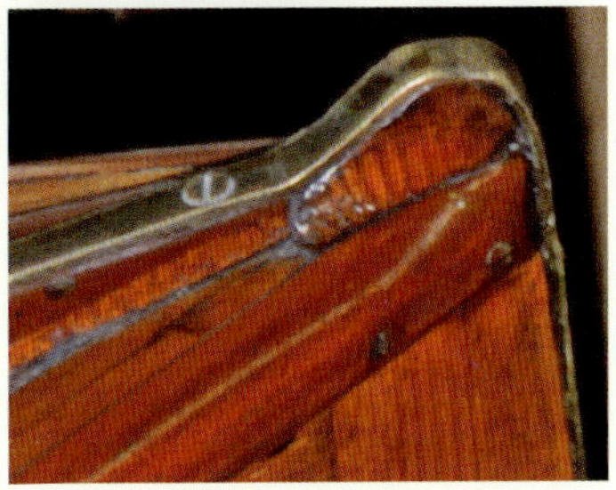

Figure G-10 Stem posts (a) A narrow stem post, typically having a width less than 1/2 inch. (b) A wide stem post, typically the full thickness of the stem. (c) A stem post with a metal cap.

**stem-post cap**
A metal band covering the stem post, sometimes nickel-plated. In some boats they are an extension of the stem band.

**strake**
A line, or row, of planking running the length of the hull. Guideboat strakes are usually formed from two or three planks scarfed together. There are usually 7 or 8 strakes on each side.

**strongback (building rack, jig,** or **stock)**
A frame to which a boat is secured during hull construction.

**tacking**
Fastening the planks together at the seams with copper clinch tacks.

**thole pin**
Early rowlocks made from two upright wooden pins, or dowels, inserted a few inches apart on each gunwale, that the oar lies between. Also, a single pin upon which an oar with a hole bored through it is placed.

**transom**
The transverse flat piece at the stern above the waterline on a square-stern boat.

**tumblehome**
The inward rake (inclining toward amidships) of the stem. The inboard inclination of the hull above the bilge. Guideboats do not have tumblehome in the hull but do in some stems.

Figure G-11 Regional stem profiles. These guideboat stems are tumblehome to varying degrees, that is, the upper portion of the stems incline inward. (Left to right) Bloomingdale, Saranac, and Long Lake stems.

**yoke (carry yoke)**
A carved block of wood, usually cedar, hollowed to fit around the neck and over the shoulders of the guide, to carry the inverted boat. It has arms extending to either side that fit into the notches of the yoke cleat. It was adapted from the yokes used to carry buckets.

Figure G-12 A hand-carved yoke with its ends in notches of the yoke cleat.

**yoke cleats**
Wooden pieces that run lengthwise inside the hull at midship, attached to the ribs near the sheer. They have a notch, to support the yoke arms. Typically, the yoke cleats extend forward and are used as grips when the boat is carried.

Figure G-13 Yoke cleat notched to support the ends of the carry yoke.

**yoke wear plates**
Small pieces of sheet brass attached behind the yoke cleat to the sheer strake and gunwale to protect the planking from wear by the ends of the yoke.

Figure G-14 Yoke wear plate.

Stony Creek, near Spectacle Ponds. Photograph by Seneca Ray Stoddard. (Courtesy of Adirondack Museum)

# 1

## THE HISTORY OF THE Adirondack Guideboat

Map of the
NEW YORK WILDERNESS
TO ACCOMPANY
Wallace's Descriptive Guide
TO
THE ADIRONDACKS.
BY W.W. ELY M.D.
1876.
Engraved, Printed and Published by G.W.& C.B. COLTON & Co. No. 172 William St. NEW YORK.
Scale of 4 Miles p. in.
CLINTON
ST. LAWRENCE
ESSEX
LAKE CHAMPLAIN
PLATTSBURGH
TICONDEROGA
CROWN POINT
PARISHVILLE
HOPKINTON
CANTON
PIERREPONT
COLTON
RIVERDALE
BRIGHTON
FRANKLIN
HARRIETSTOWN
NEWCOMB
WILMURT
BREMEN
ATLANTIC OCEAN
LAKE ONTARIO

OVER SEVERAL DECADES IN THE MID-NINETEENTH CENTURY, a unique wilderness work boat, light enough to be carried by one person, was conceived of and built in the Adirondack region of New York. The boat soon became an icon; it is hard to imagine that it could have come into existence anywhere else. Built from readily available eastern red spruce, northern white pine, and northern white cedar, the Adirondack guideboat represents the enduring legacy of a culture that was inherently appreciative of and dependent upon the challenging environment of the Adirondacks. Until the twentieth century, it was a remote mountainous place of long winters, few roads, little arable land, and a sparse population. And yet the area was rich in water, with rain and snow melt streaming into rivers and lakes, offering livelihood and connection, *if* there was a boat!

Beginning in the 1850s, descriptions of a new type of boat, initially associated with Martin's Hotel on Lower Saranac Lake, began to appear in the sporting press and books. These boats were described as slender, with a clapboard-lapstrake hull secured to matched pairs of natural-crook ribs fastened to a flat, narrow bottom board tapered at both ends. In sleekness and the shape of the bow, they somewhat resembled birchbark canoes, although unlike canoes they had narrow, high-tucked (wineglass-shaped) transom sterns.

This distinctive boat soon became widely recognized and referred to as the "Saranac," or "Adirondack," boat. By the 1860s, with the commercial availability of screws and small copper tacks, the clapboard-lapstrake planks of the earliest guide's boats could be finely beveled to make a smooth hull surface, both inside and out. The strakes, or planks, could also be thinner, down to as little as three-sixteenths of an inch. Over time the weight of a typical guideboat went from about 120 pounds to just over 70, resulting in a more efficient craft for travel, hunting, and fishing. With its increased lightness, the Saranac boat gained popularity among hotel owners, patrons, and their guides.

The Saranac boat was the precursor of the double-ended, or classic, guideboat we know today, which made its first appearance in the 1860s. Both types, transom-sterned and double-ended, with both clapboard-lapstrake and smooth-skin hulls, were being built simultane-

**FIGURE 1-1** (Left) An example of an early (1860s) smooth-skin, transom-built guide's boat. Note the reverse-curved ribs (S-shaped ribs, convex from the bottom board, concave above). (Right) The stern post (the part extending below the waterline) is similar in shape to the bow stem below the waterline.

**FIGURE 1-2** The transoms shown are carved in three dimensions from one piece of wood. They are rabbeted, that is, a recess or groove is cut along the edge, into which the ends of the planks are fitted. (Left) A painted, high-tucked, one-piece, wine-glass-shaped, transom. (Center and Right) Exterior and interior views of a varnished transom. Note the reverse-curved ribs and the pair of scribe ribs (ribs with no foot extending across the bottom board) with ledges to support the seat cleats.

ously in the Adirondacks in the 1870s. Preferred by guides, who knew that a double ender was a better craft for travel and lighter than a transom-built boat of equal length, the double-ended boat grew in popularity. By the late 1880s, double-ended guideboats had all but replaced their transom-built prototypes, although both remained in use through the 1890s. (Hereafter, transom-built boats are referred to as a "guide's boat" and double-ended boats as a "guideboat.")

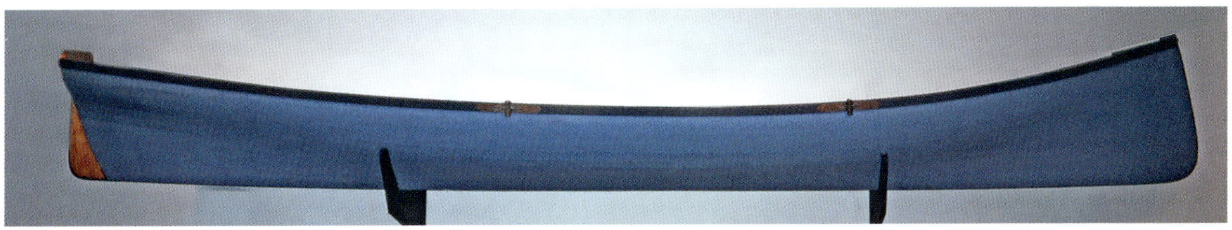

**FIGURE 1-3** A painted, smooth-skin guide's boat built by Reuben Cary of Long Lake in the 1870s. Note the transom stern and the distinctive Long Lake profile of the bow stem: a straight leading edge with tumblehome (angled inward). Note also the two sets of oarlocks for two rowing positions—when the guide is rowing alone (closer to center) or with a passenger or two (closer to the bow). Below the waterline, the boat is alike at the bow and stern. (Courtesy of Adirondack Museum)

**FIGURE 1-4** A varnished, double-ended, smooth-skin guideboat built by Caleb Chase of Newcomb in the 1890s. Note the distinctive Saranac profile of the bow and stern stems: a curvilinear leading edge with tumblehome. (Courtesy of Adirondack Museum)

**FIGURE 1-5** "The Trapper," 1870, by Winslow Homer. The handsomely shaped dugout is outfitted with a jacklight for hunting deer at night. (Courtesy of Colby College Museum of Art, Waterville, Maine)

## Adirondack Water Craft Prior to the 1850s

ROADS SCARCELY EXISTED in the Adirondacks prior to the nineteenth century, so travel was largely limited to transport on water. This was done using log rafts, dugout canoes (also called tree canoes), and bark canoes of elm and spruce made by the regional Iroquois.

Much superior to any of these was the birchbark canoe built by the Algonquian Indians of eastern Canada. The hull, made from the outer bark of the white paper birch, was impervious to water and, because of its horizontal grain, would not split lengthwise. Light, flexible, and strong, its pieces could be sewn together.

After the Revolutionary War, as European settlers became more numerous, a variety of wooden boats came into use. These included square enders (flat-bottom boats with pointed bows and rectangular, or square, sterns) and punts (flat-bottom boats with straight sides that are square at both ends, and therefore rectangular in shape).

FIGURE 1-6 A bark canoe depicted in "Camping Out in the Adirondacks," a wood engraving after Winslow Homer. *Harper's Weekly*, November 7, 1874. (Courtesy of Adirondack Museum)

FIGURE 1-7 A square ender. Note the two pairs of thole pins, or wooden pegs, on each side, that serve as oarlocks, as well as the heavy, prominent stem post at the bow and the straight upper edge of the gunwale from bow to stern, or lack of sheer. Detail from "Lake George," an engraving after J. W. Casilear, published in *Picturesque America*, 1874. (Courtesy of Adirondack Museum)

FIGURE 1-8 "The Adirondack Guide," 1894, by Winslow Homer shows a punt, with the oarlocks bolted to the oars. (Photograph ©2018 Museum of Fine Arts, Boston)

FIGURE 1-9 A punt used at the North Woods Club, founded in 1887, near Minerva, New York. It is a boat similar to those depicted in the paintings of Winslow Homer, who with his brother were charter members of the club.

The need to travel with a boat through the woods to another body of water made it essential—particularly for trappers, hunters, and fishermen—to have a boat that was light enough to be carried by one person. Such boats were called "carry boats," and the paths they were transported over were called "carries."

In 1835 professor and land entrepreneur Farrand N. Benedict of Burlington, Vermont, described the great distances traveled:

> It has long been known that hunters have transported in small boats their treasures of fish, game and fur through these waters, from the vicinity . . . of Lake Champlain to the valley of the Black River. From their accounts it appeared that the "carrying places" were few and short, and that their voyages were accomplished without much labor or hazard. My own travels over this route, which were commenced in 1835, verified these statements; and they have since been abundantly confirmed by intelligent and scientific travellers.[1]

In 1842 John Todd in his *Long Lake* wrote: "Here [at Saranac Lake] we procured a little boat, such a one as a man can carry on his head through the woods from river to river and from lake to lake."[2]

## An Early Carry Boat

The earliest builder of boats in Long Lake was William J. Austin (born in Ferrisburgh, Vermont, in 1815). He is important because he was the earliest person in the Adirondacks documented as a builder of boats for guides and sportsmen. Also, his descendants in four succeeding generations became Long Lake guideboat builders: Farrand, Merlin, Harold Sr., and Harold Jr.

Mention of Austin as a boatbuilder is from a diary by A. E. Leavenworth entitled *Journal of a Surveying Excursion to Raquette Lake & Vicinity, August 1851.* On the morning of August 19, 1851, Leavenworth and a companion arrived at the home of William and Lois Austin. He had been sent there by Farrand Benedict to survey Raquette Lake and vicinity. Leavenworth wrote:

> We rowed 9 miles [up Long Lake] and walked 5 more by 9 A.M. to Mr. Austin's at the head of the lake where we proposed to take breakfast in preference to any other place we had seen, by the advice of Prof. B. [Farrand N. Benedict]. . . . Mr. Austin's place looks well, few stones appear, the crops and grass looked well. He is rapidly acquiring wealth while his more indolent neighbors are poor. In the winter season he builds boats, about one a week, and sells them for about $15. They frequently pay for a month's work in haying.[3]

In a letter dated June 19, 1850, William Constable wrote: "You will hire three of the best small boats and see that they are perfectly *tight*. . . . Should you not be able to get all the boats you wish at the R. [Raquette Lake], send at once to Long Lake to Wm. Austin. He has very good ones to hire."[4]

A very old boat, possibly built by William Austin, was discovered, its stern submerged in mud on the shore of Brandreth Lake, west of Long Lake. The name B. Brandreth is stamped inside on a plank near the bow. At a much later date, the year "1848" was painted on its bow deck, most likely by artist Pauline Brandreth. The stern has long since been removed and the upright boat fitted with shelves for books. It's obvious that the boat had been carried by one person:

**FIGURE 1-10** The deck of the so-called "bookcase boat." Note the large, rather crude stem post typical of early boats. (Courtesy of Franklin B. Brandreth)

there are rounded notches on the tops of both gunwales, worn down by the ends of a carrying yoke. The boat was relatively short, 12 to 14 feet in length, and estimated to weigh about 120 pounds. It was rowed using thole pins rather than metal oarlocks. Its most striking feature is that its construction—a flat elliptical bottom board with ribs sawn from natural crooks—is similar to that of the Adirondack guideboat.

**FIGURE 1-11** (Left) This photograph, courtesy of the Adirondack Museum, was taken about 1890. In converting the boat to a bookcase, its lower portion has been cut off, probably to accommodate to the room's height. The boat's original length is estimated to have been 12 to 14 feet with a beam of 3 feet. Note the two blocks with thole pin holes secured to the gunwales. One pair (with three holes) about mid-level, on the inside of the gunwales, and the other pair (not easy to see) at the floor level on the outside of the gunwales. (Right) The hull is made from four strakes on each side. There is a prominent stem post, a straight deck placed betweeen the sheer planks, a clapboard-lapstrake outer hull, smooth-lapstrake inner hull, and a flat elliptical bottom board, made from two lengthwise pieces. (Courtesy of Franklin B. Brandreth)

## The Emergence of the Transom-built or Saranac Boat

### William Fortune Martin's Hotel

THE VILLAGE OF SARANAC LAKE was originally settled by Jacob Smith Moody, who arrived at the east end of Lower Saranac Lake in 1819. He had no neighbors for ten miles in any direction. Three years later Captain Pliny Miller settled nearby. In the 1840s Miller built a boarding house, the first in the region.

In 1849, William Fortune Martin came to the village from Bangor in northern Franklin County, New York, with his wife Laura, their newborn son, William Allen, and Martin's two brothers, Stephen and Henry, both of whom would later become celebrated guides. Martin leased Miller's "hotel" and used it as a departure point for sportsmen going into the woods.

> In 1851 he moved up to the foot of Lower Saranac Lake, a mile and a half distant, and in 1852 erected a two story frame building, the first in that region, expressly for a popular summer resort. The building was 30 by 38, with a wing 24 by 30, and capable of accommodating perhaps 80 guests. The Adirondacks were then unknown as a fashionable resort, and everybody called him a fool for building such a big, handsome house right in the wilderness, where none but occasional hunters and fishermen were ever seen. But Martin from the outset was full of faith that the time would come even in his day when that wilderness would be dotted with pleasure resorts and swarm with city visitors.[5]

FIGURE 1-12 Martin's hotel in the early 1870s. E. R. Wallace's *Descriptive Guide to the Adirondacks* in H. Perry Smith's *The Modern Babes in the Wood*, 1872.

According to historian Alfred L. Donaldson, Martin's "was the first hotel in the interior Adirondacks built solely to attract people of leisure and wealth."[6]

In his *Hills, Lakes, and Forest Streams*, published in 1854, S. H. Hammond wrote:

> The places I visited five years ago, are vastly easier of access now than they were then. The tourist can now go from Port Kent, on Lake Champlain, to the foot of the Lower Saranac in a day. He will travel the whole distance, save about twelve miles, on a plank road, and the balance on a tolerably smooth common road. All making the most delightful day's journey imaginable.
>
> On the banks of the Lower Saranac, literally at the end of the road, he will find "Martin's House," a new and comfortable country hotel, kept by pleasant, obliging people. Here he will hire a boatman, with his boat and tent, cooking utensils, and a store of provisions, and go a hundred miles, if he chooses, "outside of a fence," over the most beautiful lakes, and along the most delightful rivers and streams that the eye ever looked upon, but all wild, remember—all as nature threw them down there,

> among old primeval things. His journeyings will not be toilsome, he will have no tramping in the woods, save occasional short carrying places over which his boatman will march with his craft, like a great turtle with his shell on his back. . . . And if he loves nature, and takes matters easy, and gives himself time, he will come out of the woods, as I did, a stronger, healthier, and a wiser man.[7]

In his poem "The Adirondacs: A Journal Dedicated to My Fellow Travelers in August, 1858," Ralph Waldo Emerson, one of the Boston luminaries who made up the group known as the Philosophers' Camp, described using Martin's as a departure point and source of guideboats:

> We crossed Champlain to Keeseville, with our friends.
> Thence, in strong country carts, rode up the forks
> Of the Ausable stream, intent to reach
> The Adirondac lakes. At Martin's Beach
> We chose our boats; each man a boat and guide,—
> Ten men, ten guides, our company all told.[8]

E. P. Wells, in the *Williams Quarterly* (1863), wrote:

> . . .We left the steamboat at Westport, on Lake Champlain, and took [the] stage for a ride of forty miles to Saranac Lake. In this ride, we passed through, rather than over, the five ranges of mountains, which compose the Adirondac system. The peaks are numerous, lofty, and conical; and, as the road winds through the very heart of the group, the constantly shifting panorama, of the grandest mountain scenery we had ever beheld. . . . Our stage ride, as well as the road, ended at the water's edge of the Lower Saranac Lake, in the door yard of W. F. Martin, Esq., (P.O. address Saranac Lake) whose house is the rendezvous of quite a large portion of those who visit the woods. Here, too, was the end of all roads, fences, town organizations, taxes, ballot boxes (for those who live farther in neither pay taxes nor vote), black coats, white linen, calf boots, hoop skirts, long dresses, and bonnets; and the beginning of boat traveling, blue shirts, water-proof boots, bloomer dresses, camp fires, trout, and venison.[9]

And in his influential and popular 1869 *Adventures in the Wilderness; or, Camp-Life in the Adirondacks*, William H. H. Murray wrote:

> It [Martin's] is located on Lower Saranac, at the terminus of the stage route from Keeseville. It is, therefore, the most convenient point at which to meet your guides. . . . Martin is one of the few men in the world who seem to know how "to keep a hotel." At his house you can easily and cheaply obtain your entire outfit for a trip of any length.[10]

Prominent guests included scientist and educator Louis Agassiz; maid of honor to Queen Victoria, Lady Amelia M. Murray; topographical surveyor Verplanck Colvin; Adirondack mapmaker Dr. W. W. Ely; guidebook writer E. R. Wallace; and photographer Seneca Ray Stoddard. Wallace, in the fifth edition of his *Descriptive Guide to the Adirondacks (1876)*, found it a jumping-off place for "parties, including a goodly sprinkling of ladies" for excursions to nearby lakes.[11]

By 1875 Martin's hotel could accommodate 250 guests and in later years "at its height, upwards of 300 guests, advertising a wide range of recreational, social, and culinary options."[12]

## Early Builders of Transom-Built Guide's Boats

### *William McLenathen*

On first becoming an innkeeper in 1850, Martin hired William McLenathen, from Jay in Essex County, to build and repair boats for use by guides and sportsmen. McLenathen's boats were light enough to be carried by one person, primarily rowed, but able to be paddled when necessary. They were adaptations and refinements of dory, or bateau, construction, a method that was widely known, easy to master, and inexpensive to build, with narrow, flat bottom boards to allow the boat to sit upright when drawn up on land. As guides' work boats, they were fast but able to accommodate passengers and equipment for lengthy trips into the wilderness.

The 1850 census for Harrietstown, Franklin County, lists the members of the Martin household:

> William F. Martin, age 27, Inn Keeper, born in New York
>
> Laura Martin, age 26, born in Canada [wife of William F. Martin]
>
> William A. Martin, age 8 months, born in New York [son of William and Laura Martin]
>
> Henry W. Martin, age 24, Farmer, born in New York [brother of William F. Martin]
>
> William McLenathen, age 51, Boat Builder & Miner, born in Vermont[13]

FIGURE 1-13 "Log Driving on the Ausable River," from the "Annual Report of the Superintendent of Forests" in the Sixth Annual Report of the Forest, Fish and Game Commission, Albany, N. Y.: James B. Lyon, 1901. Photograph by F. A. Van Sant.

Where and from whom McLenathen learned the boat-building trade remains unknown. It is possible that he learned while living in Jay, where boats modeled on the lumberman's bateau were used in log drives on the Ausable River.

In his *History of the Adirondacks*, Donaldson wrote:

> The senior Martin used a very large number of boats in connection with his hotel because in the early days he

> hired all the available guides, and furnished each one with a boat. A man named McLenathan [*sic*] came from North Elba [Jay] every winter and spent it in the Martin boat shop, making new boats and repairing old ones.[14]

In a 1940 *Watertown Daily Times* interview, noted Saranac Lake guideboat builder Theodore S. Hanmer, nearing eighty and still building guideboats, was asked about their origin. He replied:

> [The] first boat was made by William McLenathan [*sic*] of Lake Placid [Jay], in response to demands for a craft that would be easy to carry over the frequent portages on Adirondack waterways, but yet stable enough to carry up to a ton of weight in fairly rough water.[15]

### *Nathaniel S. Graves*

A 1903 interview with boatbuilder Nathaniel S. Graves provides the earliest documentary evidence that the prototype of the traditional, double-ended guideboat had been built by 1851 and that the builder was William McLenathen. In the interview, Graves described a hunting trip he had taken in the fall of 1851, when he was seventeen years old:

> At Upper [Lower] Saranac Lake they found the only hotel in the Adirondacks, a three-room log house kept by three brothers named Martin. They hired a boat of Wm. MacClenathan [*sic*], uncle Mac they called him, who had built the first boat [of its kind] known in all the region and may be styled the father of the Adirondack guide boat. A neighbor of uncle Mac's had built a boat after his model, and these two were the only boats known to exist in the woods at that time. These boats had a narrow, square stern, but were otherwise and in a general sense the model after which all succeeding Adirondack boats have been built, says Mr. Graves.[16]

Graves spent the winter of 1851–1852 with his uncle in Keene, New York, and in the spring of 1852 "built a boat, modeled from memory, after Uncle Mac's. . . . So far as is known, this was the third boat [of that type] built in the Adirondacks."[17] Graves then went to Boston, where he remained for several years before returning to the Adirondacks. He settled in the Bog River area, at the south end of Tupper Lake, around 1856.

### *William Allen Martin*

Included among the several outbuildings at Martin's hotel was a boat shop mentioned by Joel T. Headley in an August 9, 1858, letter to the *New York Times*: "Boats, fishing rods, and guns are the staple here [at Martin's]. . . . The next morning . . . I strolled out to the boat shop and was startled to come upon [William F.] Martin."[18] It was in this boat shop that William McLenathen taught young William Allen Martin the trade of boatbuilding. "Willie" Allen, as tradition has it, built his first guideboat at the young age of sixteen, in 1865, and was to become a respected builder of guideboats. Historian Donaldson, in an interview with W. F. Martin's wife, reported:

> Young William was always to be found in this place in his spare moments, watching the work and lending a hand. When he was sixteen years old [1865] he asked permission to be allowed to build a boat all by himself. It was given rather reluctantly, but the boy turned out a bit of work that was so creditable as to surprise both his father and McLenathan [*sic*].[19]

### *Mitchell Sabattis (Attributed)*

Mitchell Sabattis (1823–1906) has long been credited with building the first traditional Adirondack guideboat, primarily due to the following statement by Donaldson:

> Its progenitors were Mitchell Sabattis and one of the Palmers, who saw the need of devising something sturdier and swifter than the canoe. Their joint product must have been put in use as early as 1842, for that was the date of Dr. [John] Todd's second visit, in recounting which he says: "we procured a little boat, such a one as a man can carry on his head, through the woods, from river to river, and from lake to lake."[20]

Donaldson provides no further documentation; however, in 1842, Ransom Palmer (1836–1923) was only six years old, and his brother Cyrus (1845–1897) had not yet been born. Mitchell Sabattis was only nineteen. Moreover, in a conversation with Kenneth Durant in 1958, Adirondack guide Willard Sutton, then aged ninety-three, stated that Sabattis "did not build boats."[21] Nor is he listed in contemporary accounts as a boatbuilder, though his son, Isaac, is.[22] Thus, it's not at all likely that Mitchell Sabattis was the "progenitor" of the guideboat.

## Early Depictions of Transom-Built Boats

On a trip to the Adirondacks in 1853, S. H. Hammond, in *Wild Northern Scenes,* was the first to describe the construction of the boats built by McLenathen at Martin's:

> Their boats are constructed of spruce or cedar boards of a quarter of an inch in thickness, 'clap-boarded,' as the expression is, upon 'knees' of the natural crook, and weigh from ninety to one hundred and ten pounds each. They are carried around rapids, or from river to river, on the back of the boatman.[23]

The earliest known drawing of a guide's boat was reproduced in an 1859 article in *Harper's New Monthly Magazine* written by T. Addison Richards. The boat, *Polly Ann,* belonged to Saranac Lake guide Harvey Moody, neighbor and friend of the Martins.

In the article, Moody says of carrying *Polly Ann*: "I'll take the boat, I carry it bottom up with a yoke on my shoulders."[24]

Harvey Moody's boat appears similar in construction to the boat of his younger brother, Cortez. A photograph of Cortez Moody and his boat is one of the earliest known of a guide's boat.

The parents of Harvey and Cortez, Jacob Smith Moody and his wife Sally, were the first settlers in the Saranac Lake area. From Unity, New Hampshire, they first settled in Keene, New York, where Harvey was born in 1808. In 1819, they moved to Saranac Lake. In 1822 Cortez Moody was the first white child born in the Saranac Lake area. Jacob Moody had six sons who all became renowned guides. In Nathaniel Graves's recounting of William McLenathen's building boats for Martin, one of the Moody brothers could very likely have been "the neighbor"

**FIGURE 1-14** A pencil sketch dated September 13, 1853, by T. Addison Richards of Harvey Moody's *Polly Ann.* It is the same basic construction as the original boat built by William McLenathen for W. F. Martin in 1850–1851. The hull is rounded, of clapboard-lapstrake construction, though not particularly slender, and the upright position indicates a flat bottom. Note the slight sheer, the yoke cleat, oarlocks pinned to the oars, and the board seat. This sketch appeared in *Harper's New Monthly Magazine,* August 1859. (Courtesy of Adirondack Museum)

who built the second boat of this type.

An early description of a Saranac boat as transom-built is found in the October 31, 1855, issue of *The Crayon* by W. J. Stillman, the man who organized the Philosophers' Camp outing three years later:

> My guide is Stephen Martin. . . . Our boat is a light, pine-built craft, somewhat on the Whitehall fashion, fifteen to sixteen feet in length, and weighing about 140 lbs. . . . One shouldered a boat and the other its cargo.[25]

(The Whitehall boat is often thought to have been a predecessor of the Saranac boat. Time and again in early sporting journals, guidebooks, and narratives, the descriptions of Saranac boats refer to a transom like that of a Whitehall. A transom is, however, the only similarity these boats share, and the shape of their transoms is quite dissimilar.)[26]

Alfred B. Street, in *Woods and Waters; or, The Saranacs and Racket* (1860), described four Saranac boats on his departure from Martin's in the late 1850s:

> Drawn half way up the green bank, near a log hut, were four Saranac boats. These boats are dark-colored, slender as a pike, buoyant as a cork, made gracefully of thin pine, with knees of fir, their weight from ninety to one hundred and twenty pounds. Each has two oars on iron pins, a paddle, and a neck yoke for the "carries." It is made for three (it can hold five), and though so small and lightly built, will live in the roughest swells.
>
> The guide balances his upward-turned craft by a wooden yoke clasping the base of his neck, the ends fitting in iron rings at the sides of the boat, and the weight also resting on

**FIGURE 1-15** A undated photograph, likely taken in the 1860s, of Cortez Fernando Moody (1822–1902) and his boat. Cortez and his brother Harvey were two of the earliest guides in the Saranac Lake region. Cortez is sitting, with fishing pole, bait bucket, and rifle, on the bow deck of his boat. Unfortunately, the stern is not shown. The boat has a narrow hull with moderate sheer and shallow depth. Yoke cleats indicate that it was light enough to be carried by one person; natural-crook ribs are evenly spaced. A flat, narrow bottom board is indicated by the boat's upright position. The hull planking is clapboard lapstrake. A tumblehome stem is evident, as is a prominent stem post. (Courtesy of Adirondack Research Room, Saranac Lake Free Library)

> his upturned arms. He thus bears his burden over the portages of the innumerable waters that make one vast Venice of the wilderness.[27]

In 1855, Lady Amelia M. Murray, a maid of honor to Queen Victoria, toured the Adirondacks in the company of Horatio Seymour, governor of New York. In her *Letters,* Lady Amelia alludes to the characteristic lightness and flat bottom of the guide's boat: "Each man carried a boat on his head. . . . One of the boats was turned upside down for a table."[28]

In the September 29, 1860, issue of the English weekly journal *All the Year Round,* edited by Charles Dickens, a visit to Paul Smith's by a party of three is described under the title "Shooting in the Adirondack" [*sic*]. The author is unnamed. (Dickens visited America in 1842 and again in 1867–1868, but he did not get to the Adirondacks.)

> We set out for Tupper's Lake, fifty miles distant . . . [with] two guides and two boats. The latter, long, graceful, lap-streaks, roomy and stiff, yet so light that a man with a neck yoke can carry one half a mile. (The canoe, since the departure of the Indian, is little used; though light to carry, it is too crank [unsteady] for comfort on a long row).[29]

W. H. Boardman, in his *The Lovers of the Woods,* described the Saranac boat as he remembered it in 1865, emphasizing that only the bow was pointed:

> It was best known as the "Saranac boat." The bow alone was pointed, the gunwale lines tapering inward on nearly a straight line from amidships to a narrow, square stern. They were clinker-built, of thin boards, each of whose lower edges lapped over the board next below. They rarely weighed less than one hundred and twenty-five pounds. . . .[30]

An account of the many guide's boats at Martin's was published in 1865:

> Moored to the bank in front of Martin's was a flotilla of small boats for penetrating the wilderness region, beautifully modeled, and of exceedingly light construction, weighing from 90 to 125 pounds, and built of cedar or spruce boards, of about a quarter of an inch in thickness. They are thus made light for transporting from river to river, and for carrying around rapids. The *modus operandi* is soon described. A "yoke" is provided, fitting to the shoulders of the guide, at the ends of which are iron projections that fit into sockets cut in the upper rave of the boat, on each side, at the center; when a "carry" is reached the boat is turned bottom up, the yoke adjusted to the shoulders, and the guide marches off with his boat like an ancient armor bearer, with a prodigious shield on his back. They are thus carried by the hardy guides sometimes 1/2 a mile without once stopping for rest.[31]

## The Spreading Use of Transom-Built Boats

The boats built at Martin's were soon to be found at other hotels in the Saranac Lake region. In 1854, Virgil Bartlett erected a small hostelry on the banks of the Saranac River between Round Lake (Middle Saranac Lake) and Upper Saranac Lake. One of the earliest known photographs of Bartlett's, inscribed 1864, shows a guide's boat partially in water; three others are overturned on the bank.

A few years later, in 1858, Apollos (Paul) Smith began construction of a hotel on the shore of Lower St. Regis Lake;

**FIGURE 1-16** This is perhaps the earliest photograph (circa 1864) of Bartlett's hotel and of a transom-built guide's boat. Note the narrow high-tucked transom boat partially in the water. This is an enlarged detail from a *carte de visite* photograph by G. H. Houghton, Brattleboro, Vermont. (Courtesy of Adirondack Museum)

**FIGURE 1-17** A wood engraving of Paul Smith's Hotel in the early 1870s. The hotel was able to accommodate 200 guests. The boathouses, on the left, could house 100 boats, and guides. (E. R. Wallace in H. Perry Smith, 1872)

it was completed in the summer of 1859. Over the next decade, Paul Smith's Hotel became nationally recognized as one of the best kept and most fashionable hotels in the Adirondacks.

The following is a vivid description of Paul Smith's in the late 1870s by A. Judd Northrup in *Camps and Tramps in the Adirondacks:*

> "Paul Smith's" is familiar to thousands of summer tourists who "take it in" along with Newport, Long Branch, and Saratoga, as well as to those veterans of the angle and the hunt, who for many years have annually resorted hither, making this the base from which to project excursions into the deeper wilderness, there to dwell in camp and tent and pursue in solitude the pleasures of the pathless woods, the limpid lakes and winding streams.
>
> The hotel stands upon a bluff looking southward out upon Lower St. Regis Lake, beyond which lie Spitfire and Upper St. Regis. It is a long, four-story, wooden edifice, with a broad verandah along its entire front. . . . The guide-house, on the shore of the lake and to the right, is a long, two story frame building, used below for housing seventy-five to one hundred trim, light and shapely boats. Above it is converted into sleeping and living rooms for the guides engaged by Mr. Smith for the season. A bowling alley still further away, and frame barns, shops and an ice-house complete this really remarkable hostelry and its appurtenances.
>
> There are social games, sober family gatherings, and flirtations in the nooks and corners, and in the office letter-writing and newspaper-reading. The fishermen and hunters who

came in, from every direction, before tea, in their fancy costumes, reappear in Scotch and broadcloth and linen, only their brown faces revealing to you that they are genuine sportsmen.[32]

As this account attests, boats were an essential part of life at Paul Smith's, whether guests traveled with guides for trips into the wilderness or remained at the hotel. A photograph of the boathouse from around 1880 shows six boats of the Saranac form.

Transom-built boats rapidly became familiar sights as they transported sportsmen and tourists in all parts of the Adirondacks. As demand grew, an independent boat-building trade began to flourish throughout the region and increasing numbers of guides and carpenters established themselves as boatbuilders.

**FIGURE 1-18** The boathouse at Paul Smith's Hotel, Lower St. Regis Lake, about 1880. Six boats (some hard to see within the boathouse) have transom sterns and are smooth-skin lapstrake, a refinement of the earlier clapboard lapstrake used in the early guide's boats. Photograph by S. R. Stoddard. (Courtesy of Adirondack Museum)

**FIGURE 1-19** Third Lake of the Fulton Chain in 1869. General Richard U. Sherman (center) with guides and members of the North Woods Walton Club (1856–1878), later to become the Bisby Club (1878–1893). Three of the guide's boats have transom sterns (view obstructed in the fourth) and all have clapboard-lapstrake hulls, consistent with early guide's boats. Photograph by R. Fred Bowdish, Boonville, New York. (Courtesy of Adirondack Museum)

## Drawings, Prints, and Photographs of Transom-Built Boats

The transom-built guide's boat was depicted in many drawings, prints, and photographs, such as those by Frederick B. Allen, Seneca Ray Stoddard, Homer Dodge Martin, and A. B. Frost.

**FIGURE 1-20** "Haystack Mountain from Upper Ausable Pond," an 1880s photograph by S. R. Stoddard. Note the narrow high-tucked transom stern and the early straight deck and deck cap. (Courtesy of Adirondack Museum)

**FIGURE 1-21** Pencil sketches dated August 1870 by Frederick B. Allen (1840–1925) (Left) Allen's father is seated in the stern of a transom-built guide's boat. (Right) On Upper Ausable Lake. (Courtesy of Adirondack Museum)

**FIGURE 1-22** "A Carry—The Start," an 1881 wood engraving after A. B. Frost (1851–1928) showing that transom-built guide's boats continued to be used into the 1880s, from *Harper's New Monthly Magazine*, October 1881. (Courtesy of Adirondack Museum)

**FIGURE 1-23** "In the Adirondacks—A Carry on the Racquette [*sic*] River" (1870), a wood engraving after Homer Dodge Martin (1836–1897). Two early clapboard-lapstrake, transom-built guide's boats are shown in this image from *Every Saturday*, September 3, 1870. Note the narrow elliptical bottom board on the boat at the right. (Courtesy of Adirondack Museum)

**FIGURE 1-24** Detail from "Outlet of Upper Saranac Lake," an 1880s photograph by Seneca Ray Stoddard of a smooth-skin, transom-built guide's boat being launched. (Courtesy of Adirondack Museum)

## Transition to the Double-Ended Guideboat

IT WAS PREVIOUSLY THOUGHT that double-ended guideboats did not make an appearance in the Adirondacks until the mid-1870s. Narrative and pictorial evidence makes clear, however, that the building of such boats had begun at least a decade earlier.

Lucia D. Pychowska described her guide and double-ended guideboat at Martin's in the summer of 1863: "our oarsman broad browed, broad shouldered, and athletic, our boat one of the fairy craft, sharp at both ends, and light as possible, borne by guides over portages from lake to lake."[33]

In *Adventures in the Wilderness,* published in 1869, William H. H. Murray referred to a double-ended guideboat, built as early as, or possibly before, 1864, as the "Adirondack boat."

> In this connection, it should be remembered that the Adirondack boats, while being models of lightness and speed, are small and will not bear overloading. On the average they are some fifteen feet long, three feet wide at the middle, sharp at both ends, some ten inches deep, and weigh from sixty to ninety pounds. Small and light as these boats are, they will sustain three men and all they really need in the way of baggage. . . .
>
> The shell in which I sat was made of forest pine, fourteen feet in length, sharp as an arrow, and weighing but seventy pounds. . . . "Little danger," I said to myself, "of snapping oar blades made of second-growth ash, and only eight feet from butt to tip. . . ."
>
> It required great care on the part of the guides to let [the boats over the shallows] gently, as their bottoms are but little thicker than pasteboard, and held by small copper tacks.[34]

FIGURE 1-25 An illustration by Harry Fenn in *Adventures in the Wilderness.* Murray makes reference to the characteristic flat bottom board of these boats. This fanciful illustration suits the tone of Murray's book, but the boat has features that do not exist in guideboats, for example, the board thwarts and the deck surrounds. A few years later, Fenn visited the Adirondacks as principal illustrator for *Picturesque America,* published in forty-eight parts and sold by subscription from 1872 to 1874. In the Adirondack Region segment, he depicted double-enders identical to those he had drawn for Murray's book.

## First Builders of Double-Ended Guideboats

### *Caleb Judson Chase*

While there is convincing evidence that the transom-sterned guide's boat was the work of William McLenathen, there is both documentation and tradition that it was Caleb Judson Chase (1830–1911) of Newcomb who built the first double-ended guideboat. The earliest reference to Chase guideboats being "alike at both ends" was published in a letter to the editor by D. W. Mandell in the March 9, 1876, issue of *Forest and Stream*:

> One of the best makers of the Adirondack guide-boat I know of is a man by name of Chase, who lives at Newcomb in Essex County, N.Y. He has the reputation among the Long Lake and Brown's Tract guides of putting together a boat in the very best manner. There are other excellent workmen at Long Lake, *viz*: Reuben Cary and Henry Stanton. I have one of Reuben Cary's make, which I have used several years, and it is about as good as new. My impression is that the Saranac men do not excel in modeling or making these boats, and I know the Saranac guides order boats from Chase, at Newcomb, and from Cary and Stanton, at Long Lake. . . . Cary's and Stanton's models differ from Chase's in being higher in the stern and somewhat squarer, while [Chase's] are not so shear and alike at both ends. There is, perhaps, a little more style to the Long Lake boats, while Chase's are somewhat stiffer.[35]

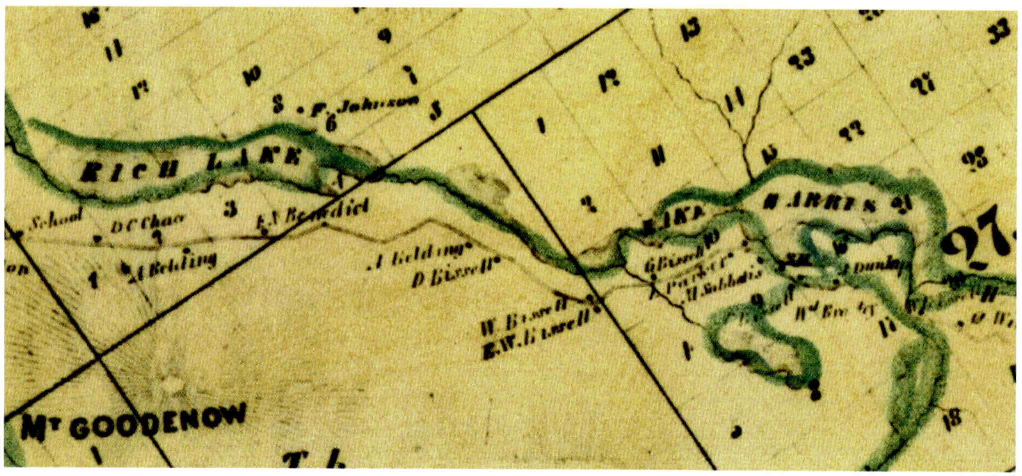


FIGURE 1-26 Detail of an Essex County map of Newcomb, New York, in 1858. Names with dots indicate the location of the person's home. Beneath the word "Rich" of Rich Lake is printed, D. C. Chase, brother of Caleb J. Chase, indicating where the Chase family lived in 1858. The third name printed beneath the word "Lake" of Lake Harris is M. Sabattis. Mitchell Sabattis and his family lived in Newcomb from 1849 to the 1870s. J. H. French, *Map of Essex County, N.Y.*, Philadelphia: E. A. Balch, 1858. (Courtesy of Adirondack Museum)

In a *Watertown Daily Times* interview of February 2, 1940, guideboat builder Theodore Hanmer of Saranac Lake, nearing his eightieth birthday, was quoted: "The first boat made with both ends alike was designed by a builder in the town of Newcomb named Chase."[36]

There is an early (1860s) double-ended, smooth-skin guideboat believed to have been built by Chase. Its hull has only four strakes of unequal widths on each side, but nevertheless it has lovely lines and sheer. The decks and deck caps are straight. The screws are iron with blunt tips, and the iron stem-bands are secured with T-headed iron nails—all traits in common with the transom-built guide's boat, with the exception of the pointed stern. The last pair of scribe ribs beneath the stern deck are half-ribs, whose upper

FIGURE 1-27 A double-ended, smooth-skin guideboat believed to have been built by Caleb Chase in the early 1860s.

ends are cut square, with a ledge to support the stern-seat cleats. These may be vestiges from guide's boats, as he refined them for more efficiency by omitting the transom. In addition, early Chase double-ended guideboats had board seats with a rectangular slot at their stern end to accommodate a narrow board backrest. These features were also commonly found in early transom-built guide's boats.

In a 1901 interview with Caleb Chase, then in his early seventies, Harry V. Radford wrote: "Chase began building boats at twenty one [in 1851] having built his first boat for Rev.[*sic*] Todd who wrote *Long Lake,* which was published in 1845. Since then the old man and his son, E. J. Chase, have built several hundred boats."[37]

### *William Henry Stanton*

According to Long Lake historian Frances Seaman, the family of William Henry Stanton (1818–1890) arrived at Long Lake in March 1849. The two boys, W. Henry (1844–1881) and George B. (1847–1935) became guides and boatbuilders when barely out of their teens. Their father was a carpenter and chair maker and the boys inherited his skill with tools. Before long they were making better and lighter boats, the stern "square" at first as was the style of the day, but later changed to double-ended. So it is not definitely known who can take credit for this change to double-ended in the skiff that became the guideboat, whether it was Caleb Chase in Newcomb or the Stanton brothers.[38] The details of this transition remain unknown.

### *William Allen Martin*

There is a long tradition that William Allen Martin, son of William Fortune Martin, was the first to build a guideboat with a smooth-skin hull. They were referred to as "Willie Allen's eggshells,"[39] a description suggesting lightness as well as smoothness. Martin, born in 1849, learned boatbuilding from William McLenathen. Whether the transition to smooth-skin hulls was the work of Martin or Chase is unknown.

Transom-built and double-ended boats, with both clapboard-lapstrake and smooth-skin hulls, were being built simultaneously in different parts of the Adirondacks in the 1860s. But by the 1880s, the building of double-ended guideboats had all but replaced that of transom-built boats. They were still seen together into the 1890s, however, on the lake shores in front of Adirondack hotels.

Visitors continued to refer to these double-ended boats as Adirondack, or Saranac, boats. In 1895, Henry Van Dyke in *Little Rivers* wrote:

> A Saranac boat is one of the finest things that the skill of man has ever produced under the inspiration of the

FIGURE 1-28 "At Martin's, Saranac Lake, Sept. 21st, 1876," a photograph by S. R. Stoddard. Four of the five boats at the shore appear to be transom-built; the other is a double ender, like the boat in the foreground. All have smooth-skin hulls. (Courtesy of Edward Comstock, Jr.)

FIGURE 1-29 The Prospect House (1864–1886), later named the Saranac Inn, at Upper Saranac Lake in the 1870s. From left to right: A guide's boat with a high-tucked transom stern; a double-ended clapboard-lapstrake guideboat; a Whitehall with its wide transom; two guide's boats with high-tucked transoms; and a smooth-skin double-ended guideboat (bow not shown). Photograph by S. R. Stoddard. (Courtesy of Adirondack Research Room, Saranac Lake Free Library)

> wilderness. It is a frail shell, so light that a guide can carry it on his shoulders with ease, but so dexterously fashioned that it rides the heaviest waves like a duck, and slips through the water as if by magic. You can travel in it along the shallowest rivers and across the broadest lakes, and make forty or fifty miles a day, if you have a good guide.[40]

For a boat of equivalent length, the double-ender was lighter and considered by guides to be a more efficient craft. Many patrons, as well, came to prefer it to its

FIGURE 1-30 An 1880s smooth-skin double-ender on a carry. (Courtesy of Edward Comstock, Jr.)

FIGURE 1-31 "The Portage—Guides Carrying the Boats and Traps," an illustration for "An August Sporting Tour" by F. S. Stallknecht and Charles E. Whitehead, in *Frank Leslie's New Family Magazine*, November 13–20, 1858. It is believed to be the earliest illustration of double-ended carry boats with flat, elliptical bottom boards, visible on the boat disappearing at the far left. (Courtesy of Adirondack Museum)

transom-built predecessor. Dwight Grant referred to short (11- to 13-foot) double-ended guideboats as "raiders" due to their lightness and ability to be easily carried in and out of fishing areas that were relatively inaccessible.

Kenneth Durant, in a 1958 conversation with Willard Sutton, guide for the Prospect House (Blue Mountain Lake) and Camp Cedars (F. C. Durant's camp on Forked Lake), asked why the guideboat was ever made with a transom stern: "I don't know," Sutton replied. "They were no good. I had one. When I could get a double-ender I just pulled the square stern up on the bank and left it there."[41]

### Early Narratives and Depictions of Double-Ended Guideboats

During the 1860s, progress was made in reducing the guideboat's weight from its planking, ribs, and bottom board. This refined guideboat is accurately described by W. H. Boardman in his 1901 book, *The Lovers of the Woods*:

> He saw, resting in stalls or pockets made of smooth poles, boats which to his unaccustomed eye seemed to be duplicates of each other. The stern and bow were alike and were decked for a foot or so from the stem toward the waist. The gunwale lines swelled sharply out from the bow and ran to amidships in a gradually softened curve, becoming nearly but not quite straight lines. They exactly repeated themselves from there to the stern. Hardy could not discover a straight line in the hull. It was a tangle of beautiful, varying curves, the result of lives of study by skillful designers and expert woodsmen. The strips of quartered pine that formed the graceful shell were, in places, less than an eighth of an inch thick. Each strip had been chisel-edged and perfectly matched, and riveted to its adjoin-

ing strip as it had been moulded and screwed to the spruce knees which had been fashioned to model the boat. The matching and finishing had been so perfectly done that the joints were not visible to him. The surface was leathery; it was a dainty, graceful, and seaworthy boat, —"built for freight, and yet for speed, a beautiful and gallant craft."

Its place was on the water, right side up, but it was well within an ordinary man's capacity to carry one of them bottom side up, over the head, balanced at the centre on a wooden yoke carved out to fit the shoulders. [Its perfection] has been a slow development, with improvements suggested by use. . . . it has been a pretty race in competitive designing by men who have used the boats as well as built them; sturdy, ingenious woodsmen who generously applauded each other's successes.[42]

The following depictions by Winslow Homer, Seneca Ray Stoddard, and Arthur Fitzwilliam Tait are representative of the many artistic renditions of guideboats, both clapboard lapstrake and smooth skin, built in the 1860s and 1870s.

### *Winslow Homer*

Winslow Homer (1836–1910) not only brilliantly portrayed nature but also captured the character of working people in his paintings. Boats were an essential part of the Adirondack culture, and his paintings included virtually every type of craft to be seen on the rivers and lakes.

**FIGURE 1-32** Two paintings by Winslow Homer. (Left) "Eliphalet Terry" (1874) is the earliest known painting of a clapboard-lapstrake, double-ended guideboat. Note the straight deck (Courtesy of The Century Association, New York). Another watercolor, "Playing a Fish" (1875), by Homer (not shown here) at the Sterling and Francine Clark Art Institute, Williamstown, Massachusetts, depicts Terry in the same boat and clearly reveals the stern to be pointed. (Right) "Boy Fishing," is a watercolor of an angler at the North Woods Club near Minerva in 1892. The boat is a circa 1860s smooth-skin, double-ended guideboat, with a prominent stem post and straight deck. (Courtesy of San Antonio Museum of Art)

FIGURE 1-33 "The Blue Boat" (1892) by Winslow Homer. The location is probably Mink Pond at the North Woods Club. The paddler is the guide Rufus Wallace and the boy in the bow is Michael Flynn. (Photograph © 2018 Museum of Fine Arts, Boston)

*Seneca Ray Stoddard*

The most prolific photographer of the Adirondacks, Seneca Ray Stoddard (1844–1917) published annual guidebooks, most notably *The Adirondacks: Illustrated,* from 1874 to 1914.

FIGURE 1-34 Photographs by Seneca Ray Stoddard. (Above) Detail of "Running the Rapids," 1880s. (Right) "Raquette River at Sweeney Carry," 1888. Note the guide setting the boat down at the end of the carry. (Courtesy of Adirondack Museum)

**FIGURE 1-35** "An Anxious Moment" by Arthur Fitzwilliam Tait, 1880. (Courtesy of Michele and Donald D'Amour Museum of Fine Arts, Springfield, Massachusetts)

### *Arthur Fitzwilliam Tait*

"An Anxious Moment" (1880) is by the English-born artist Arthur Fitzwilliam Tait (1819–1905), well known for his many paintings of Adirondack sporting life. Surprisingly, this is his only depiction of a guideboat. It shows two guides in a smooth-skin, double-ended guideboat on Long Lake, "just below Plumley's looking down the lake."[43]

FIGURE 1-36 A 22-foot transom-built family, or church, boat, built by W. A. Martin in the early 1880s. The seats are not original to the boat. Rushton and Grant offered both types of these "chair seats"—either spindle-back or cane-back.

## Other Boats of Guideboat Construction

### Family, or Church, Boats and Freight Boats

Variations on the guideboat were constructed by many builders. One type was known as a "family," or "church," boat, built to take a whole family across the lake to, for example, a chapel for Sunday services and other community gatherings. These boats were usually varnished and anywhere from 18 to over 20 feet in length.

FIGURE 1-37 (Left) A double-ended church boat built in the 1880s by Caleb Chase of Newcomb. It has three pairs of oarlock socket straps. The backrests have not been attached to the seats and are leaning up against the gunwale. (Right) A double-ended church boat built in the 1890s by Elbridge G. Ricketson of Bloomingdale.

Although also of guideboat construction, freight boats were more heavily built. They were either double-ended or square-sterned. Some double enders have subsequently had their sterns cut off and a transom added to accommodate an outboard motor.

## The Westport Boat

There is a unique freight boat, of guideboat construction, known as the Westport boat. Of all the lakes in the interior of the Adirondacks, it is found only on the Ausable lakes of the Adirondack Mountain Reserve, also known as the Ausable Club, near Keene Valley. These boats are relatively large, stable, and too heavy to be carried by one person. Who built them and why they are found only at this location has long been a mystery. It now seems likely, however, that the builder was Dennis Hayes of Westport, influenced by Frederick W. Rice, then of Essex.

By 1850, the village of Westport had become a distribution center from Lake Champlain inland to Elizabethtown, Keene, Lake Placid, and Saranac Lake. Cargo and

FIGURE 1-38 (Top) An early double-ended freight boat from Lower Chateaugay Lake. It is 22 feet, 2 inches long. The hull has only four strakes on each side. The bow deck is straight, with no deck cap or center cover board. (Center Right) Iron nails, tacked only from the outside-in, were used to secure the smooth-skin planking of the hull. (Bottom Right) The iron oarlock socket strap, a common type, resembles a design used by Rushton, among others. (Courtesy of Franklin County Historical and Museum Society, Malone, New York) (Bottom Left) A square-ended freight boat, modified for an outboard motor.

passengers arriving by way of the lake were met there by wagons and stagecoaches for the journey to the interior.

With regard to the building site of the Westport boat, in his book *A View of Westport, N.Y., on Lake Champlain*, Raymond C. Clark describes a building he remembers situated along the wharf, in the loft of which "were housed several Adirondack style rowboats built by a local craftsman, Dennis Hayes. These graceful, stable and easily maneuvered boats were rented out by the hour or day."[44] Clark's account was published in 1972; if his childhood recollections date from when he was six or seven (he was born in 1908), Dennis Hayes was still building boats in 1914–1915. The appeal of Westport as a flourishing resort back in the 1880s may well have encouraged him as a young man to begin building and repairing boats there.

In 1872 Frederick Rice, born in Hartford, Connecticut, moved to Essex, the village just north of Westport, having taken a job as a surveyor for the railroad being built along the lakeshore from Whitehall to Plattsburgh. This section of the track was completed in 1875, and so Rice decided to learn the boat-building trade in Essex, which was becoming known as a boat-building center. It is possible that Hayes in Westport and Rice in nearby Essex became acquainted sometime between 1872 and 1878, as both men shared an interest in boatbuilding.

In 1878 Rice moved with his wife and infant son to Saranac Lake to begin his career as a boatbuilder and photographer. In that year, he helped William Martin build the small steamer *Water Lily*.[45] Dennis Hayes is cited as having helped to move the *Water Lily* from Saranac Lake to Lake Placid in 1884. It is possible that Hayes could have sought out Rice in Saranac Lake at that time, for advice and instruction in the building of a sturdy livery boat—that is, a boat for hire—suitable for Lake Champlain.

Another possible influence on Dennis Hayes, and/or on Frederick Rice, in the building of the Westport boat is William Henry Stanton (1844–1881). Coincidentally, guideboat builder Stanton, from Long Lake, was also at this time building large lake boats and guideboats in Port Henry, just south of Westport. From the *Port Henry Herald*, April 5, 1877:

> Henry Stanton, a Long Lake guide, has been building at the shops of the Lake Champlain and Moriah R.R. some of the prettiest and best rowboats ever constructed along Lake Champlain. Captain Flinn says—and he is a good judge—that they are more perfect boats

FIGURE 1-39 A Westport boat. It does not have yoke cleats, as it is not meant to be carried by one person. Length 17 feet, 6 inches, width 42 inches, depth 14 inches, with minimal sheer. (Courtesy of Woodward Boat Shop)

than are built in New York City. Some of them holding three or four persons weigh but 70 pounds and can be easily carried on the back. A number of gentlemen in Port Henry are having boats built by Stanton. Tracy has got what he considers the "boss" boat, built by Stanton. It is 22 ft. long, 5ft. wide, 20 in. deep, 32 in. high at the bow and 28 in. at the stern, and a perfect model.[46]

Three years later, Dwight Grant asked Stanton, then back in Long Lake, to come to Boonville to teach him how to build guideboats. Whether he and Hayes or Rice ever met is unknown.

All nine of the boats in the Ausable Club's boathouse have a unique construction "signature" typical of the guideboats built by Frederick Rice. The first two pairs of scribe ribs are chamfered at their bottom-board ends, at both bow and stern. Until observed in the Westport boats, this characteristic had not been seen on any other builder's boats other than those by Rice and his son. The lines and measurements of one of the original Westport boats were recorded by guideboat builder Christopher Woodward of Saranac Lake, who built two Westport boats in 2005 and 2007.

Other characteristics of the Westport boat are an extremely large pie-piece-shaped deck cap covering about two-thirds of the deck's surface, the unique shape of the seat cleats, and in some boats the absence of a stem post.

In 1891 a notice posted on the gate at the Adirondack Mountain Reserve stated:

**FIGURE 1-40** Characteristics of the Westport boat. (Top) The deck cap is very large and there is no stem post. (Center Left) A stem post is present on this boat. (Center, right) The design of the seat cleat is unique to these boats. The arms of the seat frames fit into the two notches. (Bottom Left and Right) The first two pairs of scribe ribs are chamfered at the bottom board. The stem foot is sharply pointed. This boat was built using alternating light and dark planking.

"Boats and Boat-house Cottages"

A number of new boats of approved model for safety have been placed upon the lower lake. These may be rented by the hour or day. On Sundays . . . boats will not be rented.

"Charge For Boats"

The authorized guides have their own boats on both lakes.

Persons desiring to hire company boats on the lower lake will be charged for them:

| | |
|---|---|
| For one-half hour or less | $0.25 |
| First hour or fraction of an hour | .35 |
| Second and subsequent hours or fraction | .20 |
| For the day | 1.00 |
| | $1.80 |

Boats must be returned by 6:30 p.m., except under special agreement.

Company boats on the upper lake hired only with special permit and key at one dollar for any part of a day.[16]

This notice may represent the original delivery of Westport boats to the Ausable lakes.

The following photographs show the popularity of the Westport boat on Lake Champlain in the early 1890s.

FIGURE 1-41 Detail of a photograph, circa 1892, of Westport boats, three in the foreground and three in the background, beached at Barber's Point, just south of Westport. All have light-colored hulls with dark gunwales. (Courtesy of Erwin Barber)

FIGURE 1-42 Detail of an undated postcard, circa 1910, of a Westport boat. It also has a white hull, dark gunwales, and large deck caps. The boat is on the Vermont side of the lake, opposite Westport. The caption reads: "River scene on Otter Creek, mouth of Old Dug Way, used in letting American Fleet out of Otter Creek, War of 1812, Lake Champlain, N.Y., No. 21." (Courtesy of Edward Comstock, Jr.)

## Construction and Distinctive Components of the Guideboat

TRAVEL IN THE ADIRONDACKS in the nineteenth century was often easier by water than by land. Workboats had the same role as pickup trucks do today. Small-craft historian John Gardner pointed out:

> [Small boats] were built without benefit of designers' lines, and mostly by amateurs. By "amateur" I mean those not regularly working at boatbuilding as their main occupation.
>
> The nails and lumber for a skiff or a wherry were easily come by, and farmers and fishermen could and did build themselves boats in their barns and dooryards at odd times when they didn't have any thing else to do.[48]

When William F. Martin, the pioneering Adirondack hotel owner, foresaw the need for guides and boats to develop his business, he turned to local woodsmen, including boatbuilder William McLenathen, who had the ability and knowledge to produce the needed craft. No new techniques or innovations other than the design were introduced. The early guideboats were flat-bottomed, with a graceful sheer line. The hull had a sharp bow that flowed into a gently curving middle section and then to the high-tucked transom stern.

FIGURE 1-43 Two quarter-patterns of a bottom board. One would be traced four times, once in each quadrant, to form the shape of a single elliptical bottom board. Laid side by side, as shown, they form a half-section. A single (complete) or a half-pattern of the bottom board is more commonly used. A single bottom board is a distinctive feature of the Adirondack guideboat. Patterns such as these are copied, usually onto white pine, which is then sawn and beveled along each edge to conform to the deadrise (angle) of the ribs when fastened into place.

The basic components of the guideboat are bottom board, ribs and stems, and planking. A flat bottom board, natural-crook ribs, and overlapping planking are hardly innovations; they are almost as old as boatbuilding itself. A boat from the third century A.D. has been discovered in Denmark that made use of these techniques.[49]

### Bottom Board

The backbone of the guideboat is its flat "plank keel," or bottom board.[50] It is made from an inch-thick white pine board, planed to 3/4 inch or less. It is elliptical in shape, about 8 inches at its widest, usually at the middle, narrowing at the ends to about 3/4 inch.

FIGURE 1-44 An elliptical bottom board. (Courtesy of Woodward Boat Shop)

FIGURE 1-45 Ribs are sawn from the natural crooks of spruce roots. (Left) Spruce stump. (Right) Root section. (Courtesy of Woodward Boat Shop)

FIGURE 1-46 (Left) A root crook, or knee, sawn from a stump. Ribs have been penciled in ready to be cut. (Right) A set of guideboat ribs and stems cut from spruce roots. (Courtesy of Woodward Boat Shop)

## Ribs

Ribs are made from the natural curves of the root crooks of red spruce stumps. In early days the grubbing out of stumps was an everyday chore. It was essential labor done with a shovel and hoe to clear the woods, creating fields for plow and pasture. The stumps would then be split into root sections with wedges and mauls or sawn with two-man crosscut saws. These sections would be sawn into slabs, or they might be cut at the local sawmill. Cutting out ribs from the slabs was accomplished with a frame, or buck, saw. Guideboat builders use wooden patterns to determine the exact shape of the ribs, stems, oars, and bottom board. It is these patterns that allow a builder's boats to be so consistent over time.

Once sawn to the shape of the pattern and meticulously finished, the ribs are fastened to the bottom board, forming the frame of the boat. There are twenty-four to thirty pairs of ribs required for the standard 16-foot guideboat. Because they are sawn to follow the grain, they do not lose their shape and therefore no internal cross-bracing is needed.

The stem is made from the same crooks as the ribs. The early boats had a high-tucked transom carved from a solid section of the stump; it required skill and effort to shape. An axe was used to rough out the lower stem and outer face while the inner face was sawn. Fine shaping and fitting was done with a hand plane and chisel. The earliest boats were wider forward of the middle, making the forward section more buoyant, giving them what is called a "cod-headed" hull.

**FIGURE 1-47** (Above) A frame saw made by Merlin Austin that was used for cutting out the ribs. (Courtesy of Harold M. Austin, Jr.) (Right) The frame saw was replaced by a treadle-powered scroll saw, or jigsaw, and then, in the early 1900s, by an electric-powered band saw. (Courtesy of Adirondack Museum)

**FIGURE 1-48** (Above) The patterns of thirteen ribs, some of which have reversed curves. At the bottom is the foot, the part of the rib that is attached to the bottom board. (Right) A stem pattern laid out on a 2½ inch-thick slice of root crook, or knee plank.

## Planking

Early guide's boats such as those built by McLenathen and Chase in the 1850s were made of relatively thick planks (½ inch), overlapped in a clapboard manner. Clear quarter-sawn pine and cedar boards for the bottom and planking were readily procured at the mill. Fashioning the planking from the boards was done with a frame saw or a hand saw. Decks, gunwales, cleats, and seats were also sawn from boards and fashioned with hand saws and planes. Hand planes were used for the planking bevels. The fastenings were

FIGURE 1-49 The Wallace Emerson boat shop in Long Lake in the 1930s. (Above) The bottom board, ribs, and stems have been secured on a boat-building stock to prepare for planking. (Below) A guideboat on a boat-building stock, in the process of being planked. (Courtesy of Adirondack Museum) (Left) A bottom-board view of a guideboat skeleton, ready for planking. The bottom is not level, but has an arc built into it from stem to stem, called a "rocker," that helps the boat turn. (Courtesy of Thomas Bissell)

mostly small iron nails clinched, or bent over. Planks were nailed to the ribs with iron nails, or screwed with blunt-tipped iron screws, and the lap was clinched together with a single row of iron nails tacked from outside to inside and bent over. Holes for the nails were either punched with an awl or bored with a hand drill. A small hammer and clinching iron were used to clinch the planking seams together.

By the late 1850s, commercial production made available clenchable copper tacks and sharp-pointed screws that could be machine-produced in smaller sizes. This allowed the builders to use thinner (⅜ inch) planking and ribs, reducing the weight of the boat substantially.

The development of feather lapping by beveling the upper and lower edges of hull planks was initially accomplished with planks that were ¼-inch thick or greater. Experimentation resulted in varying degrees of smoothness with some overlap visible (a modified clapboard appearance), until complete smoothness was achieved. To further reduce weight, planking was thinned to the lowest practical limit of its construction strength, about 3/16 inch. The resulting boat was not only lighter but also quieter and faster for hunting and fishing, without compromising its strength and load-carrying capacity. The tacks used were longer than the plank is thick, so the point of the tack extended through the plank. By holding a clinching iron against the point as it was tapped in with a light hammer, the point was not just bent over but turned back onto itself in the form of a J, with the tip burying into the wood. To protect this delicate edge from splitting when the tack is driven through it, a small awl with a diamond-shaped point is used to punch a hole, severing the fibers of the plank. The lap edge is double-tacked from both the inside and outside, in a staggered pattern. By the late 1860s, this was the building method of choice.

Further weight reduction took place by making the size of the individual pieces, such as ribs, seats, cleats, and oars, smaller. A significant reduction in weight was achieved by discarding the transom in favor of a sharp stern, making the boat pointed at both ends—a double ender.

FIGURE 1-50 (Top) A plank beveled along both edges of its length. Beveled overlapped planking is the hallmark of the Adirondack guideboat. (Center) Both upper and lower edges are beveled to a feather edge, resulting in a smooth skin. The plank is then screwed to the ribs, and the seam between the planks is tacked. Three planks are shown in this photo; the bottom one has not yet been tacked. (Bottom) The lap has been tacked from the outside-in along its seam. The inside edge of the lap has not yet been tacked. Note the tacked scarph joint in the upper plank, where two planks are joined together to make one full-length strake. (Courtesy of Woodward Boat Shop)

FIGURE 1-51 A smooth-skin feather-beveled guideboat planked to its fourth strake. (Courtesy of Woodward Boat Shop)

As more boats were built, patterns were made for each component. Individual pieces were planed thinner as the refinementof the boats continued, boat by boat. The construction process did not vary so much as the dimensions did. As the boats were used, their strengths and weaknesses were exposed, to be reinforced or corrected in the subsequent build. The overriding concern was with making the boat lighter for the carry while maintaining its structural integrity.

In the water, the boat's strength is at its greatest. It is at the landings and carries that it is at its most fragile and sustains the most damage.

The earliest guide's boats might seem to be roughly built compared to the refined boats built in the 1870s and 1880s. However, as Willard Hanmer observed:

> There were no light, high speed woodworking machines in those days such as I have in my shop today, and even hand tools like ratchet screw drivers and better grade planes and chisels were not to be had. Even the sandpaper was of poor quality. In spite of all this, most of the boats built by these old timers were so well built that I wonder when my last boat is completed, how well I will have qualified to stand with those who have finished their boats and gone before me.[51]

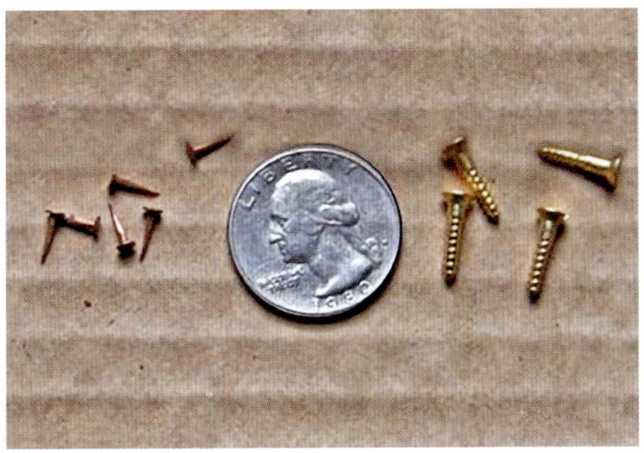

FIGURE 1-52 (Left) Hull planks are attached with about four thousand 5/16 inch copper tacks and about two thousand ½ inch screws. (Center) The tacking tools used in early guideboat construction by Long Lake builder Merlin Austin: a coffin-shaped smoothing plane, a tacking hammer, a clinching iron, and two awls. (Courtesy of Harold M. Austin, Jr.) (Right) The lap is double-tacked in a staggered pattern. The view from inside the hull of the two rows of tacks (between two ribs). The top row shows four tack heads. These tacks were driven from the inside feather edge and clinched on the outside. The lower row shows five clinched tack points. They were driven from the outside at the feather edge and clinched inside. (Courtesy of Woodward Boat Shop)

FIGURE 1-53 Early 1880s machinery used by Theodore and Willard Hanmer of Saranac Lake. (Top) A Williamsport Machine Company thickness planer. (Bottom) A band saw. (Courtesy of Woodward Boat Shop)

Through the 1870s and 1880s, as the population in the Adirondacks grew, mechanized tools such as saws and thickness planers became available. Advances in steel manufacturing made higher-quality chisels and planes available, which allowed builders to further refine each component of the boat. The guideboat was thinned down to its practical limits and reached its peak of refinement. But throughout, construction methods did not change. Hand tools were still primarily used to build the boat. That is true even today.

In 1935, Talbot Bissell, after repeated visits as a young man to Warren Cole's boat shop in Long Lake, wrote:

> [Nothing] but the simplest of hand tools [were used]: draw knives, gouges, spoke-shaves, chisels, shiny from years of use and all of unbelievable sharpness. Planes of various sizes and shapes and purposes—planes from which cedar shavings delicate as the finest tissue curled and fell into the ever growing pile at the end of the bench. Other tools were homemade to fit some particular job.
>
> The amount of hand labor entering the construction of a guideboat is simply unbelievable to anyone who has never watched one being built. Machinery is of little use here even today; mass production is impossible. In this machine age it is one field where man the craftsman is still supreme and always will be.[52]

## Carry Yoke and Cleats

Early boats were carried upside-down with or without a carry yoke. The width within the gunwales of most of these carry boats was 36 to 38 inches, which comfortably accommodates the outstretched arms of an average person.

The carry yoke used for guide's boats was modified from the hand-carved one-piece yoke that has long been used to carry buckets of water, milk, or maple sap. Depictions of such a carrying device can be seen on the walls of ancient Egyptian tombs. The ends of the earliest boat yokes were simply placed across the top of the mid-gunwales, where a semi-circular notch had been carved.

The following description published in the *Spirit of the Times* tells of an 1843 trip into the central Adirondacks. At the end of Fourth Lake of the Fulton Chain, the party prepared for the carry to Fifth Lake:

**FIGURE 1-54** One of the earliest depictions of a short, double-ended carry boat. This wood engraving illustrated "A Visit to 'John Brown's Tract'," an account by journalist/artist T. B. Thorpe in *Harper's New Monthly Magazine*, July 1859.

> We had to transfer our packs, etc. from the boat to our backs, each carrying about 50 lbs., and Higby [carried] the boat by means of a yoke rigged across the gunwales, turned downside up, with his head inside.[53]

By the early 1850s, the ends of the yoke were provided with iron extensions that lodged in the rounded notches, or sockets, cut into the top of the gunwales. S. H. Hammond on an Adirondack trip in 1853, described them:

> A "yoke" is provided, such as every man in the country, especially all who have visited a "sugar bush" at the season of sugar making, has seen. At the end of this yoke is a round iron projection, made to fit into a socket in the upper rave [gunwale] of the boat. The craft is turned bottom upwards, the yoke adjusted to the shoulders, the iron projections fitted into the sockets, and the boatman marches off with his boat, like a turtle with his shell upon his back. He will carry it thus sometimes half a mile before stopping to rest.[54]

Also from the *New-York Tribune*, in 1850, noted under the heading "Summer Retreats:"

> At the home of Mr. Austin the tourist finds a *home*—neatness and civility make the entertainment a luxury after the rough travel of the wilderness. With Robinson, an experienced hunter for guide, we pushed off in a light skiff for the Raquette. . . . The manner of getting round the rapids, or over the "carrying places," with boat inverted upon the shoulders of the guide, and the rest loaded with baggage . . . is a comical sight and a tiresome march.[55]

A significant refinement by Adirondack builders soon replaced the gunwale method of securing the yoke. Narrow horizontal wooden pieces were screwed to the upper portions of the center ribs, with a U-shaped notch in their upper border to accommodate the yoke ends. These pieces are referred to as yoke cleats in the Adirondacks. The term "cleats" (elsewhere known as "risers") is also used to refer to the narrow pieces that support the seats at the bow, center, and stern.

The word "cleats" was mentioned by S. H. Hammond as early as 1853: "I tied the end of the line to the cleets [*sic*] across

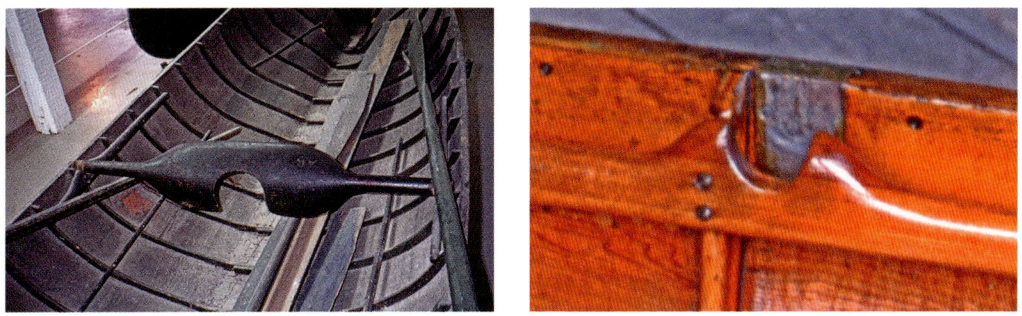

**FIGURE 1-55** (Left) A hand-carved yoke with its ends in notches of the yoke cleat. Cleats supporting the yoke are screwed to the ribs. The longer "arm" of the yoke cleat is directed toward the bow in order to accommodate varying lengths of the forward reach. (Right) A brass plate behind the notch protects the sheer strake.

the knees of the boat."[56] And in an 1857 trip, T. Addison Richards referred to the carry yoke:

> Leaving the Lower Saranac we will pass pleasantly along some half a dozen miles—then make a short portage, the guide carrying the huge boat by a yoke on the back, to the Middle Saranac.[57]

W. H. Boardman described the presence of yoke cleats and offered one of the earliest specific descriptions of how a boat was carried:

> The oars were laid in the boat, with the handles forward and the blades aft and tied fast with buckskin thongs. The yoke was set in its notches inside each gunwale [the yoke cleats] and made fast with thongs. Hardy tucked his hat and coat under the forward deck and then carefully imitated the form he had watched but had never before attempted. He stood at the starboard side and, leaning over the boat, grasped the port gunwale with his right hand, the starboard gunwale with his left hand, and lightly lifted the boat over his head. When the yoke nestled to a firm bearing on his shoulders, he cheerfully said good bye and strode off on the trail with a confident feeling that everything was all right.[58]

As travel over the carries increased, sledges and wagons were employed to transport the boats at the more accessible sites. In 1893 the State Forest Commission noted:

> A guide in traveling through the lakes generally carries only one person in his boat, but will, if asked to do so, take an additional passenger without extra charge. The boats, which by some unwritten law are painted blue, are from fifteen to seventeen feet long, weigh from sixty-five to seventy-eight pounds, and cost about sixty-five dollars. The oarsman sits near the bow, with his passenger in the stern, and the extra passenger, if any, on the middle seat. On landing at a "carry" the guide picks up the boat and, turning it bottom upwards, places it over his head, with its weight resting on his shoulders, using a neck-yoke for that purpose. The passenger is expected to carry his own "duffel" or luggage, which should be limited to a small hand-satchel and a rubber coat. Sometimes a party will employ an extra guide to run a baggage boat, in which

**FIGURE 1-56** Inscribed "Round Lake, Bartlett's," the view of a boat-wagon at the carry between Round Lake (Middle Saranac) and Upper Saranac Lake is by an unknown photographer, circa 1890. Virgil C. Bartlett established a modest hostelry on this much-traveled route in 1854. The fare to transport a guideboat was fifty cents in 1892 according to that year's *Map of the Adirondack Wilderness* by S. R. Stoddard. (Courtesy of Adirondack Research Room, Saranac Lake Free Library)

case he looks after the duffel. Where the portages are short the guide carries his boat across; but on some of the longer ones, roads have been made, and a boat-wagon, rigged for this particular purpose, is used to transport the boats and baggage across, a fee, varying from seventy-five cents to one dollar and fifty cents, being charged for the service in each case. This fee must be paid by the tourist, instead of the guide. There are some long carries, however, on which there are no boat-wagons—Bottle Pond Carry, on the Tupper Lake route, for instance, which is over four miles long—and over which the guides carry their boats on their heads the entire distance.[59]

## Oars

From the *International Maritime Dictionary:*

> **Oar:** A long shaft of wood with a blade or thin enlarged surface at one end and a handle at the other, the portion between being called the loom. It is in theory a lever . . . The blade immersed in the water forms the fulcrum, and the resultant pressure against the handle, applied to a rowlock or fixed pin in the side of the boat at some point on the loom, drives the boat forward.[60]

FIGURE 1-57 (Left) An 8-foot Long Lake guideboat oar. From top to bottom: the blade, the neck, the outboard loom between the oarlock and the blade, the oarlock pin, or yoke, the inboard loom between the handle and oarlock, and the handle or grip. The outboard loom transitions from octagonal to round about half way up its length. (Top Center) The neck, or the transition from the loom to the blade. It is ovoid in shape, being wider than it is thick. (Second From Top Center) The transition between the octagonal and the round or oval shaft of the outboard loom. The taper of the inboard and outboard loom contributes to the flexibility that is characteristic of guideboat oars. (Second From Bottom Center) The four-sided area, the "land," where the oarlock yoke is mounted. The chamfering stops below the oarlock and begins again above it. (Bottom Center ) The handle and the octagonal inboard loom. (Top Right) The blade as viewed on edge, showing the taper. (Bottom Right) The blade with a center spine for stiffness. (Courtesy of Woodward Boat Shop)

Guideboat oars are made from red (soft) maple or spruce 1 ⅜ inches thick, and are sawn, or carved, from a solid plank, rather than turned on a lathe. The blades are 5 to 6 inches wide and 21 to 25 inches long. The neck is narrow and there is a short, rounded shaft transitioning into a square loom that has been chamfered into eight sides. About 27 inches from the end of the handle, or grip, the chamfering stops and there is a four-sided "land" where the oarlock yoke is attached. Two to three inches inboard of that, the upper or inboard portion of the loom is chamfered again to eight sides, until it transitions into the grip. The oar is tapered its whole length, with the extra mass of the upper loom counter-balancing the longer lower loom and blade. Guideboat oars are designed to be light but strong, and are usually 8 feet in length for a 16-foot boat. The outboard loom is shaved down to a point that the oar becomes limber and acquires flexibility. This characteristic gives a kick at the end of each stroke, which provides an extra impetus, propelling the boat forward.

> A good Adirondack guide-boat oar is a tough one to improve, since the outer loom and blade usually are already shaved to the limit of light weight for the "carry."[61]

Like the other principal components of the guideboat (ribs, bottom board, and stems), oars were made from patterns and were designed to be light and efficient. Guideboat oars evolved to fit both of these needs to perfection. In order to gain maximum leverage, the inboard portion needed to be longer than half the width of the boat, resulting in overlapped, or cross-handed, rowing. The narrower the boat, and the longer the oar, the greater the overlap.

As Kenneth Durant noted:

> The well-made guide-boat oar is almost as complex and ingenious in design as the boat it propels. The oars had to be properly balanced to exert the utmost propulsive force with the least exertion. They had to be strong to hold the boat in the rapids or to make a dash after a swimming buck. Like the boat, the oars had to be light because they were carried over the portages. The noise they made in the rowlocks when the oarsman rowed vigorously had to be silenced through gentle strokes when he approached a trout hole.[62]

## Oarlocks

An oarlock, or "rowlock," is a generic term for the various arrangements used to provide a fulcrum for an oar in rowing. There are many varieties. It may consist simply of a pair of thole pins (upright wooden dowels mounted on the top of the gunwale), an outrigger supporting the oar, or a single pin passing through a hole in the oar.

The oarlock, also called a "swivel rowlock," consists of a forked shank that fits into a socket attached to the gunwale.[63] In the Adirondacks, it is a two-part system made of cast iron, brass, or bronze consisting of an:

> **Oarlock socket strap**, the piece attached to the gunwale, typically a plate 10 inches long by 1¼ inches wide fastened to the gunwale with ten screws. It has at its center a 2-inch-long vertical barrel with a ½-inch hole to accept the:

> **Oarlock pin** ("yoke," "horn"), the piece attached to the oar, by means of a yoke that surrounds the flat sides of the oar, from which a pin, ½ inch in diameter, extends and fits into the hole in the barrel of the oarlock socket strap, thus

**FIGURE 1-58** (Top Left) An early iron oarlock socket strap. (Top Center) A plain brass or bronze strap. (Top Right) A brass or bronze oarlock socket strap with a scroll design. (Bottom Left) An Adirondack oarlock with an iron pin attached to a disk-shaped brass yoke that clasps the oar. (Bottom Right) An oar with its attached oarlock in the socket strap that is screwed to the gunwale. (Courtesy of Woodward Boat Shop)

forming a mechanical lever to propel the boat.

Stealth and quiet were requisite for hunting at night and for approaching holes to fish for wary trout. Shipping the oars (taking them into the boat) makes noise and takes time. By having oars fixed to the boat, the rower is able to let go of the oars and instantly pick up gun or rod while the oars, trailing in the water alongside the boat, remain in position for use. Because the Adirondack oarlock holds the blade of the oar perpendicular to the surface of the water, it is not possible to feather the oars (turning the oars after a stroke so that the blade is parallel with the surface of the water until it is back in position to dip into the water for the next stroke). The oar is held snugly between the sides of the oarlock yoke so that there is no slop, or sideways movement. Not only does this transfer the force applied to the oar more efficiently, but, more important for hunting and fishing, it is noiseless. Andrew Steever wrote that "the efficiency of the non-feathering lock, such as the . . . pinned yoke of the guide boat, is the highest, maybe 97%, and there is not much potential improvement."[64]

As early as 1848, pinned oars and oarlock socket straps were a familiar sight in Hamilton County, as described by "M" in 1849 in the weekly sporting journal *Spirit of the Times*:

> One peculiarity about their boats or skiffs is that the oars are fastened to the old-fashioned iron rowlock, which turns on a pivot in the gunwale,

and are not used with thole-pins as in ordinary skiffs. . . . Then taking his oars, which all the time hang over the boat, attached to it by the iron row-lock, he gives a few smart strokes, and you dart rapidly ahead.[65]

And in 1860 Alfred B. Street felt it worthy of comment to note: "Each [of four Saranac boats] has two oars on iron pins."[66]

**FIGURE 1-59** An early hand-forged oarlock. (Courtesy of Woodward Boat Shop)

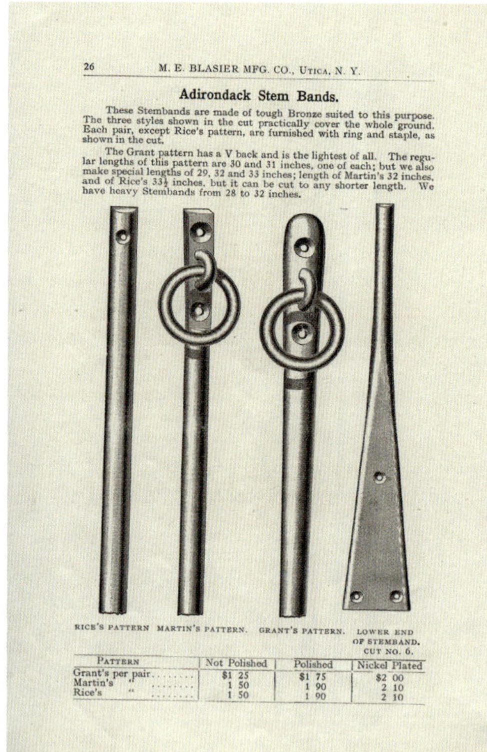

26 M. E. BLASIER MFG. CO., UTICA, N. Y.

## Adirondack Stem Bands.

These Stembands are made of tough Bronze suited to this purpose. The three styles shown in the cut practically cover the whole ground. Each pair, except Rice's pattern, are furnished with ring and staple, as shown in the cut.

The Grant pattern has a V back and is the lightest of all. The regular lengths of this pattern are 30 and 31 inches, one of each; but we also make special lengths of 29, 32 and 33 inches; length of Martin's 32 inches, and of Rice's 33½ inches, but it can be cut to any shorter length. We have heavy Stembands from 28 to 32 inches.

RICE'S PATTERN MARTIN'S PATTERN. GRANT'S PATTERN. LOWER END OF STEMBAND. CUT NO. 6.

| PATTERN | Not Polished | Polished | Nickel Plated |
|---|---|---|---|
| Grant's per pair........ | $1 25 | $1 75 | $2 00 |
| Martin's " ........ | 1 50 | 1 90 | 2 10 |
| Rice's " ........ | 1 50 | 1 90 | 2 10 |

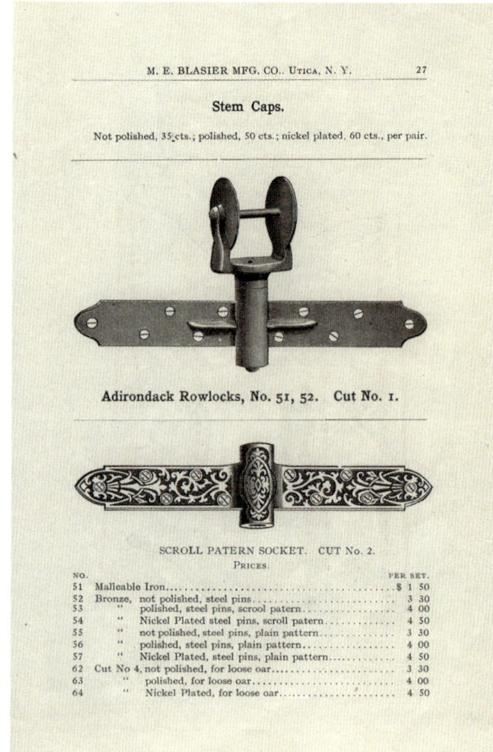

M. E. BLASIER MFG. CO., UTICA, N. Y. 27

## Stem Caps.

Not polished, 35 cts.; polished, 50 cts.; nickel plated, 60 cts., per pair.

Adirondack Rowlocks, No. 51, 52. Cut No. 1.

SCROLL PATERN SOCKET. CUT No. 2.

PRICES.

| NO. | | PER SET. |
|---|---|---|
| 51 | Malleable Iron........ | $ 1 50 |
| 52 | Bronze, not polished, steel pins........ | 3 30 |
| 53 | " polished, steel pins, scrool patern........ | 4 00 |
| 54 | " Nickel Plated steel pins, scroll patern........ | 4 50 |
| 55 | " not polished, steel pins, plain pattern........ | 3 30 |
| 56 | " polished, steel pins, plain pattern........ | 4 00 |
| 57 | " Nickel Plated, steel pins, plain pattern........ | 4 50 |
| 62 | Cut No 4, not polished, for loose oar........ | 3 30 |
| 63 | " polished, for loose oar........ | 4 00 |
| 64 | " Nickel Plated, for loose oar........ | 4 50 |

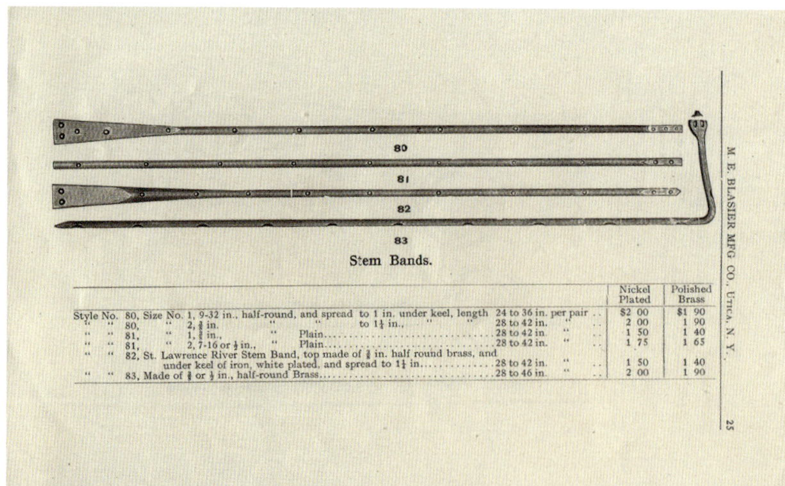

80

81

82

83

## Stem Bands.

| | | Nickel Plated | Polished Brass |
|---|---|---|---|
| Style No. 80, Size No. 1, 9-32 in., half-round, and spread to 1 in. under keel, length | 24 to 36 in. per pair .. | $2 00 | $1 90 |
| " " 80, " 2, ⅜ in. " " to 1¼ in., " " | 28 to 42 in. " .. | 2 00 | 1 90 |
| " " 81, " 1, ⅜ in., " Plain........ | 28 to 42 in. " .. | 1 50 | 1 40 |
| " " 81, " 2, 7-16 or ½ in., " Plain........ | 28 to 42 in. " .. | 1 75 | 1 65 |
| " " 82, St. Lawrence River Stem Band, top made of ⅜ in. half round brass, and under keel of iron, white plated, and spread to 1¼ in........ | 28 to 42 in. " .. | 1 50 | 1 40 |
| " " 83, Made of ⅜ or ½ in., half-round Brass........ | 28 to 46 in. " .. | 2 00 | 1 90 |

M. E. BLASIER MFG. CO., UTICA, N. Y. 25

**FIGURE 1-60** Excerpts from the 1907 *Boat, Canoe, and Yacht Hardware* trade catalogue of the M. E. Blasier Manufacturing Company of Utica, New York. The stem bands show the patterns of three prominent builders: Rice, Martin, and Grant. This was the catalogue's 15th annual edition. Blasier was the successor to the R. A. Moore hardware company of Kensington, Connecticut, that offered guideboat hardware in a catalogue published in 1883. (Courtesy of Edward Comstock, Jr.)

FIGURE 1-61 An 1870 pencil sketch of the Upper Ausable Lake by Frederick B. Allen. This is the earliest known depiction of cross-handed rowing. Inscribed at the lower right: "Upper Ausable L./ Looking N. E./ Aug. '70." (Courtesy of Adirondack Museum)

## Cross-Handed Rowing

In order to gain greater mechanical efficiency, the inboard length of the oar is increased. In a narrow boat, this results in cross-handed rowing. Kenneth Durant commented:

> The distance from the rowlock to the end of the handle is somewhat more than half the guideboat's beam, so that the handles cross at mid-stroke. This is one of the guideboat's most distinctive characteristics, seldom mentioned and frequently unobserved. The oars overlap on their inboard ends and are therefore rowed with the rower's arms crossed, one oar handle over the other.[67]

In cross-handed rowing the ends of the oars held by the rower usually overlap each other by about the width of the hands (about four inches) but sometimes by as much as eight to twelve inches. As Andrew Steever reminded rowers: "Just remember to keep your thumbs off the oar ends, and . . . your knuckles away from the opposite [oar], particularly if the . . . boat is lively on rough water."[68]

Depictions of cross-handed rowing can be seen in a sketch by Frederick B. Allen and a photograph by Seneca Ray Stoddard.

FIGURE 1-62 "The Way It Looks from the Stern Seat," an 1888 photograph by S. R. Stoddard, depicting cross-handed rowing. (Courtesy of Adirondack Museum)

## The Transition of Adirondack Guideboats, 1860s to 1890s

FIGURE 1-63 The "Chase Lake" boat (Lewis County), builder unknown, is an example of an early clapboard-lapstrake, transom-built guide's boat with a prominent stem post. (Courtesy of Adirondack Museum)

FIGURE 1-64 A smooth-skin, transom-built guide's boat. Earlier models have clapboard-lapstrake hulls. Built by Reuben Cary, Long Lake, in the late 1860s to early 1870s.

FIGURE 1-65 (Left) A smooth-skin double ender with straight decks and deck caps at bow and stern, thought to have been built in the mid- to late 1860s. Builder unknown.

FIGURE 1-66 An early (1870s) smooth-skin, double-ended guideboat. Note the straight bow deck and the shallow arced stern deck, providing a more comfortable position for the stern passenger, and the pie-piece-shaped deck caps. Note also the board seats, and the hole in the bow deck to hold a jacklight. Black (or blue) and green were the most common paint colors. Builder unknown.

FIGURE 1-67 The perfected guideboat, built in the early 1890s by Warren W. Cole of Long Lake. A varnished double ender with a smooth-skin hull, pie-piece-shaped deck caps, arc decks at bow and stern, and caned seats and backrests. All components are original.

## Endnotes


1. Kenneth Durant, ed., *Guide-Boat Days and Ways*, Blue Mountain Lake, NY: Adirondack Museum, 1963:15.
2. John Todd, *Long Lake*, Pittsfield, MA: E. P. Little, 1845:11.
3. A. E. Leavenworth, "Journal of a Surveying Excursion to Raquette Lake & Vicinity, August 1851," Adirondack Museum, microfilm:50, 53–54.
4. William Constable, Letter to his brother John, June 19, 1850, in Edith Pilcher, *The Constables*, Utica, NY: North Country Books, 1992:59–60.
5. "Noted Men and Women of the Champlain Valley and the Adirondacks," *Essex County Republican Annual for the Year 1892*, Keeseville, NY: W. Lansing & Son, 1892.
6. Alfred L. Donaldson, *History of the Adirondacks*, New York: Century, 1921, I:298.
7. S. H. Hammond, *Hills, Lakes, and Forest Streams*, New York: J. C. Derby, 1854:vii–viii.
8. Ralph Waldo Emerson, "The Adirondacs," *May-Day and Other Pieces*, Boston: Ticknor and Fields, 1867:43.
9. E. P. Wells, "The Adirondack Wilderness," *Williams Quarterly*, July 1863:244.
10. William H. H. Murray, *Adventures in the Wilderness; or, Camp-Life in the Adirondacks*, Boston: Fields, Osgood, 1869:47.
11. E. R. Wallace, *Descriptive Guide to the Adirondacks*, 5th ed., New York: Forest and Stream, 1876:115.
12. Bryant F. Tolles, Jr., *Resort Hotels of the Adirondacks*, Lebanon, NH: University Press of New England, 2003:102.
13. Federal Census for 1850, Harrietstown, New York.
14. Donaldson, 1921, II:305.
15. "Theodore Hanmer, Fifty Years Boat Builder, Still Active," *Watertown Daily Times*, February 2, 1940.
16. "Juvenal," "One of the Veterans," *Forest and Stream*, October 17, 1903:295.
17. "Juvenal," 1903:295.
18. Joel T. Headley, Letter to the Editor, *New York Times*, August 9, 1858.
19. Donaldson, 1921, I:305.
20. Donaldson, 1921, II:79.
21. Willard Sutton, Interview, 1958, Adirondack Museum, Durant Collection.
22. *Proceedings of the Board of Supervisors of the County of Hamilton for the Year 1885*, Hope, NY: Hamilton County Press Print, 1886:4.

23. S. H. Hammond, *Wild Northern Scenes; or, Sporting Adventures with the Rifle and the Rod*, New York: Derby & Jackson, 1857:35–36.
24. T. Addison Richards, "A Forest Story," *Harper's New Monthly Magazine*, August-September, 1859:316.
25. William J. Stillman, *The Crayon*, October 31, 1855:280–281.
26. Refer to Hallie E. Bond, *Boats and Boating in the Adirondacks*, 1995:136–138.
27. Alfred B. Street, *Woods and Waters; or, The Saranacs and Racket*, New York: M. Doolady, 1860:27, 65.
28. Amelia M. Murray, *Letters from the United States, Cuba, and Canada*, New York: G. P. Putnam, 1856:373.
29. "Shooting in the Adirondack," *All the Year Round*, London: September 29,1860:585–588.
30. W. H. Boardman, *The Lovers of the Woods*, New York: McClure, Phillips, 1901:80.
31. *Saranac & Raquette Journal*, Brooklyn: S. and R. Topographical Society, September 1, 1865:3.
32. A. Judd Northrup, *Camps and Tramps in the Adirondacks*, Syracuse, NY: Davis, Bardeen, 1880:110–113.
33. Lucia D. Pychowska, "To Saranac and Back—Sketches of American Life and Scenery," *The Continental Monthly*, December, 1864:666.
34. William H. H. Murray, 1869:27, 76, 80.
35. D. W. Mandell, "Letter to the Editor," *Forest and Stream*, March 9, 1876:74.
36. *Watertown Daily Times*, February 2, 1940.
37. Harry V. Radford, Letter in "Adirondack Department," *Field & Stream*, September 1901:408.
38. Frances Seaman, "Passing Years Made Guiding Obsolescent," *Tupper Lake Free Press*, August 20, 1980.
39. Donaldson, 1921, I:306.
40. Henry Van Dyke, *Little Rivers*, New York: Charles Scribner's Sons, 1895:67.
41. Durant Collection.
42. Boardman, 1901:78–80.
43. Warder H. Cadbury and Henry F. Marsh, *Arthur Fitzwilliam Tait*, Newark, DE: University of Delaware Press, 1986:252–253.
44. Raymond C. Clark, *A View of Westport, N.Y., on Lake Champlain; 1902–1972*, Elizabethtown, NY: Denton Publications, 1972:n.p.
45. *The Shore Owners' Association of Lake Placid*, Lake Placid, NY: 1973:23–24.
46. *Port Henry Herald*, April 5,1877.

47. "The Adirondack Park; Elizabethtown, Keene Valley and Wilmington Route," *Annual Report of the Forest Commission of the State of New York for 1891*, Albany, NY: James B. Lyon, 1892:161–162.
48. John Gardner, "The Wherry," in *Building Classic Small Craft*, Camden, ME: International Marine, 1977:181–182.
49. Romola and R. C. Anderson, *The Sailing Ship, Six Thousand Years of History*, New York: W. W. Norton, 1963:66–69.
50. René de Kerchove, *International Maritime Dictionary*, Princeton, NJ: D. Van Nostrand, 1948:539.
51. Durant, 1963: 235.
52. Talbot Bissell, "42 Pounds to Portage," in *The Skipper*, January 1967, Durant Collection.
53. Durant, 1963:17.
54. Hammond, 1857:36.
55. P. C. H., "Summer Retreats," *New-York Tribune*, August 29, 1850.
56. Hammond, 1857:58.
57. T. Addison Richards, *Appleton's Illustrated Hand-Book of American Travel*, New York: D. Appleton, 1857:169.
58. Boardman, 1901:86.
59. "Adirondack Guides," *Annual Report of the Forest Commission for the State of New York for 1893*, Albany, NY: James B. Lyon, 1894, I:346.
60. de Kerchove, 1948:496.
61. Andrew B. Steever, *Oars for Pleasure Rowing, Their Design and Use*, Mystic, CT: Mystic Seaport Museum,1993:71.
62. Kenneth and Helen Durant, *The Adirondack Guide-Boat.* Camden, ME: Adirondack Museum/International Marine, 1980:142.
63. de Kerchove, 1948:496, 606.
64. Steever, 1993:51.
65. M, "Hints on Trolling for Trout," *Spirit of the Times*, February 10, 1849:608.
66. Street, 1860:27.
67. Durant, 1980:84.
68. Steever, 1993:36.

# 2

# Guideboats and Their Builders

Part 2 is the result of innumerable trips to the Adirondacks over a period of twenty years. Initially intrigued by the region's history, the author developed a growing fascination for the Adirondack guideboat. Hands-on inspection, note-taking, and research regarding the boat and its builders soon characterized each visit.

## Emerson's Tribute to the Guides

THE MAJORITY of guideboat builders were guides—"the doctors of the wilderness"—as memorialized in this excerpt from Ralph Waldo Emerson's poem, "The Adirondacs."[1]

In Adirondac lakes,  
At morn or noon, the guide rows bareheaded:  
Shoes, flannel shirt, and kersey trousers make  
His brief toilette: at night, or in the rain,  
He dons a surcoat which he doffs at morn:  
A paddle in the right hand, or an oar,  
And in the left, a gun, his needful arms.  
By turns we praised the stature of our guides,  
Their rival strength and suppleness, their skill  
To row, to swim, to shoot, to build a camp,  
To climb a lofty stem, clean without boughs  
Full fifty feet, and bring the eaglet down:  
Temper to face wolf, bear, or catamount,  
And wit to trap or take him in his lair.  
Sound, ruddy men, frolic and innocent,  
In winter, lumberers; in summer, guides;  
Their sinewy arms pull at the oar untired  
Three times ten thousand strokes, from morn to eve.

Look to yourselves, ye polished gentlemen!  
No city airs or arts pass current here.  
Your rank is all reversed: let men of cloth  
Bow to the stalwart churls in overalls:  
*They* are the doctors of the wilderness,  
And we the low-prized laymen.

1 Ralph Waldo Emerson, "The Adirondacs," in *May-Day and Other Pieces,* Boston: Ticknor and Fields, 1867:47–49.

Cortez Fernando Moody, one of the guides for Emerson and "The Philosopher's Club" in 1858. This studio photograph was taken in the 1890s by G. F. Marvin, Keeseville, NY. (Courtesy of Adirondack Museum)

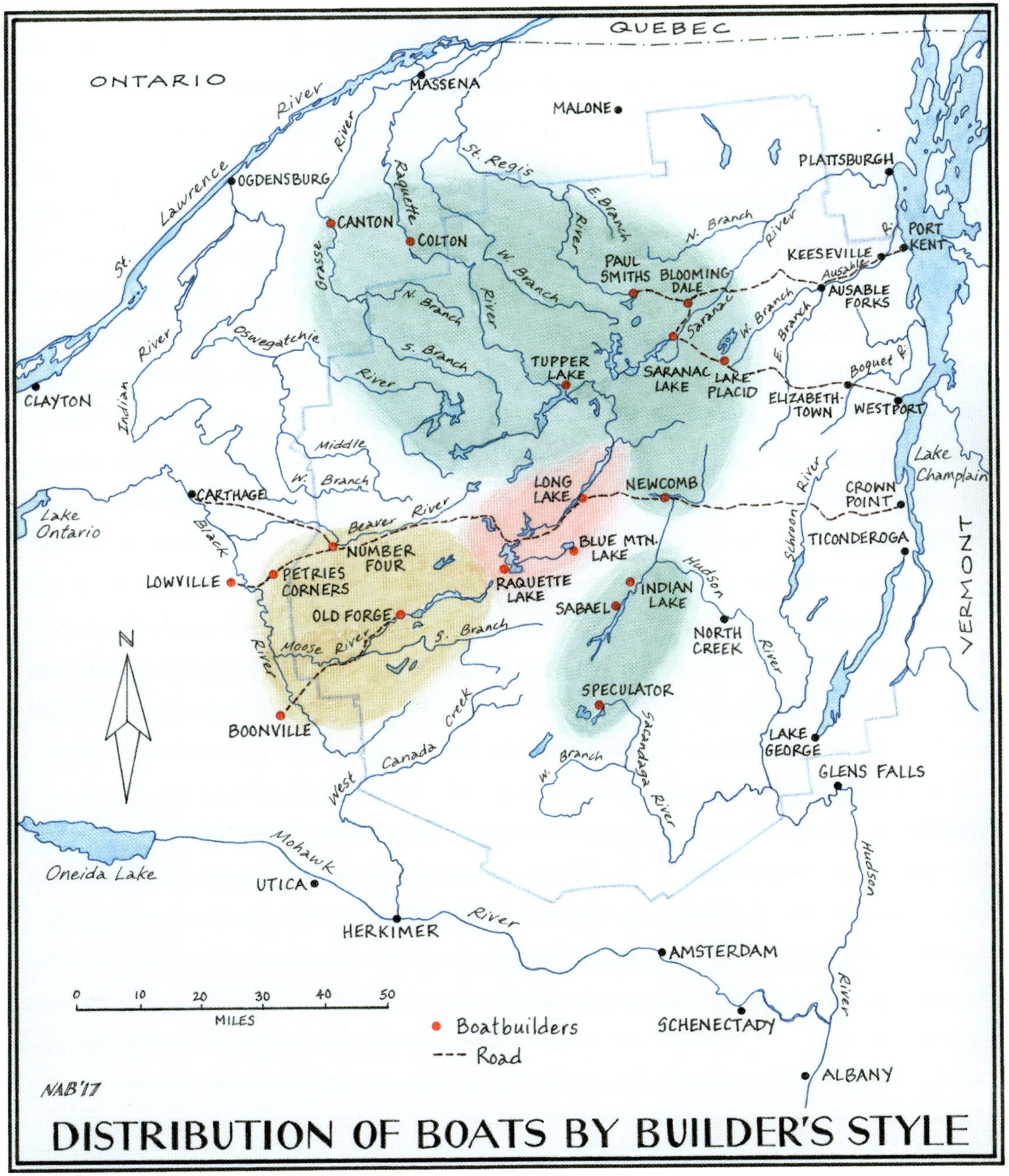


**FIGURE 2-1** This map shows the regions of the three guideboat styles. Green is the Saranac style, red the Long Lake style, and yellow the Brown's Tract style. The red dots identify boatbuilders' locations. The builders at Indian Lake, Sabael, and Speculator built in the Saranac style.

## Builders of Adirondack Guideboats Listed Chronologically by Region

THE FOLLOWING GUIDEBOAT builders are listed in chronological order, from the earliest to the most recent, and are grouped into the communities in which they worked. The list is incomplete, due not only to the absence of builders who remain unrecognized but also to the not inconsiderable number of guides who built only one or two boats, primarily for their own use.

Historically, there are three main lineages, or styles, of guideboats. It is possible to discern whether a guideboat was built in the Saranac, Long Lake, or Brown's Tract region. The identifying characteristics of these three styles include: stem-post width, stem profile, deck design, rib shape, number of strakes to a side, and the type of planking construction.

### REGIONAL CHARACTERISTICS OF GUIDEBOAT CONSTRUCTION

**Saranac style:** Tumblehome stem profile with a curvilinear inward rake, narrow stem posts, seven strakes to a side, non-reverse-curved ribs at bow and stern, feather-bevel lap hull construction, and straight or "pie-piece"-shaped deck caps on a one-, two-, or multi-piece deck. Strip decks with or without a center cover board are not uncommon.

**Long Lake style:** Tumblehome stem profile that is nearly plumb with a straight leading edge, wide stem posts, eight strakes to a side, reverse-curved ribs, feather-lap hull construction, and straight, pie-piece-shaped, or shield-shaped deck caps on a one- or two-piece deck.

**Brown's Tract style:** Stem profile has an outward rake, wide stem posts with a metal stem post cap, eight strakes to a side, reverse-curved ribs, modified-bevel lap (Grant lap) hull construction, and a center cover board on a two-piece deck.

In the following list, the bold names of towns under one of the three primary building styles indicate that the boats built there are typical of that style. The builders named are those for whom at least one extant guideboat has been identified. Biographies of these builders and the characteristics of their boats follow, along with the dates of their active building years, based on censuses, business directories, and other sources. A single year indicates the date of the builder's listing in a publication. The dates are often estimates, since only rarely does one find credible evidence of precisely when a builder entered or left the trade. A thorough and systematic search of all sources has yet to be completed.

Italicized names, indented, are documented boatbuilders for whom no boats have yet been identified. In parentheses are the birth and death dates of these builders.

The notation at the far right indicates the sources of information about these builders.

BBF: Adirondack Museum, Boatbuilders' Files

DC: Adirondack Museum, Durant Collection

ARR: Adirondack Research Room, Saranac Lake Free Library

CC: Edward Comstock, Jr. Collection, Saranac Lake

AC: Author (Steven B. Sulavik) Collection

For further information, refer to Kenneth and Helen Durant's *The Adirondack Guide-Boat*, and Hallie E. Bond's *Boats and Boating in the Adirondacks.*

## SARANAC STYLE

### Saranac Lake

William McLenathen: 1851~1875
Nathaniel S. Graves: early 1850s
*John Wesley Miller (b. 1832): 1860~1889, Harrietstown* CC
*Chester W. Peck (1826–1904): 1860~1889, Harrietstown* ARR/CC
*James A. Philbrook (b. 1836): 1870~1889* BBF
William Allen Martin: 1872–mid-1890s
Adirondack Boat Building Company: 1885–1908
William Allen Martin: 1885–mid-1890s
Henry Kilburn Martin: mid-1890s–1908
Frederick William Rice: 1874–1903
*Jesse Boula (1857–1946): 1880s~1890s* ARR
Alric B. Moody: 1880s–early 1900s
*Warren J. Slater (1849–1921): 1880s* CC
Herbert L. and Wright Salisbury: 1890–1894
*Charles E. Shaw: 1890s* BBF/CC
Henry Kilburn Martin: mid-1890s~1915
Theodore Salter Hanmer: 1898–1945
*George Rice: 1902* CC
*G. H. Putnam: 1908* CC
Frederick Marsh Rice: 1905–1931
Willard J. Hanmer: 1927–1962
Carl George Hathaway: 1963–1991
Ralph R. Morrow: 1970–2007
Christopher H. Woodward: 1987–

### Newcomb

Caleb Judson Chase: mid-1850s–1908
*Lewis Abbott: 1860~1875* AC
*Ellsworth Hayes (b. 1848): 1880s* BBF
*George Lincoln: 1864* CC

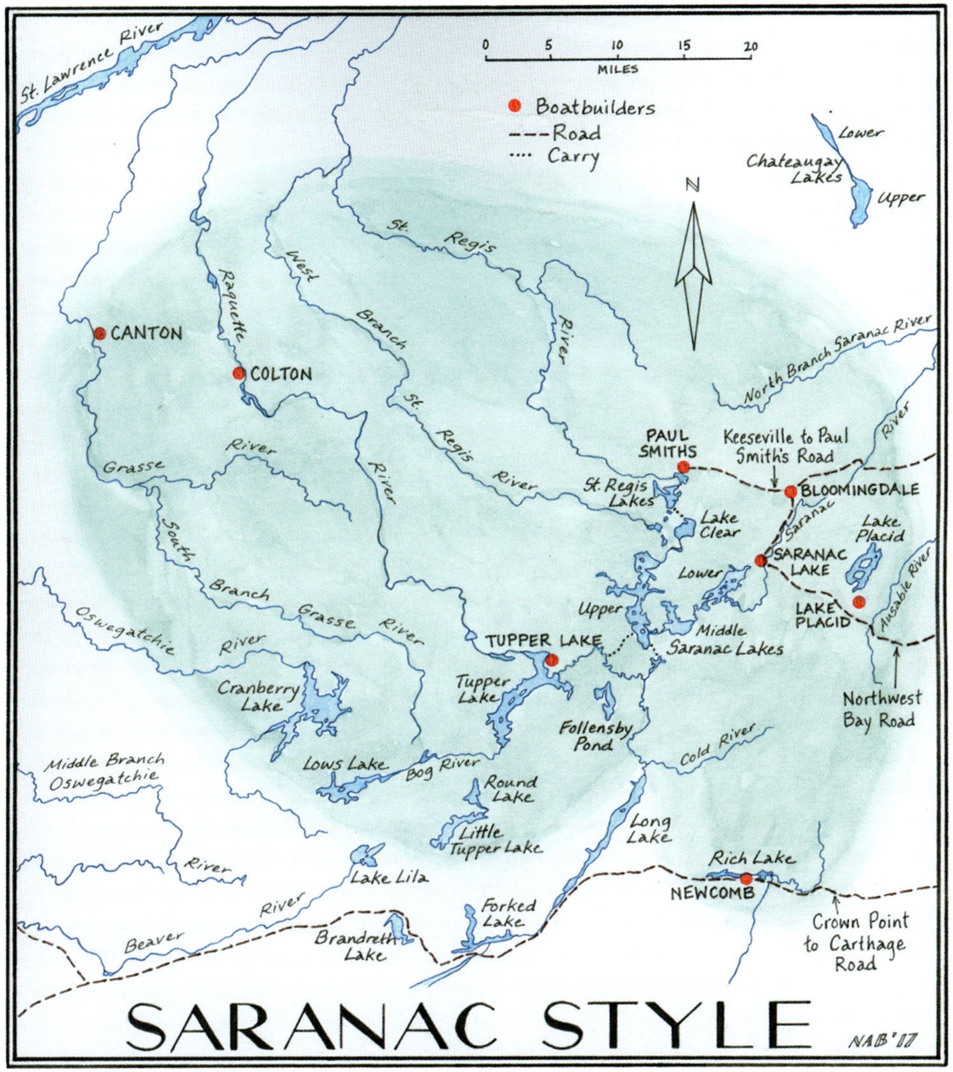


**FIGURE 2-2** The Saranac style region is located within Essex, Franklin, St. Lawrence, and Hamilton counties.

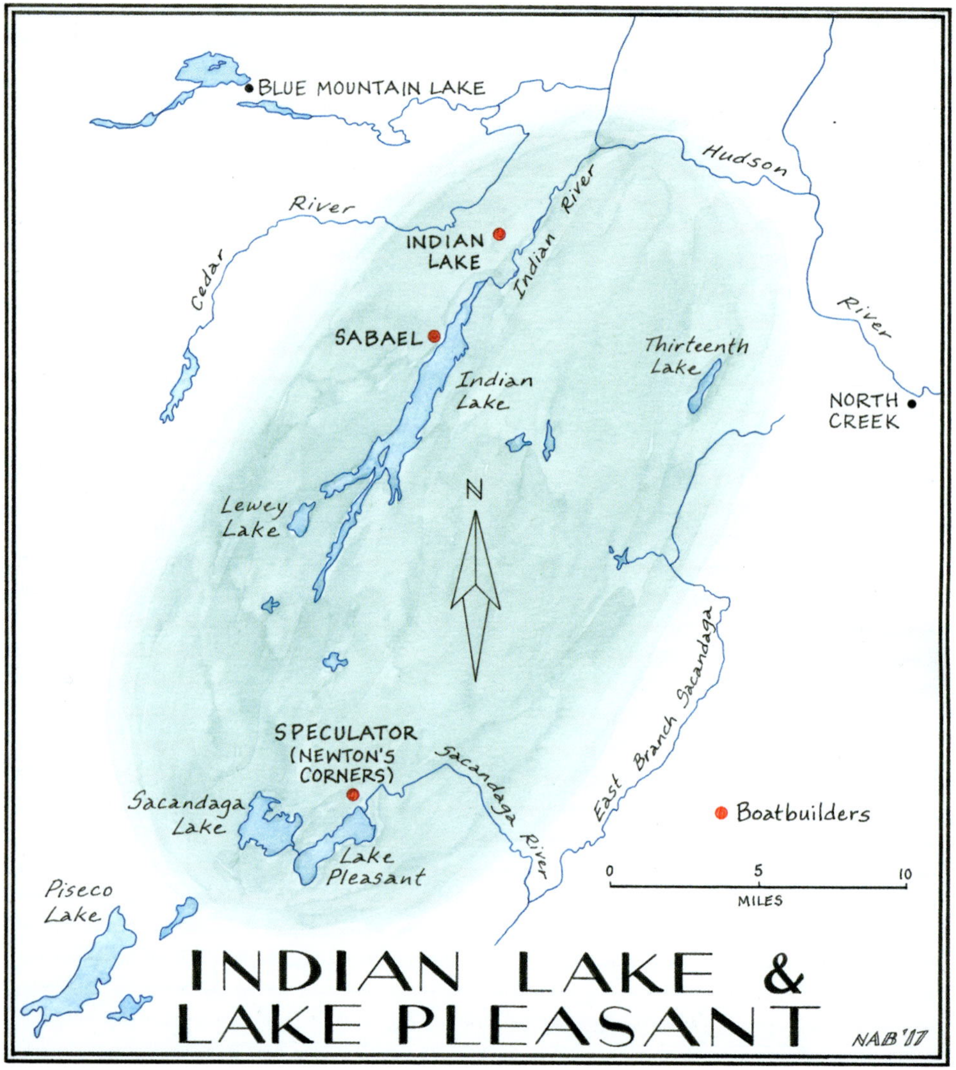


**FIGURE 2-3** Saranac style boats were also built at Indian Lake and at Speculator on Lake Pleasant, both in Hamilton County.

William M. Alden: early 1870s–early 1880s
Edmund Judson Chase: 1911~1923

### Tupper Lake

Nathaniel S. Graves: late 1850s–1860s
Leonard Anderson: 1902~1925
Alric B. Moody: 1903~1920
*Luther W. Owen (1852–1908): 1890s~1902* BBF/CC
*Daniel Hinkson (1861–1946): 1890s* BBF
*Henry E. Huntington: 1892~1910* BBF
*Earl Owen (1881–1943): late 1890s, West Potsdam; 1895–1940* BBF
*Warren J. Slater (1849–1921): early 1900s* CC
*Dyton Owen (b. 1908)* BBF
Robert W. Frenette: 1983–

### St. Regis/Paul Smiths

Elbridge Gerry Ricketson: 1870s
*James M. Cross (1844–1908): 1867~1890s* ARR
William McCaffrey: 1880s
James Fletcher Cameron: 1984–

### Bloomingdale

Elbridge Gerry Ricketson: late 1870s–mid-1890s
William McCaffrey: mid-1880s–1903
William Vassar: late 1890s–mid-1920s

### Lake Placid

Albert Henry Billings: early 1880s–1903
Frederick Marsh Rice: 1902–1903
George & Bliss: 1904–1927

### Canton

John Henry Rushton: 1888–1916
Hurst & Nickerson: 1890–1895
Isaac Abraham Hurst: 1896–1910
Myron Augustus Nickerson: 1896–1907

**Colton**

*W. W. Wright: 1864* CC
*C. C. Felton: 1862~1882* AC
*Charles Day: 1870~1885* AC
*James Cook: 1870~1885* AC
Edward Harvey: 1910s~1930s

**Vermontville**

Fuat Latif: 1985–

**Lake Clear**

Allison Wood Warner: 2011–

**Lake Pleasant/Speculator**

*Charles Letson: 1862~1889* AC
*Alvah G. Dunning (1816–1902): 1867* CC
*William H. Reedes: 1867* CC
*W. Country: 1870~1885* AC
*B. Page: 1870–1885* AC
*F. Buyce: 1874* CC
*Henry Rudes: 1874* CC
John F. Buyce: 1889–1940s
*Alvah Buyce: 1904–1940s*

**Sabael**

William Bartlett Kerst: 1895–early 1940s

**Indian Lake**

*Elijah Fish (b. 1842)* AC
Raleigh Raymond Fish: late 1960s–early 1970s

## Long Lake Style

**Long Lake**

*William Austin: early 1840s~1855*
*Asa T. Kellogg: 1864~1879* CC
*Ransom J. Palmer: 1864* BBF
*William Preston: 1867~1882* CC

FIGURE 2-4 The Long Lake style region is located within Hamilton County.

Cyrus Hale Palmer: mid-1860s~1895
Reuben Cary: mid-1860s–1910
*William Henry Stanton II (1844–1881): 1866; 1877, Port Henry; 1879, 1880, Boonville* BBF/CC
*George B. Stanton (1847–1935): mid-1870s* BBF
Mitchell Sabattis: late 1860s–1870 (attributed)
*John E. Plumley: 1872* BBF
*Alba Cole: 1874–1890s* DC
*Simeon Cole (b. 1846): 1874–1890s* DC
Farrand Benedict Austin: 1880s–1890s
Herbert L. and Wright Salisbury: early 1880s–1889
*Isaac Sabattis: early 1880s–1890* BBF/CC
*Robert J. Peck: mid–late 1880s* BBF
George Washington Smith: 1888–1926
*Orello E. Boyden: 1890–1910* CC
*Charles Henry Marsha (1863– ): 1890s* BBF/CC
Warren William Cole: 1892–1909
*Charles Cole: 1890–1898* BBF
Lewis Austin: 1893–1900
Wallace Franklin Emerson: 1905–late 1930s
Merlin Edward Austin: 1910–1930
Charles J. Hamner: 1920s–mid-1950s
Harold Merlin Austin, Sr.: 1925–1955
Harold Merlin Austin, Jr.: 1965–2015
Fred C. Burns: 1968–1983

## Blue Mountain Lake

Nathaniel S. Graves: 1896–1903
John H. Blanchard: 1898–1907
*Duane Fuller (1830–1903): 1880s* CC
Allison Wood Warner: 2003–2011

## Raquette Lake

*Jerome Wood (1840–1923): early 1880s–late 1890s* BBF
*Wesley Bates: 1880s~1900s* AC
Nathaniel S. Graves: 1904~1912
John H. Blanchard: 1908–1941

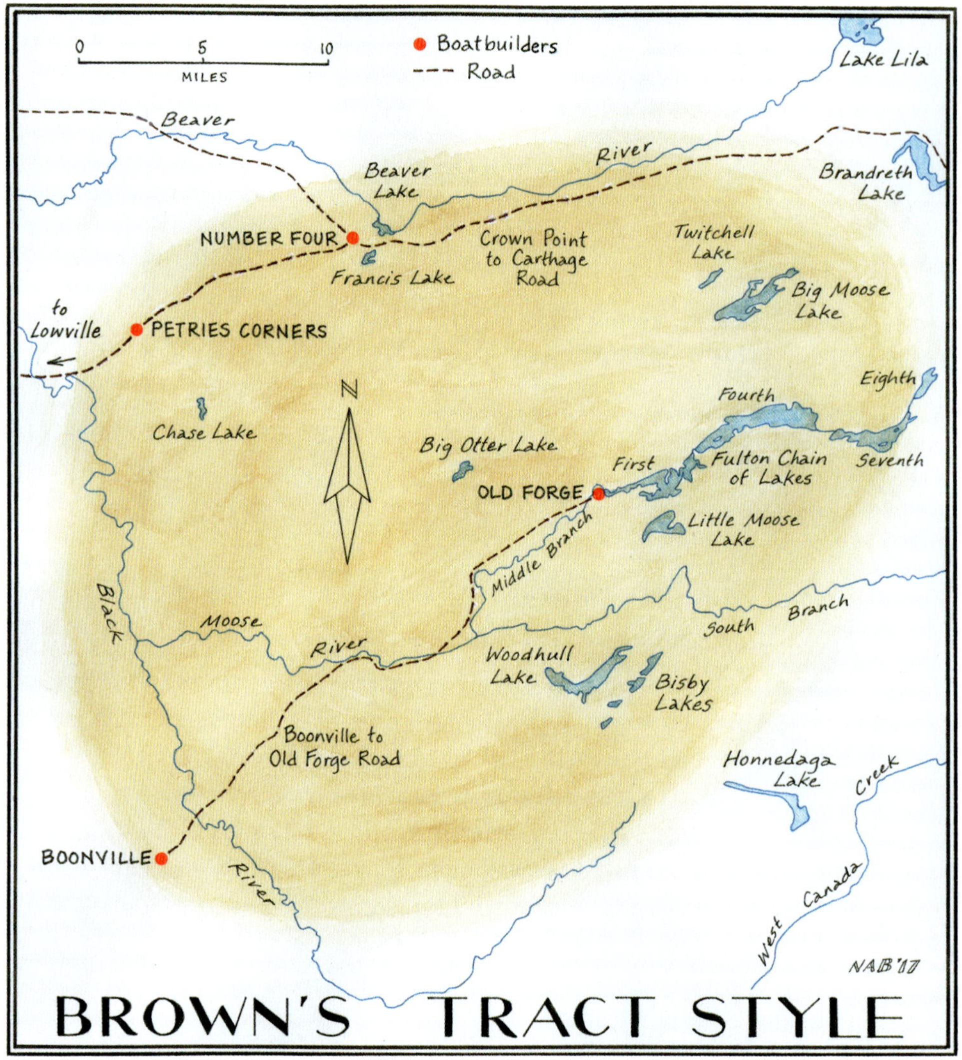


FIGURE 2-5 The Brown's Tract style region is located within Herkimer, Oneida, and Lewis counties.

## Brown's Tract Style

### Boonville

Henry Dwight Grant: 1880–1906

Lewis Lawrence Grant: 1916–1934

### Old Forge

Seeber & Parsons (Theodore Seeber and Riley Parsons): 1890–1895

Theodore Seeber: 1896–1902

Parsons & Company (Riley, Ira H., and R. Benjamin Parsons): 1896–1903

Parsons & Roberts (Ira and Ben Parsons with John E. Roberts): 1903–1909

Old Forge Boat Company (Theodore Seeber): 1903–1909

Parsons Brothers: 1910–1945

### Petries Corners

Ansel C. Wilder: late 1880s–early 1900s

### Lowville & Number 4

Oren George Fenton: early 1900s–early 1920s

*Earl B. Chapman: circa 1927* BBF

## Other

### South Boston, Massachusetts

Frederick D. Graves: 1870s–1890

### Clayton

*St. Lawrence River Skiff, Canoe, and Steam Launch Company: 1894–1895* CC

### Schroon Lake

*Jesse T. Foster: 1862~1882* AC

*Stephen C. Sherman: 1864–1874* CC

*Erastus Richardson: 1870~1885* AC

### Westport

*Dennis Hayes: circa 1890s*

### Whitehall

*Whitehall Rowboat Manufactory: circa 1890s* CC

### Contemporary Regional Builders Not Included in Biographical Sketches

*All are Saranac style builders:*

### Plattsburgh

Joseph Rector: (1962– ) 1981–

### Saranac Lake

Joseph J. Spadaro, Jr.: (1942– ) 1981–2012

Timothy Doyle: (1955–2012) late 1980s–2012

Anthony Duprey: (1942– ) 1989–2012

### Tupper Lake

William Crouse: (1928– ) 1985–2012

### Keene

William Michelfelder: (1947– ) 1988–

### Lake Clear

Curtis A. Reynolds: (1962– ) 1989–

# Builder's Active Dates: 1850-2015

Saranac Style
Long Lake Style
Brown's Tract Style

Figure 2-6: Builders listed chronologically. There was a tenuous hold on the continuation of the knowledge, skill, and craft of guideboat building in the early 1960s as evidenced by the single block between Willard Hanmer, who died in the winter of 1962, and Carl Hathaway who took over the shop in 1963. At the time this was the only building and repair shop left.

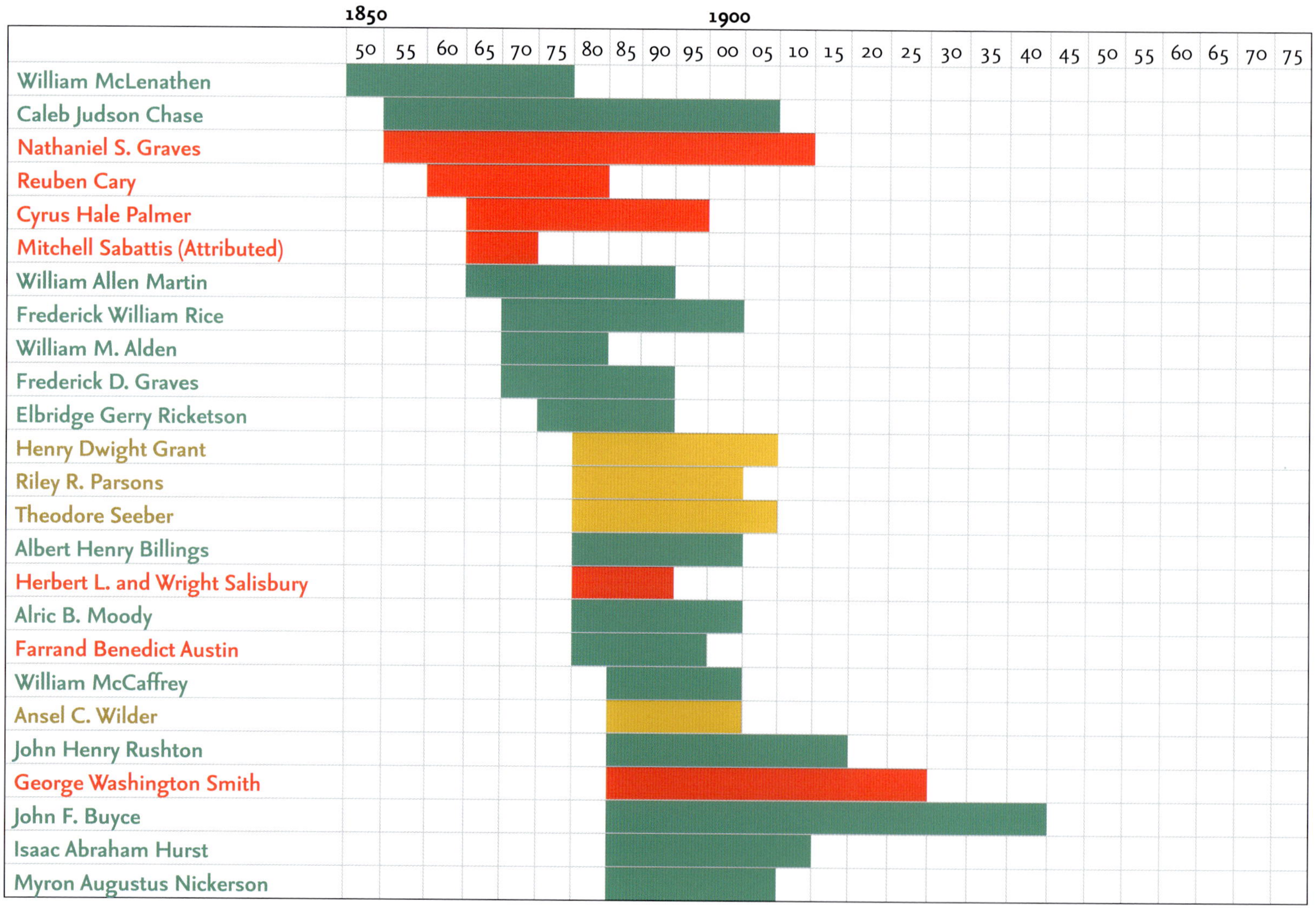

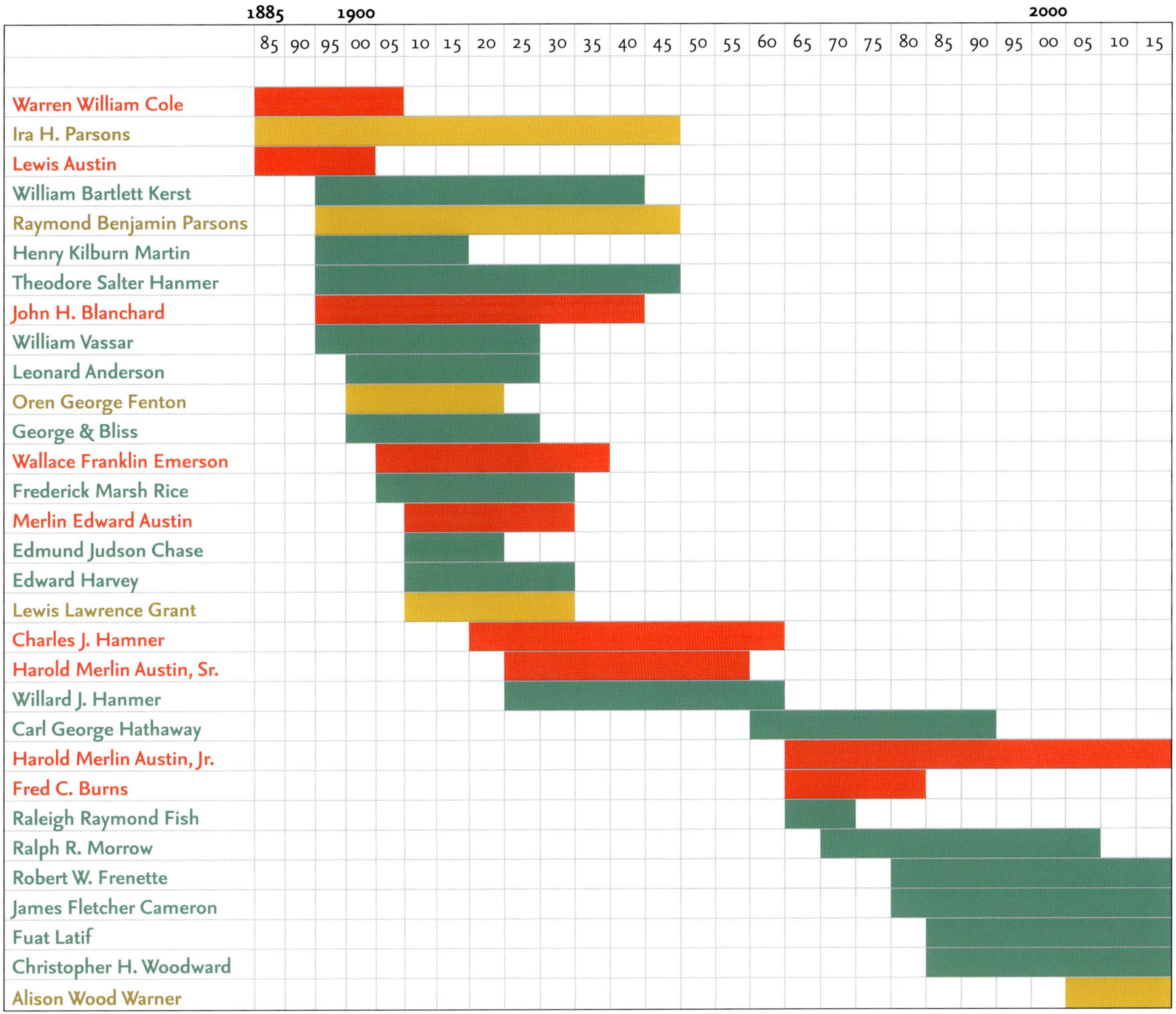
1885
1900
2000
85 90 95 00 05 10 15 20 25 30 35 40 45 50 55 60 65 70 75 80 85 90 95 00 05 10 15
Warren William Cole
Ira H. Parsons
Lewis Austin
William Bartlett Kerst
Raymond Benjamin Parsons
Henry Kilburn Martin
Theodore Salter Hanmer
John H. Blanchard
William Vassar
Leonard Anderson
Oren George Fenton
George & Bliss
Wallace Franklin Emerson
Frederick Marsh Rice
Merlin Edward Austin
Edmund Judson Chase
Edward Harvey
Lewis Lawrence Grant
Charles J. Hamner
Harold Merlin Austin, Sr.
Willard J. Hanmer
Carl George Hathaway
Harold Merlin Austin, Jr.
Fred C. Burns
Raleigh Raymond Fish
Ralph R. Morrow
Robert W. Frenette
James Fletcher Cameron
Fuat Latif
Christopher H. Woodward
Alison Wood Warner

Willard Hanmer in his shop, Saranac Lake, NY, circa 1950s. (Courtesy of Adirondack Museum)

# Builders' Profiles and the Characteristics of Their Guideboats

## Introduction

Each profile opens with the location and date of the builder's birth and death, as well as an estimate of his or her active building period and the number of guideboats built. A **Biographical Sketch** follows.

The profiles are in alphabetical order, with the following exceptions: **(a)** There are families in which sons followed their fathers in the boatbuilding trade. Examples are Austin, Chase, Grant, Hanmer, and Martin. The members of a family are listed in chronological order. **(b)** Old Forge was the location of a number of builders and companies associated with Theodore Seeber and Riley Parsons and his two sons. They have been grouped under *Old Forge Guideboat Builders and Companies.*

After the **Biographical Sketch** are **Guideboat Characteristics** describing the features of that builder's boats. Finally, brief **Field Notes** list characteristics and structural information that were compiled on site.

Only those components considered original to the boat are described. Determining which parts are original is crucial but may be difficult. Components not integrally fastened to the boat and therefore subject to replacement over time, such as oars, paddles, yoke, seats, and backrests, require close inspection. Other components subject to chronic wear and tear, such as stem posts, stems, decks, seats, and cleats, might also be repairs or replacements. Many replacements might be the design of the restorer, not the original builder. Occasionally, custom variations, requested by the buyer, might have been incorporated.

It is difficult, and often impossible, to obtain accurate information, often harking back a century or more, about many builders and guideboats. Guides who were not builders by trade also built boats, a number of which still survive. Since such boats lack builder's plates or records, it is almost impossible to determine who the builder was.

New information about builders and their boats is very much welcomed. Please direct any corrections or additional information to the Adirondack Museum.

## WILLIAM M. ALDEN

**Date of birth:** 1848
**Date of death:** April 3, 1885
**Active:** Early 1870s–early 1880s
**Location:** Newcomb, Essex County
**Estimate of guideboats built:** More than 20
**Number reviewed:** 1 (attributed)
**Builder's plate:** Not used

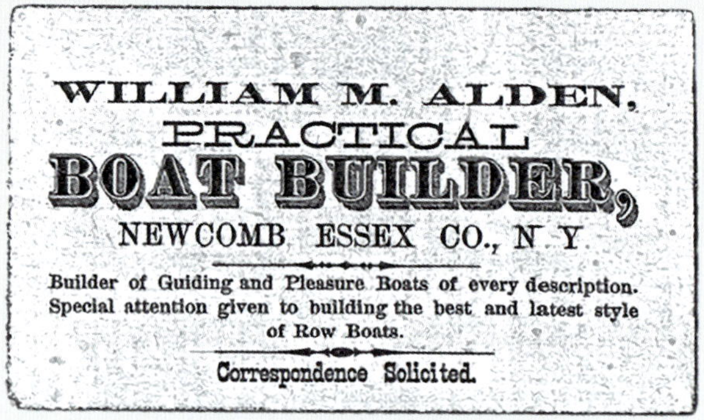
WILLIAM M. ALDEN,
PRACTICAL
BOAT BUILDER,
NEWCOMB, ESSEX CO., N. Y.

Builder of Guiding and Pleasure Boats of every description.
Special attention given to building the best and latest style of Row Boats.

Correspondence Solicited.

FIGURE 2-7 William M. Alden trade card (Courtesy of Adirondack Museum)

### Biographical Sketch

William M. Alden was the son of Rev. Willard Alden and Alice Eggleston Alden. His father arrived with his family in Long Lake in the 1850s; he was the first pastor (1855–1860) of the Long Lake Wesleyan (Methodist) Church, a church that had great influence on many Long Lakers, including early guides and guideboat builders such as Mitchell and Isaac Sabattis, and Cyrus and Ransom Palmer.[1]

William Alden entered the service in defense of his country during the Civil War. In 1874, he married Mary Jane Chase, the daughter of Newcomb guideboat builder Caleb J. Chase. The Aldens had four children, the last born only one year before William's early death.

Despite suffering from progressive pulmonary tuberculosis, he was a justice of the peace for the Town of Newcomb and supervisor in 1883 and 1884. Until his death, "he was engaged in the mercantile business, and by careful attention to business had built up quite a little trade."[2]

Alden is listed in the federal census for 1880 and in his obituary as a "boat builder." In S. R. Stoddard's editions of *The Adirondacks: Illustrated,* he is listed as a Newcomb guide.[3] His boatbuilding period extended from the early 1870s to the early 1880s. He died of "phthisis pulmonatis" (pulmonary tuberculosis) at the age of thirty-seven in 1885.[4]

1 Long Lake Wesleyan Church, *Long Lake Wesleyan Church History,* https://longlakewesleyan.wordpress.com/history-of-llwc/, 2013.
2 "Obituary," *Elizabethtown Post*, April 23, 1885.
3 Seneca Ray Stoddard, *The Adirondacks: Illustrated,* Albany, NY: Weed, Parsons, 1874:153. Additional listings are found in later editions.
4 "Obituary," *Elizabethtown Post.*

## Guideboat Characteristics

Alden's boats have structural characteristics typical of boats built by his father-in-law. These similarities include: the narrow, long, low, stem post; a pair of scribe ribs beneath the bow deck; and, at the stern, a pair of partial-length scribe ribs, cut square across the top, with a projecting ledge to support the stern-seat cleats. Chase was the only other builder known to use such stern scribe ribs for his double-ended guideboats. Other characteristics include rib feet that are finely rounded and tapered and do not extend across the bottom board to the opposite garboard, nearly identical to those by Chase from the 1870s on. The rounded stem foot is similar; however, it lacks the raised ridge and pointed end typical of Chase.

The shield-shaped deck cap at bow and stern is typical of the nearby Long Lake builders, as is the use of eight strakes on each side of the hull.

## Field Notes

**Bow:** One pair of scribe ribs beneath the deck. The next pair of ribs are footed and inboard of the deck.

**Decks:** One piece, let into the gunwales.

FIGURE 2-8 (Top) The narrow, long, low, rectangular stem post, (worn down at the front end). (Bottom) The scribe ribs at the stern have a ledge to support the seat cleat. This feature was common in transom-built guide's boats.

FIGURE 2-9 (Top) The stem-foot end at the bottom board is similar to those of Caleb Chase in its rounding and tapering, but lacks the lateral raised ridge and the more pointed end, characteristic of Chase. (Bottom) The deck cap is shield-shaped, unlike Chase's "pie-piece"-shaped deck cap.

## LEONARD ANDERSON

**Date of birth:** 1873 (Pierrepont, St. Lawrence County)
**Date of death:** 1941
**Active:** 1902~1925
**Location:** Tupper Lake (Moody), Franklin County
**Estimate of guideboats built:** More than 50
**Number reviewed:** 10
**Builder's plate:** Not used

### Biographical Sketch

Leonard Anderson came to Tupper Lake "shortly after the fire of 1899." He then "worked for some time [1899 to 1902] with Alric Moody, boatbuilder of Tupper Lake," after which he established his own boatbuilding shop in Moody, just south of Tupper Lake.[1]

According to Frederick Culley, an elderly former native of Tupper Lake who moved away in 1929, Anderson was likable, about 5 feet 8 inches tall, slim, with a "heavy" mustache, and charged $75 for his guideboats. Culley recalled that Anderson began building guideboats in the late 1890s and was still building them in 1922. Anderson was often seen wearing a cowboy hat, having spent time in Denver, Colorado.[2]

Bessie and Leonard Anderson had four children. Their daughter Alice was married to Bower Logan of Moody Road, and in 1967 the couple donated many of Anderson's boatbuilding patterns to the Adirondack Museum. Penciled on a distinctive wooden yoke-cleat pattern is "Yoke cleat L. Anderson 1902" and on a paddle pattern "1910." There are no written records for the guideboats that Anderson built.

Anderson cut his own spruce stumps and worked alone. He built guideboats for many of the private preserves in the area, such as Read and Strange, Kildare Club, and Litchfield Park. He also guided in the Tupper Lake region for many years.[3] He continued to be active as a boat builder into the 1920s, building a wide-beamed guideboat for a paraplegic member of the Read family in 1923.[4]

### Guideboat Characteristics

Anderson's guideboats are distinguished by the design of his yoke cleats, as well as the absence of stem posts in most of his strip-deck models. His stem-foot end is a horizontal rectangle. Most of his guideboats are built with strip decks, center cover boards, and narrow, non-tapered coamings. A western red cedar sheer strake was frequently used on his strip-deck models. Two Anderson boats were observed with two-piece decks, each placed between the sheer strakes, and

1 Adirondack Museum accession 67.26.1
2 Frederick Culley, *Personal communication*, 2002.
3 Adirondack Museum accession 67.26.1
4 Culley, 2002.

with pie-piece-shaped deck caps. Two others had two-piece decks, center cover boards, and coamings. Except for the presence of his distinctive yoke cleats, Anderson guideboats with two-piece decks and stem posts are similar to some of the boats built by his neighbor Alric Moody. Stem posts are rare on Anderson's strip-deck boats.

Anderson varied his deck designs. They included strip-built decks with center cover boards and coamings, with or without stem posts; two-piece decks with center cover boards and coamings, or with teardrop-shaped deck caps, with stem posts; and a few one-piece decks with a stem post.

**Figure 2-12** (Left) A strip-built deck with a center cover board and coaming but no stem post. The center cover board extends to the stem front. The coaming is rounded and not tapered. (Right) The end of the stem foot at the bottom board is a horizontal rectangle.

**Figure 2-10** The pattern for the distinctive Anderson yoke cleat. The longer arm of the cleat points towards the bow. (Courtesy of Adirondack Museum)

**Figure 2-13** (Right) A strip-built deck with a center cover board and coaming with a stem post. (Bottom Right) A strip deck, without a stem post, made of alternating maple and black cherry strips, eleven on each side at the stern and thirteen at the bow. There are two pairs of scribe ribs at both bow and stern. In this boat there is a copper air tank beneath the bow deck for increased buoyancy.

**Figure 2-11** An Anderson yoke cleat installed. Below the yoke cleat is the middle-seat cleat.

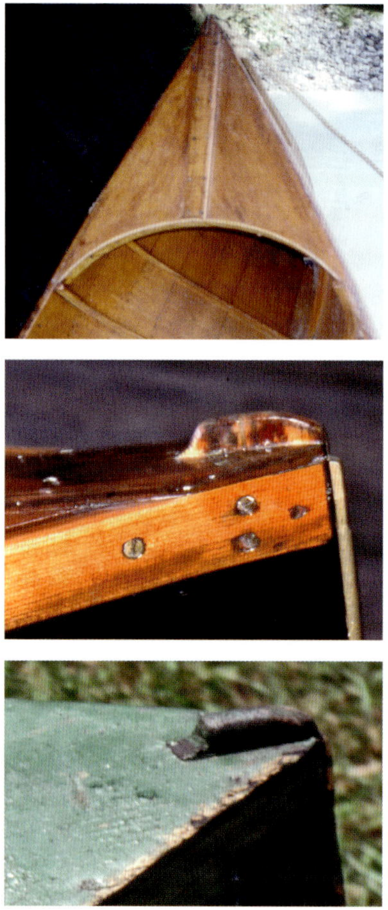

## Field Notes

**Stems:** Tumblehome (Saranac profile); stem-foot end is a horizontal rectangle.

**Ribs:** Footed rib ends are beveled and do not extend across the bottom board.

**Hull:** Number of strakes on each side: 7; feather-lap construction.

There is a guideboat, with some evidence of having been built by Anderson, whose hull is strip-built. It is the earliest known guideboat to be built in this way. It has a one-piece deck mitered into the gunwales, a method almost solely used by builders in Long Lake and Blue Mountain Lake.

FIGURE 2-15 (Left) Leonard Anderson paddles. Note the variation in the grips. (Courtesy of Robert Frenette)

FIGURE 2-14 (Top Left) A two-piece deck with a center cover board and coaming. The deck pieces are set between the sheer strakes. (Center Left) A two-piece deck with a center cover board surrounding a narrow stem post (length about 2 ½ inches, width ⅜ inch, height ½ inch). (Bottom Left) A one-piece deck with a narrow stem post. It has a concave back; the front is worn.

FIGURE 2-16 Two-piece deck with a teardrop-shaped deck cap with a stem post. There is no coaming.

FIGURE 2-17 A guideboat with a strip-built hull, using the carvel method, that is, the planks, or strips, are butted edge to edge, rather than overlapped. Length overall is 15 feet 5 1/2 inches; bottom board width is 8 1/8 inches. It has 24 strips per side, each 3/4 inches wide and 3/8 inches thick. They are edge-fastened to each other and to the ribs with steel nails, one nail per rib.

FIGURE 2-18 (Above) The strip-built hull, with the distinctive yoke cleat above the seat cleat. (Left) Stem post, pie-piece-shaped deck cap, and one-piece deck mitered into the gunwales. A metal air tank is beneath the bow and stern decks.

## Field Notes

(Guideboat with a strip-built hull only)

**Stem post:** Narrow; length 2 inches, height ½ inch, width ⅜ inch; front, slight angle; sides, vertical; back, concave; top, slightly rounded.

**Stem profile:** Tumblehome (Saranac profile).

**Ribs:** Slight reverse curve; rib spaces vary from 6 ⅜ inches to 7⅛ inches; rib cross section is ⅞ inch by ¾ inch; feet do not extend across the bottom board.

**Decks:** One piece, mitered into gunwales; extend slightly beyond the carlins.

**Deck caps:** Pie-piece; convex, tapered inboard edge; steel screws used.

**Gunwales:** Top and bottom edges slightly rounded; 1⅛ inches wide at center, tapering to 1 inch at ends.

**Stem bands:** Brass, fastened with round-head wrought-iron nails.

**Shoes:** Two iron strips.

## FARRAND BENEDICT AUSTIN

**Date of birth:** 1852
**Date of death:** Unknown
**Active:** 1880s–1890s
**Location:** Long Lake, Hamilton County
**Estimate of guideboats built:** 10
**Number reviewed:** 2
**Builder's plate:** Not used

FIGURE 2-19 Farrand Benedict Austin. Photograph by J. F. Holley. (Courtesy of Adirondack Museum)

### Biographical Sketch

Farrand Austin was the son of William J. and Lois Austin. The William Austins came to Long Lake from Vermont about 1840,[1] likely recommended by their friend Farrand N. Benedict.[2]

In the 1850s the Austins moved east to Moriah in Essex County. The 1860 census showed "Farand" to be eight years old. The 1880 census shows him back in Long Lake, listed as "Hiram" Austin, a twenty-eight-year-old guide with a three-year-old son, "Merten" (Merlin), and his wife, Almira Keller, twenty-seven years old. Farrand Austin was listed as a Long Lake guide in Stoddard's guidebooks for 1878, 1881, and 1882, as well as in the *State Forest Commission Report* for 1893.[3]

1 George and Robert Shaw, *Tahawus—Newcomb and Long Lake, 1842–1900*, Howard I. Becker ed., Rexford, NY: 1955: n.p.
2 Farrand N. Benedict (1803–1880) was a professor of mathematics and engineering at Burlington College (now University of Vermont). As a surveyor, he first visited the Adirondacks in 1834 and returned every summer for many years.
3 *New York State Annual Report of the Forest Commission for the Year 1893*, Albany, NY: James B. Lyon, 1894, I:359.

## Guideboat Characteristics

Although Farrand Austin built only a few guideboats and did not do so as a trade, there is evidence that his boats were superbly built. They have two distinguishing features. The first is the shape of the stem post, which is a truncated pyramid.

The second distinguishing feature is the type of fitting used to secure the middle-seat backrest to the seat. Kenneth Durant, referring to the middle seat of the Warren Cole guideboat he had donated to the Adirondack Museum, wrote:

> The original yoke and middle seat have been lost. The present middle seat appears to be one from a boat formerly owned by Ethel Durant and built by Farrand Austin, who made fine boats of excellent design. The back rest of the Austin middle seat fits into two slots and is held in position by rigid wooden rods. Thus it is always in an upright position, but it compels the stern passenger to step over it in walking toward the bow of the boat in order to get out. [4]

**FIGURE 2-20** Austin's distinctive stem-post design consists of a pyramidal shape on a rectangular base with a narrow, flat top. Length 2 ½ inches, bottom width ⅞ inch, top width ¼ inch, height ½ inch.

**FIGURE 2-21** Center seat with two rectangular slots in the rear cross frame, into which the center-seat backrest fits.

## Field Notes

**Stems:** Slight tumblehome with straight leading edge (Long Lake profile); tapering of upper stem begins 1 to 1½ inches below lower gunwale edge.

**Ribs:** Reverse-curved ribs at bow and stern; one pair of scribe ribs under bow deck; no ribs under stern deck; foot ends are beveled and do not extend all the way across the bottom board.

**Decks:** One piece (bow and stern); set square in gunwales and sheer strakes; circle deck at bow; C-shaped deck at stern (similar to Warren Cole).

**Deck caps:** Pie-piece-shaped with moderate taper.

**Hull:** Number of strakes on each side: 8; feather-lap construction.

4 Kenneth and Helen Durant, *The Adirondack Guide-Boat*, Camden, ME: International Marine, 1980:60.

FIGURE 2-22 Artotype photographs by Edward Bierstadt in the 1880s at Camp Cedars, Frederick Clark Durant's camp on Forked Lake. (Opposite) Accessories for the Austin guideboat. Wooden rods, instead of leather straps, are used to hold the backrest of the center seat in an upright position. This type of middle-seat construction was, as far as is known, only used by Farrand Austin. (Above) Showing three different views of the Austin guideboat. The boat is widest forward of center in what is called "cod-headed," typical of the earlier boats. (Courtesy of Adirondack Museum)

## MERLIN EDWARD AUSTIN

**Date of birth:** 1875 (Long Lake, Hamilton County)
**Date of death:** May 5, 1951 (Long Lake)
**Active:** 1910–1930
**Location:** Long Lake
**Estimate of guideboats built:** 30
**Number reviewed:** 2
**Builder's plate:** Not used

FIGURE 2-23 Merlin Edward Austin.

### Biographical Sketch

Merlin Austin, born in Moriah, Essex County, the son of Farrand and Almira Austin and grandson of William Austin. On September 5, 1901, he married Lorinda A. Hamner of Long Lake, daughter of Charles and Leona Plue Hamner.

The federal census for 1900 lists him as a twenty-two-year-old carpenter. The New York State censuses for 1915 and for 1925 list him as a boatbuilder. According to his grandson: "He worked out of his father's shop, down on what was then known as the Kickerville Road. . . . Gramp's main occupation after the decline in popularity of the guideboat was contract carpentry." [1]

Austin also had an interest in building design. He was listed as architect and building supervisor of the cobblestone gatehouse, the principal entry to Cedarlands Park on the western shore of Long Lake, built about 1910.[2]

### Guideboat Characteristics

The guideboat described below is characterized by the design of the stem post and stem foot, and also by its shallow C-shaped stern deck (similar to those of Warren Cole). The decks are mitered into the gunwales and sheer strakes, a signature of most Long Lake builders. It has beaded gunwales and carlins (also used by Warren Cole and Nathaniel Graves), and round-head screws for the deck and deck cap. The rib placement at bow and stern are also similar to those of Cole.

1 Harold M. Austin, Jr. *Letter to Mrs. Kenneth Durant, October 7, 1978*, Adirondack Museum, Durant Collection.
2 Richard C. Youngken, Application to the Division for Historic Preservation, New York State Parks and Recreation, October 26, 1979. Copy at Adirondack Museum.

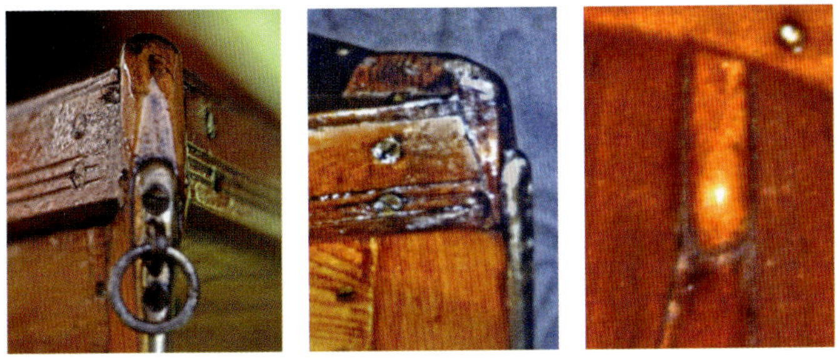

**Figure 2-24** (*Left and center*) Front and side views of the stem post, length 2 inches, width 9⁄16 inch, height ½ inch; front end, chamfered sides, slightly worn; back end flat, slight angle; top round. The gunwale is beaded. (*Right*) The rounded-over stem foot is bull-nosed.

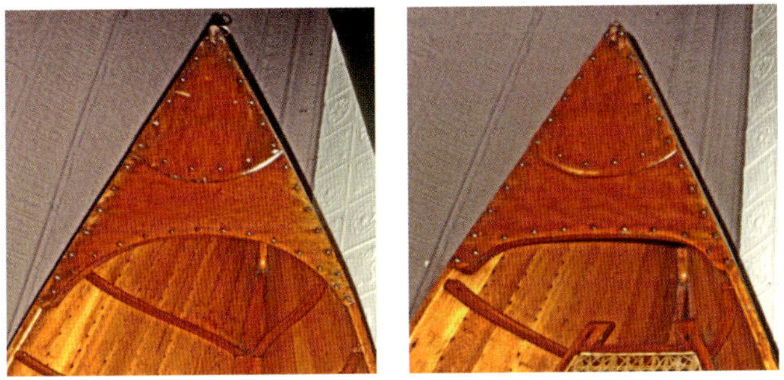

**Figure 2-25** (*Left*) Arced bow deck with a pair of scribe ribs beneath it. (*Right*) Shallow C-shaped stern deck. The pie-piece-shaped deck cap with a rounded-over inboard edge. The scribe ribs are just inboard of the stern deck.

**Figure 2-26** Beading of lower gunwale and carlin. Note the rounded deck-cap edge and the round-head screws.

## Field Notes

**Ribs:** Reverse-curved ribs at bow and stern. Scribe ribs: One pair under bow deck; one pair just inboard of stern deck. No footed ribs under decks. Rib feet ends are beveled and do not extend across the bottom. Rib spaces are 6 inches.

**Decks:** One piece, mitered into the gunwales. Arced deck at bow, shallow C-shaped at stern. Both decks extend slightly beyond the carlins.

**Deck caps:** Pie-piece-shaped with rounded inboard edge.

**Hull:** Number of strakes on each side: 8; feather-lap construction. Cod-headed (wider toward the bow with a narrower stern).

**Carlins:** Beaded.

**Figure 2-27** (*Left*) Austin's claw hammer, tack hammer, clinching iron, and plane. (*Right*) A Merlin Austin stem pattern shown lying in a guideboat. (Courtesy of Harold M. Austin, Jr.)

## HAROLD MERLIN AUSTIN, SR.

**Date of birth:** 1906 (Long Lake, Hamilton County)
**Date of death:** 1967 (Long Lake)
**Active:** 1925–1955
**Location:** Long Lake
**Estimate of guideboats built:** 5
**Number reviewed:** 0
**Builder's plate:** Not used

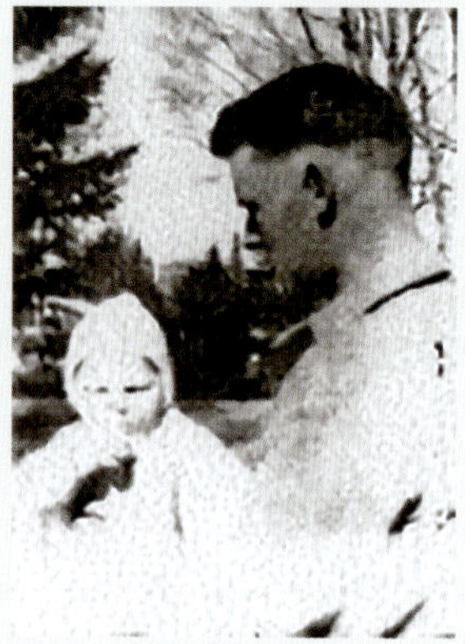

FIGURE 2-28 Harold Merlin Austin, Sr.

### Biographical Sketch

Harold Austin, Sr., was the great-grandson of William Austin, an early settler of Long Lake. He built PT boats in Norfolk, Virginia, during World War II, while living in Deep Creek, Virginia. A carpenter by trade, he also built and repaired guideboats until about 1955. His son Harold Jr. remembers "sticking tacks" for his father's guideboats. Harold Sr. worked out of Merlin's shop on Kickerville Road. The stem-post design used by Harold Sr. was also used by Harold Jr. No information exists as to the whereabouts of any of the guideboats built by Harold Sr.

FIGURE 2-29 Harold Merlin Austin, Jr.

## HAROLD MERLIN AUSTIN, JR.

**Date of birth:** June 29, 1928
**Active:** Intermittently between 1965 and 2016
**Location:** Long Lake, Hamilton County
**Estimate of guideboats built:** 8
**Number reviewed:** 3
**Builder's plate:** Not used
**Adirondack Museum accession:** 75.235.1

### Biographical Sketch

Harold Merlin Austin, Jr., learned the carpentry trade at an early age from his father and grandfather, both carpenters and guideboat builders. He is the great-great-grandson of early Long Lake settler and boatbuilder William Austin. In 1948 he married Evelyn Bump, whom he met in high school.

Austin joined the United States Marines in 1951, received his wings in 1955, and flew jets for some thirteen years before retiring in 1971 with the rank of major. While in the Marine Corps he built his first guideboat in 1965 at Cherry Point, North Carolina, having brought all of the required materials by pickup truck from Long Lake.

In 1971 Austin and his wife returned to Long Lake. In 1972 he became Superintendent of Buildings and Grounds at the Adirondack Museum. In 1981, at the age of fifty-four, he received a bachelor of theology degree from United Wesleyan College in Allentown, Pennsylvania. He "pastored" in Brant Lake until 1992, when he left for Germany to do missionary work. In 1995 he and Evelyn returned to Long Lake and, although formally retired, he continues to do "pulpit fillings" for the Wesleyan Church. He also continued the family tradition of building and restoring guideboats.

## Guideboat Characteristics

Austin uses the stem, bottom board, and rib patterns of earlier builders in various combinations. His stem posts resemble those of his father. His decks are made from two, three, or four pieces, all with deck caps of a shield-shaped design. The stem profile of his boats has a straight leading edge, or Long Lake profile. The Grant lap was used for the planking of one guideboat; the others are feather lapped.

FIGURE 2-30 (Left) A three-piece deck with a shield-shaped deck cap. The side pieces are mitered into the gunwales. (Right) A shield-shaped deck cap on a four-piece deck, all made of cherry.

### Field Notes

**Stems:** Slight tumblehome with straight leading edge (Long Lake profile) from the same pattern as his grandfather, Merlin. Stem narrowing begins about 2½ inches from lower edge of gunwale.

**Ribs:** Reverse-curved ribs; one pair of scribe ribs under bow and stern decks; rib feet ends are beveled and do not extend all the way across the bottom board.

**Hull:** Number of strakes on each side: 8; feather-lap construction.

FIGURE 2-31 The stem post is a rectangle upon which is carved a smaller, flat-topped rectangle with concave ends and sides. Its length is 2 ½ inches, width ¾ inch, and height ¾ inch to 1 inch. The front end of the stem narrows halfway down the sheer strake.

## LEWIS AUSTIN

**Date of birth:** January 1866
**Date of death:** June 20, 1901
**Active:** 1893–1900
**Location:** Long Lake, Hamilton County
**Estimate of guideboats built:** 10
**Number reviewed:** 2
**Builder's plate:** Not used
**Adirondack Museum accession:** 56.67.1

### Biographical Sketch

Lewis Austin was the son of Henry D. and Mary Austin. From the little that is known about this family, they were not related to the family of William Austin, one of the earliest settlers and boatbuilders of Long Lake. The 1892 New York State Census lists Austin as a twenty-seven-year-old carpenter. The 1900 federal census lists Henry D. Austin as a sixty-three-year-old farmer and his son Lewis as a thirty-four-year-old boatbuilder, living in Hamilton County. Though he died at thirty-five, Lewis Austin left a legacy as an accomplished guideboat builder.

One of his guideboats is in the Adirondack Museum collection. It was built for Dewitt Clinton Flanagan, whose well-known guide was Willard Sutton. John Gardner, small boat historian, wrote of this guideboat in a 1966 letter to Kenneth Durant:

> By the way I like the Long Lake stem. It is esthetically pleasing. My favorite guide-boat at the Museum is the 1894 Lewis Austin boat donated by Thomas T. Bissell. The decks are especially beautiful, the curves of these most harmonious, the three overlapping segments of which suggesting the petals of the conventionalized Japanese chrysanthemum.[1]

1 John Gardner, *Letter to Kenneth Durant, September 11, 1966*, Gardner-Durant Collection.

## Guideboat Characteristics

The stem-post design and the sharply pointed stem foot are distinctive features, as are the three-piece cambered deck caps and decks.

The length of Lewis Austin's guideboat at the Adirondack Museum is only 13 feet 3 inches, with a beam of 36 inches.

## Field Notes

**Stems:** Slight tumblehome with straight leading edge (Long Lake profile).

**Ribs:** Reverse-curved ribs are present. Scribe ribs: At bow, one pair under deck; at stern, one pair at and one pair just inboard of the gunwale/deck junction. No footed ribs under bow or stern deck. Rib feet ends are beveled and do not extend all the way across the bottom board.

**Hull:** Number of strakes on each side: 8; feather-lap construction.

**Gunwales:** Rounded upper and lower edges; the gunwale ends are chamfered in line with the stem post.

**Heel plates:** One-piece; rounded lateral margins.

FIGURE 2-32 Lewis Austin's stem posts. Length is about 2 ½ inches, width ⅞ inch, and height ½ inch. Both sides of the stem post are chamfered at the front end, and the back end is slightly concave. The sides are vertical, and the top is rounded.

FIGURE 2-33 The distinctive pronounced ridge and pointed end of the stem foot.

FIGURE 2-34 Three-piece cambered deck and deck cap. (Left) The deck is set between the gunwales. (Right) The deck cap is pie-piece-shaped, cambered, and the inboard edge is tapered.

Figure 2-35 Albert Henry Billings.

Figure 2-36 A. H. Billings builder's plate.

## ALBERT HENRY BILLINGS

**Date of birth:** 1853 (Windsor, Vermont)
**Date of death:** 1903 (Montreal, Quebec, Canada)
**Active:** Early 1880s–1903
**Location:** Lake Placid, Essex County
**Estimate of guideboats built:** 50
**Number reviewed:** 13
**Builder's plate:** 8

### Biographical Sketch

Albert Billings was born in Windsor, Vermont, in 1853, the son of Alonzo Billings. He moved to North Elba in 1876 where his older half-brother, George W. Billings, had come to live five years earlier. In that year Benjamin T. Brewster built the first hotel in what was to be the village of Lake Placid. It was named the Lake Placid House but was more commonly called Brewster's.

In 1875 George Billings married Elsa Brewster, and in 1877 Albert married Elsa's sister Ella; both were daughters of Benjamin Brewster. "As a wedding present, Brewster gave Albert and Ella a piece of land he owned on the east shore of Mirror Lake, now a part of the Lake Placid Club complex."[1] Years before, Brewster had purchased 517 acres of land bordering on Mirror Lake from Gerrit Smith, abolitionist, reformer, and philanthropist.

Exactly when Billings began to build guideboats is not known. We do know that prior to 1885 he acted as guide for summer guests at Brewster's, was occupied as a carpenter, and served two terms as town auditor. His daughter Ida Billings Lockwood, born in 1883, recalled:

> I do not remember that my father ever built the square stern boat. As a very

1 Mary MacKenzie, *Albert H. Billings*, Unpublished biography, July 30, 1988.

young child it was my privilege to 'stick tacks' in the boats as they were assembled, and I very distinctly remember the whole process of the building, from the gathering of the stumps in the fall of the year for ribs, bows, and sterns to the finished product.[2]

Albert Billings was listed as a guide in S. R. Stoddard's Adirondack guidebook in 1878 and 1881,[3] as well as in the State Forest Commission Report for 1893.[4] He may have begun boatbuilding in the early to mid-1880s. The work was carried out in the upper part of his boathouse on Mirror Lake.

An advertisement for Billings & Molloy in the July 13, 1894 issue of the *Mountain Mirror* indicates a boatbuilding partnership. The author is aware of one guideboat that has a "Billings & Molloy" builder's plate.

**Figure 2-37** Billings & Molloy advertisement in the Mountain Mirror, Lake Placid, July 13, 1894. (Courtesy of Mary MacKenzie)

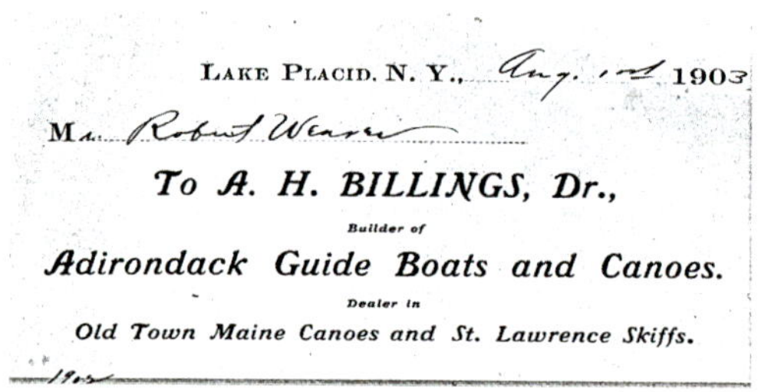


**Figure 2-38** 1903 billhead. (Courtesy of Mary MacKenzie)

The late Lake Placid/North Elba historian Mary MacKenzie noted:

> I am inclined to believe he was Walter Molloy, who owned Echo Lodge far up on the west shore of Lake Placid, since no other Molloy resided here. Molloy sold the camp in 1895 and I believe left Lake Placid at that time. . . . There is no evidence that Molloy ever had a hand in actually building the guideboat. My guess would be that he provided managerial or financial assistance in the business.[5]

Their partnership was apparently brief, since an A. H. Billings letterhead dated July 18, 1896, shows his name only, as does a billhead dated August 1, 1903.[6]

In the *Adirondack Directory* for 1902–1903, Lake Placid section, Billings is listed as the owner of a boat livery and in the display advertisement as "Builder of Adirondack Guide Boats, Canoes, Oars, Paddles and Cane Seats."[7]

Mary MacKenzie further noted:

> Albert and Ella sold their place to John Fraser and moved over to the west shore of Mirror Lake, where the village of Lake Placid was evolving. In the 1890s they built a house on Mirror Lake Drive. It is still standing, enlarged and modernized, and is now known as the Colonial Cottage of Mirror Lake Inn [torn down in 2007 and rebuilt as the Colonial House].
>
> John Fraser and his wife turned the old Billings farmhouse into a boarding house and christened it "Bonnieblink." In 1895 "Bonnieblink" became the first clubhouse of what was to be Melvil Dewey's famed Lake Placid Club. Renamed Lakeside and greatly enlarged, the building was torn down in 1946, and the original Billing's boathouse some years later.
>
> In 1897, on the site of the present

2 Ida Lockwood, Letter to Dr. LeRoy H. Wardner, October 13, 1958, Adirondack Museum, Boatbuilders' Files.
3 Stoddard, *The Adirondacks: Illustrated*, 1878,1881:216.
4 *State Forest Commission*, 1894, I:356.
5 MacKenzie, *Albert H. Billings*
6 MacKenzie, *Albert H. Billings.*
7 Jos. Mannix and Geo. H. Fay, comps., *Adirondack Directory for 1902–1903*, Saranac Lake, NY: 1902:119,128.

> Holiday Harbor, Albert established a boathouse-marina on Lake Placid and named it Billings Landing. Here he ran a boat livery and provided docking facilities for rowboats, canoes and the early motor boats of camp owners on the lake. Here he also continued building his Billings guide boat and other non-standard rowboats, besides repairing and refinishing boats of the camp owners. His boathouse was enlarged in 1899 and 1902.
>
> Albert Billings died in 1903. According to the Malone Farmer, October 2, 1903, he died in a Montreal hospital wither he had gone for an operation for cancer of the stomach. . . . Two of his employees, Thomas H. George and C. Heman Bliss, the latter chief boatbuilder for Albert, ran the business for Mrs. Billings for a year. In 1904 they purchased the entire establishment and the business became known as George and Bliss. The building of rowboats [and guideboats] at the old Billings Landing continued only a few more years. In February 1919, the entire marina, greatly expanded by George Bliss, was destroyed by fire but was quickly replaced.[8]

There were three Billings daughters: Ida, Marian, and Beth. According to the *Lake Placid News* of November 2, 1934, the second wood-burning steamboat on Lake Placid was captained by Albert Billings and named in honor of his daughter Ida. Albert's wife Ella died in 1931. He and his wife are buried in the North Elba Cemetery.

8 MacKenzie, Albert H. Billings.

## Guideboat Characteristics

Billings built guideboats with both strip decks and two-piece decks. Both models had center cover boards with coamings. The unique characteristic of a Billings guideboat is the decorative deck beam with multiple scallops. His stem posts are narrow with a rounded concave back, and the stem foot is a low horizontal rectangle. Yoke cleats were often omitted since most of his boats were built for summer residents, who used them principally on Mirror Lake or Lake Placid, with little need to be carried. The boats are quite stable.

Billings used seven or eight strakes on each side. The rectangular shape of the stern and center-seat backrests is also characteristic of his guideboats.

### Field Notes

**Stems:** Tumblehome (Saranac profile).

**Ribs:** *With strip decks:* No reverse curve. No scribe ribs. One pair of footed ribs under bow deck, no footed ribs under stern deck.

*With two-piece decks:* No reverse curve. One pair of scribe ribs under bow and stern decks, one pair of footed ribs un-

FIGURE 2-39 (Above) A strip-built deck with a multiple-scalloped deck beam. (Right) A two-piece deck with a center cover strip and coaming and no decorative deck beam. The two deck pieces are set in the sheer strakes.

der bow deck, no footed ribs under stern deck. Rib feet ends cut square and extend all the way across the bottom board.

**Decks:** *Strip decks:* Not V-grooved. Decks extend beyond carlin at bow and stern. Number of strips on each side: bow, 17; stern, 13. Coamings are narrow and are not tapered. Center cover board surrounds the stem post.

**Hull:** Number of strakes on each side: 7 or 8; feather-lap construction.

FIGURE 2-40 The multiple scalloped design of the deck beam. Although most of the decks built by Albert Billings were strip built with a center cover board and a narrow coaming, some have two-piece decks, a center cover board, and a narrow coaming, as in this photograph. The deck pieces are set between the gunwales.

FIGURE 2-42 (Right) Albert Billings and two guideboats in what appears to be the boathouse adjoining his shop. Note the absence of yoke cleats and the rectangular shape of the backrests. (Courtesy of Adirondack Museum)

FIGURE 2-41 (Above) The stem post is narrow and rectangular, with a rounded concave back and a slightly rounded top. The center cover board surrounds the stem post. (Right) The stem foot is a low horizontal rectangle.

FIGURE 2-43 (Above) The center-seat backrest is T-shaped with parallel sides. The same designs were used by Billings's successors, George & Bliss. This boat is equipped with yoke cleats. (Right) Stern-seat backrest. The side of the frames are almost parallel, and the "ears" are pointed.

**Figure 2-44** John H. Blanchard.

## JOHN H. BLANCHARD

**Date of birth:** 1878 (Blue Mountain Lake, Hamilton County)
**Date of death:** 1948
**Active:** 1898 ~ 1941
**Estimate of guideboats built:** 50
**Number reviewed:** 17
**Builder's plate:** Not used
**Adirondack Museum accessions:** 57.122.1, 60.37.1, 2001.037.1 (attributed)

### Biographical Sketch

According to Raquette Lake historian Ruth Timm, John H. Blanchard was the son of Charles William and Harriet (Baty) Blanchard. In 1873 Charles and Harriet lived on the peninsula known as Green Point, on Raquette Lake, along with early settler Samuel Payne. There, Charles built "Blanchard's Wigwams," a successful hostelry attracting hunters and fishermen. An early map indicates that Charles may have also resided on Beecher's Island (on Raquette Lake's Outlet Bay) as early as the 1860s.[1]

John Blanchard was born, married to Nancy Hughes, and made his first home, at Blue Mountain Lake, where he began to build guideboats in the late 1890s. His shop was a short distance "down the road" from where the Adirondack Museum is now located.[2] On the site today is a small building owned by the museum, known as Blanchard Cottage. James Blanchard recalls that his grandfather's early guideboats were cod-headed (wider toward the bow); that cedar and pine were used for planking and cherry for cleats and seats; and that his father Paul was also a guideboat builder, having built four.[3]

In 1908 the Blanchards moved to Raquette Lake. They purchased a house

1 Ruth Timm, *Raquette Lake; A Time to Remember*, Utica, NY: North Country Books, 1989:39.
2 Louis Little, *Letter to Kenneth Durant, November 1, 1958*, Durant Collection.
3 James Blanchard, *Personal communication*, November 23, 1998; July 30, 2001.

and parcel of land on which a guideboat shop and boathouse were built. The only other boatbuilders on Raquette Lake when the Blanchards arrived:

> were "Old Man Graves" [formerly of Blue Mountain Lake] who lived in the bay on the south side of Big Island, and "Charley Cole" [son of boatbuilder Alba Cole] who lived in Lonesome Bay. . . . As he [John Blanchard] was a highly skilled and sought after boat builder, the construction of boats during the winter months became a family project. John's wife, Nancy, and daughter Ruth caned the seats while [son] Paul assisted with other phases of the development process. John also built launches and power boats as well as repairing engines. During the summer they ran a tourist home.[4]

James Blanchard, an accomplished carpenter, and his wife, Mary DeShaw, today live in the homestead on Raquette Lake. Background of the Blanchard family may be found in Ruth Timm's *Raquette Lake: A Time to Remember*.[5]

## Guideboat Characteristics

It was in Blue Mountain Lake that an elderly Nathaniel S. Graves had already established himself as a builder of guideboats.[6] According to John Blanchard's daughter, Ruth Dymond, Graves and Blanchard became friends, and it was Graves who taught Blanchard how to build guideboats.[7] According to Wright Cole, his father Warren W. Cole sold his guideboat patterns to "a man named Blanchard of Blue Mountain Lake."[8] Indeed, some of Blanchard's guideboats do have a C-shaped stern deck and most have mitered decks, characteristic of Cole's guideboats. To further complicate matters, in a letter to Kenneth Durant, Louis Little wrote: "He [John Blanchard] learned the boat building trade from [George W.] Smith at Long Lake and was there in the 1890s."[9] The construction differences, however, between guideboats built by Smith and by Blanchard are great, not only in stem-post design, stem profile, and deck design and placement, but also in rib type at bow and stern, and rib-foot length.

The three builders, Smith, Graves, and Blanchard, are linked, however by a minor observation: Pointed scribe ribs under the bow deck are a signature of all three builders. Guideboats built by Graves and Blanchard have scribe ribs that are pointed at their lower ends. Such ribs in Smith's boats are pointed at their upper ends, just below the deck. Also, early Smith's guideboats were cod-headed as were a few of Blanchard's.

Blanchard was strongly influenced by Long Lake construction, that is, wide stem posts, reverse-curved ribs, and decks mitered or let into the gunwales. Smith, however, did not let his decks into the gunwales; they were set between the gunwales.

There was once a controversy about who built the *Alfred B. Thacher:* John Blanchard or George Smith. This guideboat was chosen to be exhibited in the United States Pavilion at the 1967 International and Universal Exposition (Expo 67), in Montreal, Canada. It was selected by the organizers as: "an American indigenous object of sculptural quality." The boat was built for New York City attorney Alfred B. Thacher, of South Orange, New Jersey, who summered at Blue Mountain Lake in one of the earliest camps built on the lake.

It is now accepted that the *Alfred B. Thacher* was built by John Blanchard.

4 Timm, 1989:50.
5 Timm, 1989:39–52.
6 Arpad G. Gerster, *Notes Collected in the Adirondacks, 1895 & 1896*, Sidney S. Whelan, Jr., ed., Blue Mountain Lake, NY: Adirondack Museum, 2005:85, 90.
7 Nancy Dymond, *Letter to Kenneth Durant, April 16, 1969*, Durant Collection.
8 Kenneth Durant, *Letter to Louis Little, May 10, 1959*, Durant Collection.
9 Little, 1958.

This has been confirmed by Blanchard's daughter Ruth, and his grandson, James.[10]

The following news release, dated July 20, 1967, provides more information.

> The controversy over the U. S. Pavilion at Expo 67 may continue for months, but Adirondackers are unanimous on one point. They're proud to be one of the few regions of this country to have specific representation at the Montreal fair.
>
> A guide-boat from the collections of the Adirondack Museum is on display at the entrance to the theater in the U. S. Pavilion, the giant, geodesic dome that is recognized as the architectural triumph of the fair. The boat is spotlighted as one of the functional creations in American life which also reflect a rare degree of skill and beauty.
>
> Strangely enough, the Adirondack guide-boat made its way to Expo via a New England boat expert, John Gardner. He was called by Cambridge Seven Associates of Cambridge, Massachusetts, the firm that organized and designed the interior structures and exhibits for the U. S. Pavilion. The representative said they wanted to include a New England dory in the exhibition, explaining that they were looking for typical American objects of sculptural quality.
>
> Mr. Gardner has been a consultant for the Adirondack Museum for several years and is one of the leading small boat specialists in the country. He replied in his "Down East" accent, "Well, you can get a dory, but 'tisn't what you really want. What you need is an Adirondack guide-boat."
>
> This now rare workboat of the Adirondacks is much sought by modern outdoorsmen as well as by many people who just love beautiful things. . . .[11]

There is a guideboat in the Adirondack Museum collection attributed to Arthur Blanchard, John's older brother. Its construction, however, is typical of John Blanchard's boats. According to John's grandson, James, and his nephew Ernest, Arthur Blanchard did not build guideboats.[12] John Blanchard's son Paul, did, however.

John Blanchard's guideboats are all finely built. His decks are one piece and most, like those of Long Lake builders, are mitered into the gunwales. The stem posts are wide. His main signature is that his scribe ribs are pointed at the bottom.

**FIGURE 2-45** (Top) The Alfred B. Thacher, exhibited in the United States Pavilion at Expo 67 held in Montreal. (Bottom) The Thacher monogram on the deck cap and the Blanchard stem post. The bottom board length is 13 feet and the boat's length overall is 14 feet 6 inches.

10 Dymond; Blanchard, *Personal communication*, 1995.
11 *News Release from Adirondack Museum*, July 20, 1967.
12 Blanchard, 1998.

**Figure 2-46** (Top and Bottom) The stem posts of Blanchard guideboats, seen here in two views, are wide. Length about 2 inches, width about 1 inch, height about ½ inch. The back is slightly concave. The stem post is chamfered on both sides at the front.

**Figure 2-47** (Above) The scribe ribs are pointed at their lower ends. The stem foot is bull-nosed. The ends of the rib feet are beveled and extend all the way across the bottom board. (Above Right) The ribs are reverse curved.

**Figure 2-48** (Above Left) Most Blanchard guideboats have pie-piece-shaped deck caps at the bow and stern; a few, however (Above Right), have a shield shape.

## Field Notes

**Stems:** Slight tumblehome and straight leading edge (Long Lake profile). Tow holes may be present at bow and/or stern, reinforced by a brass grommet. Upper stem narrows below gunwale. The end of the stem foot at the bottom board is bull-nosed.

**Decks:** One piece at bow and stern. Bow and stern decks are mitered or, rarely, let into the gunwales.

**Ribs:** A single pair of scribe ribs, pointed at the bottom board, under the bow deck. There may be one pair of scribe ribs under, or just inboard of, the stern deck, also pointed at the bottom board. No footed ribs beneath either the bow or stern decks.

**Hull:** Number of strakes on each side: 8; feather-lap construction.

**Heel plates:** Three-piece, with lateral corners cut off.

(Right) Three slightly different stern-seat backrests. (Courtesy of James Blanchard)

**Figure 2-49** Fred C. Burns. (Courtesy of Raymond W. Smith)

**Figure 2-50** Burns builder's plate.

## FRED C. BURNS

**Date of birth:** January 29, 1892 (Union Hill, New Jersey)
**Date of death:** June 8, 1988 (Saranac Lake, Franklin County)
**Active:** 1968–1983
**Location:** Long Lake, Hamilton County
**Estimate of guideboats built:** 13
**Builder's plate:** 3
**Adirondack Museum accession:** 2011.037.1

### Biographical Sketch

Fred Burns arrived at Long Lake in 1909 and became well known for his paintings of forest scenery and for building guideboats. He served in the Air Service, United States Army, in World War I and was married to Elsie Stanton on December 9, 1921. Over the years, he worked at Deerland Lodge and for Dr. LeBoutilier at nearby South Pond.

His wife Elsie's father was George Stanton. It was his brother, Henry Stanton, Jr., who taught the boatbuilding trade to Dwight Grant of Boonville. Both Stanton brothers were guideboat builders. Henry died at an early age in 1881 but George continued to build guideboats, and his tools were later passed on to his son-in-law.

### Guideboat Characteristics

The following is from a letter by Richard Dechene, Fred Burns's grandson:

> . . . my grandfather was the type of man who kept everything and recycled it. My guideboat has plywood decks. I believe all of his boats had them but I am not one hundred percent sure. He built thirteen boats, usually in the winter in his shop. His jig was homemade using large wire spool ends for his circular ends and drilled holes through them so he could angle the boats however he wanted. His tools were always in great shape and very sharp. As a child I knew never to

**Figure 2-51** (Top Left) A wide, rectangular stem post with a concave front. The sides and back are straight while the top is rounded. There is a loop in the upper stem band, acting as a painter ring. Note that the gunwale does not extend to the stem front. (Bottom Left) A wide, rectangular stem post. The stem band extends across the top of the stem post.

> touch them. The handles were always varnished and commonly colored rings were painted around the base of them. I think the most interesting thing about [my grandfather's] boats was that they were totally built with hand tools. He owned a few power tools but very rarely ever used them. I can remember spruce stumps in the woods that would be covered up with canvas tarps. He had prepared these so he could cut his ribs from them with his cross cut saw.
>
> My father would usually get the planks for the sides and grandfather would hand plane them into tapered boards. There were always piles of curly shavings on the floor which made a great fire starter. In the spring, launching day was always a big event for us. [Grandfather] would set his new boat on his homemade cart and pose for pictures. Then he would walk it to the town beach, about a quarter of a mile away, and launch it. He'd take it for a spin to see how it handled and then returned to see if anyone else wanted to test it out. This was always fun for us.[1]

Fred Burns is the only person known to have begun building guideboats as a serious endeavor at the age of seventy-six, in 1968. He built a total of thirteen, one each year. No two were exactly the same. The distinguishing feature of most is a stem band with a triangular projection, or loop, meant to serve as a painter ring. Unlike other Long Lake builders, he used seven rather than eight strakes for his hulls. Most of his decks and deck caps were made from plywood. Most of his stem posts are rectangular in shape; one has a prominent indentation in its upper front, (similar to those of Wallace Emerson). One boat has an extension of the stem band on top of the stem post. His deck caps varied between shield-shaped and, occasionally, pie-piece-shaped.

**Figure 2-52** Shield-shaped deck cap. Note the three-piece deck and the builder's plate.

### Field Notes

**Stems:** Slight tumblehome with straight leading edge (Long Lake profile). The stem narrows about 2 inches below the gunwales.

**Ribs:** Slight reversed-curve. One pair of footed ribs under the bow deck. No ribs under the stern deck. Feet extend across the bottom board.

**Decks:** One-piece and three-piece decks; most made from plywood; mitered into gunwales.

**Hull:** Number of strakes on each side: 7; feather-lap construction.

1 Richard Dechene, Letter to Author, January 29, 2011.

FIGURE 2-53 Buyce builder's plate. (Courtesy of Gerald Buyce)

FIGURE 2-54 John F. Buyce

## JOHN F. BUYCE

**Date of birth:** May 28, 1869, (Speculator, Hamilton County)
**Date of death:** 1947 (Speculator)
**Active:** 1889–1940s
**Location:** Speculator
**Estimate of guideboats built:** 12–15
**Number reviewed:** 1
**Builders plate:** Used

### Biographical Sketch

John F. Buyce, the son of Fitch and Deborah Parslow Buyce, was born in Newton's Corners (renamed Speculator in 1896), on May 28, 1869. He completed grade school, but a high school education was not then available in Newton's Corners, so he began to work in his father's sawmill as a carpenter's helper. The 1900 federal census for the Town of Lake Pleasant, Village of Speculator, indicated that John F. Buyce was married to Jennie Slack in 1891 and that they had one child, Luther Milton, born August 1, 1898.

In June of 1889 Buyce built his first workshop on the shores of Lake Pleasant. His primary trade was blacksmithing, but he was also engaged in general carpentry and boat building.[1]

An undated advertisement issued sometime after 1896, promoting his livery service rowboat, "The Lake Pleasant," notes that Buyce had been a boatbuilder since 1889. An indication of his multiple talents and versatility is a printed letterhead dated May 24, 1905.

Buyce built not only boats, but also ornate fireplace sets, wooden snowplows, huge rollers (8 feet high by 12 feet wide) to pack down snow, three-seat buckboards, lumber wagons, and bolsters for hauling

1 Charles J. Murphy, "John Buyce Will Mark 50th Year as Speculator 'Smith,'" *Morning Herald,* Gloversville, NY: June 3, 1939.

**Figure 2-55** John F. Buyce (left) and his son L. Milton Buyce in their combined blacksmithing and boatbuilding shop. Note the boat under construction at right. (Courtesy of Adirondack Museum)

**Figure 2-56** Buyce business envelope. (Courtesy of Adirondack Museum)

logs. Buyce's son L. Milton Buyce recalls that a sign in front of the shop read: "Odds and Unusual Things that You Can't Get Done at the Other Place."[2]

Working with John Buyce from 1904 into the 1940s was Alvah Buyce, his younger brother, as blacksmith, but more often as a boatbuilder.[3]

John Buyce was a respected member of the Speculator community, not only for his metal and wood craftsmanship but also for his civic mindedness. He held a number of county and town positions, including mayor of Speculator.[4]

**JOHN F. BUYCE**

Practical Horseshoer, Sleigh and Wagon Maker
Repairing in all its Branches

Dealer in Agricultural Implements and Hardware Specialties

**SADDLERS' HARDWARE**

Manufacturer of Lake Pleasant Row Boats, Oars, Paddles and Boat Fittings

Paint Shop in Connection In the Adirondacks

Courtesy of Edward Comstock, Jr.

2 L. Milton Buyce, *Personal communication to Nancy Dymond, April 15, 1969,* Adirondack Museum Boatbuilders' Files.
3 Ted Aber, and Stella King, *History of Hamilton County,* Lake Pleasant, NY: Great Wilderness Books, 1965:728.
4 Aber and King:737.

## Guideboat Characteristics

Although Buyce began building boats in 1889, he was most active in the 1920s. In 1939, the Gloversville paper noted: "Since 1920, with the decline in the use of so large a number of horses in this section, Mr. Buyce has centered much of his attention on wood-working, his specialty being rowboats, which have become famous on all lakes in the Adirondacks . . . ."[5]

The majority of Buyce boats were heavily built livery rowboats, with either natural-crook or steam-bent ribs. The most popular was the Lake Pleasant model, characterized by a clapboard-lapstrake hull, two-piece decks with a center cover board, a coaming, and board seats.

Whether Buyce ever built a boat with a smooth-lapstrake hull is not known. In a letter to a prospective buyer, he wrote of a boat he had for sale: "One 12½ ft long, 36 in beam of 3/16 cedar and copper fastened and very light, weighs only 45¾ lbs. $35.00."[6]

Buyce built about twelve or fifteen of these boats that were both light in weight and of guideboat construction, according to his son Milton. They were about 12 feet long and "were made to weigh no more than 50 pounds and included yoke cleats and a neck yoke."[7] The bottom board was said to be cypress. All had hulls that were clapboard-lapstrake planked, and were nailed or tacked outside-to-inside only, a characteristic of most Buyce boats. The one-piece decks were a solid thick board with an arc or straight inboard edge, and the deck caps were a distinctive diamond-like or pointed oval shape, although in some boats a deck cap was absent. Some had double stems. The stem posts and stem feet were rectangular.

The comment made by Milton Buyce that the bottom boards of his father's guideboats were made from cypress may be correct and would certainly be unique. It has also been stated by his son that Buyce never used iron screws,[8] however iron screws and tacks were commonly used in the lesser-quality livery boats.[9] Buyce also built boats of carvel-hull construction with inner battens.

Although his seats were usually rectangles, some had U-shaped cut-out ends, with the arms of the U supported by the seat cleats. He also built boats with a narrow V-shaped transom to accommodate an outboard motor.

**Figure 2-57** Buyce livery boat with natural-crook ribs and a typical clapboard-lapstrake hull. Except for its weight, it closely resembles a guideboat. Buyce also built shorter, lighter boats of this model, weighing only 50–60 pounds.

5 Murphy, 1939.
6 John F. Buyce, *Letter to J. H. Hanson, May 24, 1905*, Edward Comstock, Jr. Collection.
7 Milton Buyce, 1969.
8 Milton Buyce, 1969.
9 John F. Buyce, 1905.

**Figure 2-58** Buyce decks, all three of which are placed between the sheer strakes. (Left) Deck with an arced inboard edge and builder's plate. (Center) The deck is straight; the deck cap has a pointed oval, or diamond shape, and a larger builder's plate. (Right) Straight deck and the typical Buyce deck cap.

**Figure 2-59** (Above) Deck and stem post, with no deck cap. The stem post is a narrow, horizontal rectangle. (Right) The stem foot at the bottom board is a horizontal rectangle. In the middle of the stem is a screw securing a double stem. Only footed ribs are seen at the bow.

**Figure 2-60** (Above) The seat design for Buyce's higher-grade livery rowboats.

**FIGURE 2-61** James F. Cameron in his shop. (Courtesy of James F. Cameron)

**FIGURE 2-62** Cameron builder's plate.

## JAMES FLETCHER CAMERON

**Date of birth:** July 5, 1953 (Jackson, Wyoming)
**Active:** 1984–
**Location:** Upper St. Regis Lake, Franklin County
**Estimate of guideboats built:** 30
**Builder's plate:** Used

### Biographical Sketch

The author's introduction to the guideboat took place at Upper St. Regis Lake in the early 1990s, where he and his wife first met Jim and Lynn Cameron. On subsequent visits many guideboats were examined at several of the lake's camps.

James Cameron, the youngest of five boys, was born and raised in Jackson, Wyoming. He worked there as a cabinetmaker until 1980, when he moved to Northpoint Camp, on Upper St. Regis Lake, the former camp of Anita McCormick Blaine, daughter of Cyrus H. McCormick, Sr., inventor of the mechanical reaper. In 1984 he married Lynn Marvin of Rapid City, South Dakota. They live year-round at the lake.

Cameron's maternal grandfather, Dr. Edward Peterson of New York City, had purchased a camp on Upper St. Regis Lake in 1921. For the first nine years of his life, Cameron spent every other summer at his grandfather's camp, and from age ten on, every summer. He participated in the first class (1980–1981) of the Adirondack Guideboat Apprenticeship Program, offered by North Country Community College of Saranac Lake and dedicated to preserving the craft of building traditional guideboats. It was taught by master boatbuilders Carl Hathaway and Ralph Morrow.

Upon finishing the course, Cameron

**Figure 2-63** (Left) A Cameron guideboat. (Right) The Bloomingdale stem and half-moon-shaped stem post. (Courtesy of James F. Cameron)

**Figure 2-64** Note the unique deck designs and the one-piece center cover board and arrowhead deck caps. The stem bands extend over the stem posts. (Courtesy of James F. Cameron)

became a boatbuilder and repairer. Since 1984 he has built a guideboat every year and repaired hundreds. In 2011, one of his guideboats took Best in Class at the Saratoga Wooden Boat Show. He also specializes in the maintenance and repair of the local racing class sailboats, the Idem. He has sailed as a mainsail crewman for more than twenty-one years.[1]

Cameron's boat shop is in the camp's boathouse, one of only three buildings to survive a devastating fire in 1941. Boathouse Woodworks is located on the northern shore of Upper St. Regis Lake.[2]

## Guideboat Characteristics

Cameron uses William Vassar patterns and the Bloomingdale style stems. His own unique deck designs feature a one-piece center cover board and a deck cap in the shape of an arrow. His stem bands loop over a half-moon-shaped stem post, also a characteristic of Vassar. He uses a variety of deck designs with handholds beneath the decks. The bull-nosed stem foot is similar to Vassar's.

**Figure 2-65** (Above) The handhold just beneath the deck, the deck pattern, and the stem band covering the stem post. (Left) The stem foot is rounded over (bull-nosed).

1 In 1899, members of the newly formed (1897) St. Regis Yacht Club commissioned Clinton H. Crane (1873–1958) to design a class of wooden sailboats specifically for the purpose of racing in the light winds of Upper St. Regis Lake. They were named Idem-class racing sailboats—"idem" meaning "the same" in Latin. Only twelve were built and to this day eleven of them still engage in summer racing. They represent the oldest class of actively racing sailboats of the same design in the United States, perhaps in the world. The twelfth Idem, *Water Witch,* is on display at the Adirondack Museum in Blue Mountain Lake, New York

2 James F. Cameron, *Personal communication*, 1992–2012.

**FIGURE 2-66** Reuben Cary. (Courtesy of Adirondack Museum)

## REUBEN CARY

**Date of birth:** February 11, 1845 (Long Lake, Hamilton County)
**Date of death:** July 13, 1933 (Long Lake)
**Active:** mid-1860s–1910
**Location:** Long Lake
**Estimate of guideboats built:** 100
**Number reviewed:** 2
**Builder's plate:** Not used
**Adirondack Museum accession:** 61.68.1

### Biographical Sketch

Reuben Cary was the son of Thomas R. Cary, from Vermont, one of the earliest settlers of Long Lake, and Jane M. Dornburgh, daughter of one of the early Mohawk Valley Dutch pioneers. Thomas Cary built one of the first hunting and fishing camps at Beach's Lake (later Brandreth Lake), a location with which his son Reuben would become well acquainted.[1] In 1861 Thomas Cary became the third proprietor of the Raquette Lake House, constructed in 1856.[2] There, Reuben worked as a guide, spending the winters at the Cary homestead near the village of Long Lake.[3] In about 1870 the elder Cary returned permanently to his home at Long Lake and Reuben succeeded him as proprietor of the Raquette Lake House, until it closed in 1873.[4]

Reuben was the oldest of five children (four boys and a girl). As a young man, he was "adept in the use of firearms, a skillful fisherman and an ingenious trapper." He soon became a sought-after guide. His sterling character, his fishing and hunting prowess, and his extraordinary woodsmanship are well documented.[5]

1 Paul Brandreth [pseud.], *Trails of Enchantment*, New York: G. Howard Watt, 1930:101, 104.
2 Timm, 1989:63.
3 Reuben Cary, *Testimony, Record on Appeal, NYS vs. M. Hasbrouck*, Supreme Court, Appellate Division, 1907, Adirondack Museum, Charles E. Snyder Papers.
4 Timm, 63.
5 Paul Brandreth [pseud.], "Reuben Cary—Forest Patriarch," *Forest and Stream*, June 20, 1914:821–822; June 27:854–855.

In 1872 he married Estella R. Helms and they had five children. (She died of tuberculosis in 1896.) He moved to Raquette Lake in 1878 and remained there until 1881, when he moved to Brandreth Lake.[6]

Cary guided for several prominent visitors, including Dr. Benjamin B. Brandreth and the artist Arthur Fitzwilliam Tait. In 1851, Dr. Brandreth had purchased all of Township 39 in the Totten and Crossfield tract, that was mostly virgin forest. It included Beach's Lake, named after Matthew Beach, who had built the first cabin on the lake. In time it became known as Brandreth Lake. In 1880, Dr. Brandreth died, and the following year his son Franklin Brandreth (a colonel in the New York State Militia) asked Reuben Cary to "take charge of the place for the present and I will pay you $35.00 a month."[7] Cary thereby became the caretaker and game warden of the Brandreth Park and lived on the shores of the lake until retiring forty-nine years later, in 1930, at the age of eighty-five. He died three years later.

In addition to being a renowned guide and woodsman, Reuben Cary was well-known as a builder of guideboats. When he began to build them, and by whom he was taught, are not known; however, two members of his wife's family were guideboat builders, George and Henry Stanton. It is likely that he began building guideboats with transom sterns at Long Lake in the mid-1860s. He continued to build them, as well as double-ended guideboats, until about 1910, although fewer after becoming caretaker of the Brandreth Park in 1881. In an 1885 list of Grand Jurors for the Town of Long Lake, Reuben Cary's occupation is given as "Boat Builder."[8]

Fox B. Conner, Colonel Franklin Brandreth's grandson, recalled that:

> Reuben Cary worked as superintendent and lived on the Brandreth land for many years. He built guide boats there in the winter, and built several models; square stern, regular double end, and a lap strake double end that I have seen. His double end boats were narrow and inclined to be cranky.[9]

Mention of Cary as a boatbuilder appears in several different publications. From *Forest and Stream* in 1876:

> There are other excellent workmen at Long Lake, viz. Reuben Cary and Henry Stanton. I have one of Reuben Cary's make which I have used several years, and it is about as good as new. My impression is that the Saranac men do not excel in modelling or making these boats, and I know the Saranac guides order boats from Chase at Newcomb, and from Cary and Stanton at Long Lake. Reuben Cary is making me another boat this year. . . . Cary's and Stanton's models differ from Chase's in being higher in the stern and somewhat squarer, while his are not so sheer and alike at both ends.[10]

From Charles Hallock's *Sportsman's Gazetteer* in 1877:

> C. J. Chase, Newcomb, Essex Co. New York, Reuben Cary and Henry Stanton, of Long Lake, W. E. Martin, E. Peck, and G. Philboots [*sic*], of Saranac Lake, are all good builders. . . . There is perhaps a little more style to the Long Lake boats while Chase's are somewhat stiffer.[11]

From the *Boonville Herald* in 1881: "Jack Shepard [a Brown's Tract guide] has gone to the Raquette after a new boat, built by Reuben Cary."[12]

6 Orlando B. Potter III, and Donald B. Potter, *Brandreth: A History of Brandreth Park, 1851–2010*, Bennington, VT: Two Loon Media, 2011:65.
7 Franklin Brandreth, *Letter to Reuben Cary, November 12, 1881*, Copy from Franklin B. Brandreth to author.
8 *Proceedings of the Board of Supervisors of the County of Hamilton, NY*, List of Grand Jurors, Hope, NY: Hamilton County Press Print, 1886:4.
9 Fox B. Conner, *Letter to Kenneth Durant, September 6, 1962*, Durant Collection.
10 D. W. Mandell, "Adirondacks Boats," Letter to the Editor, *Forest and Stream*, March 9, 1876:74.
11 Charles Hallock, *Sportsman's Gazetteer*, New York: Forest and Steam Publishing, 1877:634.
12 *Boonville Herald*, March 31, 1881.

**Figure 2-67** (Left) A transom-built boat by Cary. (Below Left) A carved one-piece high-tucked transom. It has undergone a repair in the upper righthand corner and has had its lower planking replaced. A name plate will be attached in the inset. (Center Right) The ribs are reverse curved. (There is one pair of scribed and one pair of footed ribs at the bow.) The stem-foot end is a low horizontal rectangle. (Below Right) The wide, half-barrel shaped stem post, vertical in front and back.

## Guideboat Characteristics

Reuben Cary and William Allen Martin of Saranac Lake straddled the transom-stern and double-ender eras of guideboat building, having built both during their careers. Boats of both types by Cary or Martin survive and have been examined by the author. The transoms they built were narrow, high-tucked, and wineglass-shaped, carved in one piece from the stump of a black spruce. They are artistic accomplishments of high order.

### Transom-Built

Although two transom-built boats attributed to Reuben Cary are known, only one is well documented. It is 16 feet 1 inch long (stem post to transom). Its beam is 40 inches. The sheer strake is ¼ inch thick. The rib spacing is about 6½ inches on center. There are eight strakes on each side. The transom is ⅞ inch thick at the top.

## Field Notes

**Stem post:** Wide and rectangular. Top has a half-barrel shape.

**Stem:** Slight tumblehome with straight leading edge (Long Lake profile); begins to narrow at lower edge of sheer strake.

**Ribs:** Reverse-curved ribs. One pair of scribe ribs and one pair of footed ribs under the bow deck. At the stern one pair of half-length scribe ribs without a stern-seat cleat supporting ledge. This rib ends, slightly beveled, at the fifth strake. Foot ends are beveled and do not extend all the way across the bottom board.

**Bow deck:** Let into gunwales. This documented boat originally had a straight deck that was replaced by an arced deck.

**Gunwales:** Extend to bow stem fronts.

**Hull:** Number of strakes on each side: 8; feather-lap construction. Widest beam is forward of boat center (cod-headed).

**Heel plates:** Three-piece. Lateral margins are rounded.

**Yoke cleats:** Missing but screw holes in ribs indicate that they were once present.

### Double Ender

The author is aware of only one documented double ender built by Cary. The stem post and design of the bow and stern decks are unique to Cary. As stated by Fox Conner: "He [Cary] didn't build the same boat twice."[13]

## Field Notes

**Stems:** Slight tumblehome with a straight leading edge (Long Lake profile). Stems narrow about 4 inches below the gunwales. Stem feet at bottom board are square with rounded upper edges.

**Ribs:** Reverse-curved ribs. One pair of scribe ribs under the bow deck. No ribs under the stern deck. Feet ends do not extend all the way across the bottom board.

**Gunwales:** Extend to stem fronts.

**Hull:** Number of strakes on each side: 8; feather-lap construction.

**Heel plates:** Three-piece; rounded upper lateral margins.

FIGURE 2-68 The stem post of a restored Reuben Cary double ender. The uppermost portion of the stem narrows to form the stem post. The deck cap ends rest upon the wide portion of the stem, a construction method also used by Wallace Emerson in some of his guideboats. This stem post may have been reshaped as a result of restoration.

FIGURE 2-69 Deck and deck cap. The one-piece deck is let into the gunwales. The contour of the inboard edges of the decks is distinctive. The bow and stern decks overlap the carlins, and the deck cap is pie-piece-shaped. The hole in the deck is for a jacklight staff. The plate on the deck cap is a name plate, not a builder's plate.

13 Fox Connor was also the first to use fiberglass to build guideboats. His Allcock Manufacturing Company of Ossining, New York, built fiberglass boats molded from Wallace Emerson guideboats, from 1957 until 1962, when the company was purchased by Thomas Bissell of Long Lake and renamed the Bissell Manufacturing Company. Adirondack Museum accession: 60.39.1

**Figure 2-70** Caleb Judson Chase. (Courtesy of Adirondack Museum)

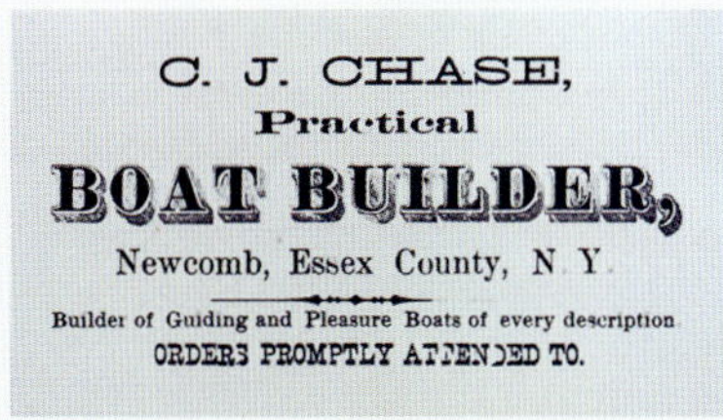


**Figure 2-71** C. J. Chase trade card. (Courtesy of Adirondack Museum)

## CALEB JUDSON CHASE

**Date of birth:** March 2, 1830 (Ticonderoga, Essex County)
**Date and place of death:** February 3, 1911 (Newcomb, Essex County)
**Active:** mid-1850s ~ 1908
**Location:** Newcomb
**Estimate of guideboats built:** More than 200
**Number reviewed:** 24
**Builder's plate:** Not used
**Adirondack Museum accessions:** 57.240.1, 72.21.1, 72.21.3

### Biographical Sketch

Caleb Chase was born on March 2, 1830, the son of Ebenezer Chase of Fisherfield, New Hampshire, and Sarah Cheney Chase, sister of John Cheney, a renowned Adirondack hunter and guide. After moving to Ticonderoga, Ebenezer died at an early age, leaving a wife and six children, including Caleb, an infant of ten months.

According to Harry V. Radford, founder and publisher of the quarterly magazine *Woods and Waters,* and a writer for *Field & Stream,* in a 1901 interview with Caleb Chase: "He removed to Newcomb with his brother, [Daniel] Cheney Chase, fourteen years his senior, about the year 1842, where he resided ever since."[1]

In Newcomb the brothers joined their uncle, John Cheney, who had a farm a

1 Harry V. Radford, "Letter Concerning Caleb Chase," *Field & Stream,* September 1901:408.

mile below the Lower Works (Tahawus) of the Adirondack, or McIntyre, Iron Works, a mining and smelting company.[2] John Cheney had located an additional iron source for the Works, northwest of Lake Sanford. He also provided a team to transport visitors to the company's Upper Works, acted as hunting and hiking guide for the company's many distinguished visitors, and with his legendary hunting skills provided food for their workers. For these services the Iron Works had presented Cheney with his farm.[3]

Caleb's older brother, Daniel, became superintendent of a portion of the Iron Works soon after his arrival. He was Newcomb's justice of the peace and served as town supervisor on multiple occasions—the first in 1845.[4] In that year Mitchell Sabattis, an Abenaki Indian who became renowned as a guide, and his wife moved from Long Lake to Newcomb. A friendship developed between Caleb Chase and Sabattis. It was here that young Caleb's hunting, woodcraft, and guiding skills developed, as well as his proficiency as boatbuilder and gunsmith. Radford again noted:

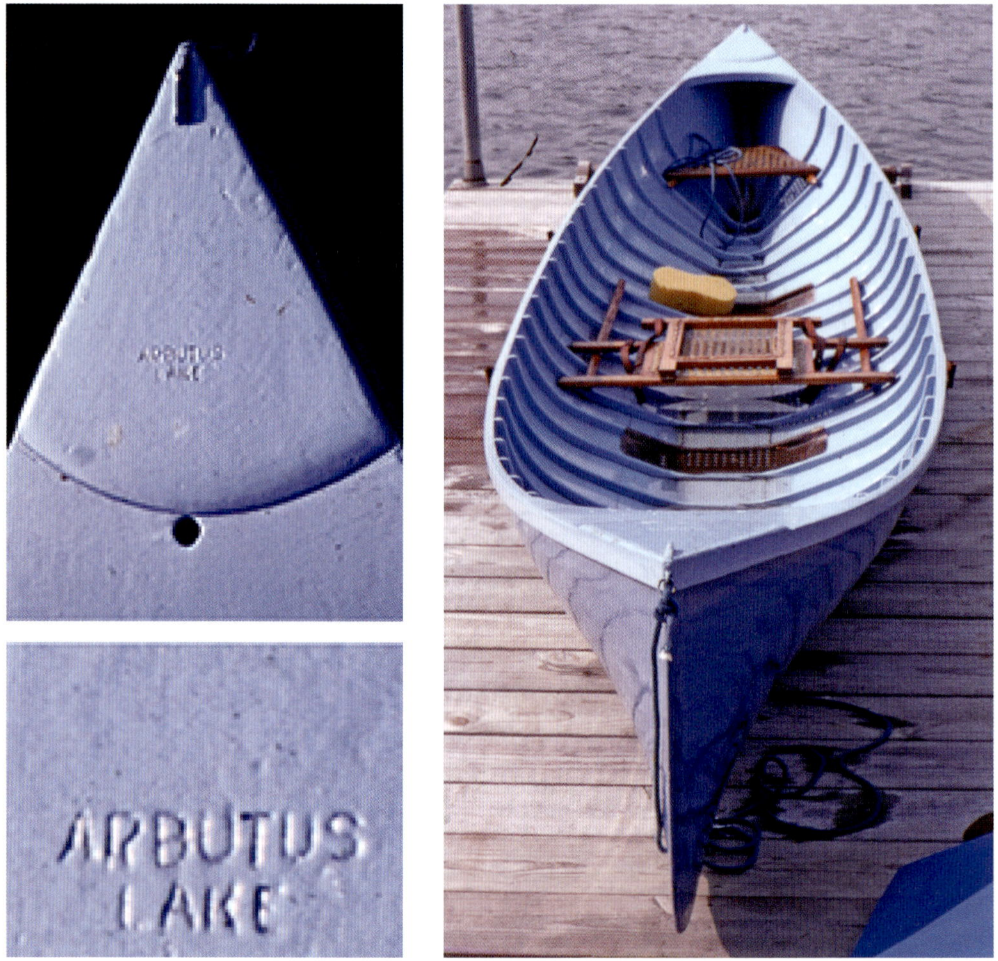


**Figure 2-72** (Right) The restored *Arbutus Lake*, built in the late 1870s by Caleb Chase. (Top Left) A narrow stem post, a pie-piece-shaped deck cap, a hole in the deck to accommodate a jacklight staff, and "ARBUTUS LAKE" stamped on the deck cap. (Bottom Left) A closeup of the stamped name. (Adirondack Museum accession: 2009.64.1)

2 "Obituary Notice of Danial Cheney Chase," *Adirondack News*, Newcomb, NY: March 1895.
3 Alfred L. Donaldson, *History of the Adirondacks*, New York: Century, 1921, I:170.
4 *Adirondack News*, March 1895.

**Figure 2-73** Chase's stem posts are narrow, low, and long: length 2¾ to 3 inches, width ⅜ inch, and height ½ inch. The front is angled; the back is almost vertical. The top is a rounded ridge.

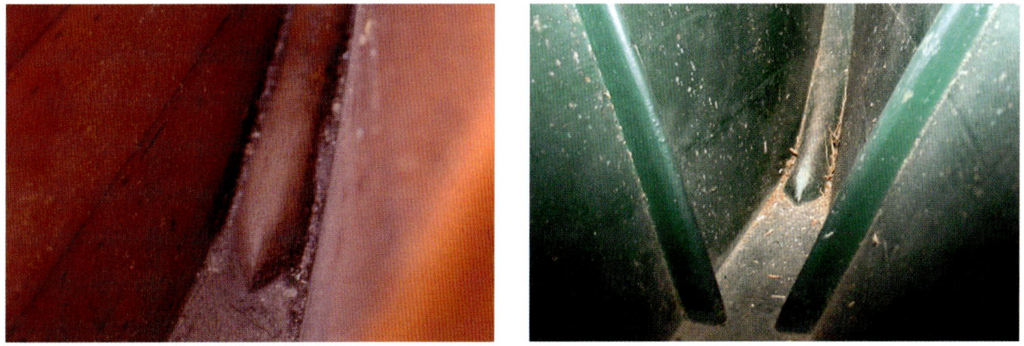

**Figure 2-74** Two views of the stem foot at the bottom board. The stem foot has a raised ridge with a pointed end. This stem-foot shape is unique to Caleb Chase and his son, Edmund.

> Caleb told me that he learned his woodcraft and huntercraft from the famous Indian guide, Mitchell Sabattis, who was about six years older than he. I have often heard the old men of Newcomb and surrounding hamlets tell of the rivalry which existed between Sabattis and Chase and of the wonderful skill of both.[5]

In January of 1853 Caleb married Thankful Preston, a schoolteacher in Newcomb, whose family had moved in 1847 from Strafford, Vermont, to Fishing Brook, midway between Long Lake and Newcomb.[6] The Chases had seven children.

In August of 1853, Caleb's brother Daniel purchased the James Chandler farm, near the western end of Rich Lake, now the site of the SUNY ESF Adirondack Ecological Center.[7] Soon afterwards, Caleb, newly married, occupied the house and farm of Farrand N. Benedict, near the eastern end of Rich Lake. He eventually purchased the house and the remaining property from Benedict, and: "In 1863 he bought his present farm, which contains eighty-eight acres of productive land; and through his energetic efforts . . . rendering it one of the best kept homesteads in this section."[8]

In the 1860 federal census for Newcomb, Caleb Chase is listed as a thirty-year-old gunsmith with three children, owning no real property, with $385 worth of personal property. Ten years later he is listed as a forty-one-year-old farmer with five children, with real property of $1,000 and $600 of personal property.[9] He was a gunsmith during the "muzzle loader" period, which sharply declined with the advent of the factory-made breechloader. In the late 1860s and 1870s, according to H. J. Swinney, gun historian and former Adirondack Museum director: "the trade in muzzle loading guns was winding down as breechloaders were being introduced, and Chase may have been glad to increase his boat-building as gun

5 Radford, 1901:408.
6 "Caleb J. Chase," *Biographical Review, Leading Citizens of Essex and Clinton Counties, New York*, Boston: Biographical Review Publishing, 1896:446. Also Marvin Bissell, Bissell family research, unpublished, *Personal communication*, 1999.
7 Leslie Rist, Unsourced newspaper article, May 7, 1983.
8 Biographical Review:446.
9 H. J. Swinney, *Letter to Miss Lois Chase, Newcomb, August 27, 1971.*

work became scarcer and scarcer—to trade trades, so to speak." Only two rifles stamped "C. J. Chase Newcomb NY" have been found.[10]

Chase's gunsmithing and boatbuilding periods overlapped. He is recorded as a gunsmith in the federal Census for 1860 but as a boatbuilder in the 1880 Census. The *New York State Business Directory* lists him as a boatbuilder in 1864, a gunsmith in 1870, and a boatbuilder in 1874 and 1876.[11] In the 1901 interview Radford wrote: "Chase began building boats at twenty one [in 1851] having built his first boat for Rev. Todd who wrote *Long Lake,* which was published in 1850 [1845]. Since then the old man and his son, E. J. Chase, have built several hundred boats."[12]

Todd's last trip to the Adirondacks was in 1854.[13] So it is reasonable to believe that Chase did build a boat for Todd in 1851. He, William Austin of Long Lake, and William McLenathen of Saranac Lake were the earliest documented boatbuilders in the region.

Chase's earliest boats probably had transom sterns, as did most others built prior to the late 1870s. A few small double-ended guideboats were built by the 1860s, however—more than a decade earlier than previously thought.

The first documentation of a double ender built by Chase is found in the previously cited article in *Forest and Stream*: "Cary's and Stanton's models differ from Chase's in being higher in the stern and somewhat squarer, while his [Chase's] are not so sheer and alike at both ends."[14] Chase's reputation as a guideboat builder is summed up by D. W. Mandell: "I know of a man by the name of Chase, who lives at Newcomb, Essex County, New York. He has the reputation among the Long Lake and Brown's Tract guides of putting together a boat in the very best manner . . . and I know the Saranac guides order boats from Chase at Newcomb."[15]

Decades later, historian Alfred Donaldson wrote: "A Chase boat in the woods ranked with a Brewster buggy in the city."[16]

A Chase guideboat was built for William West Durant in the late 1870s. The name *Arbutus Lake* was later stamped on its bow deck cap. To quote Harold K. Hochschild, author of *Township 34:*

> One of the oldest guide-boats in the central Adirondacks is the *Arbutus Lake*, built by Chase in the 1880s [late 1870s] for W. W. Durant, then living at Camp Pine Knot. She followed her owner to Camp Uncas, to Sagamore Lodge, to the Essex County lake for which she was named and, in 1901, to Eagle Nest [Hochschild's camp on Eagle Lake], where she has been in service ever since.[17]

## Guideboat Characteristics

The first boats built by Caleb Chase were most likely clapboard-lapstrake, with transom sterns. Next came transom-built guide's boats with smooth-lapstrake hulls, and eventually, double enders.

Chase's double-ended guideboats may be divided into three periods: early (1860s), middle (1870s), and late (1880s until the mid-1920s). His son, Edmund, continued with the late style after his father's death. Throughout these periods there are three identifying characteristics of a Caleb Chase guideboat that remained constant: the shape of the stem post, the stem foot, and a ledge on the stern scribe rib to support the stern-seat cleat.

10 H. J. Swinney, *New York State Firearms Trade*, Tom Rowe comp., Rochester, NY: Rowe Publications, 2003:I, 366.
11 *New York State Business Directory*, Boston: Sampson, Davenport, 1864, 1870, 1874. See also Boyd's *New York State Business Directory* for 1876.
12 Radford, 1901:408.
13 Warder H. Cadbury, "Introduction," in John Todd, *Long Lake*, 1845, Reprint ed., Harrison, NY: Harbor Hill Books, 1983: xxiii, xxiv.
14 Harry V. Radford, "Letter Concerning Caleb Chase," *Field & Stream*, September 1901:408.
15 Mandell, 1876:74.
16 Donaldson, 1921, II:80.
17 Harold K. Hochschild, *Township 34*, New York: Private printing, 1952:380.

## SUMMARY OF PERIOD CHANGES

| PART | PERIOD |
|---|---|
| RIBS | **Early (1860s)**<br>Slight or no reverse-curved ribs. One pair of scribe ribs under bow deck; one pair of half-length scribe ribs (square-cut top) with a seat-cleat supporting ledge at stern. Rib feet ends are beveled and do not extend all the way across the bottom board.<br>**Middle (1870s)**<br>Slight or no reverse-curved ribs. One pair of scribe ribs under bow deck; one pair of half-length scribe ribs (square-cut top) with ledge at stern.<br>Most rib feet ends are beveled, some are finely tapered, and they do not extend all the way across the bottom board.<br>**Late (1880s)**<br>Slight or no reverse-curved ribs. One pair of scribe ribs under bow deck; one pair of full-length scribe ribs with ledge at stern. Footed rib feet ends are finely tapered and do not extend all the way across the bottom board. |
| DECKS | **Early**<br>One-piece straight decks at bow and stern; let into the gunwales.<br>**Middle**<br>One-piece deck let into the gunwales; moderate arc at bow and shallow arc at stern.<br>**Late**<br>One- or two-piece deck set between gunwales; moderate arc at bow, shallow at stern. |
| DECK CAPS | **Early**<br>Straight with rounded inboard edge at bow and stern.<br>**Middle (transition from early)**<br>Pie-piece-shaped deck cap at bow and stern with straight decks; stern may have a shallow deck arc with a pie-piece-shaped deck cap.<br>**Middle and Late**<br>Pie-piece-shaped deck cap at bow and stern. |
| HULL | **Early to Late**<br>The oldest guideboat examined had only 4 strakes on each side; each strake made from 2 lengthwise planks scarfed together. Others have been observed with 6, 7, 8, or 9 strakes; most common is 7; feather-lap construction. |

The three periods may be recognized by certain changes in the deck and its placement, the deck cap, the scribe rib, and the shape of the ends of the rib feet.

Early Chase double-ended guideboats are generally about 14 feet long, with relatively wide bottom boards. This size was not uncommon among early builders. After the Civil War, with the introduction of luxury family hotels, his guideboat lengths increased to 15–16 feet to accommodate sportsmen plus a guide and gear for long stays in the woods.

**Figure 2-75** The interior of the stern of an early period (1860s) Chase double-ended guideboat. The stern pair of ribs are half-length scribe ribs, square-cut at the top, with ledges to support the stern-seat cleats, similar to the earlier transomed square-stern boats. The next pair of ribs are full length and footed; the ends are cut square. Note the four strakes on each side, the smooth-lapstrake construction; a one-piece straight deck, let into the gunwales and a straight deck cap with a rounded inboard edge. The straight deck and deck cap are characteristic of early transom-built and double-ended guideboats. During the early period, the stem bands were made of iron secured with iron T-shaped nails.

**Figure 2-76** An early-period (1860s) Chase double ender. (Left) The stern board seat has a rectangular slot to support a backrest. Both deck and deck cap are straight. (Right) At the bow the staff of a jacklight could be put through the hole in the deck and secured in the hole at the center of the block attached to the bottom board. During the middle and late periods, the seats and backrests were caned.

**Figure 2-77** A guideboat from Chase's middle period (1870s), showing a pair of half-length, square-cut stern ribs with ledges. There are seven or eight strakes, and an arced stern deck; a transition into the middle period.

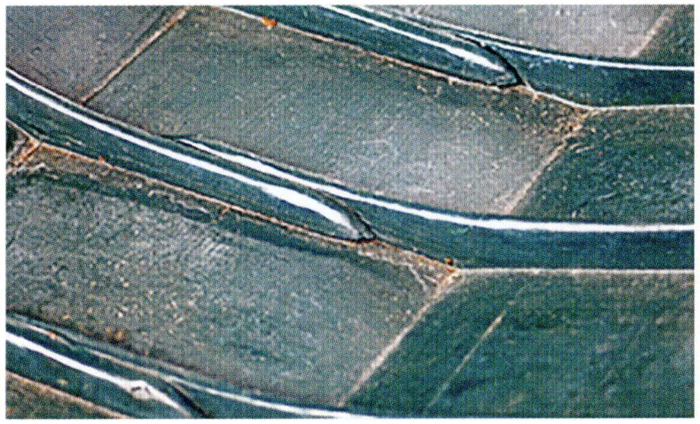

**Figure 2-78** In guideboats from Chase's middle and late periods (1870s and 1880s), the rib feet are rounded and pointed. Most guideboat builders either beveled the ends of ribs or cut them square.

**Figure 2-79** A late period Chase guideboat. The pair of scribe ribs at the stern are full length with ledges for seat cleat support; the two-piece decks are set between the gunwales. The deck is arced and crowned. Note the carlin and the pie-piece-shaped deck cap. There are nine strakes (seven or eight is the usual number). The rib feet ends are rounded. The end of the stem foot is pointed in the shape unique to Chase.

**Figure 2-80** Caleb Chase paddles with distinctive handles.

**Figure 2-81** The initials "C J C" occasionally are found stamped below the paddle handle.

**Figure 2-82** A late-period Chase guideboat with original components, including seats, cleats, backrests, yoke, paddles, and oars.

# EDMUND JUDSON CHASE

**Date of birth:** January 5, 1863 (Newcomb, Essex County)
**Date of death:** March 1, 1928
**Active:** 1911 ~ 1923
**Location:** Newcomb
**Estimate of guideboats built:** More than 50
**Number reviewed:** 17
**Builder's plate:** Not used

## Biographical Sketch

Edmund Chase was the fifth child of Caleb J. and Thankful Preston Chase of Newcomb. He married Anna M. Louks of Witherbee, Essex County, and they had seven children. Edmund guided at the Upper Works of the Adirondack, or McIntyre Iron Works, and also for the Caughnawauga Club on Catlin Lake, and for Harry V. Radford, the explorer, game conservationist, and writer.[1] He became an authority on wildlife, and "practiced taxidermy for many years."[2] During the winter months Edmund helped his father build guideboats. He may have done most of the building for several years before Caleb's death at the age of eighty-one in 1911. Edmund continued to build guideboats into the 1920s. Puzzling, however, is that while his obituary cites him as an authority on wildlife and taxidermy, it makes no mention of him as a boatbuilder.

1 Radford, 1901:408.
2 Edmund J. Chase, Obituary, source unknown, 1928.

## Guideboat Characteristics

Edmund Chase built guideboats using his father's patterns, so their characteristics are typical of Caleb Chase's late period. These include: the placement of the bow and stern decks between the gunwales, the rounded and pointed ends of the rib feet, and the scribe ribs at the stern, which are full length with a ledge supporting the stern-seat cleat.

At least ten guideboats were built by Edmund Chase in the early 1900s for

**FIGURE 2-83** Guideboats Arbutus 2 (Left) and 9 (Right) were built by Edmund Judson Chase. (Center) The guideboat with Arbutus 8 and *Beaver* designations was built by Warren Cole of Long Lake. It is the only guideboat in the Arbutus series not built by Edmund Chase. Note the difference between the long, narrow stem posts of Arbutus 2 and 9, and the short, wide stem post of Cole's Arbutus 8.

Archer M. Huntington. The *Arbutus* series was named after the wildflower, trailing arbutus (*Epigaea repens*), which in turn was the name of the estate purchased from William West Durant in 1898–1899 by Huntington, the adopted stepson of the railroad magnate Collis P. Huntington. The *Arbutus* guideboats are identified by a brass plaque with the name *Arbutus* and a serial number on the bow deck cap. A name in brass letters, often of an animal, is found along the convex arc of each deck cap. They should not be confused with the guideboat named *Arbutus Lake* built by Edmund's father Caleb for Durant in the 1870s.

The *Arbutus 2* is in the small-craft collection of the Mystic Seaport Museum in Mystic, Connecticut. It was built for Anna Hyatt Huntington, an internationally known sculptress.[3] It was probably built sometime after 1923, since Archer Huntington was divorced from his first wife in 1918 and married Anna Hyatt in 1923.[4] *Arbutus* was also the name of the Huntingtons' yacht and may have been the first of the *Arbutus*-named series.

*Arbutus 9 Mariposa* and *Arbutus 10 Peacock* are similar in construction to *Arbutus 2*. The author is aware of an *Arbutus 4* backrest and an *Arbutus 5* oar. Henry J. Houghton, caretaker since 1918 at Hewitt Lake near Newcomb, is quoted as having worked for "Ed Chase getting out knees [for guideboat ribs]."[5] Gustav L. Stewart III, author of Hewitt Lake and the Sage Family, wrote: "Most of the guide boats at Hewitt were made by E. J. Chase in Newcomb."[6]

3 Thomas L. Cheney, *Letter to John Gardner, Mystic Seaport Museum, September 19, 1975*, Copy to author.
4 Raymond D. Masters, *Huntington Wildlife Forest*, Utica, NY: North Country Books, 1993:57.
5 Kenneth Durant, *Letter to John Gardner, August 18, 1958*, Gardner-Durant Collection.
6 Gustav L. Stewart III, *Hewitt Lake and the Sage Family*, Fitchburg, MA: Smith Printing, 1979.

## WARREN WILLIAM COLE

**Date of birth:** July 11, 1854
**Date of death:** November 20, 1922
**Active:** 1892–1909
**Estimate of guideboats built**: About 225
**Number reviewed:** 26
**Builder's plate:** 12
**Adirondack Museum accessions:**
57.192.2, 69.154.1, 72.21.4, 77.191.1

FIGURE 2-84 Cole builder's plate.

FIGURE 2-85 Warren W. Cole.

### Biographical Sketch

Warren W. Cole was the son of Augustus Cole, who was killed in the Civil War battle of Drury's Bluff, Virginia; the same battle in which H. Dwight Grant, the Boonville guideboat builder, was captured by the Confederates. Warren's grandfather, Michael Cole, is said to be the first settler of Tupper Lake, where, in about 1840, he built a log cabin "near the Raquette River, where modern [day] Raquette River Drive turns and goes up a long hill."[1] Michael Cole's last name was originally Charbonneau, which he anglicized to Cole.[2] According to Warren Cole's son Wright, Michael Cole was a nephew of the French Canadian trapper Toussaint Charbonneau, who was the interpreter for the famous Lewis and Clark Expedition of the western United States from 1804 to 1806.[3] His Shoshone wife Sacagawea played an important role in the success of the expedition.

After Augustus Cole's death, his widow moved the family to Potsdam where

1 Frances B. Seaman, "The Story of Warren Cole: Builder of Guideboats," *Hamilton County News*, March 10 and 17, 1982.
2 Louis J. Simmons, *Mostly Spruce and Hemlock*, Tupper Lake, NY: n.p., 1976:26.
3 Wright Cole, *Personal communication with Kenneth Durant, May 20, 1959*, Durant Collection.

young Warren worked as a logger on the Raquette River. He settled in Long Lake in about 1872 when he was eighteen and became a guide. He was appointed Town Constable in 1877. It was from his uncles, Simeon and Alba Cole, who ran a boat shop in Long Lake, that he learned carpentry and the building of guideboats.[4] During this time he married Agnes Wright, who had come to Long Lake from Vermont. They had two sons: John, born in 1890, and Wright, born in 1892.[5]

> During the winters of 1890 and 1891 Cole worked repairing guideboats at Frederick C. Durant's Camp Cedars on Forked Lake, and at the Prospect House on Blue Mountain Lake. In 1892, he purchased the Long Lake shop of Orren B. Lapell, "who had planned to build boats, but did not."[6] The shop was located "just north of the entrance to the Rocky Dell Camps [now the Shamrock Motel]."[7]

Over the ensuing years a young man named Talbot Bissell, who lived across the lake at Endion, a summer hotel, made frequent visits to the Cole shop and became fascinated with it and with all aspects of guideboats, their construction, and their history. In 1935, under the title "Their Little Boats," Bissell wrote of his early memories. His writing captures the essence of a boatbuilding shop at that time and place. What follows are excerpts, published in 1967 in the magazine *The Skipper*:

> The writer [Talbot Bissell] recalls countless winter afternoons of his boyhood spent in the shop of Cole, greatest of them all in the matter of honest workmanship. The nearest thing to a power tool he possessed was an antiquated foot-treadle jig-saw—a leg-weary contrivance that somehow reduced the ungainly planks the local sawmill had cut out of huge roots of virgin spruce, to delicate, graceful ribs that would eventually form the skeleton of a boat.
>
> Otherwise, nothing but the simplest of hand tools: draw knives, gouges, spoke-shaves, chisels, shiny from years of use and all of unbelievable sharpness. Planes of various sizes and shapes and purposes—planes from which cedar shavings delicate as the finest tissue curled and fell into the ever growing pile at the end of the bench. Other tools were homemade to fit some particular job.
>
> The amount of hand labor entering the construction of a guideboat is simply unbelievable to anyone who has never watched one being built. Machinery is of little use here even today; mass production is impossible. In this machine age it is one field where man the craftsman is still supreme and always will be.
>
> We cannot do better than watch Cole build one of these boats. Enter his shop from the biting cold of an Adirondack winter day and you feel suddenly enveloped in a fluid warmth flowing out from the great iron stove in the corner. Enveloped, too, in a strange odor one will smell nowhere else in the world—a satisfying mixture of fragrant cedar shavings, resinous spruce, fruity black cherry, shellac, paint, and wood-smoke all combined in an unforgettable sense of well-being.
>
> Along one side of the shop stands a curious framework—'stocks' on which the boat is assembled. Pivoted at either end, it can be turned in any position needed in the course of put-

4 Wright Cole, May 20, 1959.
5 Frances Seaman, 1982.
6 Wright Cole, May 20, 1959.
7 Wright Cole, *Letter to Kenneth Durant, April 2, 1959*, Durant Collection.

ting the endless parts of the boat together. Along the wall hang dozens of patterns—thin wood patterns, brown and glistening from age and handling. Each represents some component part of the boat-to-be, for each piece is cut from a pattern perfected through years of service: patterns of the ribs, the strips of siding, the seats, the bottom board, the bow and stern stems.

In racks near the ceiling, great wide boards of thin white cedar are drying in the warmth. They have been drying for years—dried to an almost impalpable lightness. It may have been three or four years since they were growing in some almost inaccessible swamp, eventually to fall to the axe and to be hauled miles away to a mill through snow and cold. In a corner of the shop is a rack of knee planks—grotesque curved boards possibly five feet long and an inch thick. These, too, have been seasoned since the day they were grubbed out of frozen ground around the base of some giant spruce, split loose from the butt of the trunk after the tree toppled, and hauled away to the mill where a sawyer knew the trick of turning these giant boomerang-shaped segments into knee planks.

**Figure 2-86** Tom Bissell with his model of a Cole guideboat.

On the table of the foot-power jigsaw, Cole now has one of these planks on which he has traced the pattern of perhaps four sets of ribs. His heavy shoulders, stooped from a lifetime of toil at bench and oar and axe, are hunched over his work, his deep blue eyes guiding the dancing blade along the penciled lines.[8]

Talbot Bissell's son Thomas has been a teacher, a local historian, and a former supervisor for the Town of Long Lake. He has carried on his father's love for and knowledge of guideboats. An accomplished carpenter, he has built a model of a Lewis Austin guideboat and donated the original to the Adirondack Museum. He has also built a model of a Warren W. Cole guideboat.

From 1892 to 1909, Warren Cole built boats in the winter months and guided

8 Talbot Bissell, "42 Pounds to Portage," *The Skipper*, January 1967, Durant Collection.

during the spring, summer, and fall. In 1889 he was elected vice-president of the Adirondack Guides' Association and a decade later exhibited one of his guideboats at the Fifth Annual Sportsman's Show in Madison Square Garden in New York City. In 1909, his eyesight failing, Cole gave up boatbuilding. According to his son, during his sixteen years of guideboat building Warren Cole had built about 225 boats.[9]

In 1910, he moved to Vermont and in 1920 joined his son in Poughkeepsie, New York. Every fall, he and Wright would return to the Adirondacks, where, on November 20, 1922, Warren Cole died while hunting deer.[10]

## Guideboat Characteristics

Warren Cole's guideboats are distinguished by their stem-post design—wide and low with a rounded concave back, and the shallow C-shaped inboard edge of the stern deck, rather than an arc. Cole decks are typically one piece, mitered into the gunwales. The ribs are reverse curved.

While most Cole decks were one piece, two exceptions have been seen, both with builder's plates. One boat has

**Figure 2-87** Warren Cole, right, with his guideboat at the fifth annual Sportsman's Show, Madison Square Garden, New York City in 1899 at which the Adirondack Guides' Association exhibited. In addition to Warren Cole, guideboats builders A. H. Billings of Lake Placid and Edmund J. Chase of Newcomb attended in 1899 and 1900, respectively. (Courtesy of Adirondack Museum)

9 Wright Cole, May 20, 1959.
10 Durant, 1980:60.

eleven-piece bow and stern decks; the other had an eleven-piece bow deck and a nine-piece stern deck. Both boats have beaded gunwales; two beads on the upper edge and one on the lower.

Four Cole guideboats have been seen with short reinforcing ribs with feet between the regular-length ribs. Although other builders sometimes used reinforcing ribs, they were usually fewer in number and placed at the bow and stern.

## Field Notes

**Stems:** After about 1900, slight tumblehome with straight leading edge (Long Lake profile); a more Saranac profile before 1900. The narrowing of the stem begins below the gunwale edge.

**Ribs:** Reverse-curved ribs. One pair of scribe ribs under bow deck; may have one pair of scribe ribs inboard of stern deck. No footed ribs under bow or stern decks. Rib feet ends are beveled and do not extend all the way across the bottom board.

**Gunwales:** Extend to stem fronts.

**Hull:** Number of strakes on each side: 8; feather-lap construction.

**Heel plates:** Three-piece with rounded lateral borders.

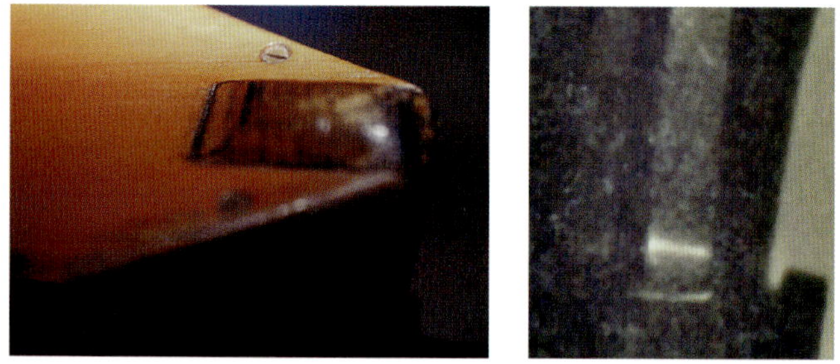

FIGURE 2-88 (Left) The stem post is wide and low with a rounded top. (Center) The rounded top with a concave back. (Right) The stem foot is rounded over in a bull-nose shape.

FIGURE 2-89 (Left) The inboard edge of the bow deck is an arc. (Right) The stern deck is shaped like a shallow C. The inboard edge of the pie-piece-shaped deck cap is tapered.

FIGURE 2-90 The distinctive notch of the yoke cleat. The enlargement shows the brass plate protecting the sheer strake from the yoke end.

**FIGURE 2-91** Stern-seat and center-seat backrests. (Left) The three-scalloped top rail and the "ears" of the stern-seat backrest; also, the rounded front frame of the seat. (Right) The top rail of the center-seat backrest also has three scallops.

**FIGURE 2-92** In four Cole guideboats, reinforcing ribs were placed between the regular ribs throughout the boat. The reinforcing ribs extend up each side across the third strake and are footed. The rib feet extend all the way across the bottom board and are beveled. They are in between every full-length rib throughout the interior. The extra ribs were added to strengthen the hull for carrying a heavier load.

**FIGURE 2-93** (Top) Multiple-piece decks, with 11 pieces at the bow and 9 at the stern, and a tapered deck cap. (Bottom) The Warren W. Cole builder's plate is centered on the bow deck cap, which is secured to the deck with round-head screws.

## WALLACE FRANKLIN EMERSON

**Date of birth:** November 1874 (Long Lake, Hamilton County)
**Date of death:** October 9, 1953 (Long Lake)
**Active:** 1905–late 1930s
**Estimate of guideboats built:** About 100
**Number reviewed:** 22
**Builder's plate:** Not used
**Adirondack Museum accessions:** 69.166.1, 2004.023.1

FIGURE 2-94 Wallace Franklin Emerson.

### Biographical Sketch

The late Franklin B. Brandreth supplied this (edited) profile in 1994:

> Wallace Emerson was the fourth child of Benjamin Franklin Emerson and Livonia Stanton Emerson [daughter of George Stanton, a Long Lake guideboat builder]. In the summer of 1891 he went to Brandreth Lake to work for Reuben Cary and returned every year thereafter until 1946. He guided for Col. Franklin Brandreth and later his son Courtenay. As a young man Wallace worked during the winters for his uncle, George Stanton, building guideboats. In 1905 he opened his own shop, which still stands today [now razed], on Deerland Road [and in which boats continued to be built until the beginning of the World War II].
>
> Some of the guests and family members at Brandreth Lake complained about the unstable guideboats being used for fly fishing. Thus when Wallace started to build boats he made up his own patterns to produce a wider, more stable guideboat.
>
> He married Ann Harper of Ossining, New York, and they had four children. In 1910 Wallace took over his father's lodge, then known as "Emerson's Boarding House." In 1929 he built "Long View Lodge" after the former lodge burned down.
>
> During the 1930s the outboard engine became reliable, and as a result the market for guideboats diminished substantially. Thus Wallace turned to flat bottom boats with a rectangular transom to accommodate an outboard engine. He stopped building altogether in the early 1940s[1].

1 Franklin Brandreth, Wallace Franklin Emerson, November 1874–October 1953, Unpublished profile to author, 1994.

## Guideboat Characteristics

Characteristic of an Emerson guideboat is the prominent rounded concave front of the wide stem posts. On a few boats, the stem post is narrower, rather than being left the full width of the stem. Thus, the ends of the deck cap rest upon part of the stem and the ends of the gunwales. This method was also used by Reuben Cary and Ralph Morrow.

The stem foot is a low horizontal rectangle with a rounded-over top edge, and his decks are one- or two-piece, mitered into the gunwales with either a pie-piece or shield-shaped deck cap. The stems are Long Lake profile. Ribs are reverse curved.

Many Emerson guideboats have wide beams for stability. It is possible that these were influenced by the boatbuilder Herbert Salisbury, who was briefly in Long Lake in the late 1880s. A boat in the collection of the Adirondack Museum, named *Cub* (accession 63.165.1), was built by Salisbury sometime in the late 1880s for Colonel Franklin Brandreth, son of Dr. Benjamin and Virginia Brandreth. The *Cub's* beam is 49 inches and its stem post has a prominent rounded concave front, two unusual characteristics found in Emerson boats.

It is said that Colonel Brandreth ordered such a stable boat from Salisbury for his three young daughters, so that they might row safely across Brandreth Lake. According to Fox Conner, Brandreth subsequently ordered boats from Emerson that would be stable enough to accommodate the growing number of guests interested in fly fishing. Emerson may well have patterned his boats after the *Cub*, located in the Brandreth boathouse, to which he had ready access. Colonel Brandreth's grandson, Franklin, confirmed that Emerson took the lines from the *Cub* and began building wider guideboats, sometimes referred to as a "fishing guideboat."[2]

Some Emerson wide-beamed guideboats were too heavy to be carried by one person and therefore did not have yoke cleats. He built many short and standard-length guideboats as well.

**Figure 2-95** (Top) The most common type of Emerson stem post: wide with a concave front. The ends of the gunwales do not extend to the front of the stem. (Center) This stem post has been narrowed above the gunwales resulting in a shoulder that the deck cap (not in place) rests upon. The rounded forward indentation is present. This design, used occasionally by Emerson, was also used by Reuben Cary and Ralph Morrow. (Bottom) The stem foot is a low horizontal rectangle with a rounded-over upper edge.

2 Wallace Emerson, Adirondack Museum Boatbuilders' Files, 1985.

## Wallace Emerson in His Boat Shop in the 1930s

**FIGURE 2-96** (Top Left) Penciling a rib pattern. (Bottom Left) Finishing a rib. (Above) Planing a bottom board.

**Figure 2-97** (Far Right) Securing the bottom board to the ribs. A manual drill is used to drill holes for the screws through the bottom board and into the rib feet. A set of Emerson-made clamps, seen here, are used to hold the ribs securely in place. (Right) Using an early treadle-powered scroll saw to make a stem. (Above) Making a rabbet for a stem.

**Figure 2-97** (Top Left) The bottom board, ribs, and stems, make up the skeletal frame of the guideboat. (Top Right) Tacking the hull planks with a tack hammer and a clinching iron. The planking is feather lapped. (Left) A carlin (the curved piece supporting the inboard portion of the deck) and a transverse deck beam are shown. (Right) Holes for the caning of the stern seat being drilled by Emerson's son John. (James W. Aughiltree, photographer, Courtesy of Adirondack Museum)

## Field Notes

**Stems:** Slight tumblehome with straight leading edge (Long Lake profile). Stems begin to narrow about an inch below the gunwale. The stem feet are horizontal rectangles with a rounded upper edge.

**Ribs:** Reverse-curved ribs. One pair of scribe ribs under bow deck; no scribe ribs under stern deck. One pair of scribe ribs at, or inboard of, the deck/sheer strake junction. No footed ribs under bow or stern decks. Note that in very short Emerson guideboats, no scribe ribs were used. Rib feet ends are beveled and usually extend all the way across the bottom board.

**Decks:** One- or two-piece, mitered in the gunwales and sheer strakes. Decks slightly overlap carlins at bow and stern.

**Hull:** Number of strakes on each side: 8; feather-lap construction.

**Heel plates:** Three-piece with rounded lateral ends.

FIGURE 2-99 (Left) Deck not in place. The gunwale and sheer strake on both sides have been beveled. (Right) The deck pieces are mitered to a corresponding bevel, resulting in an invisible seam.v

FIGURE 2-101 Emerson's yoke cleat pattern. (Courtesy of Adirondack Museum)

FIGURE 2-100 A shield-shaped deck cap on a one-piece deck at both bow and stern.

FIGURE 2-102 Emerson yoke and seat cleats. Note the flat tops of the yoke-cleat notch.

FIGURE 2-103 Emerson stern- and center-seat backrests. The top rail is a mirrored ogee design typical of Long Lake builders.

## OREN GEORGE FENTON

**Date of birth:** April 13, 1874 (Pine Grove, Lewis County)
**Date of death:** August 10, 1949 (Lowville, Lewis County)
**Active:** Early 1900s–early 1920s
**Location**: Winters in Lowville, summers at Number Four, Lewis County
**Estimate of guideboats built**: More than 10
**Number reviewed**: 1
**Builder's plate:** Not used

FIGURE 2-104 Oren George Fenton.

### Biographical Sketch

Oren Fenton was the son of John and Imogene (Strickland) Fenton of Lewis County. His first wife was Mary Schwendy, and his second wife, Edna Graves.[1] Oren was the grandson of early settler Orrin B. Fenton (1784–1870), who in 1826 built the first house in Number Four on the Beaver River, known as the Fenton House. It soon became a welcome hostelry in this section of the North Woods.[2] At age eighteen Fenton went to live with his uncle Charles Fenton, builder and proprietor of the second Fenton House. Oren learned carpentry from his uncle, who was a carpenter by trade and supervised the building of many summer camps at Beaver Lake and nearby Francis Lake. He spent the summers in a house he built at Number Four and winters at his home in Lowville. Although he built two or three guideboats each year during the winter months in his garage, he was better known as a carpenter and contractor.

### Guideboat Characteristics

Only one Fenton guideboat, based upon credible provenance, has been reviewed.[3] It closely resembles guideboats built by nearby Brown's Tract builders Grant,

1 Biographical information was provided by Sylvia Schaab Virkler, Oren Fenton's granddaughter.
2 Nathaniel B. Sylvester, *Historical Sketches of Northern New York*, Troy, NY: William H. Young, 1877:190.
3 Patrick H. Brown, *Personal communication*, date unknown.

Parsons, and Seeber. While modeled after the later Grant guideboats, it lacks their refinements. The similarities are its deck and center cover board design, stem profile, and the stem post shape. Fenton's hull construction is a modified-bevel shiplap, also used by these builders.

The characteristics that distinguish the Fenton guideboat from other Brown's Tract builders are: lack of a metal stem-post cap, no reverse-curved ribs, the absence of a bead on the lower edge of the gunwales, and outside-to-inside hull tacking only.

## Field Notes

**Stems:** Slight outward rake (Brown's Tract profile). Upper stem begins to narrow 1½ inches beneath the lower edge of the gunwale. The upper end of the stem beneath the gunwale is 1¼ inches wide, and the greatest width of the lower end is 2 inches.

**Decks:** The two-piece deck is let into the gunwales, with a center cover board and coaming.

**Center cover board:** Butts to the stem post.

**Hull:** Number of strakes on each side: 8; modified bevel construction (Grant lap).

FIGURE 2-105 The stem post, without a metal cap, is about 1 inch wide, length about 1½ inches, height about ½ inch; it slopes down to the center cover board. The center cover board butts to the stem post. There is no limber hole. The gunwale does not extend to the stem front and is not beaded. The stem band shown may be a replacement.

FIGURE 2-106 At the stern there is a two-piece deck, center cover board, and coaming. The stern deck extends to the second pair of ribs, with one pair under the deck. There are no scribe ribs. The bow deck extends to between the second and third pair of ribs with two pair under the deck. The ribs are not reverse curved. The type and number of ribs beneath the decks are unlike those of Grant, Parsons, or Seeber.

FIGURE 2-107 The outside of the hull showing the outside-to-inside-only tacking in the planking laps.

# RALEIGH RAYMOND FISH

**Date of birth:** 1903 (Sabael, Hamilton County)
**Date of death:** April 27, 1977 (Indian Lake, Hamilton County)
**Active:** Late 1960s–early 1970s
**Estimate of guideboats built:** 8
**Number reviewed:** 4
**Builder's plate:** 4

FIGURE 2-108
Raleigh Raymond Fish.

## Biographical Sketch

Raleigh Fish was the grandson of Indian Lake boatbuilder Elijah Fish, who settled in Indian Lake in 1872. Elijah taught boatbuilding to his son Ernest and Ernest's brother-in-law, William Kerst (1874–1950) of Sabael. Ernest (1877–1935) became a repairer and builder of boats but did not build guideboats. Raleigh worked as a guide for many years but also learned the boatbuilding trade from his father.[1]

1 Raymond Fish, *Personal communication*, date unknown.

## Guideboat Characteristics

During the late 1960s and early 1970s, Fish built eight guideboats, one with spruce hull planking, all of which remain in the family. A serial number is stamped on the stem foot in Roman numerals.

The identifying characteristic is the distinctive stem post. He also used plywood for the decks and red cedar for the sheer strakes.

FIGURE 2-109 Fish builder's plate centered on the carlin.

## Field Notes

**Stems:** Tumblehome (Saranac profile). The end of the stem foot at the bottom board is a rectangle.

**Ribs:** Slightly reverse curved. One pair of footed ribs under the bow and stern decks; no scribe ribs. Rib feet are cut square and do not extend all the way across the bottom board.

**Decks:** One-piece decks overlap the carlins at bow and stern and are made from plywood.

**Deck caps:** The pie-piece-shaped deck caps have a vertical inboard edge. Some were made of mahogany.

**Hull:** Number of strakes on each side: 7 or 8; feather-lap construction. Sheer strakes are made of red cedar; the hull planks of one guideboat were made of spruce.

**Heel plates:** One piece with rounded lateral borders.

FIGURE 2-110 Fish's stem posts are narrow, high, and steeply sloped to the deck cap.

## ROBERT W. FRENETTE

**Date of birth:** April 27, 1956 (Tupper Lake, Franklin County)
**Active:** 1983–
**Location:** Tupper Lake, Franklin County
**Estimate of guideboats built:** 9
**Builder's plate:** Used

FIGURE 2-111
Frenette builder's plate.

FIGURE 2-112 Robert W. Frenette.

### Biographical Sketch

Robert W. Frenette is the son of James and Susan Hull Frenette of Tupper Lake. He is the third of nine children: four brothers and four sisters. His father was a school teacher and his uncle William Frenette was the town historian. On his mother's side Adirondack guides go back three generations.

Each different season would find young Rob exploring the waterways and mountains of the region, noting the flora and fauna. He became a registered guide. He was familiar with guideboats and soon became interested in their construction. He first attempted to repair a late nineteenth-century boat built by Theodore Hanmer. "I tried restoring it myself and soon realized my carpenter skills weren't that good. I started researching and ended up going to a boat school in Maine to learn boatbuilding." From 1980 to 1982 he enrolled in the Atlantic Marine Boat Building School in Boothbay Harbor. "I rode my bike back from Maine to Tupper Lake and even hitchhiked to get there another time. I also slept in a tent for 4 months, as I couldn't afford housing. Good memories!" He took a traditional guideboat in need of repair to school, at which his teachers (builders of coastal boats) marveled, as they had never seen one.

In 1983 Frenette established Raquette River Outfitters and Spruce Knee Boat Building on High Street in Tupper Lake. Ten years later he moved to Moody (a part of Tupper Lake) with Anne Fleck

**FIGURE 2-113** A newly built guideboat with cherry sheer strakes in the Frenette boat shop. (Courtesy of Rob Frenette)

**FIGURE 2-114** (Left) The Frenette stem post design. (Center) The bow deck with a pie-piece-shaped deck cap and a pair of chamfered scribe ribs beneath the deck. (Right) The stem foot. (Courtesy of Rob Frenette)

of Lewiston, Niagara County, who is his partner and coworker.[1]

*Adirondack Life* magazine, in the October 2000 issue, featured him in "Handcrafted Traditions: The Guideboat," an introduction to the history and construction of the traditional guideboat.[2] This is the only description of the building of a guideboat since that in H. Dwight Grant's circa 1890 trade catalogue. In the early 2000s, Frenette taught Allison Warner to build guideboats.

## Guideboat Characteristics

The characteristics of Frenette guideboats include the graceful design of the stem foot, the stem posts, and the two pair of scribe ribs, chamfered at the bottom (similar to F. W. Rice), at bow and stern. His decks vary in design according to the wishes of the purchaser.

**FIGURE 2-115** The Frenette stern deck, deck cap, and two pairs of chamfered scribe ribs inboard of the deck. The scribe-rib design at the bow and stern is similar to that of Frederick W. Rice. (Courtesy of Rob Frenette)

1 Robert Frenette, *Personal communication*, 1996–2015.
2 Darby Knox, "Handcrafted Traditions: The Guideboat", *Adirondack Life*, September/October 2000:50–57.

## GEORGE & BLISS

**Partnership formed:** 1904

**Active:** 1904–1927

**Location:** Lake Placid, Essex County

**Estimate of guideboats built:** More than 50

**Number reviewed:** 12

**Builder's plate:** 4

FIGURE 2-116 George & Bliss builder's plate on the coaming.

### THOMAS H. GEORGE

**Date of birth:** unknown
**Date of death:** 1949

### C. HEMAN BLISS

**Date of birth:** unknown
**Date of death:** 1927

## Biographical Sketch

Thomas H. George and C. Heman Bliss, prior to forming a boatbuilding partnership, worked for Lake Placid boatbuilder Albert Billings. According to local historian Mary MacKenzie:

> In 1897, on the site of the present [1988] Holiday Harbor, Albert [Billings] established a boathouse-marina on Lake Placid and named it Billings Landing. Here he ran a boat livery and provided docking facilities for rowboats, canoes and the early motorboats of camp owners on the lake. Here he also continued building his Billings guideboat and other non-standard rowboats, besides repairing and refinishing boats of the camp owners. His boathouse was enlarged in 1899 and 1902.
>
> Albert Billings died in 1903. Two of his employees, Thomas H. George and C. Heman Bliss, the latter the

> chief boat-builder for Albert, ran the business for Mrs. Billings for a year. In 1904 they purchased the entire establishment and the business became known as George & Bliss. . . . On February 18, 1919, the entire marina, greatly expanded by George & Bliss, was destroyed by fire but was quickly replaced.[1]

General Hugh W. Rowan, in a talk given at the Lake Placid–North Elba Historical Society in the mid-1970s recalled:

> Heman Bliss was the chief boatman and was regarded as the absolute expert. By looking at a boat he could tell in two minutes who made it, how old it was. No one would think of buying a boat without getting Heman's OK.
>
> In 1904, a young man by the name of Tom George came around to see Heman. He said, "I have the opportunity to buy the old Billings boat livery on Lake Placid. I can get the capital and know the business end, but I'm not so hot on boats and need a thoroughly good expert to go in with me." So Heman did that and the firm of George & Bliss was founded, based upon the fact that Tom George was a man with a lot more education than Heman but Heman was a boat expert. Tom was the administrative expert and Heman was a boat man. In five or six years the shoe was on the other foot. Motor boats began to come along, and Tom knew more about them than Heman. Luckily Heman was in at the start of the thing and was always one of the founding partners.[2]

As to the final disposition of George & Bliss, local historian David H. Ackerman, wrote:

> After Heman Bliss died in 1927, the business of George & Bliss continued under Thomas H. George, with Bliss' son Kenneth continuing to hold an interest. After George's death in 1949, his son Thomas Jr. headed the firm. In 1962, George & Bliss merged with Grote's Boatlanding, Inc. . . .[3]

Various owners later ran the business; eventually all of the original George & Bliss buildings were razed.

## Guideboat Characteristics

George & Bliss guideboats follow the pattern of Albert Billings. Their decks are strip-built with center cover boards and narrow coamings. The stem-post shape is a low rectangle, the gunwales do not extend to the stem front, two-piece stems are used occasionally, and the stem foot is a low horizontal rectangle with the upper edge rounded over. The main distinguishing feature is the mirrored ogee design of the decorative deck beam. Other features include eight strakes on each side, and the shape of the outer part of the stern-seat frame extensions. The rectangular shape of the stern and center-seat backrests are the same as Billings.

George & Bliss, like their predecessor Albert Billings, also built guideboat-constructed canoes.

## Field Notes

**Stems:** Tumblehome, Saranac Lake profile. May have two-piece stems. Stem-foot end is a horizontal rectangle.

**Ribs:** No reverse-curved ribs. With one exception, no scribe ribs under the bow or stern decks. At the bow: two pairs of footed ribs, one under the deck and one at the gunwale/deck junction. At the stern: no footed ribs under the deck, one pair of footed ribs at the gunwale/deck junction.

1 Mary MacKenzie, *Albert H. Billings.*
2 Hugh W. Rowan, *History of Boating on Lake Placid*, Lecture, Lake Placid/North Elba Historical Society, [circa 1975], Mary MacKenzie Papers, Lake Placid Public Library, Lake Placid, NY.
3 David H. Ackerman, *Placid Lake: A Centennial History, 1893–1993*, Lake Placid, NY: Shore Owners' Association of Lake Placid, 1993:54.

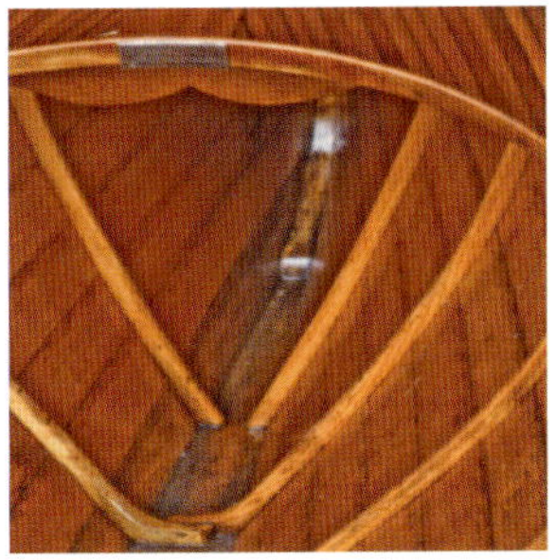

**Figure 2-117** (Left) A George & Bliss stem post. It is narrow and rectangular, about 1½ inches long, about ⅜ inch thick and about ½ inch in height above the center cover board. The front, back, and sides are straight. The top is flat with rounded edges. The gunwales do not extend to the front of the stem post. (Center) The horizontal rectangle stem-foot end is similar to Billings. (Right) The shape of the George & Bliss mirrored-ogee deck beam (at bow and stern) resembles that of J. H. Rushton. Screw heads in the stem indicate the presence of an inner and outer stem, referred to as a two-piece stem.

Rib-feet ends are beveled and extend all the way across the bottom board.

**Decks:** All are strip decks with no V-grooves. Number of strips on each side: bow 14–16; stern 10–12. The center cover board with beveled edges surrounds the stem post. The coaming is narrow, of even width.

**Gunwales:** Extend to stem fronts.

Hull: Number of strakes on each side: 8 (7 in one boat); feather-lap construction.

**Heel Plates:** Corner ends cut off.

**Figure 2-118** (Above) There are eight strakes to a side. Among the Saranac style builders only Theodore Hanmer and George & Bliss routinely used eight strakes; Albert Billings used seven or eight strakes. Other builders in the Bloomingdale, Saranac, and Tupper Lake areas routinely used seven strakes. (Above and Below Right) Stern seat with a distinctive indentation at the aft ends of the frame extensions.

**Figure 2-119** A George & Bliss canoe, built like a guideboat. A mirrored-ogee deck beam is present at the bow and stern but cannot be seen in this photograph. (Courtesy of Adirondack Museum)

## HENRY DWIGHT GRANT

**Date of birth:** October 5, 1833 (Boonville, Oneida County)
**Date of death:** May 27, 1911 (Boonville)
**Active:** 1880–1906
**Location:** Boonville
**Estimate of guideboats built:** 358
**Number reviewed:** 28
**Builder's plate:** 1 only, *Ghost*, 1882
**Adirondack Museum accessions:** 57.229.1, 71.141.1, 73.113.1, 91.42.1

FIGURE 2-120 Henry Dwight Grant (Courtesy of Adirondack Museum)

### Biographical Sketch

Henry Dwight Grant was the son of Nelson C. and Philora Grant, of Boonville, and the grandson of Elisha Grant, Jr., the first Constable and Collector of Boonville. Born on a nearby farm in 1833, young Grant became a carpenter, millwright, woodsman, and guide. He was listed as a guide in the *Boonville Herald* in 1856,[1] in the North Woods Walton Club yearbook for 1858,[2] and as a "Fulton Chain Guide" in E. R. Wallace's *Descriptive Guide to the Adirondacks* in 1872.[3] In 1858 he married Mary Jane Meeker of Boonville. They had three sons: Sidney, Floyd, and Lewis. In 1862, he volunteered for the Army. Of his years of service during the Civil War, his son, Lewis, wrote:

> ...father enlisted in the Union Army as a private in Company 1 of the 117th Regiment, New York Volunteers. He was promoted to first lieutenant and was taken prisoner at the battle of Drury's Bluff on May 16, 1864 [May 15, 1862]. I have a diary he kept in Libby Prison and in box cars and stockades as the Confederates retreated before the Union Army. He escaped once and was recaptured and then was exchanged. He was mustered out of the army in September of 1865.[4]

1 *Boonville Herald*, 1856.
2 *North Woods Walton Club*, Utica, NY: Curtiss and White, 1858:13.
3 E. R. Wallace, *Descriptive Guide to the Adirondacks*, in H. Perry Smith, *The Modern Babes in the Wood*, Syracuse, NY: Watson Gill, 1872:441.
4 Durant, 1963:224.

Civic-minded and well-informed in matters of business and government, Grant was elected Boonville Town Supervisor for 1876–1878. In 1879 he was elected to the State Assembly at Albany and served on the County Committee of the Republican Party.[5] In the words of Joseph F. Grady:

> [Grant] was then a man of scholarly and distinguished appearance, a thoughtful, effective speaker, profoundly versed in affairs of the forest which he loved. At Albany he gained the immediate confidence and respect of his associates as he had done in the woods. By exerting his influence in behalf of conservation of the State's wild life he effected a notable revision of the game laws. As the "Honorable H. Dwight Grant" he continued to follow his multiple vocations of guide, builder and business man, frankly declaring that he cherished his good name as a guide more than his title of Honorable.[6]

In his novel, *The Lovers of the Woods* (1901), William H. Boardman portrays Grant as an accomplished woodsman and inventor of a "medicinal" for dyspepsia, the "mountain ash cocktail:"

> . . . you can condense the medical treatment into one sweet moment of medicinal bliss if you will scrape a little of the tender bark of the mountain ash and make an extract with two ounces of whiskey. Two ounces of spring water and a lump of sugar mixed with this in a tin cup. . . .[7]

In this connection Lewis Grant wrote of his father:

> . . . and the men for whom he guided never forgot his mountain ash cocktails. He would crush the inner bark of the ash in liquor, and it gave the drink a sharp tang. I have not heard of anyone making a mountain ash cocktail in fifty years.[8]

It was not until 1879, when he was forty-six, that Grant, aware that the greatest need of his fellow guides was boats, seriously considered boatbuilding as a viable trade. He invited Henry Stanton, a Long Lake boatbuilder, to Boonville in the fall 1879 to discuss the removal of spruce stumps and the making of patterns, and again early in 1880 for assistance in guideboat building. The earliest record indicating that the:

> Hon. H. D. Grant had begun to build "Saranac boats" was published in the March 11, 1880, issue of the Boonville Herald. In the article, a fifteen-foot, fully equipped guideboat, weighing about eighty pounds, and able to carry three persons and duffel, was mentioned. According to the Herald: "Mr. Henry Stanton is assisting Mr. Grant . . . several boats of this kind for navigating the lakes and streams in the northern wilderness will be built this season."[9]

One year later the Boonville paper noted:

> We happened into the boat factory of our neighbor, H. Dwight Grant, lately and found him hard at work, constructing his peculiar water-craft now in such great demand among the piscatorial and pleasure-seeking visitors to the lakes and streams of "Empire Park," or the "North Woods." These tiny and fragile skiffs are made of a very light pine board for a keel from which nee [are born] the flaring sides of light, strong boards, lapped and fastened with copper rivets. Out of gnarled, knotty spruce stumps are sawn the knees of proper shape to give swell and strength to the frail structures, and these receive the siding firm-

5 Durant, 1963:222.
6 Joseph F. Grady, *The Adirondacks: Fulton Chain-Big Moose Region, The Story of a Wilderness*, Little Falls, NY: *Journal & Courier*, 1933:213–214.
7 William H. Boardman, *The Lovers of the Woods*, New York: McClure, Phillips, 1901:118–119. See also mountain ash cocktail in *Fourteenth Report of the Commissioners of Fisheries*, Albany, NY: Weed, Parsons, 1886:116.
8 Durant, 1963:224.
9 Durant, 1980:167.

ly fastened with brads and screws. These are all smoothed and finished to perfection and when well painted and caulked become a buoyant shallop, floating lightly, and capable of carrying three men and supplies for quite a voyage. So light are they a stalwart guide shoulders one with ease and bears it over portages from lake to lake, and around rapids of several miles in length without inconvenience or weariness. Each boat is worth about fifty dollars or over, and the great demand for them is with difficulty supplied. Mr. Grant will have eight of these in readiness for the sporting season and we have the promise of a ride in one when first we go "fishing."[10]

FIGURE 2-121 A photograph of a Grant guideboat beside his boat shop. Left to right: Theodore Seeber, Lester Fox, and Dwight Grant. The tumblehome stem profile indicates a date between 1884 and 1887. (Courtesy of Edward Comstock, Jr.)

According to Lewis Grant, his father built the front part of his boat shop in October through December of 1881 and started building guideboats there on January 21, 1882. Twenty-one guideboats and one sailboat were built during the 1881–1882 season by his father and three helpers, Theodore Seeber, Lester Fox, and Robert Bartlett.

The only season to exceed this number was 1890–1891, when twenty-five boats were built, with the help of six other

10 "Saranac Boats," *Boonville Herald,* March 31, 1881.

workers: "Grant and Lester Fox built the boats; the five other carpenters made ribs, oars, paddles, yokes, and decks, and did the sanding, varnishing, and painting. Gus Syphert, a snowshoe-maker, caned the seats and back rests."[11]

Lewis Grant has provided his father's estimate of the time needed for one person to build a sixteen-foot guideboat, not counting the retrieval of a stump from a spruce tree:

> Father figured that there were twenty-one ten-hour days in the making of a sixteen-foot guide-boat, with three cane seats, one cane back rest for the stern seat, one pair of eight-foot oars, paddle and carrying yoke. Such a boat, painted or varnished three coats, would weigh seventy pounds complete with oars and other equipment. It would hold three people and their sporting duffel, and was not too heavy to carry.[12]

Among the guideboats built in the spring of 1882 was one named *Ghost*, said to have been built for his son, Sidney. In September of 1882, *Ghost*, entry 2113, was exhibited at the State Fair at Utica and took "First Premium."

> Entry 2113 was built under the influence of Henry Stanton. Painted white and appropriately named the *Ghost*, the boat was 16 feet 4 inches overall and was characteristic of the Long Lake models of its day, somewhat in the manner of the Saranac tumblehome. Ribs, decks, and siding were heavier than in Grant's later models. The laps of the planking were visible and feathered-edged. The strakes were fastened with iron screws. The decks were perhaps somewhat longer than those of conventional Long Lake boats, with a more sweeping curve along the gunwale, and there was more than ordinary room in the stern seat. Though it lacked the rake of bow and stern characteristic of the later Grant models, it was a craft of delicate beauty.[13]

It is the only Grant guideboat known to have a builder's plate.

No guideboats were built during the 1882–1883 winter season; Grant was occupied building an addition to his boat shop as well as the *Hunter*, the first steamboat to ply the Fulton Chain of Lakes, for his brother-in-law Jonathan Meeker.[14]

Grant, and his son Lewis after him, kept a written record of their boatbuilding activities; these are the only such builder's records known to exist:

> All boats built during the winter of 1883–84 and after were tallied on a series of slender, fine-grained, half-inch pine panels. Dwight Grant noted dimensions, weight, number of ribs, and other details, and frequently added the names of the purchasers. These tally boards, now preserved in the Adirondack Museum, offer a comprehensive record of progress in design and production for 23 years. The tallies were interrupted in 1906 when Dwight Grant retired, but they were resumed by Lewis Grant in 1917.[15]

In 1896, Grant was again elected Boonville town supervisor. In 1897 he became the manager of the Adirondack League Club (ALC) Mountain Lodge at Little Moose Lake. On March 8, 1898, the Brown's Tract Guides' Association was formed at a meeting held at Grant's boat shop. He was made a member of the executive committee. In 1900 he became Superintendent of the ALC, which included clubhouses on Little Moose, Bisby, and Honnedaga lakes. With increas-

11 Durant, 1980:49.
12 Durant, 1963:225–226.
13 Durant,1980:47.
14 Durant, 1963:225.
15 Durant, 1980:49.

**Figure 2-122** Grant's earliest deck designs. (Left) The bow and stern have one-piece straight decks. The deck cap at the bow is heart-shaped, while at the stern it is pie-piece-shaped. The upper stem narrows just below the gunwales. Note the rounded top of the stem post and the single bead on the lower gunwale edge. (Center) The bow deck cap is heart-shaped. (Right) The stern deck cap is pie-piece-shaped. Stern and bow decks are straight. No limber holes are present in these early models.

ing commitments at the ALC after 1900, much of the boatbuilding was carried on by his sons, Floyd and Lewis, the latter having assisted his father since 1890. When Grant resigned from the ALC in 1906 due to failing health, the Boonville shop was closed. Floyd Grant left Boonville to work for General Electric in Schenectady, and Lewis Grant took over his father's position as the ALC superintendent. Five years later, on May 27, 1911, H. Dwight Grant died.[16]

## Guideboat Characteristics

The earliest published description of the sequence of construction of a traditional guideboat is H. D. Grant's trade catalogue *The Famous Adirondack Guide Boats,* circa 1890. He also compiled a complete price list "regulated by the grade and style of finish and trimmings used." For a thorough description of the building of a Grant guideboat, with line drawings by John Gardner, see Kenneth and Helen Durant's *The Adirondack Guide-Boat.*

Over his twenty-five-year career as a boatbuilder (1881–1906), Grant made some notable alterations in the designs of his boats. A chronological narrative will be used to describe these innovations. Historian Edward Comstock, Jr., described Grant's innovative building approach:

> Grant stands apart from other builders by thinking things through in small ways that made a difference. His addition of the metal stem post cap is an example. It adds weight, but it protects the top of the vulnerable stem from carry wear and tear.

16 Durant, 1980:50.

**FIGURE 2-123** (Left) Ghost, built in the spring of 1882. (Above) The two-piece circle deck, the coaming, and the center cover board represent a departure from earlier Grant decks. (Right) The barrel-shaped or half-cylindrical stem-post design had not changed. The center cover board is tapered and butts to the back of the stem post. (Courtesy of Adirondack Museum)

> In addition, the accessory components of a[n] Grant boat have an inherent elegance not often found on the comparable components of other builders. The bentwood backrest, the shoulders on the seat frames, and the molded seat cleats all are examples. So too is the gunwale with its molded bead. This sort of thinking sets him apart.[17]

Grant's earliest guideboats (1880–1881) were built with one-piece straight decks at bow and stern, set between the sheer strakes. His son, Lewis wrote: "… father's first-made boat had wooden seats and just a plain strait [*sic*] deck, not a circular deck, and those things made the difference in the price of the boat."[18]

Two of these early guideboats have deck caps that were heart-shaped at the bow and pie-piece-shaped at the stern. His early boats also had wide, rectangular, barrel-shaped stem posts until 1888–1889, and tumblehome stems until 1893–1894. Throughout his building career, Grant used reverse-curved ribs, gunwales whose ends did not reach the stem fronts, and a single bead along the lower edge of the gunwale.

During the 1881–1882 building season,

17 Edward Comstock, Jr., *Personal communication*, July 12, 2011.
18 Lewis L. Grant, *Letter to Kenneth Durant, 1959*, Durant Collection.

**Figure 2-124** Between 1883 and 1888, a limber hole was added. The early shape of the Grant stem post (front worn), the tapered center cover board, the single bead on the lower gunwale edge, and gunwales that don't extend to the stem front. The narrowing of the stem begins just below the gunwale.

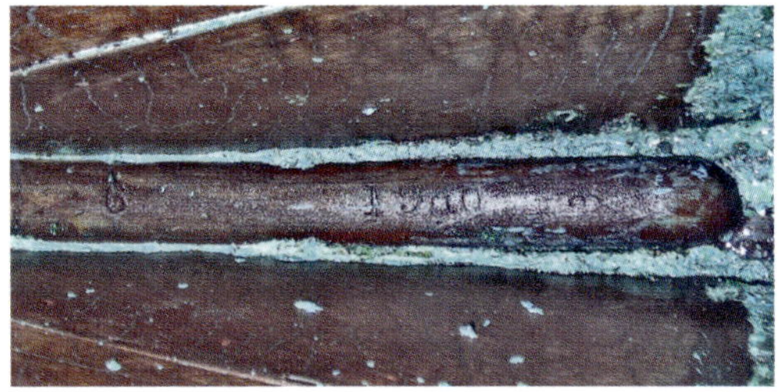

**Figure 2-125** The identification system used by H. D. Grant and his son, Lewis. (Above) The sixth guideboat of the winter building season of 1899–1900, stamped with the serial number and year "6–1900" on the stem foot. (Right) The third guideboat built during the building season of 1901–1902, stamped with the serial number and year "3–1902" on the back side of the yoke cleats.

Grant introduced a dramatic change in deck design. The bow and stern decks became two-piece, let into the gunwales, and their previously straight inboard edge was replaced by a concave crescent or arc shape (referred to as a "circular" or "circle" deck by Grant's son, Lewis),[19] accompanied by a wide coaming that tapers toward its ends. At bow and stern, the center line where the two pieces of the deck meet is covered by a tapered center cover board that butts up against the stem post. Center cover boards used by the other Brown's Tract builders, J. H. Rushton, and more recently, Ralph Morrow of Saranac Lake, also butt against the stem posts.

Grant may have been inspired by the circle-deck designs of the St. Lawrence skiffs and the boats of J. H. Rushton of Canton. The American sailing and racing canoe vogue of the 1880s featured many craft with circle decks, center cover boards, and coamings.

Between the fall of 1883 and the spring of 1888, four significant changes were noted:

**(a)** A hole was drilled through the center cover board and deck to let water run out when the boat was overturned. This hole, just behind the stem post, is called a limber hole,[20] though Lewis Grant refers to this as a "drain hole."[21] No limber hole was present in the *Ghost,* built in 1882, but it did exist in two later boats built between 1883 and 1888.

**(b)** About 1886, Grant first began to stamp, with a steel die, the year the boat was built and that boat's number among the boats built during that season. The year stamped was the spring of the building season. For example, a boat built in the winter of 1886–1887 would be stamped 1887. These numbers were stamped on the stem feet at both bow and stern, and

19 Durant, 1980:46.
20 W. A. McEwan and A. H. Lewis, *Encyclopedia of Nautical Knowledge,* Centreville, MD: Cornell Maritime Press, 1953:296.
21 Durant, 1980:139.

on the back side of the yoke cleats. The numbers may also be found on the underside of seats, the stern-seat backrest, and on the yoke itself. The dates, and measurements of each boat were written on tally boards, beginning with the "Winter of 1883–1884." The original purchaser's name, occupation, and location is often included.[22]

**(c)** Also in 1886, Grant made an important change in the planking bevel of his hulls. Like most builders, his planking, including that of the *Ghost*, had been feather-beveled; that is, the upper and lower edges of the planks had been beveled to a fine feather edge and then joined. According to Lewis Grant, boat number 14 of the fifteen "built in 1886" was of a modified-bevel shiplap hull construction, "fitting as perfect as the bark to a tree."[23]

Although the shiplap method of joinery had been known for centuries, it was first used by canoe builders in Peterborough, Ontario, Canada, in the late 1870s because it was easier than the tongue-and-groove method for smooth-hull canoes. By the fall of 1882, Fletcher Joyner, then of Glens Falls, had designed a modified, beveled-shiplap method, which he called a "novelty ship-lap joint"[24] and used it in building smooth hulls for his canoes and lightweight hunting boats. In the September 30, 1886, issue of the sporting journal *Forest and Stream,* titled "Notes on Practical Canoeing," Joyner wrote:

> The inner edge of each plank is not tapered to a feather edge, but is left with a square shoulder inside to hold the swell of the timbers and to support the fastenings as well. I have used this same joint in all my lapstreak work for four years, especially below the water, with a heavy varnish or a mixture of varnish, japan and lead in the joint; and when thoroughly dried it is the strongest and tightest joint possible.[25]

In the spring of 1886, with boat number 14, Grant designed a special plane that allowed him to use a modified beveled method of hull construction, on planking as thin as 3⁄16 inch, similar to the one Fletcher Joyner had first employed four years earlier.

Of these methods of building smooth-lapstrake hulls, only the bevel lap (also called feather-edged), and

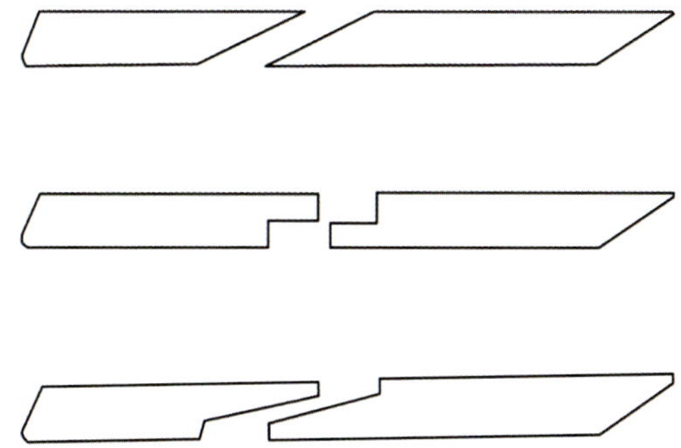

**Figure 2-126** Smooth-lapstrake construction methods. (Top) Feather-lap, or bevel-edged, lapstrake; (Center) Shiplap, or half-lap, lapstrake; (Bottom) Modified beveled, or Grant lap

the Grant-lap method were used for Adirondack guideboats. Kenneth Durant noted "We know of no link between Grant and Joyner. . . . Lewis Grant said he never heard his father mention Joyner."[26]

**(d)** In the 1888–1889 building season, Grant reshaped his stem post. Its new sloping shape was covered by a nickel-plated cast brass cap fastened to the deck by a single screw. The limber hole was located forward of the screw. Most, if not all Grant guideboats built from 1889 onwards had brass stem-post caps.

**(e)** Beginning about 1889, all Grant guideboats had two reverse-curved scribe

22 Durant, 1980, *Appendix A, The Grant Tally Boards*, 167.
23 H. Dwight Grant, *The Famous Adirondack Guide Boats*, Boonville, NY: Boonville Herald, n.d., circa 1890:3.
24 Fletcher Joyner & Son, *Catalogue and Price List for 1885*, Glens Falls, NY: West Bros., 1885:2.
25 Fletcher Joyner, "Notes on Practical Canoeing," *Forest and Stream*, September 30, 1886.
26 Durant, 1980:125.

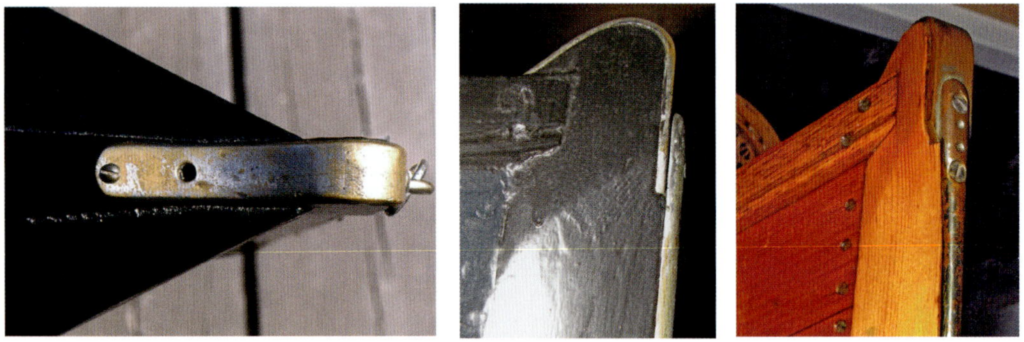

**Figure 2-127** A later (after 1889) Grant stem post with its thick cast-brass cap at both bow and stern. (Left) One hole for a screw and one limber hole. (Center and Right) The stem-post cap is recessed into the front portion of the stem post to accommodate the overlapping stem band. A painter ring was riveted onto the stem band at the bow; a ring was not used at the stern.

ribs with non-pointed ends beneath both the bow and the stern decks.

(f) During the 1880s, Grant continually widened the outward flare of his boats' ribs, providing more room within the boat. This, however, resulted in a blunt-nose appearance, corrected in 1894 by adding outward rake to the stems. Lewis Grant addressed this:

> His early boats, such as the *Ghost* at Bisby Lake, had stem patterns which curved inward at the top like the Saranac boats and the boats which Stanton and others built on Long Lake. Father changed his stem pattern in 1894. Flaring the ribs at the top, as he did, had given bow and stern a kind of podgy look. Father overcame this by raking the stem forward with a sharper outline to the decks. This change was just for looks. It made no difference in the hull at the waterline, and so did not affect the running of the boat.[27]

Grant's earliest stems were relatively wide and tumblehome in profile (Saranac/Long Lake). By 1889–1890, the width of the stem was narrowed and the tumblehome diminished. In 1893–1894, the stems were "let out," resulting in an outward-raked stem with no tumblehome.

Lewis Grant described how Seeber and Parsons also let out their stems:

> They both worked for my father building guide-boats, before leaving Boonville to make their homes in Old Forge in 1890. They got the rib shapes from one of my father's boat[s]. They also put the tip of the stems out an inch or a little more than father's last model, so they would not look just like the Grant guide-boat. I just repaired a very old Seeber & Parsons guide-boat and father's first rib patterns fit that boat.[28]

Since it was not until 1894 that Grant "raked his stems forward," the outward rake originated with Seeber & Parsons two years earlier and not with Grant, as is commonly held. (One cannot help but wonder what Dwight Grant thought of Seeber and Parsons, two valued workers who had learned the trade in his shop, leaving to move closer to the market and building guideboats that were essentially replicated from his patterns.)

Other distinctive changes during this period involved the design of the stern-seat and middle-seat backrests, the seat

27 Durant, 1963:227.
28 Lewis Grant, 1959.

**Figure 2-128** Typical Grant rib pattern and placement after 1888–1889. There are two pairs of reverse-curved scribe ribs, cut square at the bottom board, under both bow and stern decks.

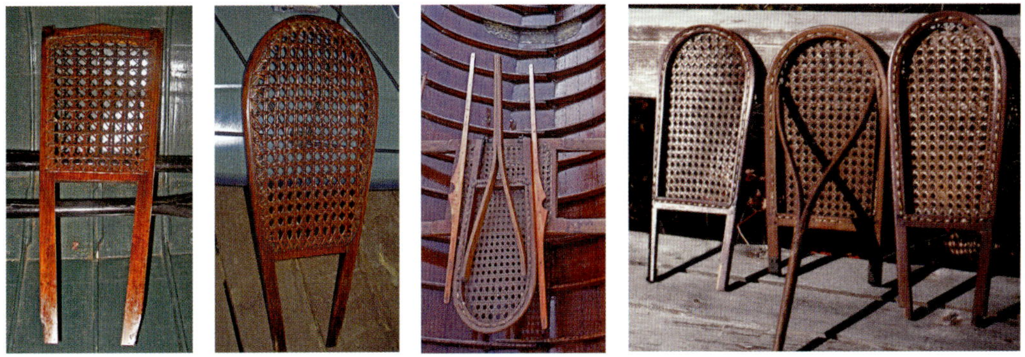

**Figure 2-129** (Left) A four-piece Grant stern-seat backrest dating from 1882 to 1889. (Center Left) A two-piece stern-seat backrest dating from 1890 to 1906. This pattern was subsequently adopted by Seeber & Parsons, Parsons & Company, Theodore Seeber, Parsons & Roberts, Parsons Brothers, Old Forge Boat Company, and Grant's son, Lewis. (Center Right) A Grant center seat. On top of the seat are a pair of yoke cleats, the seat's backrest, and the backrest support. (Right) A Grant center-seat backrest with its attached support, and two stern-seat backrests on either side. (Courtesy of Edward Comstock, Jr.)

1882 **(a)** 1884–1887 **(b)** 1889–1890 **(c)** 1889–1890 **(d)** 1896–1897 **(e)**

**Figure 2-130** Grant stem profiles. A slight tumblehome profile with a wide stem **(a)** and **(b)**. The tumblehome profile is retained but the stem width is narrowed **(c)** and **(d)**. The outward rake of the stem began to be used in 1893–1894 **(e)**. This is known as the Brown's Tract profile.

**FIGURE 2-132** Seats and seat cleats. (Top) The shape of the stern seat's projecting ends. (Bottom Left) Note the distinctive design of the moulded ends of the seat frames. The frame ends of the stern, middle, and bow seats have the same design. (Bottom Right) A detail of the seat-frame ends and the molded seat cleat. This style was adopted by Theodore Seeber and Riley Parsons after they left the Grant shop.

**FIGURE 2-131** Grant's molded seat cleats, a design subsequently used by Theodore Seeber and Parsons.

cleats, and the seats. In Grant's earlier stern-seat backrests, the almost rectangular frame was built with four pieces; later the top and sides of the frame were one steam-bent piece attached with a bottom rail. This backrest and the deck coamings were the only steam-bent parts of the boat.

Grant's early seat cleats were rectangular with rounding of the top edge. He later had them molded, thus reducing their weight without sacrificing strength.

Grant's offered both board or caned seats and backrests. The projecting ends of the stern seat that held the backrest have a distinctive shape. All his seat-frame extensions have rounded shoulders.

A unique wraparound, or weave-like, pattern of seat caning has been observed in a few guideboats built by Grant.

Grant's yoke and cleats are distinctive and were adopted by the other Brown's Tract builders. Grant was also known for his paddles with their unique ovoid grips.

Grant built about fifty-four short guideboats. Their length overall was 13½ feet or less. Lewis Grant wrote:

> Father called all guideboats with bottom boards 12 ft long or less "RAIDERS," as they were used mostly by one or two men, to make a raid on a distant hard-to-get-to lake, pond, or river spring hole and get some real fishing.[29]

William H. Boardman was a friend of Dwight Grant's, so the term "raider" was familiar to him. In Boardman's *The Lovers of the Woods*, the guide Alonzo, says: ". . . I put the raider over my head and took him to Round Pond."[30] Lon's guideboat had a bottom-board length of 11 feet, the same as guideboat number 7, purchased by Boardman from Grant in 1891.[31]

H. Dwight Grant, Lewis L. Grant, Theodore Seeber, Riley Parsons and his sons, Ben and Ira, all used the same patterns and designs for their guideboats and the decks, seats, backrests, yokes, cleats, and oars.

29 Durant, 1980:49.
30 Boardman, 1901:84.
31 Durant, 1980:178.

## Field Notes

**Stem posts:**
**1881–1888** Wide, barrel-shaped (cylindrical), no stem-post cap.
**1884–1886** One limber hole added at bow and stern.
**1889–1906** Stem post sloped, cast brass stem-post cap added.

**Stem profile:**
**1881–1893** Slight tumblehome. (Henry Stanton, Long Lake)
**1894–1906** Incorporation of an outward rake. (Brown's Tract profile)
**1896–on** Bow and stern height made equal.

**Stem-foot end at the bottom board:**
**1883–1906** Low, flattened, circular.
**1886–1906** Year and serial number stamped on lower portion of stem feet.

**Stem bands:**
**1882–1906** Grant pattern; V-grooved to fit the stem and remove weight.

**Decks:**
**1880–1881** Straight at bow and stern; one-piece, let into the gunwales.
**1882–1906** Two-piece, let into the gunwales, or partially mitered, with center cover board. Deep circle decks at bow and stern.

**Deck caps:**
**1880–1881** Heart-shaped at the bow and pie-piece-shaped at the stern.

**Center cover board:**
**1882–1906** Tapered, butts to the back (inboard) end of bow and stern stem posts.

**Coamings:**
**1882–1906** Wide, tapered at both ends.

**Carlins:**
**1882–1906** Rounded at the back bottom edge.

**Ribs:**
**1881–1906** Reverse-curved ribs.
**1889–1906** Two pairs of scribe ribs (not pointed at bottom board) under bow and stern decks; rib feet are beveled and do not extend all the way across the bottom board.

**Hull:**
**1881–1882** Feather-lap planking; 8 strakes on each side.
**1886–1906** Modified-bevel planking (Grant lap); 8 strakes on each side.

FIGURE 2-133 A Grant yoke carved from a block of cedar. Its shape is readily distinguished from other builders' yokes. It also was the design used by Seeber and Parsons.

FIGURE 2-134 This wraparound method of seat caning has been observed in some Grant-built guideboats. These seats may have been influenced by those of furniture maker F. A. Sinclair and his popular camp and porch chairs, made in Mottville, a hamlet north of Skaneateles, New York.

FIGURE 2-135 Paddles designed by Grant. Note the ovoid-shaped handles. (Courtesy of Edward Comstock, Jr.)

## LEWIS LAWRENCE GRANT

**Date and of birth:** August 4, 1878 (Boonville, Oneida County)
**Date and place of death:** September 27, 1960 (Boonville)
**Active:** 1916–1957
**Location:** Boonville
**Estimate of guideboats built:** 20
**Number reviewed:** 3
**Builder's plate:** Not used

**FIGURE 2-136** Lewis L. Grant, F. A. Moore photographer, Boonville, New York. (Courtesy of Edward Comstock, Jr.)

### Biographical Sketch

Lewis Lawrence Grant was the youngest son of Henry Dwight Grant and Mary Jane Meeker. He was named after Lewis Lawrence, a prominent lumberman and native of Utica. Dwight Grant was a longtime caretaker of Lawrence's camp (Camp Lawrence) on the north shore of Fourth Lake of the Fulton Chain.

Lewis's development as a carpenter began in boyhood, "making sleds and toboggans from the thin sides of great circular cheese boxes." His most enjoyable early days were spent hiking in the woods and fishing with his father, for whom he had the greatest respect and admiration. In 1895, at the age of seventeen, he began work in his father's boat shop "putting on decks, shaping ribs, and making oars, paddles, and seat frames. Soon he became adept at the difficult task of shaping and fastening the siding."[1] From 1900 until 1905, when Dwight Grant was involved full time as superintendent of the Adirondack League Club, Lewis and his brother, Floyd, ran their father's boat shop.

In 1906, H. D. Grant, in ill health, retired from the club and Lewis took over his

1 Durant, 1980:54.

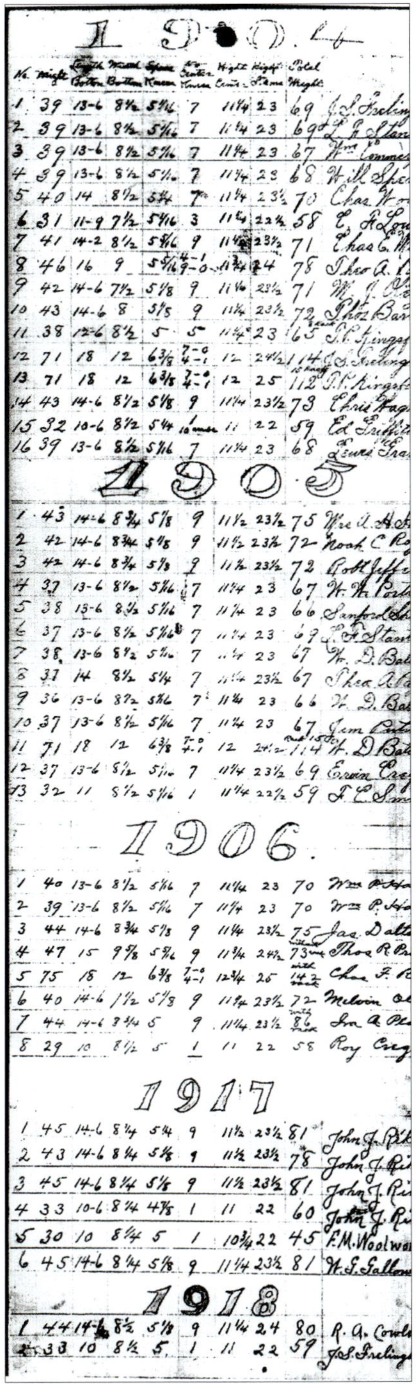

father's position as superintendent. The Boonville boat shop was closed. In 1916, Lewis returned to Boonville to care for his aging mother and reopened the shop. He wired it for electricity and had some machinery installed. His mother, at age eighty-four, was pleased to be of help by "sticking tacks" as her son clinched them. Between the 1917 and 1923 seasons, Lewis built nineteen guideboats. His twentieth, and last, guideboat was built in 1934 ". . . when I had used up what rib timber my father left in the shop. . . . However, I continued to repair guideboats and built a lot [116] of flat-bottom boats of pine and marine plywood (referred to as Bisby Lake guideboats)." Lewis built his last boat in 1957, at the age of seventy-nine.[2]

## Guideboat Characteristics

Lewis L. Grant's guideboats, like his father's, are stamped for the year they were built and their serial number in that year. They follow his father's patterns. Lewis explains: "I did not make any changes in patterns or dimensions after father's death and I have never seen any improvements made by anyone else."[3]

Identification of a guideboat built by Lewis Grant can be made by locating, on the stem foot or the back side of the yoke cleat, a year stamped 1917 or later and a serial number. The purchaser and boat dimensions are recorded on the Grant shop tally boards that may be found in Kenneth and Helen Durant's *The Adirondack Guide-Boat,* Appendix A.[4]

**Figure 2-137** Copy of a photograph of Lewis Grant's original tally sheet. On it are listed every guideboat built during a given year, its purchaser, its shell weight (hull weight, when taken off the rack, without the decks, gunwales, cleats, and seats) and total weight (finished), its bottom board length and width, the "space knees" (the distance on center between each pair of ribs), the number of pairs of ribs, the "depth center" (the vertical distance from the bottom board to the top of the gunwales at the center of the boat), and the "stem height" (the vertical distance from the bottom board at bow and stern to the top of the stem post). The tally lists the guideboats built during five particular years in Lewis Grant's handwriting. (Courtesy of Edward Comstock, Jr.)

2 Durant, 1980:229–230.
3 Durant, 1963:227.
4 Durant, 1980:167–199.

## FREDERICK D. GRAVES

**Date of birth** March 31, 1835 (Unity, New Hampshire)
**Date of death:** Unknown
**Active:** 1870s–1890s
**Location:** South Boston, Massachusetts
**Estimate of guideboats built:** Unknown
**Number reviewed:** 2 (Attributed, each with the Graves patented oarlock straps)
**Builder's plate:** Unknown. Oarlock straps embossed with name and patent date (1875) are known.
**Adirondack Museum accession:** 2004.079.1

### Biographical Sketch

Frederick Graves lived and worked in South Boston, Massachusetts. He is the only person known to have built guideboats outside of New York State. Whether Frederick ever even visited the Adirondacks is not known, but, as described in Part I, his brother Nathaniel stayed as a young man at Martin's Hotel on Lower Saranac Lake in 1851–1852, where he not only observed William McLenathen, the pioneering boatbuilder, build the first Saranac boat, but also, in 1853, before returning to Boston, built one modeled after it. It is likely, therefore, that Frederick learned to build Adirondack boats from his brother, Nathaniel.

Nathaniel returned to the Adirondacks in the late 1850s and lived for some time at the head of Tupper Lake. After adventures out west he returned again, living in Blue Mountain Lake and then Tupper Lake, and became a well-known builder of guideboats. Another brother, William, became in the 1860s the proprietor of Graves Lodge, a hotel on the western shore of Tupper Lake that catered to hunters and fishermen.[1]

Information about Frederick Graves's early life is from the *Boston City Directory* for 1860: "Graves, Fred D. pianomaker, boards 44 Hudson."[2] The same directory for 1860 and 1861 lists "Graves, (Samuel) & Co., mus. inst. Maker . . .,"[3] which may

1 In 1871, while attempting to drive a deer to shore on nearby Horse Shoe Pond, William Graves's boat capsized and, unable to reach shore, he drowned. See E. R. Wallace, 1872:420.
2 *Boston City Directory*, n.p., 1860:175.
3 *Boston Almanac*, Brown and Taggard, 1861:174.

have a family connection. "Graves, F. D." is also listed under "Boats and Boat Builders" for a number of years between 1879 and 1893 in the *Boston Almanac and Business Directory.*[4]

In 1875 Graves was granted a patent for an "improved noiseless rowlock." While the socket strap for this rowlock has been identified, by its embossed name and patent date, no oarlock pins have been discovered.

A Graves "Adirondack boat" with his "improved noiseless rowlock," together with a model of the boat, were exhibited in 1876 at the Centennial Exposition in Philadelphia. It was described as representing "one of the finest of sporting boats."[5] As it was feared that the full-length boat "could not be trusted to a sea voyage," the model only was exhibited in 1880 at the International Fisheries Exhibition in Berlin, Germany.[6]

William H. H. Murray's weekly newspaper, *Golden Rule,* in 1878, mentions Graves and his Adirondack boat:

> Advertisement: "Adirondack Boat, for sporting purposes made by Frederick D. Graves care of Bradford & Anthony 374 Washington Street,"

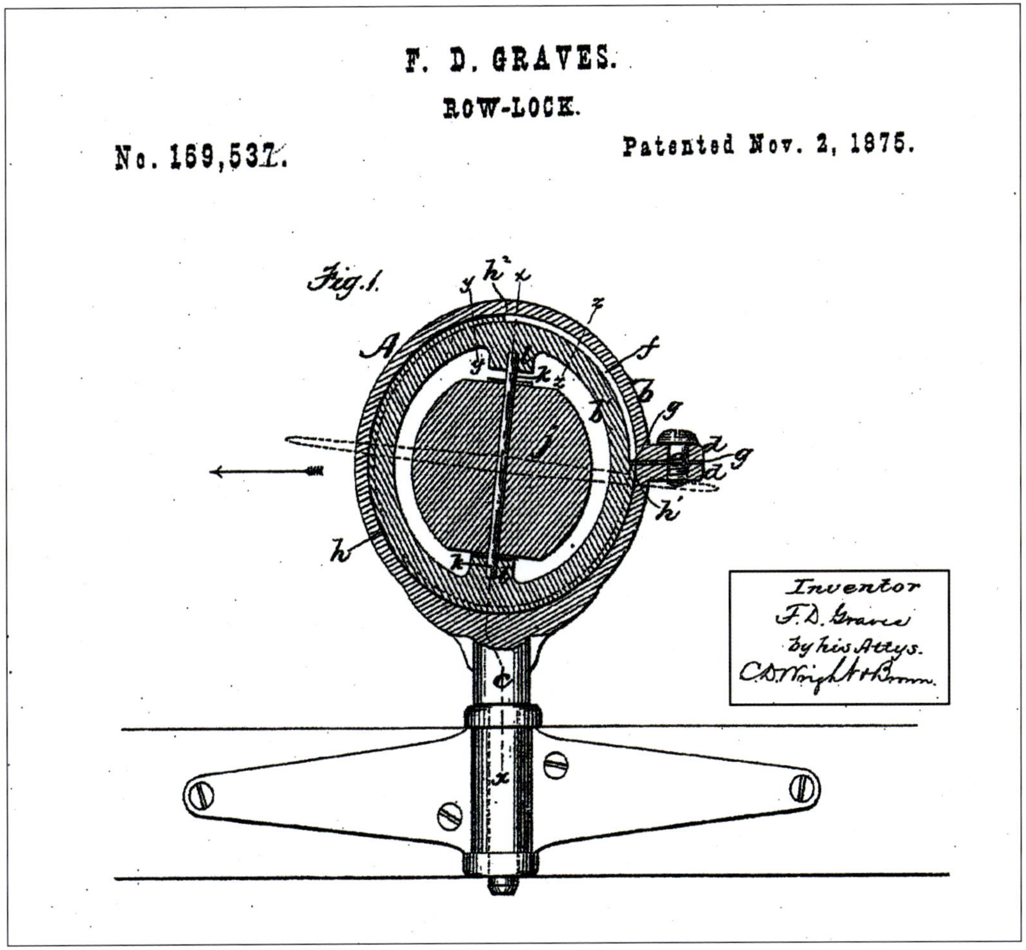


**FIGURE 2-138** Graves Improved Noiseless Rowlock (Patent No.169,537, November 2, 1875). Its purpose was to allow the oars to be feathered.

4 *Boston Almanac and Business Directory,* Boston: Sampson, Davenport, 1879:180.
5 G. Brown Goode, *Philadelphia Centennial Exposition, 1876; Catalogue of the Collection,* Washington, DC: Government Printing Office, 1879:147.
6 G. Brown Goode, "The Fisheries and Fish Culture of the United States of America," in *International Fisheries Exhibition, Berlin, 1880,* Washington, DC: Government Printing Office, 1880, Paper 21, Bulletin 18.

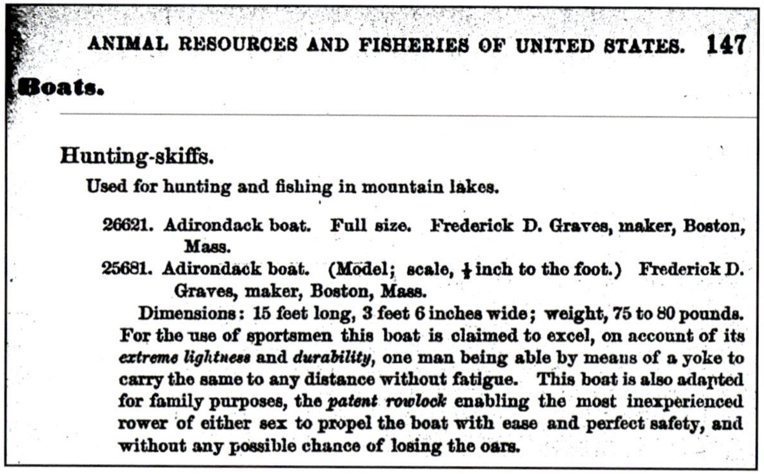
ANIMAL RESOURCES AND FISHERIES OF UNITED STATES. 147

**Boats.**

**Hunting-skiffs.**

**Used for hunting and fishing in mountain lakes.**

**26621. Adirondack boat. Full size. Frederick D. Graves, maker, Boston, Mass.**

**25681. Adirondack boat. (Model; scale, 1/4 inch to the foot.) Frederick D. Graves, maker, Boston, Mass.**

**Dimensions: 15 feet long, 3 feet 6 inches wide; weight, 75 to 80 pounds. For the use of sportsmen this boat is claimed to excel, on account of its *extreme lightness* and *durability*, one man being able by means of a yoke to carry the same to any distance without fatigue. This boat is also adapted for family purposes, the *patent rowlock* enabling the most inexperienced rower of either sex to propel the boat with ease and perfect safety, and without any possible chance of losing the oars.**

**Figure 2-139** The catalogue entry for Hunting-skiffs in the Centennial Exposition, Philadelphia, 1876. The identical entry appeared in the International Fisheries Exhibition, Berlin, 1880. The boat and model, now lost, were part of the Smithsonian Institution's Miscellaneous Collections.

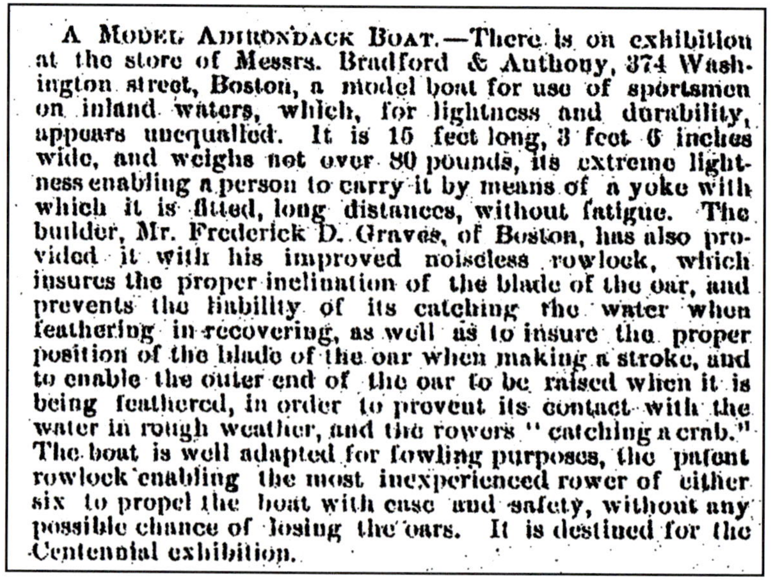
A Model Adirondack Boat.—There is on exhibition at the store of Messrs. Bradford & Anthony, 374 Washington street, Boston, a model boat for use of sportsmen on inland waters, which, for lightness and durability, appears unequalled. It is 15 feet long, 3 feet 6 inches wide, and weighs not over 80 pounds, its extreme lightness enabling a person to carry it by means of a yoke with which it is fitted, long distances, without fatigue. The builder, Mr. Frederick D. Graves, of Boston, has also provided it with his improved noiseless rowlock, which insures the proper inclination of the blade of the oar, and prevents the liability of its catching the water when feathering in recovering, as well as to insure the proper position of the blade of the oar when making a stroke, and to enable the outer end of the oar to be raised when it is being feathered, in order to prevent its contact with the water in rough weather, and the rowers "catching a crab." The boat is well adapted for fowling purposes, the patent rowlock enabling the most inexperienced rower of either six to propel the boat with ease and safety, without any possible chance of losing the oars. It is destined for the Centennial exhibition.

**Figure 2-140** A notice for the Graves Adirondack boat on exhibit at Bradford & Anthony's sporting goods store in Boston in the March 9, 1876, issue of *Forest and Stream*. Later that year it was exhibited at the Centennial Exposition in Philadelphia.

**Figure 2-141** Embossed oarlock strap reads: F. D. GRAVES; NOV 2 1875; on the socket barrel: PAT (vertical). Made of galvanized cast iron. (Courtesy of Rick Stys)

**Figure 2-142**. The guideboat attributed to F. D. Graves. The boat is 14 feet in length and 37½ inches in width. The donor stated that the boat was used on the Charles River in Dedham, Massachusetts. (Adirondack Museum accession: 2004.079.1)

**Figure 2-143** (Above) Bull-nosed stem foot. (Top Left) Graves stem post. (Bottom Left) The deck is straight and let into gunwale. The diamond-shaped deck cap is a replacement.

and under "Our Advertisers" on the same page:

> An Adirondack boat, as all old Adirondackers know, is a "thing of beauty and joy forever." We never knew but one man out of the woods that could build one properly, and he is Frederick Graves, brother of the [William W.] Graves of Tupper Lake, whose [Graves Lodge] was so well known to tourists, and whose untimely death was so widely mourned by Adirondackers. We doubt if there is any other way in which sixty dollars can be invested so profitably by dwellers on our seaboard as in one of these famous boats.[7]

It does not appear that any Graves's boats made it to the Adirondacks. Each Adirondack region had its own builders with guides and sportsmen loyal to them. However, Graves's boats were seen on northern New England waters. Charles A. J. Farrar noted in his 1887 guidebook *From Lake to Lake—A Narrative of The Wilds of Maine*:

> We found six or seven boats at the landing, but they were all heavy but one. Some of them also were deficient in oars and rowlocks, and when I fortunately stumbled upon a light "Graves" boat of the Adirondack pattern, I told Jack that he need not spend any more time looking over the boats, for that was the craft for us, and the oars and paddle that belonged to it we found all right underneath.[8]

## Guideboat Characteristics

Of the two boats reviewed with his patented embossed rowlock straps, one was of standard guideboat construction and the other was in two sections bolted together. Neither had builder's plates, but both had rowlock straps embossed "F. D. Graves" and "Nov. 2, 1875 PAT."

The boat cut into two sections that had Graves rowlock straps was possibly built by Frederick Graves. To join the two sections, the pairs of ribs at the ends of each boat half were bolted together. The ends of the matching planks of each half were sealed with India rubber. The gunwales were made of three pieces; the center piece is short and was bolted into place, forming the connection between the two halves. It was scarfed into the other two pieces. Just below the gunwales, the boat halves were bolted together through the

7 W. H. H. Murray, *Golden Rule,* 1878:8, Durant Collection.
8 Charles A. J. Farrar, *From Lake to Lake—A Narrative of The Wilds of Maine,* Boston: Lee & Shepard, 1887:111–112.

**Figure 2-144** (Top) The two-piece guideboat. (Center Left) The junction of the halves. (Center Right) The attachment of the halves at the bottom board. (Bottom) The wooden yoke cleat bolted through the sheer strake and gunwale. (Courtesy of Rick Stys)

yoke cleats, also serving as a connection. A pair of angle irons, straddling the two halves of the bottom board, was attached to each bottom-board half. As a watertight seal, India rubber was placed between all parts of the halves in contact with each other. The six hull strakes on each side were not all equal in width. All tacks, nails, and screws were made of iron, indicating of their age: the 1870s. The planking laps were feather edged. The inboard edge of the deck cap and the carlins share a scalloped design.

Neither of these boats have any distinguishing characteristics in common other than the patented Graves rowlock straps.

## Field Notes (Adirondack Museum boat)

**Ribs:** Feet extend all the way across the bottom board.

**Decks:** Decks are one piece, let into gunwales, straight decks.

**Hull:** Length 14 feet 2 inches, beam 37½ inches. Planks ¼-inch thick. Seven strakes, feather edge bevel.

**Yoke cleats**: Missing, but residual screw holes remain.

**Figure 2-145** (Left) The bow deck is slightly crowned and the carlin and deck cap have an unusual scalloped design. The deck is one-piece with a shallow arced inboard edge. The hull has six strakes per side, and the ribs are slightly reverse curved. The stem foot has a rounded top edge (bull-nosed). (Right) The deck cap is scalloped along its arced inboard edge. Note the decorative raised collar around a hole for a flag or a jacklight staff. (Courtesy of Rick Stys)

**FIGURE 2-146** Nathaniel S. Graves, Forest and Stream, October 17, 1903.

## NATHANIEL S. GRAVES

**Date of birth:** March 23, 1832 (Unity, New Hampshire)
**Date of death:** After 1908
**Active:** 1851 ~ 1908
**Location:** Blue Mountain Lake, Raquette Lake, Hamilton County
**Estimate of guideboats built:** More than 30
**Number reviewed:** 1 (attributed)
**Builder's plate:** Not used

### Biographical Sketch

According to a 1903 interview in *Forest and Stream*, Nathaniel S. Graves, age seventy-one, was born in Unity, New Hampshire, in 1832.[1] He is listed in the New York State Census for 1905 as a boatbuilder in Raquette Lake. According to local historian Ruth Timm, he was actively building guideboats in 1908.[2] At age seventy-six he was one of the oldest known builders of guideboats. In the spring of 1851, with an uncle who lived in Keene, Essex County, nineteen-year-old Nathaniel went on his first Adirondack deer hunt. "Graves then went to relatives in Boston and spent the summer there in work."[3] That fall he returned to the Adirondacks and went on his second deer hunt. The following description of that visit, from *Forest and Stream,* represents the earliest account of the origin of the Adirondack guideboat.

> Then [Graves] with a brother and brother-in-law came to the Adirondacks on a hunting trip [in the fall of 1851]. At Upper [Lower] Saranac Lake they found the only hotel in the Adirondacks, a three-room log house kept by three brothers named Martin, one of whom [W. F. Martin] afterward kept the well-known "Martin's" on lower Saranac. . . . They hired a boat of Wm. MacClenathan (spelled according to pronunciation by Mr. Graves), Uncle Mac, they called him, who had built the first boat [of its type] known in all the region and may be styled the father of the Adirondack guide boat. A neighbor of uncle Mac's had built a boat af-

1 "Juvenal," "One of the Veterans," *Forest and Stream,* October 17, 1903:295.
2 Ruth Timm, *Raquette Lake: A Time to Remember,* Utica, NY: North Country Books, 1989:49–50.
3 *Forest and Stream,* 1903:295.

> ter his model, and these two were the only boats known to exist in the woods at that time. These boats had a narrow, square stern, but were otherwise and in a general sense the model after which all succeeding Adirondack boats have been built, says Mr. Graves.[4]

Graves spent the winter of 1851–1852 with his uncle in Keene and in the spring of 1852:

> Graves built a boat, modeled from memory, after Uncle Mac's. So far as known this was the third boat [of this type] built in the Adirondacks. After a hunt Graves went to Boston and stayed several years.[5]

Graves's stay in Boston ended sometime in the mid- to late 1850s.

> But the love of the woods was upon him; he had seen very desirable timber land around the head of Big Tupper Lake; thought he would like to live there, and when Moses A. Horrick, manager of the Underhill Hardware Co., of Boston, offered to give him 160 acres a half mile west of Big Tupper if he would move up there, he promptly took it. He then lived about Big Tupper five or six years and cut the first road to [nearby] Horseshoe Pond. About this time guiding began to come in vogue, and little by little Graves began to guide on Big Tupper and Bog River. About this time also Paul Smith came out with a white boat, guided some, and in about two years started a hotel in a little log house. This was the beginning of the now famous hostelry.[6]

Graves patented an "improved rowlock" in 1877, similar to his brother Frederick's model. It allowed for a fixed oar, like that in a guideboat, to be feathered. He also was an inveterate traveler.

> Later in life Mr. Graves had large experiences as a mining prospector in the West, and has been to the Rocky Mountains and back several times. He has been in several Indian fights and with 46 others was once captured by a large band of Apaches.
>
> A few years ago he drove with a horse and cart from near tidewater in Lower California across the Rockies and the plains to Blue Mountain Lake, New York. The journey occupied three months, during which he camped and cooked, earning money enough to buy food for himself and horse, by tinkering—cleaning hundreds of clocks and mending tinware. Mr. C. H. Downs, the skillful taxidermist at Blue Mountain Lake, bought the horse and cart, and still keeps them as curiosities.[7]

**Figure 2-147** The shop and home of Nathaniel Graves on Blue Mountain Lake as illustrated in *Forest and Stream*, 1903.

Graves was building guideboats in the mid-1890s as Dr. Arpad G. Gerster's entered into his diary for Sunday, May 24, 1896:

> When we entered Blue Mountain Lake the East wind freshened, and we had to buck quite a sea till we beached our boat at Hollands. Mr. Graves, a grizzly old Seventh Day Baptist, met us on landing, and volunteered to carry up the hill our heavy box of trout, which we gladly accepted. At Holland's we were hospitably received, and I learned that my buckboard was ordered. Graves invited us to come and see the $100 cedar boat he had just finished . . . "with *three* coats of shellac" (emphasis on three).[8]

4 *Forest and Stream*, 1903:295.
5 *Forest and Stream*, 1903:295.
6 *Forest and Stream*, 1903:295.
7 *Forest and Stream*, 1903:295.
8 Gerster, 2005:85.

**Figure 2-148** The bow of a guideboat attributed to Nathaniel Graves. It has one pair of scribe ribs at the bow and stern that are pointed at their bottom and are reverse curved. There are no footed ribs under the decks. The deck is one piece, the stem-foot end is bull-nosed, and the rib feet extend all the way across the bottom board, features that are all similar to John Blanchard's guideboats.

The entry for Wednesday, August 12, 1896, reads: "It was a hot pull, he rowing, I paddling with my fine new, heavy and large cherry paddle bought of Graves last spring."[9]

According to *Forest and Stream*:

> Mr. Graves lives at Blue Mountain Lake, in a little building he erected over the water, and which constitutes boat shop and dwelling house combined. Here he supports himself by building boats for sale and to rent. He is an earnest Christian of the Advent persuasion, and as such enjoys the respect of the community, for nothing will induce him to break his Sabbath in any way, and whatever men may believe for themselves, they respect consistency in others.[10]

Graves built boats at Blue Mountain Lake from the 1890s through 1903 and then moved to Raquette Lake. Paul Blanchard, son of guideboat builder John Blanchard, stated: "When he [my father] arrived on Raquette Lake [in 1908] there were two other boat builders on the lake, 'Old Man Graves' who lived in the bay on the south side of Big Island and 'Charley Cole' who lived in Lonesome Bay."[11] Ruth Dymond, John Blanchard's daughter, reports that a friendship existed between young John Blanchard and the elderly Graves.[12] Graves apparently played a major role in the life of Blanchard and taught him how to build boats.[13]

## Guideboat Characteristics

Only one guideboat attributed to Graves has been identified; it is similar to those built by John Blanchard. Both have reverse-curved scribe ribs, with their ends pointed at the bottom board.

**Figure 2-149** (Left) The stem post is wide, with no chamfering of the sides. The front and sides are vertical, the top is rounded, and the back slightly angled. Beading runs along the lower edge of the gunwale and the carlins are also beaded. The stem narrows just below the gunwales. (Right) The ornate shield-shaped deck cap.

Not similar to Blanchard's are Graves's stem-post and deck-cap designs, the beading of the gunwales and carlins, and the liberal use of round-head brass screws.

## Field Notes

**Stems:** Tumblehome (Saranac profile). The stem foot is bull-nosed.

**Decks:** One piece, let into the gunwales.

**Hull:** Number of strakes on each side: 8; feather-lap construction.

**Gunwales:** Extend to stem fronts; beaded, and secured with round-head brass screws.

**Heel Plates:** Three-piece; lateral corners cut off.

9 Gerster, 2005:90.
10 *Forest and Stream*, 1903:295.
11 Timm, 1989:50.
12 Ruth Dymond, *Personal communication*, August 1, 1995.
13 William Crowley, *Letter to Benjamin A. G. Fuller, Curator, December 10, 1982*, Mystic Seaport Museum, Mystic, CT.

## CHARLES J. HAMNER

**Date of birth:** June 1882
**Date of death:** 1956 (Long Lake, Hamilton County)
**Active:** 1920s–mid-1950s
**Location:** Long Lake
**Estimate of guideboats built:** More than 50
**Number reviewed:** 14
**Builder's plate:** Not used
**Adirondack Museum accession:** 69.166.1

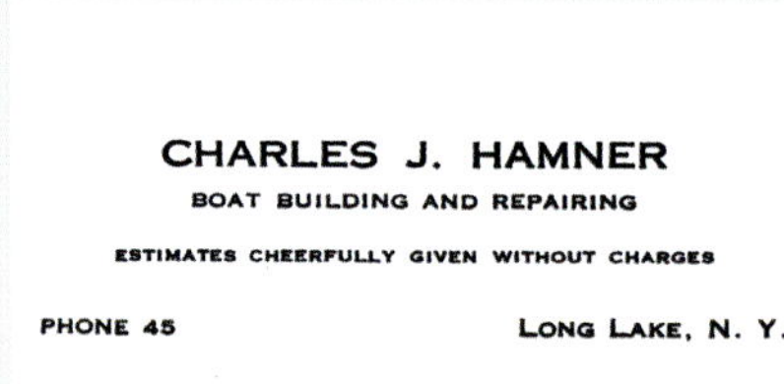

CHARLES J. HAMNER
BOAT BUILDING AND REPAIRING
ESTIMATES CHEERFULLY GIVEN WITHOUT CHARGES
PHONE 45
LONG LAKE, N. Y.

FIGURE 2-150 Charles Hamner's trade card. (Courtesy of Adirondack Museum)

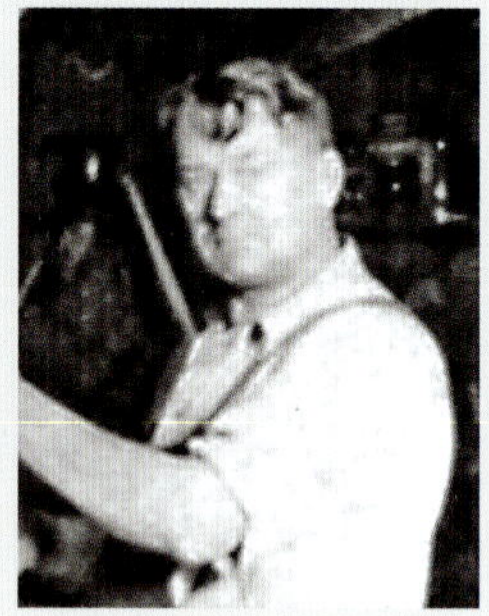

FIGURE 2-151 Charles J. Hamner.

### Biographical Sketch

Family relationships are fairly common among guideboat builders. Charles J. Hamner's wife, Katherine, was the sister of George Washington Smith's wife, Gertrude.[1] Hamner may have learned boat building from Smith. Although Hamner's guideboats differed in many construction details from Smith's, there is a similarity in their basic design, particularly their stem posts. Hamner was one of the few guideboat builders active between the 1920s and 1950s. In 1958 Frank Boone of Long Lake wrote:

> Regrettably there has been a diminishing supply of new Adirondack guide boats in the past few years. It was heartening therefore to find in recent years one source of output still active. At the busy workshop of the late Charley Hanmer [*sic*] in Long Lake Village, that old-time skilled workmanship was still being applied to the third one of these boats he had made during that winter of 1952–1953.
>
> This last specimen, 16 feet in length and 39 inches in width, had cedar sheathing sawed in strips 3 inches wide, which besides being fastened to

1 Mickie Smith, *Personal communication*, April 4, 2009.

**Figure 2-152** Stem posts and inner stem end. (Left and Center) Stem-post dimensions: length 2½ inches, width about ⅞ inch, height about ½ inch. There is a rounded indentation at the upper front. The stem begins to narrow about 2 inches below the gunwales. The gunwales do not extend to the leading edge of the stem. The gunwale is beaded on the boat at left. (Right) The bull-nosed stem-foot end.

> the ribs were copper-tacked to each other. The edges of each one was beveled to make as smooth a surface as that of a finished canvas canoe.[2]

The last guideboat built by Hamner is believed to be hanging on the wall on the second floor of Hoss's Country Corner store in Long Lake. Hamner is a variant spelling of Hanmer, and there may be a family relationship between the Hamners of Long Lake and the Hanmers of Saranac Lake.

## Guideboat Characteristics

Charles Hamner's stem posts are distinctive, though they bear some similarity to those of G. W. Smith and the boat attributed to Mitchell Sabattis at the Adirondack Museum. The upper front is concave, the top edges are rounded, and there is a concavity at its back. The stem-foot end is rounded over in a bull-nose shape. Decks are usually one- or two-piece but may have five, seven, or nine pieces. He used both pie-piece-shaped and shield-shaped deck caps, and the rounded notch of his yoke cleats have quarter-rounded sides, similar to those of Warren Cole. He commonly used round-head screws on his decks, deck caps, and gunwales. His stern-seat backrests are unique. Patterns for them survive.

2 Frank Boone, "The Adirondack Guide Boat," in *North Country Life*, Winter 1958:26.

## Field Notes

**Stems:** Slight tumblehome with straight leading edge (Long Lake profile); bull-nosed inner stem end.

**Ribs:** Reverse-curved ribs; 1 pair of scribe ribs under the bow and stern decks; may have no ribs under stern deck on short boats. Foot ends beveled and do not extend all the way across the bottom board. Spacing on center: 5½ inches.

**Decks:** One- and two-piece decks are mitered into the gunwales. Three- (and more) piece decks are set between the sheer strakes. Bow deck extends slightly beyond carlin. Stern deck is flush with the carlin. May have round-head brass screws.

**Hull:** Number of strakes on each side: 8; feather-lap construction.

**Gunwales:** The end is vertical about an inch behind the stem front; may have two beads along lower edge. May have round-head brass screws.

**Heel plates:** 3-piece with rounded lateral borders.

FIGURE 2-153 (Top) Seven-piece deck with pie-piece-shaped deck cap. (Center) The yoke cleat has a rounded notch with quarter-rounded sides.(Bottom) Five-piece deck and shield-shaped deck cap. The inboard edge of the deck cap is beveled.

FIGURE 2-154 (Top) Stern seat and backrest. (Center) Pattern for the decorative top rail of the stern-seat backrest. (Bottom) Pattern for the top rail of a center-seat backrest. (Courtesy of Mickie Smith)

**FIGURE 2-155** Theodore Salter Hanmer. (North Country Life, Spring 1957)

**FIGURE 2-156** Hanmer builder's plate. (Courtesy of Woodward Boat Shop)

## THEODORE SALTER HANMER

**Date of birth:** February 26, 1860 (Black Brook, Clinton County)
**Date of death:** April 20, 1957 (Saranac Lake, Franklin County)
**Active:** 1898–1945
**Location:** Saranac Lake
**Estimate of guideboats built:** More than 200
**Number reviewed:** 17
**Builder's plate:** Used
**Adirondack Museum accessions:** 2005.006.1, 2008.078.1

### Biographical Sketch

Theodore S. Hanmer was born in Black Brook, Clinton County, in 1860, the son of Truman and Sylvia Barnard Hanmer. He attended school in Black Brook, learned carpentry, and became an accomplished fisherman and woodsman. On February 23, 1889, he married Emma Abare of that village.[1] Later that year, after an attempt, not entirely successful, to supply the fish needed for the restaurant at Paul Smith's Hotel, Hanmer moved to Saranac Lake.[2] There, according to his son Willard, he helped to rebuild William Allen Martin's boat shop, recently destroyed by fire. He spent the following winter working in the Martin boat shop. He also worked between 1890 and 1894 in the Saranac Lake boat shop of the ailing Herbert Salisbury.[3]

According to Willard's wife, Theodore Hanmer began building boats in his own shop in 1898.[4] The local business directory for 1902 lists his occupation as "carpenter, 52 Lake [St.]"[5] and for 1910, as "boat builder, 77 Lake St."[6] He continued

1 "Veteran Adirondack Boat Builder to Break Half Century's Tradition," *Syracuse Post-Standard*, February 20, 1944.
2 "Theodore Hanmer, 50 Years Boat Builder, Still Active," *Watertown Daily Times*, February 2, 1940.
3 Robert Bruce Inverarity, *Interview with Willard Hanmer, 1961*, Adirondack Museum, Transcript of a tape recording, 1966:14, 63.
4 Mrs. Willard J. Hanmer, *Letter to Kenneth Durant, August 13,1962*, Durant Collection.
5 *Adirondack Directory for 1902–1903*:50,119,128.
6 *Adirondack Directory: Saranac Lake and Vicinity*, Saranac Lake, NY: 1910:98.

as an "active, full-time" boatbuilder until about 1927, when Willard took over most of the work.[7] Willard's shop was located a short distance away from his father's at 202 Lake Street. Theodore continued to build guideboats, though fewer each year, until the mid-1940s—his last two in 1943 and 1945, respectively.[8]

The Hanmers had eight children, two sons and six daughters. Bessie, one of the daughters, described some of the activities typical of guideboat builders' children:

> I don't think my father ever paid any of my sisters for sticking tacks, he probably did pay my brothers as they worked right along with him in learning the boat building business. But he did let us girls buy a 5 [cent] bag of peanuts at the grocery store run by Mr. Kendall in those days, and I'm sure his bill each month listed more peanuts than the groceries did. . . . My brothers and sisters that did stick tacks were from the eldest as follows: Kate, Truman, Addie, Bessie, Jennie, Belle, Willard, and Blanche; we all caned boat seats and were paid according to the size from 75 cents to $5.00—the larger seats being for cruisers and launch, a large open pleasure boat. We used to sandpaper the boats, oars, paddles, the cleats, and neck yoke. Also the seats.[9]

Bessie was a nurse and cared for her father the last seventeen years of his life. She was also a private nurse for Annie Dewey, wife of Melvil Dewey, the founder of the Lake Placid Club and the inventor of the Dewey Decimal System.

Theodore Hanmer was highly respected in Saranac Lake, as excerpts from a letter and an article attest:

> Feb. 10, 1955
>
> Dear Mr. Hanmer,
>
> I have received word that you will be 95 years old on February 26. . . . You were a fine workman. You knew and enjoyed nature. You were a good sportsman. You had a wonderful family and loved them dearly. You were never contented with less than perfection in your work. I have seen it. All of my friends in and around Saranac Lake always told me about you. They speak of you with pride of acquaintance. . . . I myself will never forget the experience of having known you. Your life could well be an example for any aspiring young man to follow. In my own memory you will live forever. Have no fear, Mr. Hanmer, God wants such as you to be with Him in Heaven.
>
> Sincerely, Henry Case[10]

From a 1980 article "Theodore: A Recollection of Theodore Hanmer, Builder of

**Figure 2-157** (Top) Hanmer stem post, a narrow, low, long rectangle. Length 2¼ to 2 ¾ inches, width about ⅜ inch, height ⅜ to ½ inch. The top is flat with rounded edges. The back is angled with a slight concave shape. The same design was used for both one-piece and strip decks. (Bottom) The stem-foot end is rounded over, or bull-nosed.

7 Hanmer, 1962.
8 Bessie L. Hanmer, *Letter to Kenneth Durant, February 4, 1964*, Durant Collection.
9 Hanmer, 1964.
10 A. Henry Case, *Letter to Theodore Hanmer, February 10, 1955*.

the Famous Adirondack Guide Boat" by John G. Homburger:

> As no other person outside of my immediate family, Theodore Hanmer ranks supreme. Father of several boys and girls, some grown, some growing, he still had time for a seven year old neighborhood sprout. Ol' man Hanmer, and I use the term reverently, was all a grandfather could be to any child. His imposing height (probably six feet two or three inches), his raw-boned frame (215–220 pounds), and his craggy features—a living image of Honest Abe—were never imposed on anyone. Mostly, it seemed, he was just there.
>
> Theodore could lead vesper services Sunday night in the Presbyterian Church, provide a subdued voice at a political gathering, or be highly observant at an auction or other assembly. In his boat shop he became a surgeon with hand tools; an artist with plank or other raw lumber; a creator of oars, paddles, seats, and yokes; and much more. No job too large, no job too small. If it was intended to float but wouldn't, that also was remedied.[11]

Having been in ill health for two years, Theodore Hanmer died at his home on April 20, 1957, at the age of ninety-seven.[12] His love for fishing and hunting never diminished. The Adirondack Museum has his fishing license that he filled out on June 30, 1956, at the age of ninety-six; he also had gone hunting that same year.

**Figure 2-158** (Left) A one-piece Hanmer deck, let into the gunwales. The shallow deck arc and the pie-piece-shaped deck cap with a vertical inboard edge. (Right) A Hanmer strip deck with a shallow deck arc and no coaming. The hull has eight strakes.

## Guideboat Characteristics

Hanmer stem posts are low, long, narrow rectangles, and the stem-foot end is bull-nosed. He built two types of decks: one-piece decks that are let into the gunwales, with a pie-piece-shaped deck cap that has a vertical inboard edge, and strip-built decks that have a center cover board and no coaming. Like the guideboats of Frederick W. Rice, from whom he received patterns in 1903, the first two pairs of ribs at bow and stern were usually scribe ribs. In some of his boats, Hanmer also used as many as three pairs of scribe ribs at bow and stern. He is the only known builder not to place any ribs under the stern deck but to place two or three non-chamfered scribe ribs inboard of it.

He was one of the few Saranac style builders to have regularly used eight strakes rather than seven. Lake Placid builder Albert Billings used eight strakes occasionally, and George & Bliss often. Hanmer may have been influenced

11 Source unknown.
12 "Theodore Hanmer, 97, Famous Boat Builder: Old Adirondacker of Guide Boat Fame Dies," *Adirondack Daily Enterprise*, April 20, 1957.

**FIGURE 2-159** (Left) No reverse-curved ribs. There is one pair of scribe ribs under the bow deck and two pairs of scribe ribs inboard of the deck. (Right) Three pairs of scribe ribs at the stern.

**FIGURE 2-160** (Above) At the stern there are no ribs under the deck. The first three pairs of ribs are scribe ribs.

**FIGURE 2-161** (Top) Stern seat and backrest. (Bottom) Center seat and backrest with replacement nylon straps.

by Herbert Salisbury with whom he worked. Although no guideboats built by Salisbury while he was in Saranac Lake have been identified, he had previously built boats in Long Lake where the use of eight strakes was the rule, as it was for boatbuilders in Blue Mountain Lake, Raquette Lake, Old Forge, and Boonville.

## Field Notes

**Stems**: Tumblehome (Saranac profile). Width from the rabbet line to the leading edge of the stem just under the gunwale; about 2½ inches; lower stem (greatest width), 3½ to 4 inches. Stem-foot end is bull-nosed.

**Ribs**: No reverse-curved ribs. Rib feet do not extend all the way across the bottom board.

**Deck caps**: For one-piece decks, the deck caps are pie-piece shaped with a vertical inboard edge.

**Center cover board**: Surrounds the stem post.

**Gunwales**: Extend to stem fronts.

**FIGURE 2-162** A guideboat-constructed canoe built by Hanmer with a carry yoke in place.

**FIGURE 2-163** Willard Hanmer builder's plates, located on the center of the carlin or deck cap. (Courtesy of Woodward Boat Shop)

**FIGURE 2-164** Willard J. Hanmer. (North Country Life, Spring 1957)

## WILLARD J. HANMER

**Date of birth:** June 30, 1902 (Saranac Lake, Franklin County)
**Date of death:** May 23, 1962 (Saranac Lake)
**Active:** 1927–1962
**Location:** Saranac Lake
**Estimate of guideboats built:** More than 100
**Number Reviewed:** 17
**Builder's plate:** 9
**Adirondack Museum accessions:** 69.195.1, 2015.35.1

### Biographical Sketch

Willard Hanmer was the seventh of eight children, born on June 30, 1902, to Theodore and Emma Hanmer of Saranac Lake. He began at the age of nine to learn boatbuilding, starting with sticking tacks, sandpapering ribs, and caning seats.[13] Like his father he was an avid hunter and fisherman. In 1926 he married Pauline Bennett, from Maine.[14] They had no children.

In 1927, at the age of twenty-five, Willard took over most of the boatbuilding responsibilities from his father. By 1930, he had built his own shop at 202 Lake Street, which he shared with his father. In "Requiem for a Craft," Roland B. Miller described Willard's shop:

> [It] consisted of a yard and storage place for the pine or cedar planking, plus a cellar for the cold keeping of the stumps and larger roots of spruce from which the boat ribs and stems

13 Angus Argyll, "Story of Guide Boats told by a Scotsman," *Adirondack Daily Enterprise*, March 5, 1958.
14 "Famed Builder of Adirondack Guide Boats Dies," *Warrensburg–Lake George News*, May 31, 1962.

**FIGURE 2-165** Willard Hanmer outside his boat shop, now the Woodward Boat Shop. It has served as a boat shop for three generations of builders: Willard Hanmer, Carl Hathaway, and currently Christopher Woodward. It is the oldest active guideboat-building shop in the Adirondacks. (Courtesy of Woodward Boat Shop)

**FIGURE 2-166** Willard Hanmer at work. (Courtesy of Adirondack Research Room, Saranac Lake Free Library)

> were cut. Over this cold storage room was his main shop, with boats in various stages of construction. Overhead was a varnish and paint loft.[1]

Willard began building boats at a time when power tools were becoming more readily available. Willard's admiration for builders like his father, who relied on hand tools, is apparent in a 1959 interview with Kenneth Durant:

> There were no light, high speed woodworking machines in those days such as I have in my shop today, and even hand tools like ratchet screw drivers and better grade planes and chisels were not to be had. Even the sandpaper was of poor quality. In spite of all this, most of the boats built by these old timers were so well built that I wonder when my last boat is completed, how well I will have qualified with those who have finished their boats and gone before me.[2]

According to his sister Bessie, Willard built his last guideboat for Dr. W. Richards of Columbia University. Dr. Richards was scheduled to give Hanmer a medical examination and collect his new guideboat on May 25, 1962. However, Willard had died of heart failure just two days earlier.

A year after Willard's death, the *Watertown Daily Times* carried this headline: "Adirondack Guideboat Race to be July 4 at Saranac Lake:"

1 Roland B. Miller, "Requiem for a Craft," *New York State Conservationist*, December–January, 1962–1963:27.
2 Durant, 1963:235.

**FIGURE 2–167** Poster for the First Annual Willard Hanmer Memorial Race, 1963. (Courtesy Adirondack Research Room, Saranac Lake Free Library)

> The Adirondack guideboat, once the most extensively used craft among guides and woodsmen and still popular today, will have a day of its own July 4 with the staging of the first annual Willard Hanmer Memorial Guideboat race, named after one of the most prominent builders of the long, sleek, double-ended craft. . . . The race will also be open to canoes and folboats, but . . . the guideboat will be the 'Prima Donna' of the event.[3]

The race in honor of Willard Hanmer was held annually for fifty years, from 1963 to 2012.

## Guideboat Characteristics

The decks of Willard's earliest guideboats were similar to his father's, with strip-decks and no coamings. There were, however, significant differences: all of Willard's have seven strakes rather than eight and they do not have scribe ribs. Also, his planks are ¼ inch cedar (his father's were $\frac{3}{16}$ inch) except the sheer strake, which is $\frac{3}{16}$ inch and often made from western red cedar.[4] What is striking about Willard's boats is their variety over time. This is true of his stem posts; his decks, center cover boards, and deck caps; his backrests; his oarlock straps; and even his boat shapes. The later incorporation of handholds in his decks at bow and stern are, however, his most recognized innovation. He also started using wooden shoes, in place of galvanized iron, in the 1940s, when iron became unavailable during World War II. He cast his own shortened oarlock straps at the same time.

How much did it cost to buy a Hanmer guideboat? Fortunately, in 1952 Willard recorded the prices he charged:[5]

13-foot guideboat: $279.40
14-foot guideboat: $290.40
16-foot guideboat: $314.60

Using guideboat construction methods and materials, Hanmer also built a number of square-stern rowboats, canoes, a racing kayak, and even a boat in the shape of an Irish curragh.

3 "Adirondack Guideboat Race to be July 4 at Saranac Lake," *Watertown Daily Times*, March 29, 1963.
4 Inverarity, 51.
5 Willard J. Hanmer, *Letter to Albert W. Allison, November 25, 1952*, Author Collection.

**FIGURE 2-168** Willard Hanmer's stem posts. (Top Left) His early strip decks are similar to his father's. (Top Right) This design, similar to F. W. Rice's, was also used on some of his early strip-deck guideboats. (Bottom Left) Later this distinctive high-pointed, sloped stem post was used. The gunwales are rounded and tapered. (Bottom Right) This style was used with a shield-shaped deck cap.

## Field Notes (all guideboat models)

**Stems:** Tumblehome (Saranac profile). Width from rabbet line to the leading stem edge: upper stems (just under the gunwale) about 2½ inches, lower stems (greatest width) 3 ½ to 4 inches. The stem foot is bull-nosed.

**Decks:** Shallow arc; V-groove construction in some later multiple-piece models.

**Ribs:** No reverse-curved ribs. Footed ribs at bow and stern; rib feet ends are beveled and do not extend all the way across the bottom board.

**Hull:** Number of strakes on each side: 7.

**Coamings:** Not used.

**FIGURE 2-169** In addition to oval handholds in the decks, another hallmark of these later guideboats is his short oarlock straps.

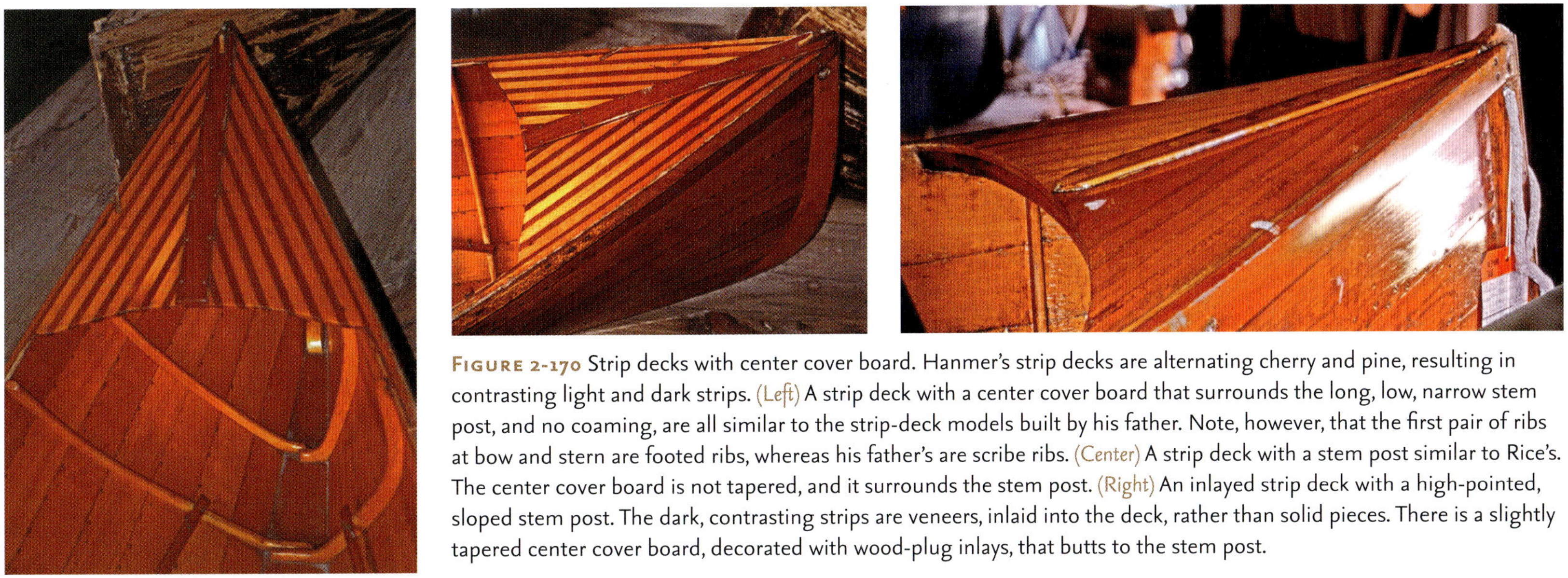

**Figure 2-170** Strip decks with center cover board. Hanmer's strip decks are alternating cherry and pine, resulting in contrasting light and dark strips. (Left) A strip deck with a center cover board that surrounds the long, low, narrow stem post, and no coaming, are all similar to the strip-deck models built by his father. Note, however, that the first pair of ribs at bow and stern are footed ribs, whereas his father's are scribe ribs. (Center) A strip deck with a stem post similar to Rice's. The center cover board is not tapered, and it surrounds the stem post. (Right) An inlayed strip deck with a high-pointed, sloped stem post. The dark, contrasting strips are veneers, inlaid into the deck, rather than solid pieces. There is a slightly tapered center cover board, decorated with wood-plug inlays, that butts to the stem post.

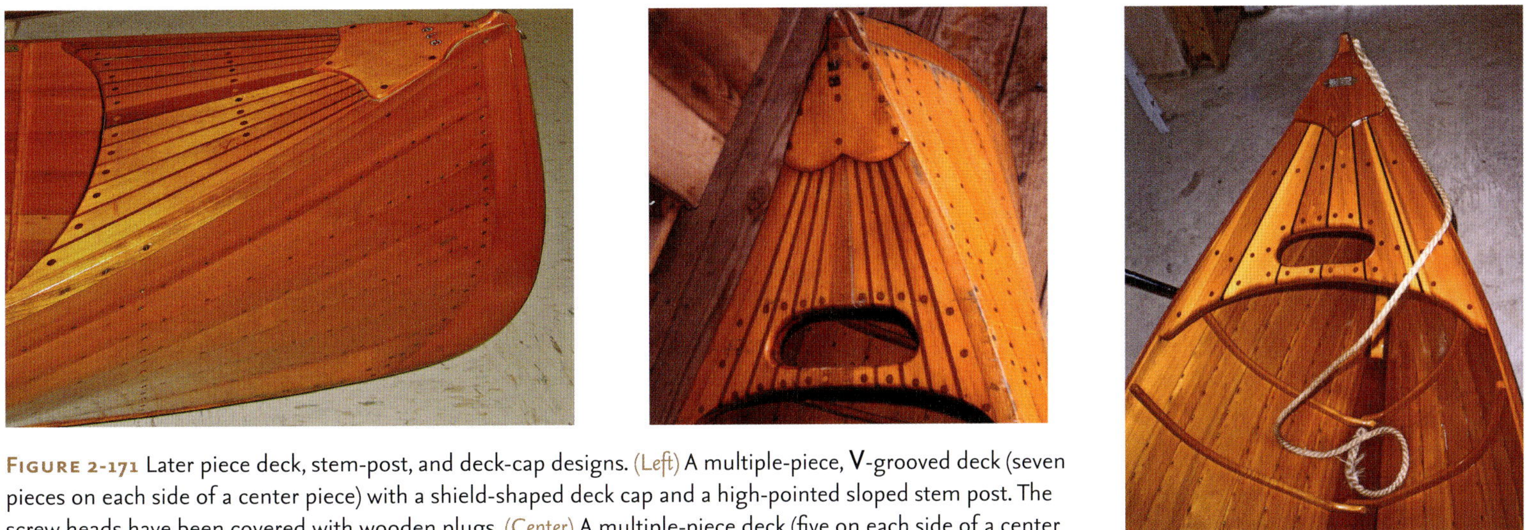

**Figure 2-171** Later piece deck, stem-post, and deck-cap designs. (Left) A multiple-piece, V-grooved deck (seven pieces on each side of a center piece) with a shield-shaped deck cap and a high-pointed sloped stem post. The screw heads have been covered with wooden plugs. (Center) A multiple-piece deck (five on each side of a center piece) with a high-pointed sloped stem post, a heart-shaped deck cap, and a distinctive oblong handhold (at bow and stern). The handholds are supported by a ¾-inch thick, solid deck beam. (Right) Six-piece, V-grooved deck. The deck cap is shield-shaped with a high-pointed sloped stem post. There are handholds at bow and stern.

**Figure 2-172** (Top and Center) Two stern seats and backrests. Hanmer used these cedar-board back rests, with or without holes on his later boats. (Bottom) Center seat and backrest.

**Figure 2-173** Examples of the boatbuilding versatility of Willard Hanmer. (Above) The guideboat-constructed Irish curragh. (Right) A square-stern rowboat. (Below Right) A guideboat-constructed canoe with a high-pointed, sloped stem post; shield-shaped deck cap; and handhold. (Below Left) Note the alternating dark and light strakes similar to some guideboats built by William Vassar of Bloomingdale.

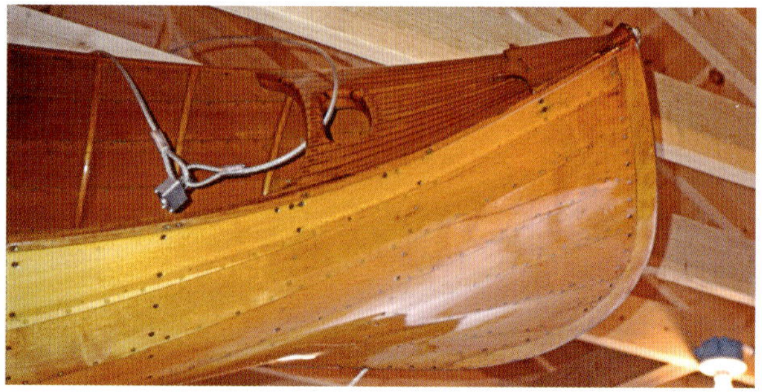

## EDWARD HARVEY

**Dates of birth:** Unknown
**Date of death:** Unknown
**Active:** 1910s–1930s
**Location:** Colton, St. Lawrence County
**Estimate of guideboats built:** 20
**Number reviewed:** 3
**Builder's plate:** Not used
**Adirondack Museum accessions:** 60.22.28, 68.148.1

### Biographical Sketch

Little is known about Edward Harvey, other than that he ran a boat livery and built and repaired boats on the Raquette River at Colton, St. Lawrence County. John P. Potter of Colton owned a boat built by Harvey that is now in the Adirondack Museum. In a letter dated October 7, 1968, Potter wrote:

> There is an old timer who lives in town [Colton] who claims to know about boats. His name is Otis Schefell, born in 1879 and has lived around here most of his life. Years ago he had a boat livery located on the Raquette River right here in Colton. He purchased the livery from an Ed Harvey whom he claims built many boats and is quite certain he built the guideboat for my father and his friend.[1]

### Guideboat Characteristics

Harvey's stem posts are long, low, and narrow. All four boats reviewed—one with steam-bent ribs—have heart-shaped deck caps at bow and stern. Two of these boats have had their hulls canvassed.

1 Source unknown.

## Field Notes

**Stems:** Tumblehome (Saranac profile); bull-nosed stem-foot end.

**Ribs:** No reverse-curved ribs. One pair of scribe ribs under the bow deck and one pair of scribe ribs under or inboard of the stern deck. No footed ribs under bow or stern decks. Rib feet are smoothly tapered and extend all the way across the bottom board.

**Decks:** One piece, let into the gunwales. The bow deck edge is either straight or arced; the stern deck edge is also slightly arced. The decks are flush with the carlin at bow and stern.

**Gunwales:** Extend to stem fronts; may be half-round.

**Hull:** Number of strakes on each side: 7.

**Figure 2-174** (Top Left) Harvey stem post and heart-shaped deck cap. (Top Right) The stem post is a long, low, narrow rectangle. (Bottom Left) Heart-shaped deck caps, at bow and stern, are Harvey's most characteristic feature. Early guideboats also had heart-shaped deck caps, but only on the bow deck, including some by Dwight Grant, William Vassar, and Willard Hanmer. (Bottom Right) One of Harvey's canvassed hulls; it may have been done to repair damage. Some Nickerson boats were also canvassed.

FIGURE 2-175 Carl G. Hathaway. (Courtesy Adirondack Research Room)

FIGURE 2-176 Hathaway builder's plate, located on the bow deck cap.

## CARL GEORGE HATHAWAY

**Date of birth:** December 30, 1929 (Tupper Lake, Franklin County)
**Active:** 1963–1991
**Location:** Saranac Lake, Franklin County
**Estimate of guideboats built:** 16
**Number reviewed:** 3
**Builder's plate:** 3
**Adirondack Museum accession:** 2014.39.1

### Biographical Sketch

The following is from an interview with Carl and his wife Valda, by Christopher Woodward, 2008–2009.

> Carl Hathaway did not set out to become a boat builder; it came about by necessity. In fact, when asked, he refers to himself as a boat restorer more so than a builder.
>
> Carl was born in Tupper Lake on December 30, 1929, the only child of Albert J. and Esther Cutting Hathaway. He lived in the house he was born in on Lakeview Street until he was five years old. At that time they moved to Upper Saranac Lake where his father became the caretaker for Colonel Wetherill at the Bucknell Camp, on Pine Point. Growing up on the lake, doing chores for his father, he was exposed to the boats and the maintenance they required. It was during these years that Carl first met Willard Hanmer, helping him from time to time on the mill as the tail man, removing and stacking the boards as they came off the saw.
>
> Carl attended school at Corey's then in Tupper Lake for high school. As Tupper Lake was 15 miles away, Carl

**Figure 2-177** Carl and Valda Hathaway, April 1967, with Carl's first boat. (Courtesy of Adirondack Research Room, Saranac Lake Free Library)

boarded with families in town, returning to camp by foot on the weekends. After high school Carl went to work for his father at the camp, cutting ice and firewood in the winter months for the surrounding camps and guiding during hunting season. Carl married Valda Ryan from Chateaugay on September 22, 1950, when he was twenty years old. They took up residence at camp, renting out a small apartment.

On November, 25, 1950, a severe southeasterly storm blew all day with winds reaching in excess of 55 miles per hour. The resulting blow-down devastated forest lands. When the state bid out contracts for the salvage of the timber, Carl went to work harvesting the logs with horses, working in the woods for the next two years.

During this time Judy, the first of his two daughters, was born. With a growing family to feed and clothe, Carl felt the need for more stable employment. When an adjacent camp owner approached him about taking over as caretaker for them, he agreed, moving his family about one mile from his childhood home across the bay to work for the Loeb family at Gull Bay camp. In 1955 he started as caretaker where he worked for the next 43 years, retiring in 1998.

While life as a caretaker has its pluses, such as year-round employment, salary, and housing, it also has its downsides, such as the lack of ownership and retirement or pension plans. Many a caretaker has been hurt, disabled, or grown too old for the demands of the job—or just due to the whims of the owners—and found themselves out of a job. So when Carl was asked by Hanmer if he would be interested in helping out during the winters at the boat shop, he took the opportunity to learn a new trade. For the winters of 1960–1961 Carl went to work for Willard. Or more precisely for Willard's wife, Pauline, known as Ben. His duties were to sand the boats smooth in preparation for her to varnish.

During the second winter there, Willard started to show Carl some of the

**FIGURE 2-178** (Left) The stem post is tall and narrow; length about 1 ½ inches, width about ⅜ inch, height ¾ inch. (Right) The stem foot is bull-nosed.

secrets of building that he had perfected over the years. Unfortunately, before Carl could complete his apprenticeship, Willard died; Carl helped Ben finish up the remaining boat. In 1963, Ben offered to sell the shop to Carl. Needing something to fall back on, Carl took the offer and bought the shop.

For the first several years Carl worked evenings and in the winters, repairing and restoring guideboats, wood canvas canoes, sail boats, skiffs, and mahogany runabouts from the surrounding lakes and camps. In 1967, Carl built his first boat using the shop patterns, and remembering what he had seen Willard do. Like all true woodsmen, using a dose of common sense, he was able to puzzle through his first boat, making an acceptable first attempt. As he had already made and replaced every part on a guideboat in one form or another, this was not that far removed from building one from the ground up. By remembering each misstep and correcting them he soon was building new boats with the confidence and ability of a master builder. However, the majority of output from the shop was in repair work. There is more money in repairs, the outlay of materials is less, and the work is steadier. Demand for new boats waxes and wanes with the economic times while repairs and restorations stay on a more even keel.

By 1980 Carl had built a dozen or more new boats and had repaired and restored hundreds more. As more work came in Carl employed several local men at one time and another. Names like Dick Bomyea, Clint Beaney, Mory Brigham, Ed Marshall, and Ralph Morrow stand out as builders and restorers in their own right.[1]

Of great importance is that Carl Hathaway, together with Ralph Morrow, played a pivotal role in preserving the practical skills of guideboat building. The Adirondack Guideboat Apprenticeship Program was created in the early 1980s through the Center for Adirondack Studies, by Dr. Murray Heller and assisted by Robert A. Klein at North Country Community College in Saranac Lake. The program was supported by the National Endowment for the Arts. Hathaway and Morrow agreed to teach groups of students (seven months for each group) to build a guideboat using traditional methods and materials. This program, apprenticing almost 65 men and women over an eight-

1 Christopher Woodward, *Interview with Carl and Valda Hathaway*, 2008–2009.

**Figure 2-179** (Left) The five-piece, deck, with V-grooves, made of pine alternating with red cedar. The deck pieces at each side are set between the sheer strakes. An oblong handhold through the bow and stern decks. (Right) Deck without V-grooves. The deck cap has been removed.

year period, was essential in preserving the craft of traditional guideboat building for another generation. Several graduates became builders, restorers, and repairers of guideboats.[2]

In 1994 Carl was recognized for his contribution to the regional culture by Traditional Arts of Upstate New York (TAUNY) and was awarded a North Country Heritage Award.[3]

## Guideboat Characteristics

A narrow rectangular stem post is characteristic of Hathaway, as is the bull-nosed shape of the stem-foot end. The most distinctive characteristic of Hathaway guideboats, however, is their five-piece decks with a pie-piece-shaped deck cap and an oblong handhold, patterned after those of Willard Hanmer. His boat lengths range between 14 and 18 feet. His 16-foot boats have a beam of 38 inches, with a bottom board width of 8 inches. The rib spacing is 6 inches on center. Stem and rib designs are similar to those of Hanmer.

## Field Notes

**Stems:** Tumblehome (Saranac profile). Width from rabbet line to leading stem edge: upper (at lower gunwale edge) about 1¾ inches, lower (greatest width) about 2¼ inches. The stem-foot end is bull-nosed.

**Ribs:** No reverse-curved or scribe ribs under the bow or stern decks. For a 16-foot guideboat, 13 pairs of footed ribs on each side of the center, or "o" pair, of ribs, for a total of 27 pairs of ribs. The rib feet extend all the way across the bottom board and are beveled.

**Deck caps:** Pie-piece-shaped with a rounded inboard edge.

**Hull:** Number of strakes on each side: 8; feather-lap construction; sheer strake ¼ inch thick; garboard ¼ inch thick.

**Gunwales:** May or may not extend to stem front.

**Seats:** Mortise and tenon construction.

**Stern-seat backrest:** Top rail smooth (no "ears"); rounded corners.

**Tacks and screws:** Tacks from W. W. Cross, New Bedford, Massachusetts; screws from Clendenin Bros., Baltimore, Maryland.

**Rowlocks and stem bands:** Cast from Hathaway's patterns by Jardine Foundry, Baldwinsville, New York.

2 Murray Heller, *Letter to the Author*, January 15, 2006.
3 North Country Heritage Award, Traditional Arts of Upstate New York, Canton, NY, 1994.

## HURST & NICKERSON

**Partnership formed:** 1890
**Active:** 1890–1895
**Location:** Canton, St. Lawrence County
**Estimate of guideboats built:** 20
**Number reviewed:** 2
**Builder's plate:** 2

### ISAAC A. HURST
### MYRON A. NICKERSON

FIGURE 2-180 Hurst & Nickerson builder's plate, located on center cover board.

### Biographical Sketch

In 1890 Isaac Hurst and Myron Nickerson left the employ of boatbuilder J. H. Rushton, to form a boatbuilding partnership, Hurst & Nickerson.[1] The *St. Lawrence Plaindealer* reported the event on May 14, 1890, under the heading "A Handsome Boat:"

> I. A. Hurst and M. A. Nickerson have entered into co-partnership in the manufacture of Saranac boats with their shop at the residence of Mr. Hurst on Judson Street (in Canton). The Saranac boat is peculiar to the Adirondack region, where it is a favorite. The boats are built with fine lines and are speedy. They are what are known as smooth skins, the siding being so joined as to make the boat smooth outside and within.

Mr. Hurst has worked for the famous boat builder Martin, at Saranac Lake, and both are experienced boat builders. The boat seen on the forms appeared perfect in every way. It was 16 feet long, of pine, with butternut and cherry trimmings, cane seats and chairs, fitted out with excellent oars and paddles. It will be a handsome craft when completed. Mr. Martin's

1 William Crowley, *Letter to James A. Williamson, September 30, 1983*, Adirondack Museum Boatbuilders' Files.

> boat factory very recently burned, and Messrs Hurst and Nickerson are hastening the completion of a load of boats which they propose to ship to the lake [Saranac Lake]. It is difficult to see why they are not a perfect boat for the kind.[2]

The Hurst & Nickerson partnership was dissolved in 1895, each becoming an independent builder. Not many guideboats were built by this short-lived partnership, and only two bearing the Hurst & Nickerson builder's plate have been located. One has been excluded from this discussion because of extensive "restoration" of the decks and hull. The remaining boat is characterized by its V-groove strip deck similar to those of Rushton.

## Guideboat Characteristics

The Hurst & Nickerson guideboat can be distinguished from those of Rushton's by the following: no metal stem-post cap continuous with the stem band; no steam-bent, red elm scribe ribs beneath the bow and stern decks; no decorative deck beam; and a non-tapered center cover board that surrounds the stem post.

2 "A Handsome Boat," *St. Lawrence Plaindealer*, May 14, 1890.

## Field Notes

**Stems:** Tumblehome (Saranac profile). The width of the stem from the rabbet line to the leading edge of the stem: upper (just below the gunwale) about 2¼ inches; lower (greatest width) about 4½ inches. A double stem may be present.

**Ribs:** No reverse-curved ribs. At bow and stern 1 pair of scribe and 3 pairs of footed ribs beneath the decks. Rib spacing is 4 ½ inches on center. Feet do not extend all the way across the bottom board and are beveled.

**Hull:** Number of strakes on each side: 7; feather-lap construction. Length is about 15½ feet. The sheer strake is made of Spanish cedar and is about $\frac{3}{16}$ inch thick.

**Gunwales:** Extend to stem fronts; may be D-shaped and tapered toward the bow and stern. Round-head brass screws are used.

**Yoke cleats:** The sides of the rounded notches of the yoke cleats have sharply pointed tips.

**Figure 2-181** (Top) The stem post of a Hurst & Nickerson guideboat is narrow, with a width about 5/16 inch, length about 1 7/8 inches, and height about 5/8 inch. It is rectangular with a slightly concave back. The front end is worn. (Bottom) The bow deck has 17 strips on each side, the stern deck 16. V-grooves are present, similar to Rushton's decks. The coaming is narrow, of equal width throughout, with rounded ends. The center cover board is 2 ¾ inches wide and non-tapered with rounded upper edges; it surrounds the stem post.

**FIGURE 2-182** Isaac A. Hurst. (Courtesy of St. Lawrence County Historical Association)

**FIGURE 2-183** Hurst builder's plate, located on the center cover board.

# ISAAC ABRAHAM HURST

**Date of birth:** Unknown
**Date of death:** Unknown
**Active:** With Myron Nickerson 1890–1895; independent after 1896
**Location:** Canton, St. Lawrence County
**Estimate of guideboats built:** More than 25
**Number reviewed:** 7
**Builder's plate:** 6

## Biographical Sketch

Isaac Hurst worked for Saranac Lake boatbuilder William Allen Martin in the early to mid-1880s. He moved to Canton in 1887 to work for J. H. Rushton. The December 1887 issue of the *American Canoeist* reported: "He [Rushton] has now a builder from Saranac Lake [Hurst] and will add the Saranac boats to his stock."[1]

In the spring of 1890, Hurst formed a partnership with fellow Rushton employee Myron Nickerson. This partnership lasted for five years. How long Hurst continued to build boats after working independently is not known. Atwood Manley recalled Hurst in his later years:

> My memory of Ike Hurst was as an employee in the old Canton Champlin Wagon Shop, where as I recall he did most of the fine finish painting work. A rather short, rather bumptious man with a black handlebar mustachio.[2]

## Guideboat Characteristics

The guideboats of Hurst and of Nickerson are similar. Both used a decorative deck beam with four concave arcs, and a shield-shaped brass plate on the forward part of the center cover board surrounding a flagpole socket. Unlike Nickerson, Hurst used two different stem posts. On some of his boats it is high and narrow and on others, low, narrow, and sloping, covered with a

1 "Builder's Notes," in *American Canoeist*, December 1887:224.
2 Atwood Manley, *Letter to George Bowditch, Curator, April 28, 1971*, Adirondack Museum, Atwood Manley Papers.

brass stem-post cap that extends onto the center cover board. His strip decks are smooth, not V-grooved; and the center cover board surrounds the stem post. There is one pair of scribe ribs at both the bow and stern. The hulls have seven strakes, and the stems are two-piece.

Although Hurst had worked for Rushton, their guideboats are not difficult to tell apart. Unlike Rushton's, Hurst's strip decks are not V-grooved, and he did not use half-round steam-bent scribe ribs. Hurst's stem post cap is not a continuous extension of the stem band; and his center cover board surrounds the stem post. His decorative deck beam has four concave arcs.

## Field Notes

**Stems:** Saranac profile. May have double stems. Width from rabbet line to the leading edge of the stem: upper (below gunwale) 2½ inches; lower (greatest width) 4½ inches. The shape of the stem foot is a horizontal rectangle.

**Ribs:** No reverse-curved ribs. There is 1 pair of scribe ribs under both the bow and stern decks. There may be 1 or 3 pairs of footed ribs under the bow and stern decks. Rib space on center is 4½ to 5½ inches. Rib feet ends are beveled and extend all the way across the bottom board.

**Decks:** No V-grooves in strip decks. There are 12 to 20 strips on each side; the strips may curve with the gunwales. The center cover board surrounds the stem post. They are about 2 ½ inches wide and not tapered, with rounded upper edges. Round-head brass screws are commonly used.

**Hull:** Number of strakes on each side: 7; feather-lap construction.

**Gunwales:** Extend to stem front; may be rounded and tapered at each end.

**Yoke cleats:** The tips of the rounded notches of the yoke cleats are sharply pointed.

**Heel plates:** Three-piece with rounded lateral ends.

FIGURE 2-184 Two Hurst guideboats that show characteristics found in both Hurst and Nickerson boats. (Top) The decorative deck beam with four concave arcs. (Bottom) The shield-shaped brass plate on the bow deck. The brass stem-post caps are not found on Nickerson guideboats.

FIGURE 2-185 (Left) A brass stem-post cap, fastened to the center cover board covers a low, narrow, sloping stem post. (Right) The short, narrow, high stem post: length about 1 ¾ inches, width about ¼ inch, height about $1\frac{9}{16}$ inches. The front end is worn; the back end has a slight angle or concavity.

**FIGURE 2-186** William Bartlett Kerst.

**FIGURE 2-187** Sign at the Kerst livery in Sabael on Indian Lake.

## WILLIAM BARTLETT KERST

**Date of birth:** 1874
**Date of death:** 1950
**Active:** 1895–early 1940s
**Location:** Sabael, Hamilton County
**Estimate of guideboats built:** 25 to 30
**Number reviewed:** 5
**Builder's plate:** Not used
**Adirondack Museum accessions:** 60.23.1, 77.175.1

### Biographical Sketch

Most of the following information was obtained through the courtesy of Jean and Grant Daniel Kerst, grandsons of William Bartlett Kerst.

William Kerst moved to Sabael, in 1895. That year he married Carrie Fish of Sabael, the daughter of Elijah Fish, a builder of boats, though not guideboats, from whom Kerst learned the trade. The year after his marriage he built a sawmill on the Indian River. In 1898 he established a boat livery on Indian Lake, specializing in pleasure boats and launches. He was the first to sell and service inboard and outboard motors on the lake. Although most of the boats Kerst built were for livery use, a few were guideboats, either made on order or used as livery boats. He built fewer than thirty.

Kerst was not only a builder but a guide. He was listed in the Hamilton County Census for 1925 as a "boat builder" and as a guide in the *Registered Guides in New York State* for 1927.[1]

### Guideboat Characteristics

William Kerst's grandson, Daniel, remembers being told that his grandfather

1 Charles K. Brumley, *Guides of the Adirondacks: A History*, Utica, NY: North Country Books, 1994:337.

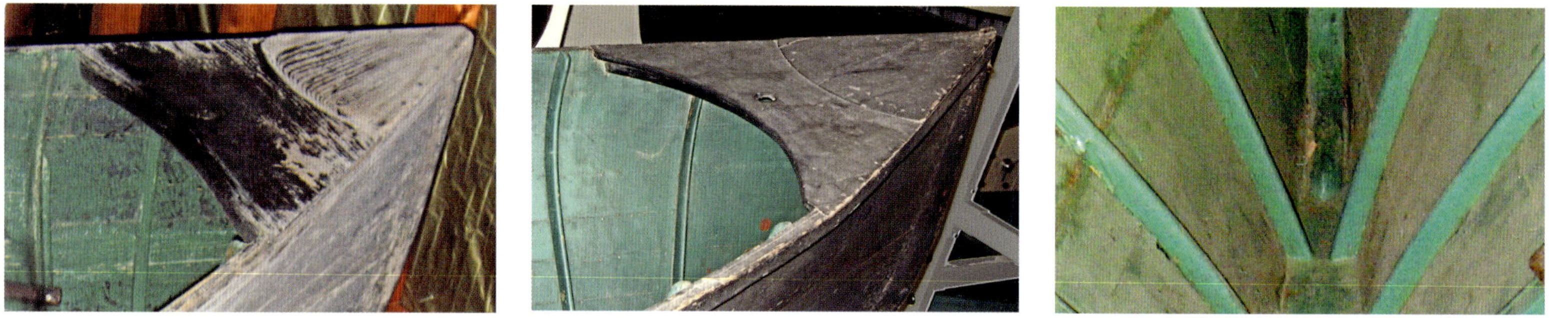

**FIGURE 2-188** (Left) A guideboat with no stem post. Leonard Anderson of Tupper Lake also omitted stem posts on some of his guideboats. (Center) A guideboat with a narrow stem post. The one-piece decks are mitered or let into the gunwales. Note the hole in the deck for a jacklight staff. The one-piece decks have a different arc in the left and center photographs. (Right) The stem foot is rounded, almost pointed. Note the rounded end of the footed ribs.

"never built the same guideboat twice."

Many Kerst guideboats lack a stem post. When stem posts are present, they are narrow, low, and rectangular. In one boat the stem foot is rounded and pointed. The one-piece decks are either mitered or let into the gunwales. Deck caps are pie-piece shaped with a tapered inboard edge. There is a hole in the bow deck for "a jacklight, not to shoot deer but to show tourists deer at night." The stem and rib feet are rounded. He used board seats. Double stems are common. The yoke cleat has a very long, slender, forward-facing arm and a short aft-facing arm; the pattern is in the Adirondack Museum.

There is one pair of scribe ribs under the bow and stern decks, that may or may not be slightly reverse curved. There are eight strakes on each side of the hull. There are short reinforcing pieces on the bottom board and along the ribs within the hull. A three-piece floorboard was common. Rib feet do not extend all the way across the bottom board to the garboard. The bow deck overhangs a rounded carlin.

## Field Notes

**Stems:** Straight leading edge (Long Lake profile); upper stem width (just below gunwale) about 2 ½ inches; lower stem width (greatest width) about 3 ½ inches.

**Ribs:** Slight reverse curve. One pair of scribe ribs under bow and stern decks; no footed ribs under either deck. Rib feet may be rounded.

**Deck caps:** Pie-piece-shaped. Inboard edge is tapered.

**Hull:** Number of strakes on each side: 8; feather-lap construction; short reinforcing rib pieces on bottom board or adjacent to hull.

**Gunwales:** Extend to stem fronts; ends may be rounded.

**Floor boards**: Commonly, three wide longitudinal pieces resting on the ribs.

**Figure 2-189** Fuat Latif.

**Figure 2-190** Latif's builder's plates.

## FUAT LATIF

**Date of birth:** October 13, 1947 (Bavaria, Germany)
**Active:** 1985–
**Location:** Vermontville, Franklin County
**Estimate of guideboats built:** 13
**Builder's plate:** Used

### Biographical Sketch

Fuat Latif was born of a Russian father and Tatar mother in Bavaria, Germany. During World War II his father and mother had been brought to Germany from Russia; his father (a member of the Russian Army) as a prisoner of war, his mother as a laborer in a work camp. There, his parents met and married.

In 1951, at the age of four, he and his family left for the United States, sponsored by the Tolstoy Foundation, and settled near the Foundation's headquarters in Nyack, New York. From 1965 to 1970, he attended Northeastern University and obtained a degree in civil engineering. From 1971 to 1995 he lived in Orwell, Vermont, starting as a carpenter's helper and eventually becoming a cabinet and furniture maker. In 1985, he built a canoe made of wood strips and fiberglass based on a how-to article, and then went on to build a dozen more. He became inspired by traditionally built wooden boats, after viewing the collection at the Adirondack Museum. Over the ensuing years, he has built a host of small wooden boats, including St. Lawrence skiffs, many Rushton models such as Nessmuk, Ugo, Vaux, Jr.; several lapstrake canoes; a replica of the fantail pulling boat that Ulysses S. Grant is said to have used on a trip to the Thousand Islands; and thirteen guideboats.

In 1995 Latif moved to Saranac Lake and then in 2005 to Vermontville, Franklin County, where he built a workshop and lived in a yurt. After the first winter—"I stayed warm but used a lot of wood"—he moved to a room in his workshop and began to build the small studio apartment that he occupies today.[1]

## Guideboat Characteristics

Latif uses the patterns and outward raked stem of a Grant boat. He has used both two-piece decks, like Grant, and, in most, a V-groove strip deck, like Rushton. All have modified bevel-lap hull construction and an extended stem band that covers the narrow, sloping stem post.

**Figure 2-191** Profile of a Latif guideboat.

**Figure 2-192** (Left) The stem and sloping stem post are narrow. The brass stem-post cap is an extension of the stem band. The center cover board butts to the stem post. A single bead runs along the lower edge of the gunwale. (Right) A V-groove deck. The center cover board, with the builder's plate, is tapered. The coaming is wide.

1 Fuat Latif, *Personal communication*, 1995–2015.

## WILLIAM ALLEN MARTIN

**Figure 2-193** Martin builder's plate, located on the coaming.

**Date of birth:** October 7, 1849 (Bangor, Franklin County)
**Date of death:** February 24, 1907 (Saranac Lake, Franklin County)
**Active:** 1865 to mid-1890s
**Location:** Saranac Lake
**Estimate of guideboats built:** More than 75
**Number reviewed:** 10
**Builder's plate:** 5
**Adirondack Museum accession:** 64.125.1

### Biographical Sketch

William Allen Martin was the son of William Fortune Martin, pioneer and legendary hotelkeeper of the Saranac region. The elder Martin came to Saranac Lake in 1849 with his wife Laura and his two brothers, Stephen and Henry, from Bangor, in northern Franklin County, the year William Allen was born. It was here that William McLenathen taught young Willie Allen Martin the fundamentals of boatbuilding. It is said that Martin built his first guideboat at the age of sixteen.[1]

Based upon advertisements in two guidebooks: Stoddard's *The Adirondacks: Illustrated* [2] and F. H. Bryant's *Nooks in the North* [3]—both stating that William Martin had fifteen years of experience—his formal career as a boatbuilder would have begun about 1872, when he was twenty-three. The 1874 *New York State Business Directory* lists a "Martin Wm. A., S.[Saranac] Lake" as a boatbuilder.[4] At about this time he married Estella E. Manning. They had one son, Henry Kilburn Martin, born in 1879, who also became a guideboat builder.

The August 17, 1867, issue of *Spirit*

1 Donaldson, 1921, I:305.
2 S. R. Stoddard, *The Adirondacks: Illustrated*, 1886:256.
3 F. H. Bryant, *Nooks in the North*, New York: New York News, 1887: n.p.
4 *New York State Business Directory*, Boston: Sampson, Davenport, 1874:356.

*of the Times* reported what may have been the first recorded guideboat race among guides. The "summary" of the article reads: "Saranac Lake, Aug. 9th, 1867—Single Scull Boat Race; course two miles. Each man rowing alone, and timed separately." The race started and ended at Hough's hotel on Upper Saranac Lake. There were six contestants, one of whom was William Martin, who tied for third with Warren Slater.[5]

In a query as to who were "good builders" of the "Adirondack boat," a comment in *Forest and Stream*, in 1876, gave three names, one being W. E. [*sic*] Martin of Saranac Lake.[6] In Charles Hallock's *Sportsman's Gazetteer* (1877), in reply to a similar query, six Adirondack boatbuilders are listed: "C. J. Chase of Newcomb, Reuben Cary and Henry Stanton of Long Lake, W. E. Martin [W. A. Martin], E. Peck [Chester W. Peck], and G. Philboots [James Philbrooks] of Saranac Lake, are all good builders."[7]

In 1878, with Frederick W. Rice, a newly arrived boatbuilder from Willsboro, on Lake Champlain, Martin completed the building of the first steamboat, *Water Lily*, to operate on Lower Saranac Lake. The launching on the Fourth of July was a special occasion: on board was the band that was playing that summer at Martin's.[8] The 1878 edition of Stoddard's guidebook reported:

> The little steamer on the Lower Saranac was built in the spring of 1878, to run in connection with the *Mattie* on Upper Saranac Lake. Its length is 36 feet; breadth of beam, 9 feet; draft, 18 inches. It is fitted with a nice cabin, will carry 40 persons, is owned by Martin & Co., and is manned by captain, engineer and one crew.[9]

In 1882 William F. Martin built a new hotel "on the high point of land where the roads from the Ampersand and Algonquin [hotels] join."[10] Across the road, in 1885, W. A. Martin and T. Edmund Krumbholz built a boat shop for their new venture, the Adirondack Boat Building Company.

As has been mentioned, Martin grew up learning from William McLenathen how to build boats. He is credited with being the first to introduce a lighter, smooth-skin transom-built guide's boat. His boats were referred to as "Willie Allen's eggshells,"[11] implying both light-

**FIGURE 2-194** Both of these Martin stem posts are narrow. (Top) Length about 2½ inches, width about 5⁄16 inch, height about 3⁄8 inch. The front end is angled; the back end concave (most common) or vertical. (Bottom) A narrow, long, and low stem post with an angled front and back.

5 "A Letter from the Adirondack," *Wilkes' Spirit of the Times*, August 17, 1867.
6 "Answers to Correspondence," *Forest and Stream*, February 17, 1876:23.
7 Charles Hallock, "Sporting Boats and Canoes," *Sportsman's Gazetteer and General Guide*, New York: *Forest and Stream*, 1877:634.
8 Donaldson, 1921, I:307.
9 Stoddard, 1878:104.
10 Donaldson, 1921, I:303.
11 Donaldson, 1921, I:306.

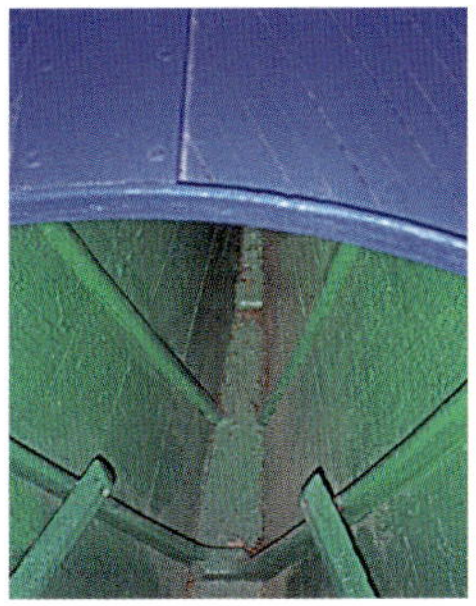

**Figure 2-195** No reverse-curved ribs. (Left) Beneath the bow deck: 1 pair of steam-bent, red elm scribe ribs and 2 pairs of footed ribs. (Right) Beneath the stern deck: 1 pair of steam-bent, red elm scribe ribs, and 1 pair of footed ribs. Rib feet are beveled and do not extend all the way across the bottom board. The stem foot is a horizontal rectangle.

**Figure 2-196** (Top Left) The one-piece deck is let into the gunwales. The pie-piece-shaped deck cap's inboard edge is cut square. The bow deck extends beyond the carlin; the stern deck is flush with the carlin. (Top Right) A strip-built deck with a pie-piece-shaped deck cap and a narrow coaming. There is a hole in the deck, surrounded by a brass collar, for a flagstaff. (Left) A strip-built deck with a center cover board and a narrow coaming. The bow deck has 15 alternating light and dark strips on each side; the stern deck has 13 such strips. The center cover board surrounds the stem post. Martin's strip decks are not V-grooved.

ness and a smooth hull. He was a leader in the evolution of the guideboat, one of the few to bridge the transom and double-ended eras of guideboat building. He continued to build boats until the mid-1890s, when his health began to fail and his son took over the business.

The development of feather lapping by shaving the upper and lower edges of hull planks was initially accomplished with planks ¼ inch thick or greater. Experimentation resulted in varying degrees of smoothness with some overlap visible (a modified clapboard appearance) until complete smoothness was achieved. To further reduce weight, plank thickness (excluding the garboard) was further reduced to the lowest limit of construction strength—3⁄16 inch. Weight reduction by shaving other guideboat parts, such as the ribs, was also taking place in other boat shops, by other builders. The final significant reduction in weight was achieved by discarding the transom in favor of a guideboat pointed at both ends—a double ender.

Noted guideboat builders who worked for, and learned from, Martin include: his son Henry Kilburn Martin, Frederick W. Rice (1878), and Theodore S. Hanmer (1888–1889) of Saranac Lake, Alric B.Moody (1886–1890) of Tupper Lake, and Isaac A. Hurst (1887) of Canton.

Of quiet demeanor, Martin was also mechanically inclined, a telegraph operator, and an accomplished "play by ear" pianist.[12]

## Guideboat Characteristics

Martin built guideboats as well as guideboat-constructed church, or family, boats. He used two different stem-post designs. A distinctive characteristic was his use of a pair of half-round, steam-bent, red-elm scribe ribs beneath the bow and stern decks (also used by his son H. K. Martin and J. H. Rushton). His decks were both one-piece and strip-built. As with some other builders, his highest-grade guideboats have round-head brass screws on the coamings, center cover boards, deck caps, and occasionally the gunwales. The sheer strakes are often made from western red cedar.

An 1883 catalogue illustrated "stem bands in three patterns named respectively for three guideboat builders: Fred W. Rice and William A. Martin, both of Saranac Lake, and H. Dwight Grant of Boonville."[13]

12 Donaldson, 1921, I:306.
13 Durant, 1980:145.

### Field Notes

**Stems:** Tumblehome (Saranac profile). The end of the stem foot is a horizontal rectangle.

**Deck caps:** Pie-piece-shaped, bow and stern. The inboard edge is square cut.

**Hull:** Number of strakes on each side: 7; feather-lap construction.

**Gunwales:** Extend to stem fronts.

**Heel plates:** One piece. The upper lateral borders are rounded.

FIGURE 2-197 Example of Martin's workmanship. (Top Left) A guideboat-constructed church or family boat in original condition, with a one-piece transom stern, carved from a spruce stump (circa late 1870s). Its length, from stem post to stem post, is 23 feet 6 inches. Beneath the bow deck are two pairs of steam-bent, red elm scribe ribs. (Top Right) A view of the two chair seats and the transom stern. (Left and Right) Two views of the one-piece, hand-carved transom and lower stem.

**Company formed:** 1885
**Location:** Saranac Lake, Franklin County
**Active:** 1885 ~ 1909
**Estimate of guideboats built:** Over 50
**Number reviewed:** 3
**Builder's plates:** 3

# ADIRONDACK BOAT BUILDING COMPANY

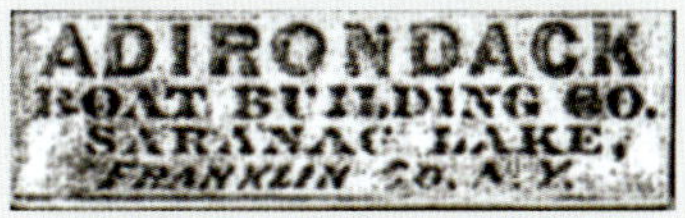


FIGURE 2-198 Builder's plate, located on bow deck cap.

**WILLIAM A. MARTIN**

**HENRY K. MARTIN**

**T. EDMUND KRUMBHOLZ**

## Biographical Sketch

In 1882, one of the first guests to stay at Martin's newly built, second hotel was T. Edmund Krumbholz, who was ill with tuberculosis. He was referred to Martin's by his Albany physician Dr. Samuel B. Ward, who knew of the work of Dr. Edward L. Trudeau in Saranac Lake.[1] Unexpectedly, and unusual in the history of advanced tuberculosis, Krumbholz's health rapidly improved.

A friendship and eventually a boatbuilding partnership was formed between Krumbholz and William Allen Martin. In 1885 they built a boat shop at the junction of Edgewood Road and Lake Street.[2] The shop was destroyed by fire in the winter of 1885–1886, but by the following summer, with financial support from friends, it was rebuilt.[3] Krumbholz financed the enterprise, but he was not a boatbuilder. In an advertisement in the 1886 edition of S. R. Stoddard's guidebook, T. E. Krumbholz and W. A. Martin were listed as co-proprietors of the Adirondack Boat Building Company.[4] Krumbholz left the partnership to begin a career as a hotel manager during the winter of 1886–1887,[5] and Martin retained the Adirondack Boat Building Company's name.[6] In F. H. Bryant's 1887 edition of the guidebook, *Nooks in the*

1 Donaldson, 1921, I:304.
2 Donaldson, 1921, I:305.
3 *St. Lawrence Plaindealer*, May 14, 1890.
4 Stoddard, 1886:256.
5 T. Edmund Krumbholz was a partner in building the Wawbeek Lodge, manager of the Ruisseaumont Hotel in Lake Placid, manager of the Sagamore Hotel on Lake George, and manager of the Kirkwood Hotel in Camden, South Carolina, among others.
6 Inverarity, 1961:2–3.

**Figure 2-199** (TopLeft and Right) Wide stern carlins. The decks are one piece and the inboard edge of the deck caps is slightly beveled. The stem posts are narrow rectangles. (Right) Closeup of the stem post.

*North,* an advertisement lists W. A. Martin as the sole proprietor.[7]

In the mid-1890s, William Allen Martin retired from boatbuilding due to failing health. He died on February 24, 1907.[8] In 1902 the local business directory listed as boatbuilders the Adirondack Boat Building Company and H. K. Martin. From 1902 until at least 1906, H. K. carried on as proprietor of the

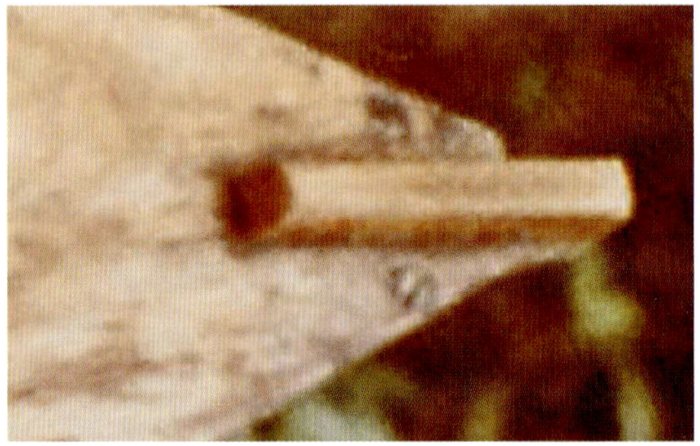

Adirondack Boat Building Company. In 1910 the company was no longer listed in the directory; however, the name H. K. Martin was listed as a "manufacturer of Adirondack Guide Boats."[9] He is also listed as a boatbuilder in the New York State Bureau of Statistics at the time of his second marriage in 1914.[10]

## Guideboat Characteristics

From 1885 until about 1909, guideboats were built in the Martin boat shop in Saranac Lake, first by the firm of Martin and Krumbholz (1885 to 1886), then by William Allen Martin (1887 to the early 1890s), and finally by Martin's son, H. K. Martin (mid-1890s to 1909). Some bear the builder's plate of the Adirondack Boat Building Company, but others have the plates of W. A. Martin or H. K. Martin. Those with the company plates were of standard grade, whereas those with Martins plates were of higher grade, and usually built to order.

A wide stern carlin is the most distinctive feature of the company guideboats. It is not present in guideboats with the W. A. or H. K. Martin plates. Features in common include: seven strakes on each side, tumblehome or Saranac stem profile, low bull-nosed stem feet, one-piece decks let into the gunwales, pie-piece-shaped deck caps with slightly beveled inboard edges, the placement of footed, almost straight, ribs under the bow and stern decks, center and stern

7 Bryant, 1887: n.p.
8 Donaldson, 1921, I:306.
9 *Adirondack Directory*, 1902–03:61, 65; 1906:79; 1910:20, 113.
10 New York State Department of Vital Statistics, "Marriages," 1914, I, 2492: n.p.

seats, and backrests and yoke cleats. The Adirondack Boat Building Company did not use steam-bent red elm scribe ribs.

## Field Notes

**Stems:** Tumblehome (Saranac profile).

**Decks:** One piece, let into the gunwales.

**Deck caps:** Pie-piece-shaped with slightly beveled inboard edges.

**Hull:** Number of strakes on each side: 7; feather-lap construction.

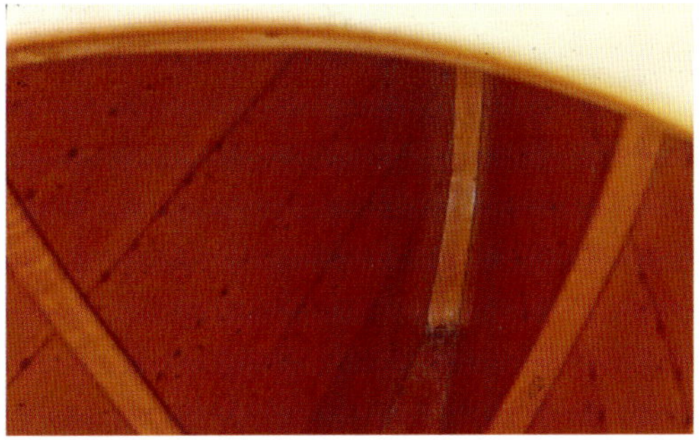

FIGURE 2-201 Note the narrow carlin at the bow. The stem foot is rounded over, or bull-nosed.

FIGURE 2-200 (Left) At the stern, one pair of nearly straight, footed ribs beneath the deck and another pair inboard of the deck. (Right) At the bow, two pairs of almost straight, footed ribs beneath the deck.

FIGURE 2-202 (Above) The stern-seat backrest. Note the pronounced "ears." (Left) The top rail of the center-seat backrest has rounded "shoulders" and leather straps that secure the backrest. These backrest designs were also used by William Allen Martin and his son. Some seats and rests are marked with the company stamp.

## HENRY KILBURN MARTIN

**FIGURE 2-203** H. K. Martin's builder's plates, located on the coaming or the center cover board.

**Date of birth:** 1879 (Saranac Lake, Franklin County)
**Date of death:** Unknown
**Active:** Mid-1890s ~ 1915
**Location:** Saranac Lake
**Estimate of guideboats built:** More than 50
**Number reviewed:** 14
**Builder's plate:** 6
**Adirondack Museum accession:** 71.24.1

### Biographical Sketch

Little is known of the life of Henry Kilburn Martin. He was the grandson of William Fortune Martin, who established Martin's Hotel on the shores of Lower Saranac Lake, and the son of boatbuilder William Allen Martin.

In the late 1890s, H. K. Martin, while still in his teens, became, due to his father's ill health, sole proprietor of his father's business, the Adirondack Boat Building Company. He continued to run the business for a few years after his father died in 1907, but thereafter built boats under his own name. In 1910, the Adirondack Boat Building Company was no longer listed in the local directory, but H. K. Martin was as a "manufacturer of Adirondack Guide Boats."[1] He was again listed as a boatbuilder in the *New York State Department of Statistics* at the time of his second marriage (he had been a widower) to Stella Woods on June 4, 1914, in Saranac Lake.[2] There is no mention of him in the records thereafter.

1 *Adirondack Directory*, 1910:20, 113.
2 New York State Department of Vital Statistics, "Marriages," 1914: n.p.

The *Ticonderoga Sentinel* reported on June 14, 1917, that pontoons for the war industry were being built at the Martin boat shop in Saranac Lake.

> SARANAC LAKE
> GETS WAR INDUSTRY
>
> Saranac Lake is to have a war industry—the manufacture of pontoons for sea planes for the government—for which the Palmer-Simpson Co. was recently organized and has secured a large contract. Work has already been begun on these pontoons or floats in the Martin boat shop on Algonquin Ave. [Lake Street]. The industry will employ a considerable number of men at high wages. The government will have about 4,000 sea planes under construction before the summer is over. Each plane requires two pontoons and a spare one or two for replacement in case of damage. The industry is established at Saranac Lake because the Adirondack guide boat builders are there. The material will be Adirondack spruce. The pontoons must be very light and very strong. The Adirondack guide boat is regarded by experts as remarkable for light weight, strength and seaworthiness; and men who can build these boats have the necessary skill for building pontoons.[3]

FIGURE 2-204 Advertisements for pontoons (1917) and hulls (1918) for "hydroaeroplanes" built in Saranac Lake by the Palmer-Simpson Company. (Courtesy of Historic Saranac Lake)

Although only pontoon construction is mentioned, additional space was later located in the O'Brian building on Olive Street, allowing both hulls and pontoons to be built for the Navy's "hydroaeroplane" (flying boat), model HS-2L.[4] This flying boat was the first American-built aircraft sent overseas during World War I.[5]

Whether the boat shop had previously been vacant or Martin had been building boats there and leased the shop to make it available for the war effort is not known. Sometime, however, between about 1915 and 1917, H. K. Martin stopped building boats.

## Guideboat Characteristics

H. K. Martin built guideboats with either two-piece or strip decks. Those with two-piece decks are less common and were probably built earlier in his career.

His boats have a wide center cover board with a wide bevel on each side. They have a pair of steam-bent, red elm scribe ribs placed beneath the decks at bow and stern, similar to those used by his father and J. H. Rushton, and a distinctive decorative deck beam with three concave arcs. In most of his boats there are two small indentations in the top of the coaming to either side of the cen-

3 "Saranac Lake Gets War Industry," *Ticonderoga Sentinel*, June 14, 1917:1.
4 "The World War I Hydroplane Industry in Saranac Lake," Historic Saranac Lake, https://localwiki.org/hsl/Palmer-SimpsonCompany.
5 Ann Cipriano Venzon, ed., *United States in the First World War: An Encyclopedia*, New York: Garland, 1995:12.

ter cover board. The sheer strakes on Martin's strip-decked boats were usually western red cedar or Spanish cedar. He also commonly used round-head brass screws for the coamings and center cover boards of these boats.

Those with two-piece decks are relatively plain, although they also have a center cover board with beveled edges, and a coaming. Their coamings lack the distinctive indentations. They also lack decorative deck beams. They may have the pair of red elm scribe ribs beneath bow and stern decks that is so characteristic of Martin's boats.

## Field Notes

**Stems:** Tumblehome (Saranac profile). Double stems may be present. The stem foot is bull-nosed.

**Ribs:** No reverse-curved ribs. Rib feet ends are beveled and do not extend all the way across the bottom board. Ribs are about 6 inches apart. There are two pairs of footed ribs beneath the bow deck and one pair of footed ribs beneath the stern deck. Boats with a strip-built deck have a single pair of steam-bent, red elm scribe ribs beneath the bow and stern decks, behind the deck beam. Only some boats with a two-piece deck have these scribe ribs.

**Hull:** Number of strakes on each side: 7; feather-lap construction.

**Gunwales:** Extend to stem fronts.

**Heel plates:** One piece, the upper lateral margins are rounded.

FIGURE 2-205 H. K. Martin's stem-post designs. (Left) A narrow stem post with length of about 2½ inches, width about ⅜ inch, and height about ½ inch. The front end has a slightly rounded angle; the back end is concave. (Right) A stem post with 3 notches, likely carved by the owner, and a concave back end. Note the wide bevel on the sides of the center cover board.

FIGURE 2-206 The decorative deck beam has three concave arcs, and there is one pair of steam-bent, red elm scribe ribs. The stem foot is rounded over or bull-nosed.

**Figure 2-207** Deck types. (Above) An early two-piece deck, a center cover board with a wide bevel on each side, and a coaming without indentations. No decorative deck beam or steam-bent, red elm scribe ribs. Deck pieces are let into the gunwales. (Right) A typical strip-deck model: The bow deck has 13 strips on each side, alternating light and dark; the stern deck has 9 strips on each side, also alternating light and dark. The coaming is narrow and of equal width throughout. There are two shallow indentations in the top of the coaming, at either side of the center cover board. There is a decorative deck beam with three concave arcs and a pair of steam-bent, red elm scribe ribs. In common with the two-piece-deck model, the center cover board has a wide bevel on each side, typical of H. K. Martin guideboats.

**Figure 2-208** (Below) Stern-seat backrest with pronounced "ears." (Bottom) Center seat and backrest.

## WILLIAM McCAFFREY

**Date of birth:** 1859
**Date of death:** 1912 (Paul Smiths, Franklin County)
**Active:** Mid-1880s ~ 1902
**Location:** Paul Smiths, Franklin County; Bloomingdale, Essex County
**Estimate of guideboats built:** More than 75
**Number reviewed:** 18
**Builder's plate:** 2

**Figure 2-209** (Top) McCaffrey builder's plate used at Paul Smith's. (Bottom) Used at Bloomingdale. The plates are located on the bow deck.

### Biographical Sketch

William McCaffrey built guideboats especially for the guides employed at Paul Smith's hotel on Lower St. Regis Lake. According to Everett Merritt Brown, the grandson of Bloomingdale guideboat builder William Vassar, it was McCaffrey who taught Vassar how to build guideboats. For a time, they shared the same shop in Bloomingdale.[1]

In 1885 McCaffrey is listed as one of the men who received payment for work at the state fish hatchery at Lake Clear for "carpenter work" and "labor" during the last three months of that year.[2] It appears that McCaffrey began his career as a boatbuilder around this time. There are similarities between his boats and those of Elbridge G. Ricketson, a Bloomingdale guideboat builder ten years his senior. It is probable that McCaffrey learned the trade from Ricketson.

William McCaffrey's boatbuilding career appears to have ended with the announcement in the *Adirondack Directory* published in 1902:[3]

1 Everett Merrit Brown, *Personal communication*, August 1, 1992.
2 *Fisheries Report*, 1886:176–177.
3 *Adirondack Directory*, 1902:168

THE BROOKSIDE HOTEL

I wish to announce to the people of Bloomingdale, Saranac Lake and vicinity that I have purchased the hotel known as the Murray Hill Hotel, and which will be known as the Brookside Hotel at Bloomingdale, N.Y., and am prepared to meet the wants of the public. New furniture has been added and the house has been thoroughly renovated from top to bottom. I hope to receive a share of your patronage and guarantee to treat you first-class in every respect.

BLOOMINGDALE, N. Y. WM. McCAFFREY. PROPR.

**FIGURE 2-210** (Left) McCaffrey's stem post: narrow, with length of about 2 ½ inches, width about ½ inch, and height about ¾ inch. Front end is vertical (slightly worn); back end a rounded concavity; top slightly rounded. (Center) The back end rounded concavity is better shown. The front also sometimes has a slightly indented angle. (Right) The stem-foot end is cut to an arch shape.

## Guideboat Characteristics

There are similarities but also significant differences between the guideboats built by McCaffrey, Ricketson, and Vassar. McCaffrey's stem posts are narrow and rectangular, with a slight rounded indentation at the back; Vassar's have a distinctive half-round shape. Also, McCaffrey's stem-foot end, like Ricketson's, is arch-shaped, quite unlike Vassar's.

A distinctive stem pattern is used by all three builders. The lower stem, from the rabbet line to the leading edge at the waterline, is unusually wide—from 4½ to more than 6 inches. This stem profile, with its tumblehome shape, is sometimes mistakenly referred to as a "ram bow." Only three earlier builders are known to have consistently used this stem pattern, all from Bloomingdale: Ricketson, McCaffrey, and Vassar. James Cameron and Christopher Woodward are contemporary builders who also use this stem profile.

Both McCaffrey and Vassar placed one pair of short scribe ribs at bow and stern that are pointed at the upper end and have a supporting ledge for the stern-seat cleats: McCaffrey's end on the fifth strake, Vassar's on the sixth.

Both builders built guideboats with two-piece decks set between the sheer strakes and strip-built decks with pie-piece-shaped deck caps. McCaffrey did not use a center cover board or coaming with his strip-built decks. A hole with a brass collar in the bow deck cap (and in some boats the stern deck cap as well) was common.

One narrow guideboat (length 15 feet 10 inches, beam 31 inches, bottom board width 5⅞ inches) built by McCaffrey, was fitted with outriggers for racing.

## Field Notes

**Decks:** The inboard edge of the bow deck is a moderate arc; the stern is a shallow arc. The bow deck extends slightly beyond the carlin; the stern deck is flush with the carlin.

**Deck caps:** Bow and stern: Pie-piece-shaped with tapered inboard edge. Strip decks also have a pie-piece-shaped deck cap. There is usually a hole (for a flag) with a brass collar at the bow, and occasionally at the stern.

**Ribs:** No reverse curve.

**Hull:** Number of strakes on each side: 7; feather-lap construction.

**Gunwales:** Extend to the stem fronts.

**Heel plates:** One piece. A short piece of the lateral pointed end is cut off.

FIGURE 2-211 (Left) Stem profile. Width from rabbet line to the leading edge: upper stem (just under the gunwale) about 2 inches, lower stem (greatest width) at the waterline, 4 ½ to more than 6 inches. (Center) One pair of scribe ribs that have pointed upper ends ending on the fifth strake. (Right) At the stern scribe rib, there is a projecting ledge supporting the stern-seat cleat.

FIGURE 2-212 (Top Left) A two-piece deck, set between the sheer strakes (the dark strips just inside of the gunwales). (Top Right) A strip deck with a pie-piece-shaped deck cap. The number of strips on each side: bow 15, stern 12 to 13. There is no coaming and no center cover board. (Left) Pie-piece-shaped deck cap with a flag-staff hole and brass collar. The inboard edge of the deck cap is tapered.

**FIGURE 2-213** McLenathen's gravestone. (Courtesy of Laura Viscome)

## WILLIAM McLENATHEN

**Date of birth:** 1798 (Franklin Falls, Franklin County)
**Date of death:** 1892 (Upper Jay, Essex County)
**Active:** 1850 ~ 1870
**Location**: Saranac Lake, Franklin County
**Estimate of guideboats built:** Unknown
**Number reviewed:** 1 (attributed)
**Adirondack Museum accession:** 56.74.1

### Biographical Sketch

Little is known of William McLenathen. (See Part I) His gravestone indicates that he was born in 1798, died in 1892, and was buried in the Mountain View Cemetery in Upper Jay, New York.

By 1850, at the age of fifty-one, he was known to be working as a boatbuilder with the Martins on the shore of Lower Saranac Lake. The 1850 federal census for Harrietstown, Franklin County, lists McLenathen amongst the members of the Martin household:

> William F. Martin, age 27, Inn Keeper, born in New York
> Laura Martin, age 26, born in Canada [wife of William F. Martin]
> William A. Martin, age 8 months, born in New York [son of William and Laura Martin]
> Henry W. Martin, age 24, Farmer, born in New York [brother of William F. Martin]
> William Mclenathen, age 51, Boat Builder & Miner, born in Vermont

By whom and where McLenathen learned the boatbuilding trade is also unknown, although cities near the Adirondack region known for boatbuilding—such as Schenectady, Albany, and even New York—are possibilities. It is also plausible that he learned to build boats while living in Jay, where boats modeled on the traditional Maine lumberman's bateau were used in log drives on the Ausable River. In October 1958, the local newspaper, *Adirondack Daily Enterprise*, contained an article titled, "Seek Builder's Name of Old Guide Boat," by Dr. Leroy Wardner, a Saranac Lake physician.

Wardner stated that "The boat is considered to be the oldest in the collection of the Adirondack Museum at Blue Mountain Lake. We seek to establish the identity of its builder and any additional information pertinent to its design and early use."[1]

The next day the *Enterprise* printed a response from a local woodsman and cabinetmaker, Russell Demerse of Saranac Lake, who wrote that he believed the boat had been built by men whom he called the McLenathen brothers of the Lake Placid area.

The boat's lack of yoke cleats, and its length (17 feet 4 inches), beam (44 inches), and weight (120 pounds), rule it out as a carry boat. However, it meets the criteria of an early freight or family boat. Wardner said, "It remained in possession of my family at a remote camp on Lake Placid from around 1880 to 1956. Until 1936, it was used regularly for fishing as well as for freighting firewood and supplies."[2]

Likely later additions are the stern deck, the storage compartment at the bow, and the metal reinforcing strips between ribs at the stern. The carved one-piece transom is wineglass-shaped. The deck is slightly cambered and the deck cap is heart-shaped. The stern-seat cleats have been removed.

**FIGURE 2-214** (Right) The unidentified boat in the 1958 *Enterprise* article. There are two rectangular slots in the far end of the stern deck. The bow deck is cambered with a slight arc. Seat cleats are present at the stern; the center-seat cleats are long, thick and able to support more than one board seat. The oars blades are being supported on the rear oarlock socket straps. The bottom board is wide and there are no yoke cleats. The stern ribs are reverse curved.

**FIGURE 2-215** (Below) The boat described in the *Enterprise* article, now at the Adirondack Museum. It is an early (1860s) transom-built guide's boat with a Saranac profile, eight strakes to a side, a high, narrow, rectangular stem post, and slight-to-moderate clapboard lapstrake planking. (Courtesy of Adirondack Museum, accession 56.74.1)

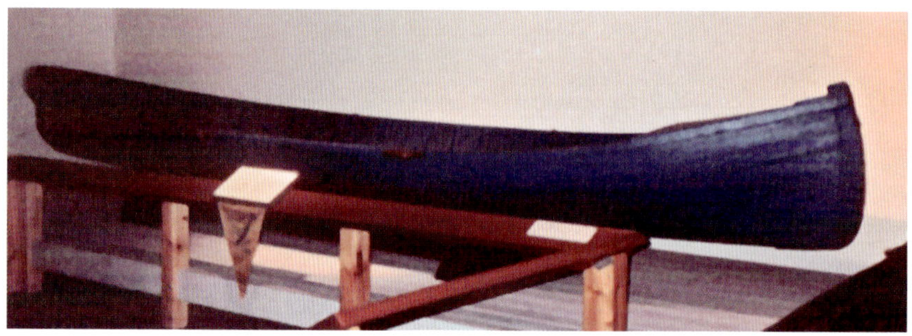

1 Dr. Leroy Wardner, "Seek Builder's Name of Old Guide Boat," *Adirondack Daily Enterprise*, October 9, 1958.
2 Wardner, 1958.

**Figure 2-216** A view of the one-piece, high-tucked transom. The boat's length is 17 feet 4 inches; beam 44 inches (outside); weight 120 pounds. Note the long seat cleats and the storage compartment at the bow. Three pairs of oarlock socket straps are present. Yoke cleats are absent. (Courtesy of Adirondack Museum)

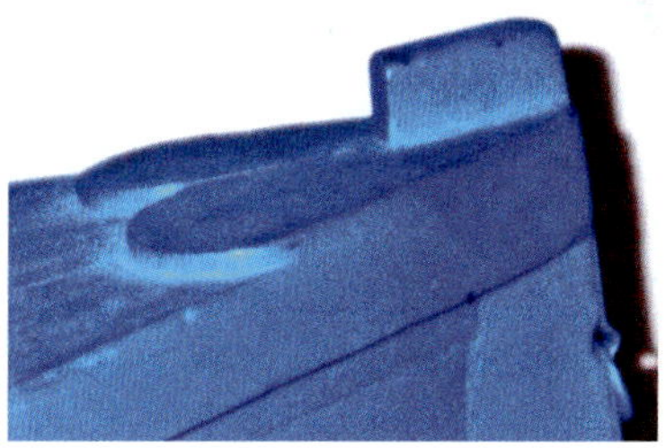

**Figure 2-217** (Above Left) The tall rectangular stem post and heart-shaped deck cap. (Above Center) The storage compartment under the bow deck; the 7-piece slightly cambered deck (probably a replacement), which rests on top of the gunwales; the heart-shaped deck cap; and the upright rectangular stem foot (barely visible). (Above Right) The bow compartment revealing a single pair of scribe ribs inside and the rounded edge of the deck.

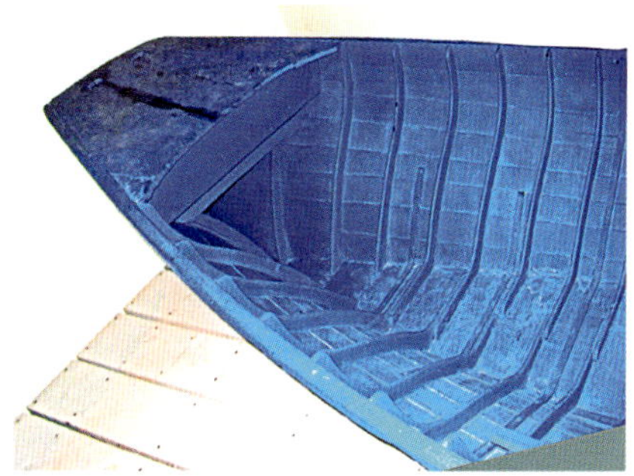

**Figure 2-218** (Top) The ribs at the stern are reverse curved, typical of transom-built guideboats. There was likely a board seat in the stern (before the stern deck was constructed). There is a pair of half-length scribe ribs, followed by two pairs of full-length scribe ribs. The stern-seat cleats have been removed. At the far end of the platform are two rectangular slots, most likely to engage the legs of a back rest. (Bottom) The inside of the hull reveals the clapboard lapstrake construction. The bottom board is wide, about 12 inches.

## ALRIC B. MOODY

**Date of birth:** March 28, 1854 (Saranac Lake, Franklin County)
**Date of death:** 1930 (Tupper Lake, Franklin County)
**Active:** 1880s–1920s
**Location:** Saranac Lake, Canton, St. Lawrence County, and Tupper Lake (Moody)
**Estimate of guideboats built:** More than 50
**Number reviewed:** 5
**Builder's plate:** Not used

### Biographical Sketch

Alric Moody was born in Saranac Lake, son of early settlers Daniel and Polly Moody, and the grandson of Jacob Moody, the first settler.

Alric's uncle, Martin, moved from Saranac Lake to Big Tupper Lake in 1868. After building an inn for sportsmen at the foot of the lake, known as the Tupper Lake House, and then losing it to fire, Martin built and managed a popular hotel, the Mount Morris House, better known as Moody's, at the northeast end of the lake. Eventually a post office was established there, giving the location the official designation of Moody, now considered part of the Town of Tupper Lake.[3]

Alric and his wife, Alfaretta (Etta) Berkeley Moody, had three daughters, Mae, Gertrude, and Bessie, and one son, Otto. By the early 1880s, Moody had achieved regional recognition as a boatbuilder. He had worked in the Saranac Lake boat shop of William Allen Martin, then by 1890 was in Canton working for

3 Donaldson, I:215.

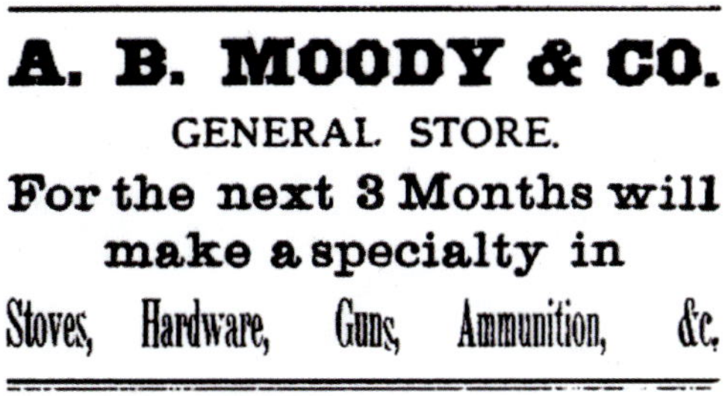


**FIGURE 2-219** A. B. Moody & Company advertisement in the *Adirondack News*, St. Regis Falls, 1896. (Courtesy of Fultonhistory.com)

**FIGURE 2-220** Moody and Anderson decks. (Left) A characteristic Moody two-piece deck with stem post, center cover board, and coaming. The deck pieces are set between the sheer strakes. (Center) An Anderson strip deck with a stem post, center cover board, and coaming. (Right) Rib type and placement for both Moody and Anderson guideboats. At the bow and stern, one pair of scribe ribs beneath the deck and one pair of scribe ribs at, or just inboard of, the deck/sheer-strake junction.

Rushton whose catalogue for 1891 noted:

> Our Saranac boats are built under the direct supervision of Mr. A. B. Moody, formerly of Saranac Lake, whose name is a guarantee of first class model and work.
>
> These boats also have considerable deadrise, and from their speed have been called the *Black Snake of the Wilderness.*[1]

An 1896 advertisement in the St. Regis Falls newspaper notes that one A. B. Moody was operating a general store there. It is possible that this was Alric. Rushton's business had been hurt by the depression of the early 1890s, so Moody may have been obliged to go into the general-store business.

In the late 1890s Moody moved to Tupper Lake and established himself there as a boatbuilder. The federal census for 1900 and the local business directory for 1902 list Alric Moody as a boatbuilder.[2] Around 1905, Moody and Warren J. Slater (newly arrived from Saranac Lake) "founded a boat-building partnership" that lasted many years.[3] During this period, from the early 1900s into the 1920s, Moody also worked as chief guide at Whitney Park, a 68,000-acre private preserve near Long Lake. His obituary in 1930 states that he was "a man of sterling integrity and loyal spirit and one of the pioneers of the sector and for a quarter of a century was in company with the late Warren J. Slater (1849–1921) as builder of Adirondack guide boats at Moody on Big Tupper Lake."[4]

## Guideboat Characteristics

In 1899, Leonard Anderson arrived in Tupper Lake and began to learn the boatbuilding trade from Alric Moody in his shop. By 1902 Anderson was building guideboats on his own. Eventually Anderson set up his own shop in Moody, just south of Tupper Lake. Not surprisingly, Moody and Anderson guideboats are difficult to tell apart.

1 J. H. Rushton, *Catalogue of Canoes, Pleasure, & Hunting Boats*, Canton, NY: 1891:3.
2 *Adirondack Directory*, 1902:157.
3 Source unknown.
4 Obituary, source unknown.

**Figure 2-221** (Left) Moody yoke cleat. (Right) Anderson yoke cleat.

They both used similar deck designs, either two-piece decks placed between the sheer strakes, which Moody favored, or strip-built, which Anderson preferred. Occasionally each man did the opposite: Moody with a strip-built deck and Anderson with a two-piece deck placed between the sheer strakes. Both used the same type and placement of ribs at bow and stern.

The distinctive difference between Moody and Anderson guideboats is the design of their yoke cleats. They are not difficult to tell apart. Moody used a conventional-styled cleat while Anderson's has a rectangular section to the rear of the notch.

Both builder's stem posts are long, low, and rectangular. Moody's stem post has a vertical back and angled front, while Anderson's has a rounded notch at the back, and is vertical at the front. If no stem post is present on a strip-built deck model, the builder was Anderson.

A smooth-skin lapstrake cedar canoe built by Moody is on display in the Charles Dickert Wildlife Collection at the Saranac Lake Free Library.[5] It is characterized by a relatively long, low, rectangular stem post, a two-piece deck, placed between the sheer strakes, with a center cover board and narrow coaming, a rectangular stem-foot end, flat steam-bent ribs with copper rivets, and eight strakes to a side.

Five guideboats and several canoes examined at Whitney Park were found to have characteristics similar to those of the canoe. Moody's close association with Whitney Park and its superintendent, Ernest H. Johnson (his uncle), supports the conclusion that these five guideboats were likely built by Moody.

5 Edmund A. Guggenheim, *Agreement with the Saranac Lake Free Library concerning the Charles Dickert Collection of Mounted Wild Life*, Saranac Lake Free Library, 1967.

## Field Notes

**Stems:** Tumblehome (Saranac profile).

**Ribs:** No reverse-curved ribs. The rib feet are beveled and do not extend all the way across the bottom board.

**Hull:** Number of strakes on each side: 7; feather-lap construction.

**Figure 2-222** (Left) Moody stem post with a straight back end. (Right) Anderson stem post with a rounded rear notch.

**Figure 2-223** The cedar canoe built by Alric Moody. The deck is two-piece, set between the sheer strakes, with a center cover strip and narrow coaming. The stem post is long, low, and rectangular. Note the flat steam-bent rib secured with copper rivets. (Courtesy of Charles Dickert Wildlife Collection, Saranac Lake Free Library)

**Figure 2-224** Ralph R. Morrow.

**Figure 2-225** Morrow builder's plate. The boat number is stamped on the plate.

## RALPH R. MORROW

**Date of birth:** November 25, 1923
**Date of death:** July 31, 2007
(Saranac Lake, Franklin County, Pine Ridge Cemetery)
**Active:** 1970–2007
**Location:** Saranac Lake
**Estimate of guideboats built:** 67
**Number reviewed:** 4
**Builder's plate:** Used
**Adirondack Museum accession:** 2012.080.1

### Biographical Sketch

Ralph R. Morrow, a resident of Saranac Lake for most of his life, was the son of Raymond, a carpenter by trade, and Lena (Barber) Morrow. He married Cecil L. Barber on April 14, 1943.

Morrow was a combat veteran of World War II, having served in the Headquarters Company, 2nd Battalion, 3rd Infantry Division. After his military service he worked at Crescent Bay Marina in Saranac Lake, repairing wooden boats. He then went to work for Carl Hathaway, boatbuilder and restorer, from whom he learned to build guideboats. In 1970 he set up his own shop in Saranac Lake.[1]

Ralph Morrow was a quiet, "no nonsense" man who worked alone; an independent thinker whose language could be "as salty as a cussed sailor's."[2] Morrow, Carl Hathaway, and Edward

1 Ralph Morrow, *Personal communication*, 2005.
2 "Practitioners of Tradition," *Watertown Daily Times*, September 19, 2004.

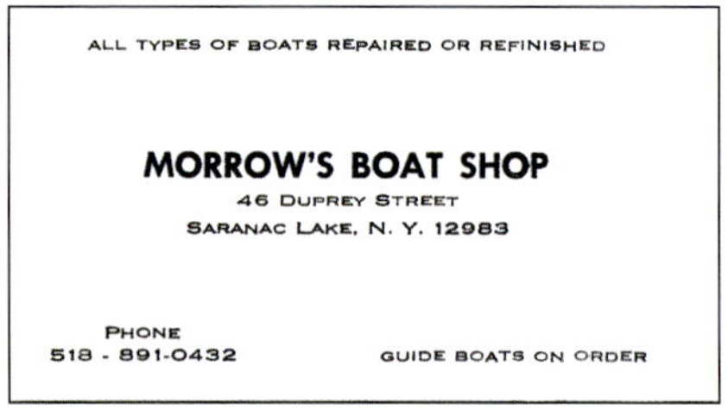
ALL TYPES OF BOATS REPAIRED OR REFINISHED

**MORROW'S BOAT SHOP**
46 DUPREY STREET
SARANAC LAKE, N. Y. 12983

PHONE
518 - 891-0432

GUIDE BOATS ON ORDER

**FIGURE 2-226** Ralph Morrow's trade card.

Marshall are due great credit for their work in passing on the craft of building traditional guideboats. They did this in a hands-on course they taught during the 1980s through North Country Community College. In 1999 Morrow was featured in an article in *USA Today*—part of a series on "Vanishing America." In September 2004, he received the North Country Heritage Award "for mastery of and creative commitment to local traditions, customs, and arts, and for dedication to community and to the teaching of others."[3]

## Guideboat Characteristics

Morrow's stem, where the gunwales overlap, is wide, in the Long Lake style. His stem posts are narrow, cut down to that width from the wider upper stem. His decks are two-piece, let into the gunwales; his center cover boards are tapered and butt to the stem post. This deck design is similar to that of the Brown's Tract builders—the guideboats that he apparently liked the best. Morrow also built a few boats with strip decks and a center cover board that surrounds the stem post.

## Field Notes

**Stems:** Tumblehome (Saranac profile).

**Ribs:** Two pairs of ribs beneath the bow deck; one pair of ribs beneath the stern deck; rib feet extend all the way across the bottom board. No scribe ribs.

**Hull:** Number of strakes on each side: 8; feather-lap construction.

**Gunwales:** Do not extend to the front of the stem.

**FIGURE 2-227** (Right) Morrow's stem posts were narrow, cut down from the wider upper portion of the stem (similar to those of Reuben Cary and Wallace Emerson). (Above) The front end of the center cover board rests on the shoulders of the wide portion of the stem. Note the strip deck.

**FIGURE 2-228** Morrow's typical Brown's Tract style deck design. (Left) A two-piece deck with coaming and a tapered center cover board whose forward end butts to the stem post. The deck pieces are let into the gunwales. (Right) The forward ends of the deck rest on the wide portion of the stem. The tapered center cover board butts to the stem post.

3 North Country Heritage Award, Traditional Arts of Upstate New York, Canton, New York, 2004.

FIGURE 2-229 Myron A. Nickerson. (Courtesy of St. Lawrence County Historical Association)

FIGURE 2-230 Nickerson builder's plate, located on the center cover board.

## MYRON AUGUSTUS NICKERSON

**Date of birth:** May 22, 1843 (Canton, St. Lawrence County)
**Date of death:** September 29, 1928 (Canton)
**Active:** With Isaac Hurst 1890–1895; independent 1896 ~ 1907
**Location:** Canton
**Estimate of guideboats built:** More than 75
**Number reviewed:** 15
**Builder's plate:** 1
**Adirondack Museum accession:** 76.97.1

### Biographical Sketch

Myron Augustus Nickerson, one of eight children, was the son of Anson Nickerson (1805–1880) who, as a youth, had come to Canton from Cape Cod, Massachusetts. Born in a log dwelling on his father's farm south of the village, Myron took up farming in his early years. On February 2, 1869, he married Harriet P. Barber. The Nickersons had one child, Zona, who married Canton optometrist W. A. MacPhee. The MacPhees had one son, Dr. Halsey Myron MacPhee, who is the source of some of the biographical information about his grandfather included below.[1]

When he was forty-three Nickerson went to work for J. H. Rushton where he learned the boatbuilding trade.[2] According to Atwood Manley, author of *Rushton and His Times in American Canoeing*:

> The Rushton workman to make the greatest success was Nickerson, the Canton farm boy. Tall, quiet, and easy-going, Myron Nickerson had an intuitive knack with tools. He became well established as a maker of fine craft.[3]

In 1890 Nickerson and coworker Isaac

1 Atwood Manley, *Letter to David W. Johnson,* July 16, 1975, Manley Collection.
2 Gilborn, 1972:1.
3 Atwood Manley, *Boat Shop Craftsmen Carry on the Rushton Tradition,* Unpublished typescript, 1975, Manley Collection.

Hurst left the Rushton shop to begin their own boatbuilding enterprise. Five years later the partnership ended, with each man setting up his own shop in Canton.

Rushton's biographer, Atwood Manley, describes a first-hand experience with one of Nickerson's guideboat-constructed canoes, named *Allegra:*

> Myron Nickerson obviously knew canoes . . . and built them with the greatest of skill. . . . the most interesting, . . .the canoe *Allegra*, . . . is neither fish nor fowl—part guide boat and part smoothskin canoe. With its high, pronounced stems at either end, it looks [in profile] like one of Leif Erikson's Viking ships. . . . it looks also very much like quite a tippish canoe. It rides high in the water, seems narrow at midship, and the two high upswing stems would seem easy prey for wind and waves. Not so!
> At the invitation of George Bowditch, Curator of the Adirondack Museum, the writer [Atwood Manley] took the bow seat in this canoe while at the Antique Boat Show at Clayton, New York in 1972. We were both wielding double-bladed paddles as we struck out for the open waters of Clayton's waterfront. That narrow, rather high-sided smooth skin slipped through those choppy waves and over the surface with the ease and seaworthiness of a gull. That brief paddle off shore was all pure joy.[4]

Also, from his conversation with Halsey MacPhee, Atwood Manley wrote:

> Halsey did tell me that as a small lad he saw his grandfather load the rack on top of a heavy lumber-type wagon with four, six or eight craft he had built during the winter, and behind the team of horses set forth up into the Adirondacks to either sell or rent the craft by the season. I was also informed that Myron was an easy-going man who trusted his friends and customers too generously; that he only made brief memo slips of his transactions, especially the craft made and then rented out here and there during the season. When Myron died it is said that his desk was profuse with these little memo slips, many of which only noted something like this: "One canoe to man on Trout Lake." Result: his estate was unable to appraise or collect on quite a large number of rental craft. Myron seems to have been more interested in building a fine craft than in making money. He had an exemplary reputation locally.[5]

## Guideboat Characteristics

Nickerson's guideboats are similar to Hurst's, his former partner. Both built only strip-deck models, and they both used a decorative deck beam with four concave arcs, and a shield-shaped plate surrounding a flagstaff socket on the forward part of the center cover board. Other than the presence of a builder's plate (many of Nickerson's boats are without them) or a metal stem-post cap (observed only in Hurst guideboats), here are ways to tell them apart:

- No scribe ribs. A pair of scribe ribs under the deck is most consistent with a Hurst guideboat. Nickerson used footed ribs beneath the decks; in fact, he may have been the only builder to have placed four pairs of footed ribs beneath the bow deck.
- The Nickerson stem post is lower and longer than that of Hurst.
- V-grooved strip decks (typical of Rushton) were observed only in Nickerson boats.
- Nickerson's guideboats may have seven or eight strakes; Hurst's have only seven.

4 Manley, *Boat Shop Craftsmen,* 1975.
5 Manley, *Letter to Johnson,* 1975.

**Figure 2-231** The Nickerson boathouse and shop, circa 1894, showing a mix of canoes, guideboats, and skiffs. Nickerson is seated in the canoe on the right. Some of the canoes have protective carpet on the floors. (Courtesy of Adirondack Museum)

## Field Notes

**Stems:** Tumblehome (Saranac profile). The horizontal width of the stem from the leading edge of the stem to the rabbet line: upper (below the gunwale) 2¼ to 2½ inches; lower (greatest width) 3½ to 4¼ inches. Double stems are common. The stem foot is a horizontal rectangle.

**Ribs:** No reverse-curved ribs. Scribe ribs are rare. There may be up to four pairs of footed ribs under the bow deck and as many as three under the stern deck. Rib spacing is about 4½ inches on center. Rib feet ends are beveled and extend all the way across the bottom board.

**Hull:** Number of strakes on each side: 7 or 8; feather-lap construction.

**Gunwales:** Extend to stem fronts. They often have a rounded upper edge or are D-shaped, are tapered at the bow and stern, and may be secured with round-head brass screws.

**Yoke cleats:** The tips of the rounded notch are pointed.

**Heel plates:** Three-piece with rounded lateral ends.

FIGURE 2-232 (Left) Nickerson strip deck with center cover board and coaming; it is not V-grooved. Note the shield-shaped plate. (Right) A V-grooved Rushton-style strip deck was sometimes used by Nickerson.

FIGURE 2-233 This Nickerson stem post is narrow and rectangular, with length about 2½ inches and width about ⅜ inch.

FIGURE 2-234 Nickerson's distinctive decorative deck beam with four concave arcs similar to that used by Isaac Hurst.

**FIGURE 2-235** Rib type and placement beneath the bow and stern decks. Nickerson rarely used scribe ribs. (Left) Four pairs of footed ribs beneath the bow deck. (Center) Three pairs of footed ribs beneath the stern deck. This number, type, and placement of ribs beneath the bow and stern decks was commonly used by Nickerson. (Right) This Nickerson guideboat has only one pair of footed ribs beneath the deck. The presence of a double stem is indicated by the screws joining the inner and outer stems.

**FIGURE 2-236** The sharply pointed tips of the yoke-cleat notch.

**FIGURE 2-237** The *Allegra*. (Courtesy of Adirondack Museum)

## Old Forge Guideboat Builders and Companies

Old Forge was the location of a number of businesses associated with Theodore Seeber, and Riley Parsons and his two sons, Ben and Ira. Their biographies have been grouped together, followed by their boatbuilding enterprises.

**THEODORE SEEBER**

**RILEY R. PARSONS**

**IRA H. PARSONS**

**RAYMOND BENJAMIN PARSONS**

**Businesses**

**Seeber & Parsons (1890–1895)**

**Theodore Seeber (1896–1902)**

**Old Forge Boat Company (1903–1909)**

**Parsons & Company (Riley, Ira, and Ben Parsons) (1896–1905)**

**Parsons & Roberts (John E. Roberts) (1906–1910)**

**Parsons Brothers (1911–1945)**

**FIGURE 2-238** Theodore Seeber, 1889. Photograph by A. B. Gardner, Utica, New York. (Courtesy of Town of Webb Historical Association)

## THEODORE SEEBER

**Date of birth:** 1848 (Germany)
**Date of death:** January 4, 1910 (Old Forge, Herkimer County, Boonville Cemetery, Oneida County)
**Active:** 1880–1909
**Location:** Old Forge

### Biographical Sketch

Theodore Seeber was born in Germany in 1848. When he was three years old, his parents came to the United States and settled in Utica, New York. (The German spelling of his name—Sieber—was anglicized by him to Seeber.) In 1875, newly married to Esther (Etta) C. Griffin of Remsen, he moved to Boonville.

In 1881, at the age of thirty-three, he began work in the boat shop of H. D. Grant. He had already become an accomplished mechanic, carpenter, and boatbuilder before joining Grant. In 1880, he had built a small steamboat that he named after his wife.[1] According to his obituary in the *Boonville Herald*, Seeber is said to have built the first Adirondack guideboat in Boonville, prior to working for Grant.[2] In the winter of 1882–1883, a small "steam yacht," *Hunter*, was built in the Boonville shop for Dwight Grant's brother-in-law, Jonathan Meeker. Originally built for use on the Black River, the *Hunter* became, in 1885, the first steamboat on the Fulton Chain of Lakes. In a sworn deposition on March 6, 1896, Seeber told of bringing the *Hunter* to the Fulton Chain:

> I brought to the Fulton Chain 11 years ago a small steamer, the *Hunter*, capacity 10 persons, cost here $900,

1 *Theodore Seeber Deposition*, March 6, 1896.
2 "With Those Who Mourn," *Boonville Herald*, January 6, 1910.

> which was drawn on sleighs from Boonville to Minnehaha and there launched. It took us then two days to navigate the boat up the Moose River to Old Forge, a run of eight miles. The *Hunter* was run for six seasons and then sunk, being not worth repairing.[3]

The second steamboat on the Fulton Chain was the *Etta S.,* which Seeber had built and named for his wife in about 1880. Again, on March 6, he recounted the event:

> In 1887 the *Eddie* [*Etta*] *S.*, capacity 15 persons, cost about $600, which was built by me at Boonville [in about 1880 for use on the Black River and the Black River Canal], was brought in [to Old Forge and the Fulton Chain]. It was run for two years, then I sold her to outside parties.[4]

In the summer of 1888, the steamer *Fulton*, "a far tidier craft than the five-year-old *Hunter,*"[5] was built by Seeber and launched into Old Forge Lake [now Old Forge Pond]. According to Seeber's March 6, testimony:

> About eight years ago I built the *Fulton*, 80 persons capacity, a cabin boat, cost $2,100, for the well-known Jack Shephard, which boat has been run ever since.[6]

The *Boonville Herald* of June 14, 1888, recorded:

> The finishing touches to the new Fulton Chain steamer *Fulton* of which Captain Jack Shephard is the owner, are now being made by the skillful artisan, Theodore Seeber.[7]

In the winter of 1888–1889, on the State Fish Hatchery grounds below the Old Forge dam, Seeber, assisted by Abe Platt, built the steamboat *Fawn* with a capacity of 50 persons. William S. deCamp, an influential Brown's Tract landowner, had contracted with Seeber to build the boat and helped him to select appropriate engines and boiler. The *Fawn* was launched early in April and used to transport passengers from Minnehaha, eight miles upstream on the Moose River, to within one mile of Old Forge. The *Fawn:*

> . . . was a double-decked side wheeler with ample deck space for passengers, freight and baggage. Its two wheels were independently reversible. Either could revolve in a forward direction as the other back paddled, thus permitting the vessel to accomplish a quick, pivotal turn as a means of avoiding obstructions suddenly encountered in the river.[8]

Beginning in 1885, various building endeavors had obliged Seeber to spend a lot of time in Old Forge.[9] He built a home there and, in 1889, leaving the employ of Grant, moved north. In 1890, with his fellow Grant worker, Riley Parsons, he formed a boatbuilding partnership.

Theodore Seeber was a respected member of the Old Forge Community. In 1898 he completed the building of St. Bartholomew's Catholic Church, and in 1907 was chosen as the chief engineer of the volunteer Fire Department, the year it was organized.[10] He became ill in the summer of 1909, and on January 4, 1910, he died of stomach cancer at age sixty-two.[11]

3 Seeber, 1896.
4 Seeber, 1896.
5 Grady, 1933:225.
6 Seeber, 1896.
7 "Adirondack Echoes," *Boonville Herald*, June 14, 1888.
8 Grady, 1933:235.
9 Seeber, 1896.
10 Helen Kennerknecht, *Letter to the Town of Webb Historical Association,* August 7, 1988.
11 *Boonville Herald*, January 6, 1910.

**FIGURE 2-239** The Seeber-built steamboat *Fawn* at Little Rapids, Minnehaha, on the Moose River, circa 1890 Photograph (detail) by A. M. Church, Boonville, NY. (Courtesy of Edward Comstock, Jr.)

## RILEY R. PARSONS

**FIGURE 2-240** Riley R. Parsons. Saturday Globe, Utica, NY, September 24, 1904.

**Date of birth:** May 4, 1839 (Leyden, Lewis County)
**Date of death:** September 17, 1904 (Old Forge, Herkimer County)
**Active:** Early 1880s–1904
**Location:** Old Forge

### Biographical Sketch

Riley R. Parsons was born in Leyden, Lewis County, in 1839. Leyden is five miles from Boonville. He became an experienced woodsman, carpenter, builder, and musician. In 1858, he married Abbie A. Thayer of Leyden. They had four children: Ira H., Ella, Jane, and R. Benjamin.

While residents of Leyden, Riley and his brother Edward became noted for their violin playing:

> Two musically gifted brothers in the party, Ed and Riley Parsons, of Leyden, had brought their violins, and the artistic William [signer of the hotel register for the group] recorded the fact by writing the word "fiddles" after their names. Each day's outing in the woods and on the lakes came to a nightly climax in the hotel parlor with the Parsons brothers tuning their instruments and swinging into lively accompaniments for the Schottische, Money Musk and Virginia Reel as the entire company joined in rhythmic execution of the steps.[1]

In the early 1880s, Riley moved his family to Boonville and, by May 1882, had completed the construction of a home there.[2] During the 1880s he worked in the Boonville boat shop of Dwight Grant,[3] while continuing to maintain his own shop advertised as "Riley Parsons, Carpenter and Builder, Shop at Red Mill Below Depot."[4] In the local directory for 1888–1889, the entry for Parsons lists "Sash, doors, blinds, also contractor and builder, 120 Schuyler. . . ."[5]

In 1890, he moved with his family to Old Forge and established a boatbuilding partnership with Theodore Seeber, a coworker from the Grant shop. In October 1890, Parsons:

> . . . had one of his limbs badly injured while working at the mill at Old Forge. He was skidding logs and one of them caught his leg, bruising it quite badly so he is unable to get around. His son Ira went to Old Forge Tuesday to look after him.[6]

The partnership dissolved in 1895, and in 1896 he formed Parsons & Company with his sons, Ben and Ira. In 1903 they partnered with John E. Roberts to form Parsons & Roberts. Parsons died September 17, 1904 and is buried in the Boonville cemetery.[7]

1 Grady, 1933:170–171.
2 "Echoes from the Adirondacks," *Boonville Herald*, May 18, 1882.
3 Grant, 1959.
4 Riley Parsons, Billhead, July 17, 1889, TWHA.
5 *General and Business Directory of Boonville*, Lyons, NY: Globe Directory Publishing, 1888:126.
6 "Adirondack Echoes," *Boonville Herald*, October 30, 1890.
7 "The Late Riley R. Parsons," *Saturday Globe*, Herkimer Edition, September 24,1904.

**Figure 2-241** Ira H. Parsons. (Courtesy of Edward Comstock, Jr.)

## IRA H. PARSONS

**Date of birth:** December 1, 1860 (Leyden, Lewis County)
**Date of death:** Unknown
**Active:** 1892–1945
**Location:** Old Forge, Herkimer County

### Biographical Sketch

Ira H. Parsons was born on December 1, 1860, the elder son of Riley and Abbie Parsons. On July 9, 1887, he married Carrie Florilla Warren of Martinsburg, Lewis County. The couple went by buckboard and boat to Cedar Island in the Fourth Lake of the Fulton Chain to spend their honeymoon and remained until early winter. They returned over the frozen lake on a handmade sled, and after brief respite at the Forge House, proceeded to make their way to Boonville. Four years later, in 1892, they returned to Old Forge and built the sixth house in that rapidly growing community.[1]

In 1892 Ira went to work for the Seeber & Parsons boat shop, of which his father was co-owner. Ira's younger brother, Ben, had already begun to work there in 1890. Ira continued boatbuilding until the 1940s under the sequential business names of: Seeber & Parsons, Parsons & Company, Parsons & Roberts, and Parsons Brothers. Ira Parsons was also for many years a member of the Adirondack Guides' Association. He is listed as a guide in New York's *Annual Report of the Forest Commission for the Year 1893*, and the *New York State Registry of Guides* for 1927.[2] At age eighty-one he was active as a boatbuilder and remained a guide and caretaker for the A. W. Soper family camp on First Lake, as he had been for forty-one years.

1 "Couple Who Built Sixth House Here, Wed 54 Years," *Adirondack Arrow*, Old Forge, July 1942.
2 *Forest Commission*, 1894, I:366; *Registry of Guides*, 1927, 1942.

## RAYMOND BENJAMIN PARSONS

**Date of birth:** June 23, 1868 (Leyden, Lewis County)
**Date of death:** March 11, 1945 (Old Forge, Boonville Cemetery)
**Active:** 1895–1945
**Location:** Old Forge, Herkimer County

FIGURE 2-242 Raymond Benjamin Parsons, 1944. (Courtesy of Town of Webb Historical Association)

### Biographical Sketch

Raymond Benjamin (Ben) Parsons was born in Leyden, Lewis County, on June 23, 1868, the younger son of Riley and Abbie Parsons. In 1872, his parents moved to Boonville where he attended school. In 1884 he settled in the Fulton Chain area. In 1890 he went to work for the newly established boat shop of Seeber & Parsons, of which his father was co-owner. Like his older brother Ira, Ben was a woodsman and guide and was a caretaker at one of the Adirondack League Club's camps on Little Moose Lake for more than thirty years. He was an active member of the Brown's Tract Guides' Association and was listed as a professional guide in New York's *Annual Report of the Forest Commission for the Year 1893*, and the *New York State Registry of Guides* for 1927 and 1942.[1]

On November 12, 1895, he married Mabel M. Thomas in Atlanta, Georgia. They had two sons, F. Waynard and Riley B., and one daughter, Jane Ann.[2]

A 1924 newspaper article, "One Contented Man," describes Ben Parsons's character and philosophy:

> In the heart of the Adirondack forest there is a man who might be said to have found . . . the meaning of peace—real peace. The winter finds him at his beloved trade, making graceful gliding craft, with which no artist can find fault. . . . In the summer he acts as guide and cares for a gentleman's camp. . . . He loves all living things and never kills anything. He guides others

1 *Forest Commission*, 1894, I:366; *Registry of Guides*, 1927, 1942.
2 "Adirondack Boat Builder," Unsourced newspaper clipping, March 1945, TWHA.

to hunt and fish, but for himself he lives and lets live. . . .

He is a quiet man—a good listener—and thus he has learned much. . . . He needs no excitement to buoy up his spirits. A glorious sunset or a perfect day, even a group of people whom he has served—these are the things that count for him. . . .

To go through life, everything you do must be within reason. When you work for anybody do your very best. . . . When you have done this you will have the satisfaction. . . .

When you think you are about to lose your temper, sum up courage and when you cool off, you will realize that you have been better for it.

Don't cheat a man out of anything, even tho it is an easy thing to do, for there is no satisfaction like knowing that you can withstand temptation. A clear conscience makes you grow old with better grace, and you have nothing on which to look back with regret.

Make the best boat you can while making it, even if it takes a day longer,

And if one wants to learn something of contentment and things worthwhile, seek out Ben Parsons, guide-boatman of Old Forge, New York.[3]

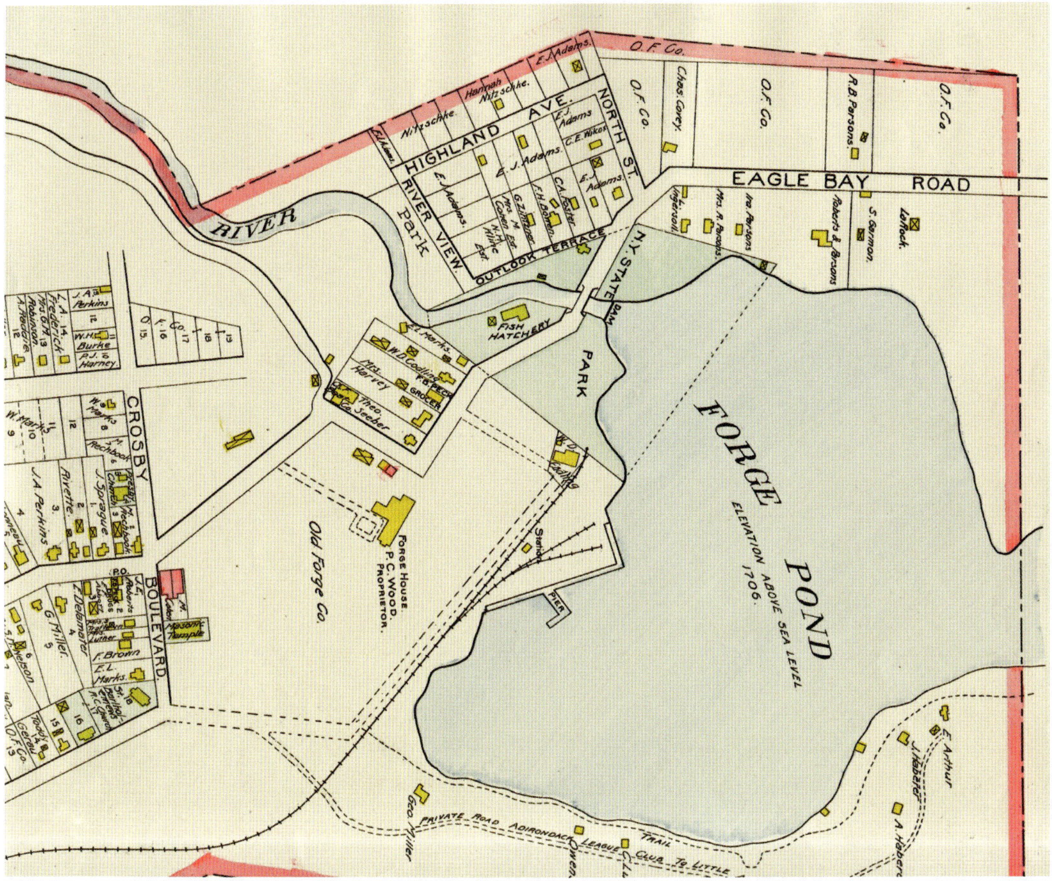


**FIGURE 2-243** Map showing the Parsons & Roberts boat shop, and the residences of Mrs. Riley Parsons, and those of her sons, Ben and Ira, on the Eagle Bay Road. It also shows Theodore Seeber's house and the Old Forge Boat Company shop close by the Forge House. Century Map Publishing Company, 1906. (Courtesy of Adirondack Museum)

3 "One Contented Man," Unsourced newspaper clipping, November 16, 1924, TWHA.

## SEEBER & PARSONS

**Partnership formed:** 1890–1895
**Location:** Old Forge, Herkimer County
**Estimate of guideboats built:** 60
**Number reviewed:** 5
**Builder's plate:** 2

FIGURE 2-244 Seeber & Parsons builder's plate.

### Business Profile

In 1890, Theodore Seeber and Riley Parsons left Boonville and the employ of Dwight Grant and formed a partnership. Old Forge, on the Fulton Chain of Lakes, had become a popular sporting and vacation center, with a number of new camps being built, and the demand for guideboats was increasing.

Riley's younger son, Ben, soon joined the boat shop, which was initially located in a third-floor mill loft near the middle branch of the Moose River. The success of the venture led them to build, in 1892, a two-story shop north of the Old Forge Dam.[1] The *Boonville Herald* for May 12, 1892, reported: "Seeber & Parsons are doing quite an extensive boat business this season at Old Forge."[2] In 1892 Ira Parsons, Riley's elder son, having returned to Old Forge with his family, also went to work at the shop. In 1894, Seeber & Parsons assisted in the building of the steamer *Stowell*. Its capacity of 150 was a sign of the increasing tourist traffic and the demand for camps on the Fulton Chain.[3]

The partnership dissolved in 1895. By the following year Theodore Seeber and the Parsonses had set up independent shops in Old Forge.

1 Grady, 1933:215.
2 [Seeber & Parsons], *Boonville Herald*, May 12, 1892.
3 Seeber, 1896.

**Figure 2-245** The Old Forge boat shop of Seeber & Parsons, circa 1890. Riley Parsons is in the left foreground. (Courtesy of Edward Comstock, Jr.)

## Guideboat Characteristics

Seeber and Parsons brought with them from Boonville a copy of the Grant modified-bevel plane as well as the Grant rib and stem patterns. Like Grant, they made their decks two-piece, let into the gunwales, with a wide coaming, and a tapered center cover board butting up to a brass-capped stem post, essentially replicating the Grant boat.

Many of Grant's design elements were retained: the stern-seat backrests steam-bent from one piece and joined by a lower rail, the limber holes, the molded seat cleats, and the distinctively shaped seat frames—all shown and described in the entry on Grant. The Grant stem bands and oarlock socket straps, supplied by the M. E. Blasier Manufacturing Company of Utica, were also used by Seeber & Parsons. Originally their stems followed Grant in being slightly tumblehome. Over time, however, they made several changes.

In the Seeber & Parsons boats after 1891, the stems were raked outward, which became the signature Brown's Tract profile, as described by Lewis Grant:

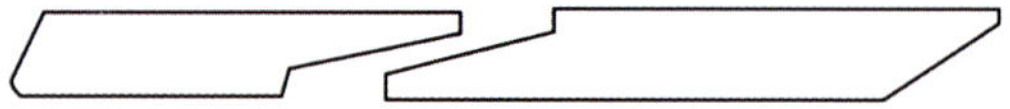

**Figure 2-245** A schematic drawing of a cross section of the Grant modified-beveled lap used by Seeber & Parsons beginning in 1890.

> They [Theodore Seeber and Riley Parsons] both worked for Father building guideboats, before leaving Boonville to make their home in Old Forge in 1890. They got the rib shapes from one of Father's boats. They also put the tip of the stems out an inch or a little more than father's last model, so they would not look just like the Grant guide-boat. I just repaired a very old Seeber and Parsons guideboat and father's first rib patterns fit that boat. . . .[4]

Initially, in 1890–1891, the design, number, and placement of ribs under the bow and stern decks were also similar to those of Grant—two pairs of reverse-curved scribe ribs ending at the bottom board. After 1891, Seeber and Parsons placed three pairs of scribe ribs beneath the bow and stern decks. The first pair, with pointed lower ends, end just above the stem foot. The second pair, usually with pointed lower ends, end at the bottom

**Figure 2-246** A Seeber & Parsons deck, center cover board, coaming, brass stem-post cap, and builder's plate. The deck is two-piece, with a wide coaming. The seam is covered by a tapered center cover board that butts to the stem post. The deck is let into the gunwales.

board. The third pair have the lower ends cut square at the bottom board. Shorter guideboats (12–13 feet) may have fewer scribe ribs under the decks and their rib ends may not be pointed.

Seeber & Parsons used thin nickel-plated brass caps secured with two screws. They were not let in to the stem fronts as were the thicker caps covering Grant's stem posts.

Without a builder's plate it is difficult

4 Grant, 1959.

**FIGURE 2-247** The Seeber & Parsons boat shop, circa 1892. Left to right: Ira Parsons, Len Ingersoll, Theodore Seeber (seen over the raised guideboat), Riley Parsons (in the foreground), and Ben Parsons. The two guideboats in the foreground were evidently built during the partnership's early period (1890–1891), before they had settled on a final model, since they have only two pairs of ribs beneath the decks—one scribe and one footed. The raised guideboat in the center is in the process of being planked. The label in the upper left reads: "Harold D. Ross, Photo Artist, Old Forge, N.Y." (Courtesy of Adirondack Museum)

to tell the difference between a Seeber & Parsons guideboat and one built by any of the subsequent Parsons companies; they all used patterns and construction methods similar to those in the final Seeber & Parsons model, built after 1891.

For a description of the seats, seat cleats, yoke cleats, yokes, and stern-seat backrests, used by Seeber & Parsons, refer to these components in the entry on Grant, whose patterns they copied.

The boats are numbered sequentially from 1 to about 60, with no year stamped.

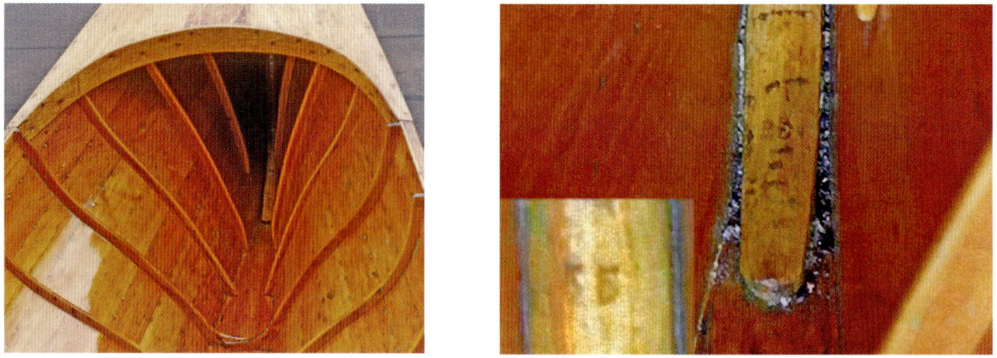

**FIGURE 2-249** (Left) The number, type, and placement of ribs in the final Seeber & Parsons model. (Right) Difficult to make out on the upper portion of the stem foot but shown in the inset at the lower left is the number 35. Seeber & Parsons guideboats were sequentially stamped irrespective of year. This is the thirty-fifth guideboat built since the partnership began in 1890. The relatively flat stem-foot end is typical of Seeber & Parsons guideboats.

**FIGURE 2-248** (Left) A Seeber & Parsons guideboat from 1890–1891, with a slight tumblehome profile. (Right) By 1891–1892, their guideboats had an outward rake.

**FIGURE 2-250** (Above) A Seeber & Parsons stem post and stem-post cap. (Right) A screw, a limber hole, and a screw (three holes) in the deck portion of the stem-post cap.

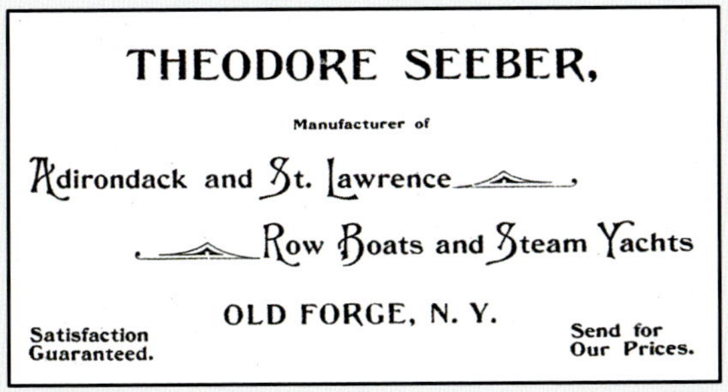

THEODORE SEEBER,

Manufacturer of

Adirondack and St. Lawrence

Row Boats and Steam Yachts

OLD FORGE, N. Y.

Satisfaction Guaranteed.

Send for Our Prices.

**FIGURE 2-251** Theodore Seeber trade card. (Courtesy of Edward Comstock, Jr.)

## THEODORE SEEBER

**Formed:** 1896
**Active:** 1896–1902
**Location:** Old Forge, Herkimer County
**Estimate of guideboats built:** Unknown
**Number reviewed:** 1
**Builder's plate:** Not used

### Business Profile

In 1896, Seeber sold his interest in Seeber & Parsons to his partner, which became Parsons & Company, and set up his own boat shop. A billhead dated November 26, 1896, indicates this.

On March 18, 1896, the *Boonville Herald* reported: "Parsons & Co. have their fourteenth boat nearly completed. . . . Seeber's boatshop is finishing the tenth boat."[1]

Five years later in February 1901:

> The two boat building shops in this place [Old Forge] are doing a more extensive business than ever before. Parsons & Co. have been putting in considerable new and expensive machinery and expect to begin building at once. Theodore Seeber has already built several boats and is now completing a handsome launch for a Mr. Clark of Connecticut. This is the first launch ever built in Old Forge. It is 22 feet long and five and one half feet beam and will be run by a five horse power gasoline engine. The hull is of pine, the deck and finishing of cherry in the natural wood. Mr. Seeber is also building a 20 foot rowboat for J. L. Connell of Philadelphia, Pa.[2]

The period between 1896 and 1902 was an active one for Seeber in the building of steamboats, launches, and St. Lawrence rowboats.

1 [Parsons & Company], *Boonville Herald*, March 18, 1896.
2 "Personal Items: Old Forge: First Launch Ever Built in the Place," *Boonville Herald*, February 28, 1901.

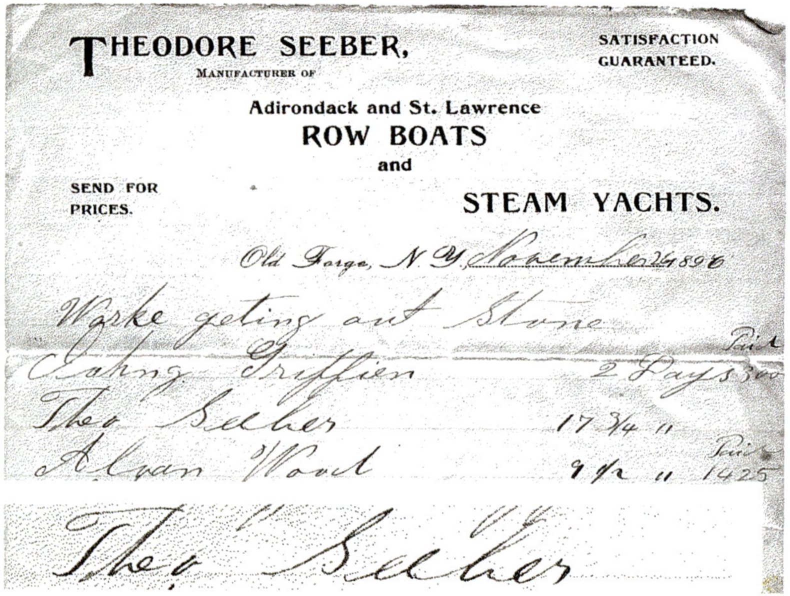
THEODORE SEEBER,
MANUFACTURER OF
Adirondack and St. Lawrence
ROW BOATS
and
STEAM YACHTS.
SATISFACTION GUARANTEED.
SEND FOR PRICES.
Old Forge, N. Y. November 26 1896
Worke geting out Stone
Cahng Griffien 2 Days 3.00 Paid
Theo Seeber 17 3/4 "
Alvan Wood 9 1/2 " 14.25 Paid
Theo Seeber

**FIGURE 2-252** The Seeber billhead for "Worke geting out stone," dated November 26, 1896. (Courtesy Town of Webb Historical Association)

## Guideboat Characteristics

One of the first boats of guideboat construction built by Seeber upon leaving the Seeber & Parsons partnership in 1895 was the *Resaca*, commissioned by former President (1889–1893) Benjamin Harrison. In October of 1895 Harrison purchased a thirty-seven-acre peninsula of land on the south shore between First and Second Lakes of the Fulton Chain. Here he built a camp, which in honor of his ancestral Virginia plantation he named Berkeley Lodge. David Beetle, author of *Up Old Forge Way*, recounting memories of Horace deCamp, then the owner of the camp, wrote:

> He [deCamp] thinks of the President as an austere, bearded gentleman who used to go fishing in the Executive Flagship, *Resaca*, a rowboat with an American flag in the stern. Harrison's other boats were *Elsa* [now in the collection of the Town of Webb Historical Association in Old Forge] and *Lohengrin*. . . .[3]

*Resaca*, purchased in 1896, was named for the Battle of Resaca, fought during the Civil War's Atlanta campaign—Harrison's first real test as a troop commander. The boat is 18 feet long with a beam of 44 ½ inches. Due to its size and weight, Harrison's rowboat, though of guideboat construction, was not meant to be carried by one person and so has no yoke cleats. It may be referred to as a family, or church, boat.

The basic characteristics of Seeber's guideboats are the same as the Seeber & Parsons boats, with the following differences: Seeber placed two scribe ribs, or one scribe and one footed pair of ribs, beneath the bow and stern decks (similar to Grant). This rib placement was continued by the Old Forge Boat Company.

Seeber's boats are numbered serially; number and year, starting with 1 each year from 1896 to 1902.

By April 1903, Seeber had completed a two-and-a-half-story, well-equipped boat shop behind his house for his new enterprise, the Old Forge Boat Company.[4]

3 David Beetle, *Up Old Forge Way*, Utica, NY: *Utica Observer-Dispatch*, 1948:92.
4 "Old Forge," *[Boonville Herald]*, undated newspaper clipping, TWHA.

**Figure 2-253** Built by Theodore Seeber, Benjamin Harrison's "flagship" *Resaca*, with its name in brass letters at the bow. The modest tumblehome of the stem is similar to Grant guideboats before 1894. Board seats and the absence of yoke cleats indicate that this is not a carry boat. It is in the collection of the Town of Webb Historical Association.

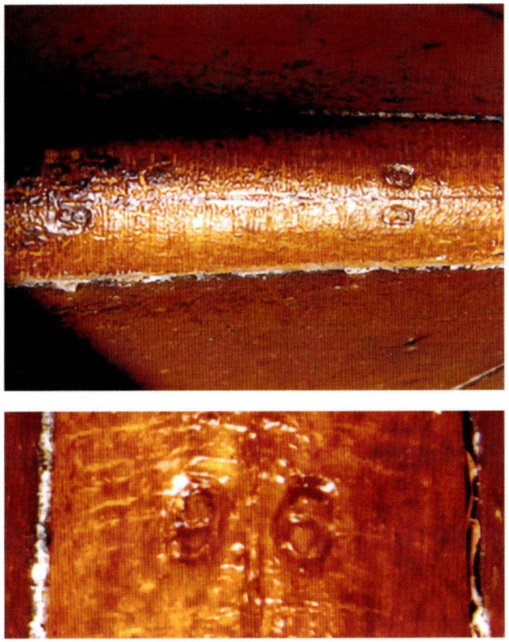

**Figure 2-254** The end of the *Resaca's* stem foot at the bottom board. (Top) The number "8" is stamped at the left, and "96" at the right. (Bottom) Magnification of "96." This is the eighth boat built during the winter of 1895–1896.

**Figure 2-255** Two non-pointed scribe ribs beneath the bow and stern decks of a Seeber guideboat. The ribs are reverse curved.

## OLD FORGE BOAT COMPANY
## THEODORE SEEBER

**Formed:** 1903
**Active:** 1903–1909
**Location:** Old Forge, Herkimer County
**Estimate of guideboats built:** More than 30
**Number reviewed:** 2
**Builder's plate:** 2

**Figure 2-256** Old Forge Boat Company builder's plate.

### Business Profile

After Theodore Seeber sold his interest in Seeber & Parsons to Riley Parsons, he continued to work independently until shortly before his death in January 1910. From 1896 to 1902 he operated under the name Theodore Seeber, and from 1903 to 1910 as the Old Forge Boat Company, a name that first appears in news articles in 1902 and 1903:

> [November] 1902: A large building, 60 x 34 feet and two and a half stories high, to be used as a boat, joiner and paint shop, is being erected on the rear of Mr. Seeber's lot by E. L. Marks, L. [*sic*] Seeber and Floyd Marks, the company known as Old Forge Boat Company.
>
> February 4, 1903: The Old Forge Boat Co. have commenced setting machinery in their new boat shop. When completed they will have one of the best equipped and most convenient shops in this section.
>
> March 1, 1903: The Old Forge Boat Company plant is nearly completed and work will begin next month. All kinds of boats will be made in a substantial and artistic manner, as well as repairing and painting.
>
> April 2, 1903: The Old Forge Boat Company has established a thoroughly equipped joiner's shop on the second floor of their factory.[1]

Where Seeber's boat shop was located before the fall of 1902, when he started working under the name Old Forge Boat Company, is unknown. A 1906 map locates the "O. F. Boat Co." on a rectangu-

1 Newspaper clippings, 1902,1903, TWHA.

**Figure 2-257** An Old Forge Boat Company guideboat with one pair of non-pointed scribe ribs and one pair of footed ribs under the bow and stern decks. The relatively flat, rounded shape of the stem foot is typical of Grant and Parsons boats.

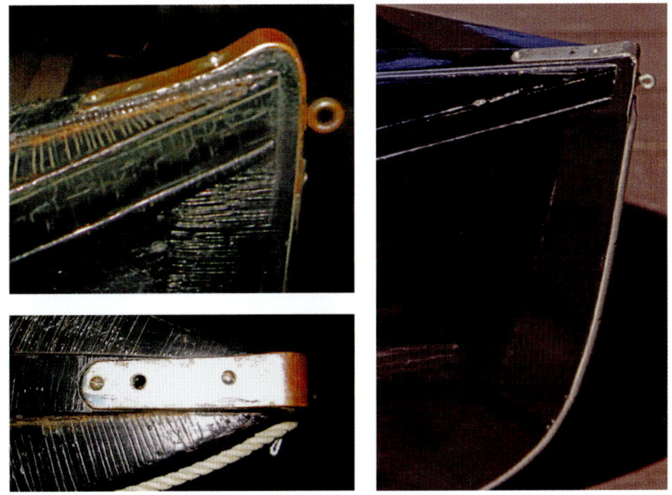

**Figure 2-258** (Top Right) A thin, brass stem-post cap that is not let into the stem front. (Bottom Right) A screw, a limber hole, and then another screw. (Far Right) An Old Forge Boat Company stem profile: a slight outward rake, not as prominent as the outward rake of Parsons guideboats.

lar plot behind his home near the Forge House. (See map, Figure 2-243.)

Seeber's billhead informs us that from 1896 on, he was not only building "Steam Yachts" and "Adirondack Row Boats," but also "St. Lawrence Row Boats."[2] The only guideboat the author is aware of is one with an Old Forge Boat Company builder's plate stamped "9 09" (the ninth boat built in 1909).

## Guideboat Characteristics

Old Forge Boat Company guideboats (including cleats, seats, backrests, and hardware) are almost identical to the Seeber & Parsons boats, with one exception: the number and placement of the scribe ribs. Old Forge Boat Company guideboats have only one pair of scribe ribs, rather than three, under the bow and stern decks. The second pair under the deck are footed ribs (but may be non-pointed scribe ribs). The outward rake of the Old Forge stem profile is not as prominent.

Old Forge Boat Company guideboats are numbered serially, starting with number 1 each year, from 1903 to 1909.[3]

## Field Notes

**Decks:** Like those of Seeber & Parsons and Parsons & Company.

**Hull:** Number of strakes on each side: 8; modified-bevel (Grant-lap) construction.

For a description of gunwales, seats, seat cleats, backrests, and yoke, see H. D. Grant.

2 Seeber billhead, 1896.
3 "Old Forge" map, 1906.

## St. Lawrence Row Boats

Two St. Lawrence Row Boats with Old Forge Boat Company builder's plates, and one without a builder's plate, were also reviewed. They are of typical guideboat construction, heavily built with a wide beam. One is in the collection of the Adirondack Museum (accession 69.106.4). It is 14 feet 5½ inches long, with a beam of 42½ inches, and weighs 97 pounds.

**Figure 2-259** (Top) A 16-foot St. Lawrence Row Boat built by the Old Forge Boat Company in the process of being restored.

**Figure 2-260** (Top Left) The two-piece deck is placed between the sheer strakes. The tapered center cover board (similar to Grant) butts to the stem post. (Top Center) Coaming and a mirrored ogee decorative deck beam (similar to Rushton). (Top Right) Beneath the decks are one pair of steam-bent scribe ribs and two pairs of footed ribs (similar to Rushton). The stem foot is a horizontal rectangle. (Bottom Left) The beam is 41½ inches. (Bottom Center) The stems have a slight outward rake. A rub rail runs the length of the boat below the gunwales. (Bottom Right) The iron stem-post cap is continuous with the stem band (similar to Rushton and the St. Lawrence skiff). A single bead runs along the lower edge of the gunwale.

**Figure 2-261** (Left and Bottom) A second St. Lawrence Row Boat in restored condition built by the Old Forge Boat Company in 1909 (length 17 feet 9 inches; beam 43 inches). There are no yoke cleats. (Top Left) The brass stem-post cap. Deck pieces are set between the sheer strakes. (Top Center) The coaming, with the mirrored ogee decorative deck beam visible beneath it, and the steam-bent scribe ribs (similar to Rushton). (Top Right) The bow showing the rub rail below the sheer strake. The stem band is continuous and forms the stem-post cap.

## PARSONS & COMPANY

**RILEY R. PARSONS**
**IRA H. PARSONS**
**R. BENJAMIN PARSONS**

**Formed:** 1896
**Active:** 1896–1903
**Location:** Old Forge, Herkimer County
**Estimate of guideboats built:** 45–50
**Number reviewed:** 8
**Builder's plate:** 5

**FIGURE 2-262** Parsons & Company builder's plate.

### Business Profile

The Seeber & Parsons partnership ended in 1895, and by the following year both men had set up independent shops in Old Forge. Parsons & Company was made up of Riley and his two sons, Ira and Ben, who had both previously worked in the Seeber & Parsons shop. The *Boonville Herald* reported on March 18, 1896: "Parsons & Co. have their fourteenth boat nearly completed," and on February 28, 1901:

> The two boat building shops in this place [Old Forge] are doing a more extensive business than ever before. Parsons & Co. have been putting in considerable new and expensive machinery and expect to begin building at once.[1]

In 1902, Riley Parsons moved his shop to a location between the Eagle Bay Road and the north shore of Forge Pond, as it was then known.[2] (See map, Figure 2-243)

### Guideboat Characteristics

The guideboats built by Parsons & Company, Parsons & Roberts, and Parsons Brothers all adhere to the patterns and designs of the final model built by Seeber & Parsons after 1891.

The hull interiors of some Old Forge and Boonville guideboats were painted a medium brown color, referred to locally as "Brown's Tract mud."[3]

The presence of an outward-raking stem profile, a builder's plate, and a serial number stamped on the stem foot are all distinguishing features of guideboats built by the various Parsons companies. Parsons & Company guideboats are numbered sequentially; number and

1 *Boonville Herald*, March 18, 1896; February 28, 1901.
2 "Old Forge" map, 1906.
3 Durant, 1980:145.

year, from 1 to about 50, for the years 1896 to 1901.

John E. Roberts, a local dealer in lumber and building materials, became financially associated with the Parsonses at this time. A 1902 Parsons & Company letterhead was signed by J. Roberts.[4] A newspaper clipping dated May 5, 1903, reports the new company's formation:

> The boat company on the north shore of the pond known as Parsons & Co. will from now on be known as the Parsons & Roberts Boat Company. The building has been enlarged. They have already completed twenty-five new Adirondack row boats and have some large orders to fill.[5]

The state of Riley Parsons's health may have had something to do with this partial transfer of ownership. Parsons died the following year, on September 17, 1904, at age sixty-five.

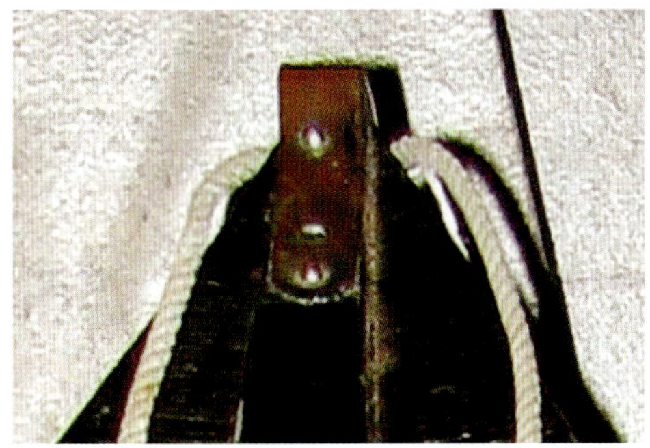

**Figure 2-263** (Above) A narrow stem with a prominent Parsons outward rake. (Top Right) A hull interior painted in the color known as "Brown's Tract mud." (Bottom Right) A brass stem-post cap typical of Old Forge builders—a screw, a limber hole, and a second screw.

4 Parsons & Company, Letterhead, 1902, TWHA.
5 "Along the Fulton Chain," *Boonville Herald,* May 6, 1903, TWHA.

## PARSONS & ROBERTS

### ABBIE PARSONS
### JOHN E. ROBERTS

**Formed:** 1903
**Active:** 1903–1909
**Location:** Old Forge, Herkimer County
**Estimate of guideboats built:** More than 40
**Number reviewed:** 6
**Builder's plate:** 4
**Adirondack Museum accession:** 77.27.1

FIGURE 2-264 Parsons & Roberts builder's plate.

### Biographical Sketch: John E. Roberts

John Eaton Roberts, son of John Roberts of Constableville, Lewis County, became financially associated with the Parsonses in 1902 and by 1903 was a partner in the boat shop.

He married Jennie M. Smith on July 7, 1905. Roberts was a director of the Old Forge Company, which in 1906 was by far the largest landowner in the village of Old Forge. A letterhead dated December 29, 1908, indicates that Roberts, while in partnership with the Parsonses, also maintained his own business as a "Retailer of Lumber and Dealer in Building Materials, Old Forge, N.Y."[1]

A Parsons & Roberts billhead for 1905 lists the owners as J. Eaton Roberts and "A. (Abbie) Parsons," Ira and Ben's mother.[2] The 1906 map (Figure 2-243) locates the Parsons & Roberts boat shop on Eagle Bay Road adjacent to the home of Ira Parsons and just across Eagle Bay Road from Ben Parsons.[3]

The partnership was brief, however, ending in 1909. The Roberts association was apparently a friendly one at a time when the Parsonses may have needed help financially to maintain their business.

### Guideboat Characteristics

See Parsons & Company. Parsons and Roberts boats are numbered sequentially starting with 1, from 1902 to 1909. The last known number is 69. Guideboats that bear the builder's plates of Parsons & Roberts are stamped 1904 and later.

1 John E. Roberts, Letterhead, December 29, 1908, Comstock Collection.
2 Parsons & Roberts, Billhead, September 30, 1905, TWHA.
3 "Old Forge" map, 1906.

## PARSONS BROTHERS

**Figure 2-265** Parsons Brothers builder's plate.

**Formed:** 1910
**Active:** 1910–1945
**Location:** Old Forge, Herkimer County
**Estimate of guideboats built:** 165–170
**Number reviewed:** 25
**Builder's plate:** 7
**Adirondack Museum accessions:** 63.183.1, 64.170.1, 66.69.1

### Business Profile

See Ira H. Parsons and Raymond Benjamin Parsons for their individual biographies.

In 1909, John Roberts withdrew from the business partnership, and Ben and Ira Parsons assumed control. They built boats for the next thirty-five years, until 1945. The following note was handwritten on a Parsons Brothers invoice dated May 18, 1941, to George Van Gorder, a camp owner on Seventh Lake:

Dear Sir:

We enclose bill for the boat; you will find it a good one. The material in this boat cost us $91. There is 2500 brass screws and nearly 4000 copper tacks and twenty days labor.

With care it is good for fifty years. A number of people have been here to look at the boat and taken pictures.

Yours Truly

Ben Parsons [1]

### Guideboat Characteristics

See Parsons & Company. Parsons Brothers guideboats are numbered sequentially from 1 to about 125, from 1910 to 1924; then sequentially from 1 to about 25, from 1925 to 1927. From 1928 to 1945, they built few guideboats. These are numbered serially, starting with 1 each year. The last known guideboat built is stamped number 1, 1945.

1 Parsons Brothers, Note on billhead, May 18, 1941, TWHA.

## CYRUS HALE PALMER

**Date of birth:** May 30, 1845 (Elizabethtown, Essex County)
**Date of death:** December 8, 1897 (Long Lake, Hamilton County)
**Active:** mid-1860s ~ 1895
**Location:** Long Lake
**Estimate of guideboats built:** 50
**Number reviewed:** 1
**Builder's plate:** Not used

**FIGURE 2-266** Cyrus Hale Palmer.

### Biographical Sketch

Cyrus Hale Palmer was born in Elizabethtown in 1845, the son of Ezekiel (1810–1886) and Harriet (Kellogg) Palmer. Cyrus was married to Emily Closson Robinson (1849–1904). They had four children: Leslie A., Lester, Bessie, and Amy.[1]

Of Cyrus's early life, little is known. The 1870 federal census and the *New York State Business Directory* for 1867 and 1874 list his occupation as boatbuilder. In the 1872 and 1880 editions of Wallace's Adirondack guidebook, he is listed as a Long Lake guide.[2] In 1885,[3] and again in 1895,[4] as a grand juror for the Town of Long Lake, he is listed as a farmer and a boatbuilder, respectively.

The *New York State Business Directory* for 1864 lists Cyrus's older brother, Ransom J. Palmer, as a boatbuilder.[5] As he was nine years older and listed as a boatbuilder three years before Cyrus, it is likely Ransom taught Cyrus how to build boats. Ransom had enlisted in the Union Army in 1861 and was severely wounded in one arm in the battle of Cold Harbor, Virginia (May–June 1864). In 1865 he moved to Viola, Minnesota. His arm had to be amputated in 1873.[6]

Henry and George Stanton, both Long Lake contemporaries, may have learned

1 Timothy Hopkins, *The Kelloggs in the Old World and the New*, San Francisco: Sunset Press, 1903, II: n.p.
2 Federal census, 1870; *Business Directory*, 1867, 1874; E. R. Wallace, 1872, 1880.
3 *Proceedings of the Board of Supervisors of the County of Hamilton for the Year 1885*, Hope, NY: Hamilton County Press, 1886:4.
4 *Proceedings of the Board of Supervisors of the County of Hamilton for the Year 1895*, Wells, NY: Hamilton County Record, 1896:18.
5 *Business Directory*, 1864.
6 Joseph A. Leonard, *History of Olmstead County, Minnesota*, Chicago: Goodspeed Historical Association, 1910.

the boatbuilding trade from Palmer.[7]

The *History of Hamilton County* suggests that Cyrus Palmer and Mitchell Sabattis may have been the first to build a guideboat. There is no credible evidence to support this.[8]

## Guideboat Characteristics

Only one Cyrus Palmer guideboat has been seen by the author. It was previously owned by Palmer's son, Leslie, and then by local historian Frances Seaman.

Originally, the Palmer guideboat was painted green, inside and out. Since then its interior has been stripped and varnished and its exterior repainted.

The identifying features of the Palmer guideboat include: half-barrel-shaped stem posts; gunwales that do not reach the stem fronts; shield-shaped deck caps at bow and stern; the absence of scribe ribs at bow and stern, and the absence of ribs beneath the bow and stern decks; decks mitered into the gunwales.

**Figure 2-267** Cyrus Palmer's boat shop in Long Lake. Cyrus is at the left; his son, Leslie, is at the right. (Courtesy of Adirondack Museum)

**Figure 2-268** A vintage photograph of Leslie Palmer rowing a guideboat built by his father Cyrus. (Courtesy of Long Lake Historical Society)

7 Lewis Grant, *Letter to Kenneth Durant, January 17, 1958,* Durant Collection.
8 Aber and King, 1965:137.

FIGURE 2-269 The restored Cyrus Palmer guideboat.

FIGURE 2-271 (Left) The bow and (Right) the stern. No scribe ribs beneath either deck. A shield-shaped deck cap. The stem foot is a horizontal rectangle. There are nine strakes.

FIGURE 2-270 A Palmer stem post that has been repaired. The front has been reshaped.

FIGURE 2-272 The deck is mitered into the gunwales.

FIGURE 2-273 (Top) Detail of yoke cleat of the original Palmer guideboat. (Bottom) Yoke cleat of the restored Palmer guideboat.

**FIGURE 2-274** Frederick William Rice.

## FREDERICK WILLIAM RICE

**Date of birth:** March 25, 1852 (Hartford, Connecticut)
**Date of death:** April 23, 1934 (Tracy, California)
**Active:** 1875–1903
**Location:** Saranac Lake, Franklin County
**Estimate of guideboats built**: More than 75
**Number reviewed:** 19
**Builder's plate:** Not used

### Biographical Sketch

Frederick William Rice was born in Hartford, Connecticut, on March 25, 1852. He was the son of Caleb Hall Rice and Jane E. Bailey. Caleb Hall Rice was named after his grandfather on his mother's side, Caleb Hall, a distinguished clergyman. In a letter mentioning his great-grandfather, Rice wrote: "[Caleb Hall] was a very strict old fashioned Methodist farmer who believed in not sparing the rod. He gave my father such a whipping that he ran away from home and learned to be a plumber. Father enlisted [in the Union Army] and wrote to me once from a hospital in New Orleans. He has never been heard from since."[1]

In 1872, Rice left Connecticut for Essex, New York, and worked as a surveyor for the Whitehall and Plattsburgh Railroad. At the inn in Essex he met Harriet "Kitty" Todd and in 1874 they were married. In 1875, when work on the railroad was completed, Rice took up boatbuilding, becoming "a builder of sailboats in Willsboro" [just north of Essex on Lake Champlain].[2]

On March 8, 1876, the first of their eleven children, Frederick Marsh Rice, was born in Burlington, Vermont.[3] In 1878 Fred Rice, his wife, and their infant

1 Frederick W. Rice, *Pedigree of Frederick W. Rice*, Letter to his children, After 1907, Adirondack Museum.
2 Donaldson, 1921, I:307.
3 Obituary, *Adirondack Daily Enterprise*, April 15, 1966.

son, "travelled to Saranac Lake on a buckboard pulled by mules. They didn't have too many belongings. The buckboard was mostly filled with tools for building boats, and an almost finished sailboat."[4]

For the first three years they lived in a log cabin on the corner of Algonquin Avenue and State Street while a house, boat shop, and ice house were being built at the end of Algonquin Avenue on Lower Saranac Lake. In early 1878 Rice and guideboat builder W. A. Martin built the steamboat *Water Lily*. It was launched on July 4, 1878, the first steamboat on Lower Saranac Lake and the first documented boat to have been built by Rice. He soon became recognized as a builder of fine guideboats.

A catalogue issued in 1883 by R. A. Moore of Kensington, Connecticut, supplier of boat hardware, advertised guideboat stem bands in three designs—one of them by F. W. Rice.[5]

Guideboat builder Theodore Hanmer of Saranac Lake stated in a 1940 interview:

> . . . the best of them was Fred Rice. . . . I've seen some of Rice's boats that after 40 years of use will not show a crack or warp along the seams. . . . The boat which I am building now is from a set of patterns that Rice devised back in the last century.[6]

One of Rice's guideboats was shown at the 1904 Louisiana Purchase Exposition at St. Louis, in the New York State Forest, Fish, and Game exhibit:

> A guide-boat of the latest style and of superior workmanship was a part of the sportsman's outfit. This boat was kindly loaned by the manufacturer, Mr. Fred W. Rice, formerly of Saranac Lake, N.Y., but now living at Seattle, Wash. His son continues the manufacture of guide-boats at Lake Placid, N.Y."[7]

Rice left a handwritten ledger, now at the Adirondack Museum, containing a trove of information listing the cost of items of everyday living, as well as guideboat components such as copper tacks, brass screws, paint, lumber, caning, etc., for the years 1879 to 1890.[8] As with other builders of his era, Rice shared his boatbuilding knowledge and skills. His daughter Ernestine Eskuche wrote: "My father . . . gave the plans to anyone who wanted them."[9] One recipient of Rice's patterns was Theodore Hanmer.[10]

While Rice's letterhead of 1903 states that he was a "Dealer in Boat Lumber and Boat Builder's Supplies," he also was a photographer.[11] His interest in portrait and landscape photography began about 1887 when he built a studio next to his boathouse.[12] He photographed Samuel L. Clemens (Mark Twain) and his family during their summer stay at Lower Saranac Lake in 1901. He did so on Clemens's condition that the photographs were not to be shown publicly while the author and his wife were alive. The agreement was kept.

During this summer, Clemens showed considerable interest in Adirondack guideboats "conversing at length"[13] with Fred Rice about the technical details of the "exquisite and practical craft."[14] Although he rarely rowed one himself, he enjoyed being rowed around the lake.

4 Madge Rice Sterns Carpenter, *F. W. Rice and Family*, Unpublished manuscript, n.d., Adirondack Research Room, Saranac Lake Free Library.
5 Durant, 1980:145.
6 *Watertown Daily Times*, 1940.
7 A. B. Strough, "Forest, Fish, and Game Exhibit," in Delancey M. Ellis, comp., *New York at the Louisiana Purchase Exposition, St. Louis, 1904*, Albany, NY: J. B. Lyon, 1907:427, 440.
8 Frederick W. Rice, *Accounts Book, 1879–1890*, Adirondack Museum, Frederick W. Rice Papers.
9 Ernestine Rice Eskuche, *Letter to Frederick Anderson, June 14, 1972*, Berkeley: University of California, Mark Twain Papers.
10 *Watertown Daily Times*, 1940.
11 F. W. Rice, Letterhead, Rice Papers.
12 F. W. Rice, *Accounts Book*, 1887:131.
13 R. L. Kellogg, "Mark Twain's Summer at Saranac Lake," *Adirondac*, August 1998:34–36.
14 C. Alexander, "Writer in Residence, Mark Twain's Adirondack Summer," *Adirondack Life*, July/August 1998:18.

**Figure 2-275** A photograph taken by Rice of the Samuel Clemens family at "The Lair" on Ampersand Bay, Lower Saranac Lake, during the summer of 1901. (Left to right) Clara Langhorne Clemens, Jane Lampton Clemens, Mrs. Olivia Langdon Clemens, and Clemens. (Courtesy of Adirondack Research Room, Saranac Lake Free Library)

In 1903 the Rices had their eleventh and last child. There were four boys and seven girls. In 1904, Frederick Rice received an inheritance from his uncle, William Marsh Rice, founder, in 1891, of the William Marsh Rice Institute for the Advancement of Letters, Science, and Art in Houston, Texas (now Rice Institute, Rice University). The uncle had gone to Texas in 1838 and there parlayed a 320-acre land grant into a mercantile business, then branched into real estate, cotton, lumber, insurance, petroleum, shipping, railroads, and banking. By 1896, he had amassed $9 million, the equivalent of hundreds of millions today.

In 1900, the eighty-four-year-old W. M. Rice was murdered with an overdose of chloroform by his lawyer and valet in a conspiracy to alter his will and confiscate the bulk of his estate. After lengthy court proceedings, the conspirators were brought to justice, though only temporarily. The considerable estate was distributed among the Rice Institute and his heirs. Frederick W. Rice received $100,000. He and his family then moved to Mercer Island, near Seattle, Washington. Three of the sons remained in the East, including the eldest, Frederick M. Rice, who followed in his father's footsteps as a boatbuilder in Saranac Lake. Frederick W. Rice later moved to Tracy, California, where he died on April 23, 1934, at the age of eighty-two.[15]

15 Eskuche, June 14, 1972.

**Figure 2-276** The first two pairs of ribs are chamfered scribe ribs, as shown here at the bow (Top) and stern (Bottom).

## Guideboat Characteristics

The decks of F. W. Rice guideboats are either one piece or strip-built, with the strip-built decked boats usually of a higher grade. Distinctive features include the angled front and back of his stem posts and the chamfered scribe ribs at bow and stern. Rice's placement of scribe ribs was used by Theodore Hanmer after Rice left Saranac Lake; Hanmer did not, however, chamfer them at their bottom board ends as Rice had done.

Such chamfering can be observed in six Westport boats on the Ausable lakes. Before coming to Saranac Lake, Rice had lived and worked in Willsboro, near Westport. In addition to surveying for the railroad, he had built sturdy Lake Champlain sailboats and had become a mentor to Dennis Hayes, who lived in Westport and was learning to build boats for hire on the lake.[16] It is possible that Dennis Hayes had borrowed Rice's chamfered scribe-rib design in constructing the heavily built Westport boats. Boats with sufficient stability and size to take heavy loads of supplies to camps on the Ausable lakes were needed, and the guideboat-constructed Westport boats filled that need. (See Westport Boats in Part 1.)

The writer has also examined one early guideboat from the late 1870s, believed to have been built by F. W. Rice. The decks were placed on top of the gunwales and sheer strakes. The inboard edge of the bow deck is a shallow arc, and the stern deck is straight.

16 Raymond C. Clark, *A View of Westport, N.Y., on Lake Champlain: 1902–1972*, Elizabethtown, NY: Denton Publications, 1972: n.p.

## Field Notes

**Stems:** Tumblehome (Saranac profile). Horizontal width from rabbet line to leading stem edge: upper stem (just below the lower edge of the gunwale) about 2 inches; lower stem about 3 inches. Stem-foot end is rectangular.

**Decks:** One-piece and strip. One-piece: Let into the gunwales and sheer strakes, with shallow arcs at both the bow and stern. The bow deck extends beyond the carlin, while the stern deck is flush with the carlin. Deck caps are pie-piece shaped with a non-tapered inboard margin. Strip: No V-grooves, with shallow arcs at bow and stern. Number of strips on each side: bow about 20, stern about 17. Center cover board surrounds the stem post; its upper edges are rounded. The coaming is wide at the center, tapering toward the ends. The deck beams have rounded lower edges.

**Hull:** Number of strakes on each side: 7; feather-lap construction. The sheer strake is often made from western red cedar.

**Gunwales:** Extend to stem fronts; may be D-shaped, particularly on strip-deck models.

**Stem bands:** F. W. Rice pattern; manufactured and sold by R. A. Moore, Kensington, Connecticut, and later by M. E. Blasier Manufacturing Company, Utica, New York.

FIGURE 2-277 A Rice narrow stem post: length about 2¾ inches, width about ¼ inch, and height about ¾ inch. It has an angled front and concave back with a flat top.

FIGURE 2-278 Rice did not use reverse-curved ribs. At the bow there are two pairs of scribe ribs, chamfered at the bottom board. One pair is under and one pair is inboard of the deck. The stern also has two pairs of chamfered scribe ribs that are both inboard of the deck. The ends of the footed ribs are beveled and do not extend all the way across the bottom board. The photograph also shows pairs of quarter-length, footed reinforcing ribs between each pair of full-length ribs. Such ribs were also used by other builders such as Warren Cole of Long Lake.

## FREDERICK MARSH RICE

**Date of birth:** March 8, 1876 (Burlington, Vermont)
**Date of death:** April 1966
**Active:** 1905~1931
**Location:** Saranac Lake, Franklin County
**Estimate of guideboats built:** Unknown
**Number reviewed:** 1
**Builder's plate:** Not used
**Adirondack Museum accession:** 64.27.1

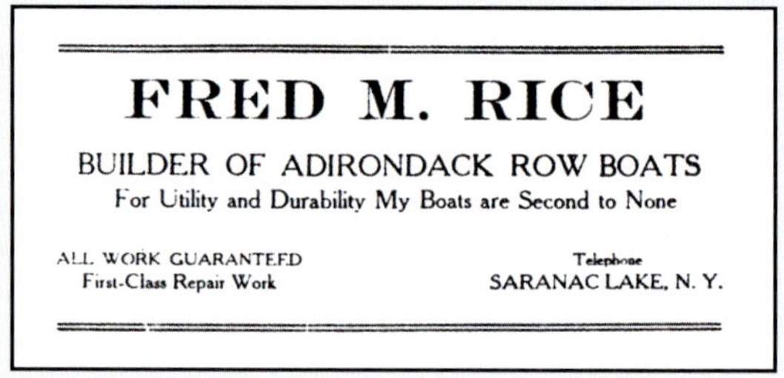
FRED M. RICE
BUILDER OF ADIRONDACK ROW BOATS
For Utility and Durability My Boats are Second to None
ALL WORK GUARANTEED
First-Class Repair Work
Telephone
SARANAC LAKE, N. Y.

**FIGURE 2-279** Cover of the Rice trade catalogue, circa 1920s. (Courtesy of Adirondack Research Room, Saranac Lake Free Library)

### Biographical Sketch

Frederick Marsh Rice, guide, naturalist, and boatbuilder, was born in Burlington, Vermont, on March 8, 1876. He was the oldest of the eleven children of Harriet Todd and Frederick William Rice. His middle name, Marsh, was taken from that of his father's uncle, William Marsh Rice, founder of Rice University in Houston, Texas. In 1878, he moved with his parents to Saranac Lake, where he remained until his death in 1966 at the age of ninety.

Rice is probably best remembered for his strong views on the superior value of "living in the woods—the curative effect of wilderness air for health seekers." In 1937, he published a booklet titled *Fifty Years in a Health Resort.* In it he stated:

> Because a real outdoor life was not easily adapted to a hospital routine it was abandoned and rest in bed was recommended as a substitute. Thus, for the sake of expediency, was sacrificed the greatest aid for these unfortunate people that has ever been known—a healthful outdoor life in a beneficial climate.[1]

In 1931, Rice placed an advertisement in the local paper: "Wanted: To get in touch with some invalid who is not improving, and who would like to go into the woods for the summer."[2] One of the people who answered the ad was Martha Rebentisch (1911–1964), who, at the age

1 Frederick M. Rice, *Fifty Years in a Health Resort*, Saranac Lake, NY: 1937:7.
2 Martha Reben, *The Healing Woods*, New York: Crowell, 1952:5.

of twenty, had already spent three and a half unsuccessful years in a cure cottage. The summer of 1931 would be the first of virtually every spring, summer, and fall for Martha to "live in the woods" until her death in 1964. From her first summer at Weller Pond (off of Middle Saranac or Round Lake) Martha kept a journal of her daily experiences and observations. The first ten years of her life in the woods were the basis for her first book, *The Healing Woods,* published in 1952 under her pseudonym, Martha Reben. The book proved successful, and the movie rights were purchased by financier Cornelius Vanderbilt Whitney. The movie never materialized, however. Two more well-received books by Reben followed: *The Way of the Wilderness* (1955) and *A Sharing of Joy* (1963).

Documentations of Fred M. Rice as a boatbuilder include his listings in the 1905 New York State Census as a "28-year-old boat builder" and the 1906 local business directory as a "boat builder."[3]

## Guideboat Characteristics

Only one guideboat examined by the writer has credible provenance that it was built by F. M. Rice; it is patterned after his father's boats. The F. M. Rice catalogue states:

> I build canoes when ordered. . . . a number of models of different styles of flat-boats—called punts, sharpies or scows. . . . I have a number of models, each one made for certain uses. One of them was in use by my father 28 years ago. This was our first guide boat and is in general use today.[4]

The *Gull,* an example of a heavy square-stern boat, designed for an outboard motor, is at the Adirondack Museum (accession 64.27.1). The first two pairs of natural-crook ribs at the bow of *Gull* are scribe ribs chamfered at their bottom-board ends, typical of the rib design and placement in his father's guideboats. The boat is 17 feet 9 inches in length, 43 inches in width, and weighs 219 pounds.

FIGURE 2-280 Frederick M. Rice and author Martha Reben. (Courtesy of Adirondack Research Room, Saranac Lake Free Library)

3 New York State Census, 1905; *Adirondack Directory,* 1906:87, 88.
4 *Fred M. Rice, Builder of Adirondack Row Boats,* Trade catalogue, Saranac Lake, NY: Adirondack Enterprise Press, circa 1920s.

## ELBRIDGE GERRY RICKETSON

**Date of birth:** 1849
**Date of death:** November 7, 1916 (Gabriels, Franklin County, Mountain View Cemetery)
**Active:** Late 1870s–mid-1890s
**Location:** Bloomingdale, Essex County
**Estimate of guideboats built:** More than 75
**Number reviewed:** 9
**Builder's plate:** 4
**Adirondack Museum accession:** 58.284.2

FIGURE 2-281 Ricketson builder's plate. (Courtesy of Woodward Boat Shop)

FIGURE 2-282 Elbridge Gerry Ricketson. (Courtesy of Elizabeth Kuter Pfenning)

### Biographical Sketch

Elbridge Gerry Ricketson, surveyor, guide, and boatbuilder, was the son of attorney William Ricketson and Abigail Hoag Ricketson (his second marriage). Abdenego Ricketson, the father of William, was among the first settlers of the Town of Brighton, Franklin County. Ricketson married Mary Alice Hall in Plattsburgh, Clinton County, on June 30, 1874. They had five children.[1] He is listed in the 1876 county atlas under "South Woods Business Notices," as "Ricketson, E. G., Surveyor, P. O. Bloomingdale."[2] He is included as a St. Regis guide in the 1878, 1881, and 1882 editions of S. R. Stoddard's Adirondack guidebooks, and as a guide in E. R. Wallace's guidebooks for 1881 and 1882. In the federal census for 1880, he is listed as a guide and boatbuilder in the Town of Brighton.[3] He is also listed in 1886 as a boatbuilder in the St. Regis Lakes and Bloomingdale section of the *Fourteenth Report of the Commissioners of Fisheries*.[4] The annual supervisors' reports of Essex County lists him as a boatbuilder for the years 1887 through 1890. He is listed as a mechanic in 1891 and then again as a boatbuilder in 1892.[5]

Elbridge Ricketson held political offices, among them Inspector of Election (1884), Auditor's Clerk (1888), and Assessor (1894). Although the Ricketson boat shop was located in the Village of

1 Elizabeth Kuter Pfenning, *Personal communication*, February 2008. Pfenning is the great-great-granddaughter of E. G. Ricketson.
2 Daniel G. Beers, "Business Notices," on the "Plan of the South Woods," in *Franklin County Atlas*, Philadelphia: D. G. Beers, 1876.
3 Federal census, 1880.
4 Stoddard, 1878, 1881, 1882; Wallace, 1881, 1882; *Fisheries Report*, 1886.
5 *Proceedings of the Board of Supervisors of the County of Essex*, Port Henry, NY: various publishers, 1887–1892.

Bloomingdale, Town of St. Armand, Essex County, his residence was in the Town of Brighton, Franklin County, about three miles away.

A Ricketson journal survives. Entries beginning on March 27, 1876, and ending in November 1882, show that he began by repairing and building guideboats in the late 1870s, mainly for guides at Paul Smith's. Ricketson describes his various day-to-day chores and his interactions with other St. Regis/Paul Smith's guides. He provides details of the sales of his guideboats, and the type, cost, and manufacturers of the tools, tacks, screws, paint, rowlocks, and other items used in building them. This documentation by a builder of terms such as "cleat" and "planing the boat knees" is notable. The journal also provides a first-hand account of rural life in Brighton.[6]

## Guideboat Characteristics

The Ricketson stem-post design is a narrow, long rectangle with a concave back and angled front. His stems are wide at the waterline with extreme tumblehome sometimes erroneously referred to as a "ram bow." This stem design was adopted by local builders William McCaffrey and William Vassar, as was his method of placing the decks between the sheer strakes. Ricketson's shape of the stem foot was also used by McCaffrey. These similarities suggest a working relationship among these three contemporaries: Ricketson (born 1849), McCaffrey (born 1859), and Vassar (born 1866). Several construction details, however, clearly differentiate among the three.

Ricketson built boats with three different deck designs: **(a)** a two-piece bow deck and a one-piece stern deck, with pie-piece-shaped deck caps; **(b)** two-piece decks, bow and stern, with center cover board and coaming; and **(c)** a strip deck with a center cover board and coaming. All three are set between the sheer strakes. Decorative deck beams with an unusual sawtooth design were sometimes used.

### Field Notes

**Ribs:** Very slight reversed curve; two pair of scribe ribs under the bow deck, no ribs under the stern deck.

**Heel plates:** One piece with rounded ends.

6 E. G. Ricketson, *Journal*, 1876–1882, Pfenning private collection. Copy in Author Collection.

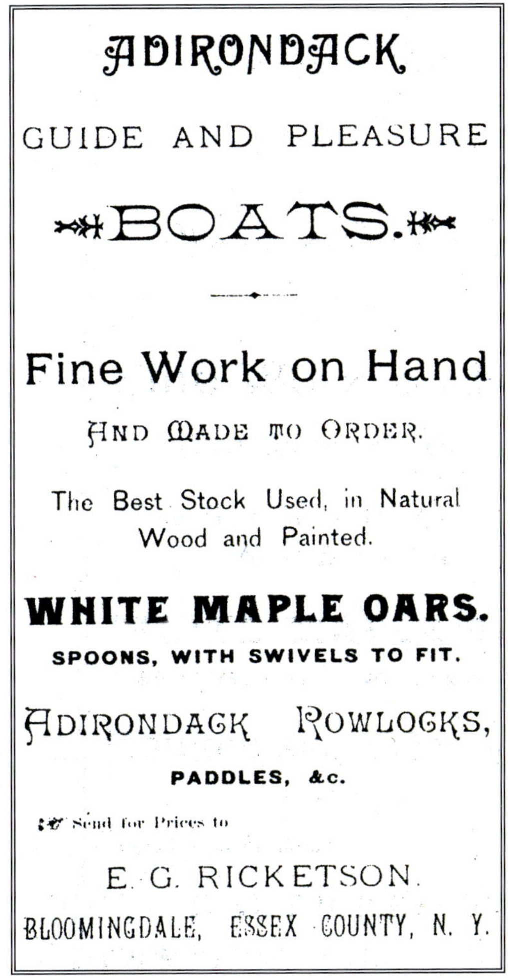


FIGURE 2-283 An advertisement from the 1889–1890 brochure: In the Adirondacks: Illustrated Railway Guide of the Delaware & Hudson and Chateaugay Railroads. (Courtesy of Warrensburg Public Library)

FIGURE 2-284 Ricketson boat shop in Bloomingdale, NY. (Courtesy of Adirondack Museum)

**Figure 2-285** The stem post is narrow, with a length of about 2 inches, height about ½ inch. The front end is flat and angled, the back end is slightly concave, and the top is slightly rounded.

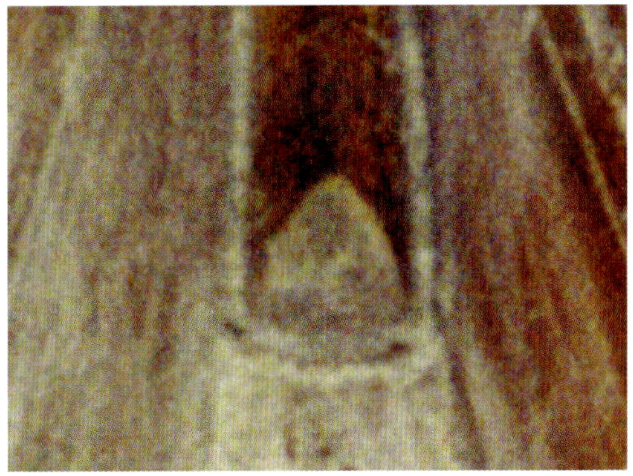

**Figure 2-287** The stem foot at the bottom board shows its characteristic arch shape.

**Figure 2-288** The decks (removed in this photograph) are set between the sheer strakes. On both sides, wooden deck supports, secured with three screws, are placed against and just below the top of the sheer strakes. Note the supporting carlin and deck beam.

**Figure 2-286** The extreme tumblehome stem of a Ricketson guideboat. The greatest horizontal width of the lower portion of the stem, from the rabbet line to the leading edge, at the waterline, is greater than 4½ inches, and in most cases greater than 5 inches. The width of the upper portion of the stem (just below the gunwale) is about 2 inches.

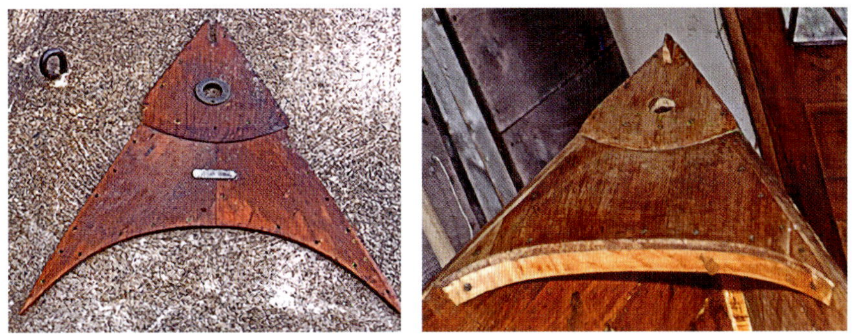

**Figure 2-289** (Left) A two-piece bow deck. (Right) A one-piece stern deck. Both are set between the sheer strakes. The bow deck extends slightly beyond the carlin; the stern deck is flush with the carlin. Deck caps are pie-piece shaped with a tapered inboard edge. Occasionally, there is a hole with a brass collar in the bow and/or the stern deck cap.

**FIGURE 2-290** (Left) A two-piece bow deck with a center cover board and narrow coaming. The center cover board surrounds the stem post. (Right) A strip deck with a wide coaming. The number of strips on each side: bow 16, stern 14. The center cover board surrounds the stem post.

**FIGURE 2-291** (Left) An unusual sawtooth decorative deck beam. The number of teeth may vary. Most Ricketson decks do not have this feature. (Right) An oarlock strap for a swivel oarlock as advertised by Ricketson.

**FIGURE 2-292** John Henry Rushton, circa 1883. (Courtesy of St. Lawrence County Historical Association)

**FIGURE 2-293** (Top) The builder's plate used before 1898. (Bottom) The builder's plate used between 1899 and 1906, located on the bow deck cap or center cover board. The builder's plate used after Rushton's death in 1906 is shield shaped.

## JOHN HENRY RUSHTON

**Date of birth:** October 9, 1843 (Edwards, St. Lawrence County)
**Date of death:** May 1, 1906 (Canton, St. Lawrence County, Fairview Cemetery)
**Active:** 1888–1916 (Shop continued after his death)
**Location:** Canton
**Estimate of guideboats built:** More than 100
**Number reviewed:** 11
**Builder's plate:** Used
**Adirondack Museum accessions:** 60.22.29, 66.161.1, 69.180.1, 71.39.1

### Biographical Sketch

John Henry Rushton was born on May 1, 1843, south of the village of Edwards, St. Lawrence County. The son of Peter and Martha Glines Rushton, he was named after his grandfather, John Henry, a wheelwright from Bolton, a mill town near Manchester, England. He had one sister, Martha, four half-brothers, and two half-sisters (from Peter Rushton's second marriage to Jane Philpot, after the early death of his first wife). In his early years, Rushton suffered from a chronic respiratory ailment. At the age of twenty he was barely five feet tall and very thin, weighing less than one hundred pounds. He nevertheless acquired a love of hunting, fishing, camping, and woodcraft.[1] In the words of one of his friends: "J. Henry Rushton was an exceedingly small man with boundless energy."

Four people had a great influence in his life: his scholarly South Edwards school teacher, Cornelius Carter; two Canton merchants, Joseph Barnes Ellsworth of the Ellsworth Boot and Shoe Store and Milton D. Packard of Packard's Dry Goods; and Tom Leonard, guide,

1 Atwood Manley, *Rushton and His Times in American Canoeing*, Syracuse, NY: Adirondack Museum/ Syracuse University Press, 1968:2, 4, 5.

boatbuilder, and the owner of Leonard's Hotel in Morley, a village five miles from Canton. In 1869 Rushton moved to Canton to work as a clerk for Ellsworth's store. After two fires devastated the store, he left Canton in the winter of 1872–1873 to work for Leonard at his hotel in Morley. Later that year, to prepare for a lengthy stay in the wilderness, Rushton decided to build a boat for his own use. With patterns loaned to him by Leonard, and likely some instruction in the fundamentals of boatbuilding, Rushton built his first two boats in a vacant barn opposite the home of his friend Ellsworth.[2] The 1878 *History of St. Lawrence County* stated:

> In 1874, J. H. Rushton engaged in boat-building on a small scale, using a model which has proved very satisfactory. The business has been gradually enlarged, until at present [1878] nearly a hundred boats per year are built, with an increasing demand from all parts of the country. A specialty is made of very light boats, for fishing and sporting purposes, and the *Rob Roy* canoe.[3]

FIGURE 2-294 The "Rushton crew" and boat shop between 1888–1889. Rushton is seated in the front row, third from the left. (Courtesy of St. Lawrence County Historical Association)

Rushton's first successful boats were light double-ended rowboats, advertised as "portable sporting boats." He employed a structural innovation described in his first catalogue, circa 1877:

> The [red elm] ribs are a neat half oval in shape, made so by being turned perfectly round and split through the centre by a machine made expressly for that purpose. They are ½ to ¾ inch wide, to ¼ to ⅜ inch thick [steam-bent] and are put into the boat but 1 ½ inches apart, thereby giving great strength with little weight.[4]

By the late 1870s Rushton had achieved national prominence as the builder of ultra-lightweight cedar canoes, made famous by "Nessmuk," the pen name for the writer George Washington Sears

2 Manley, 1968:10.
3 Henry B. Pierce and Samuel W. Durant, *History of St. Lawrence County, N.Y.*, Philadelphia: L. H. Everts, 1878:217.
4 J. H. Rushton, *Rushton's Portable Sporting Boats and Canoes*, Trade catalogue, Canton, NY: Plaindealer Steam Presses, circa 1877:4, 5.

(1821–1890), and particularly for his combination sailing and paddling canoes modeled after the English design. These canoes were a highlight of the American Canoe Association's first meet at Lake George in 1880. By this time Rushton had established a boat shop with a large number of skilled employees.

By 1882, according to the April 6 issue of *Forest and Stream,* business was flourishing: "Rushton carries in stock something like 150 canoes, and sells them like hot cakes every spring and with a score of hands cannot keep pace with the demand."[5]

On September 5, 1883, at the age of forty, Rushton married Leah Pflaum, a schoolteacher from Port Jervis, New York. Leah soon became an important asset in the Rushton enterprise:

> In designing [their] house, they planned a 'sail room,' over which Leah took charge. She became a proficient sailmaker. Located in a back ell of the house, this second-floor room afforded ample space for outlining the various types and patterns of sails—such as, lateen, Bailey rig, and leg-of-mutton—with which to outfit Rushton's skiffs and canoes. Two or three sewing machines were installed next to an outside wall. They were operated by a water-power motor. Leah hired local women to assist her.[6]

The Rushtons had two children: Joseph Henry, born in 1886, and Sidney, in 1888.[7]

Throughout his career Rushton was a committed marketer of the boats and accessories that his shop produced. His boats typically carried builder's plates, and often the brass hardware was stamped with his name. Illustrated catalogues were issued annually and he advertised widely. Major sporting goods emporiums such as Henry C. Squires and H. & D. Folsom Arms Company in New York City, and the John Wilkinson Company in Chicago, acted as his agents.

Rushton always believed that clapboard-lapstrake hulls, with closely spaced, steam-bent, half-round ribs, provided a lighter, stronger boat than any other type of construction. In 1888, however, in response to market demand, he did eventually turn to building the "Adirondack or Saranac Lake Boat," as he called it.

John Henry Rushton died of a kidney ailment on May 1, 1906. Upon his death, his son Harry became plant manager. The boat shop was incorporated under

**FIGURE 2-295** (Top) The Henry C. Squires plate on an early Rushton guideboat. (Bottom) The H. & D. Folsom Arms Company plate on a Rushton American Beauty canoe. Squires and Folsom both retailed Rushton's boats in New York City. (Courtesy of Adirondack Museum)

the title of J. H. Rushton, Inc., and Mrs. Rushton became its president. Upon her death in December 1911, Judd W. Rushton, J. H.'s half-brother, became part owner and manager.

Biographer Atwood Manley wrote:

> The once flourishing enterprise came to an end late in 1916 or in the forepart of 1917. After the closing, a former

5 William Crowley, *Rushton's Rowboats and Canoes, The 1903 Catalog in Perspective,* Camden, ME: International Marine, 1983:ix.
6 Manley, 1968:87–88.
7 Manley, 1968:103.

workman living near Canton made canoes from Rushton patterns for local people and repaired old craft. Then he too passed from the scene. In 1926 Judd sold the Boat Shop to a farmer, who tore it down and built a large dairy barn with the lumber.[8]

## Guideboat Characteristics

A review of Rushton catalogues indicates that there were three basic designs of Rushton guideboats built consecutively over twenty-eight years, beginning in 1888. The catalogues from 1888–1890 offered both 15- and 16-foot boats in one grade, the only years the shorter model was available. Thereafter until 1900, only a 16 x 37 model (16 feet by 37 inches) was built—in two grades. There were two exceptions: in 1895 Rushton also offered guideboats measuring up to 20 x 44. And in 1899, the 20 x 44 size as well as a 16 x 44 size boat could be ordered—plus square-stern variants of each. All of these were available in A or AA grade. None are known today.

**Figure 2-296** (Top Left) Rushton guideboats built in 1888–1890 had no metal stem-post cap. The stem post is narrow, length 1 inch, width 1/4 inch, front and back ends angled, and the top flat (similar to the stem posts of Frederick W. Rice). (Bottom Left) Decks are of Spanish cedar or mahogany; they are one piece and let into the gunwales. The deck caps are pie-piece shaped. The natural-crook stems and ribs are made from red spruce or hackmatack. (Right) One pair of chamfered scribe ribs beneath the bow deck and another just inboard of it. The first two pairs of ribs at the stern are chamfered scribe ribs just inboard of the stern deck. This rib design and placement are also similar to those of Frederick W. Rice. Rib spaces are 6 to 7 inches.

### The Period from 1888 to 1890

In the winter of 1887–1888, Isaac Hurst left the employ of Saranac Lake guideboat builder William Allen Martin to work for Rushton. The December 1887 issue of the *American Canoeist,* under the title "Builder's Notes," reported: "He [Rushton] has now a builder from Saranac Lake and will add the Saranac boats to his stock."[9]

Rushton's "Adirondack or Saranac

8 Manley, 1968:150–151.
9 "Builder's Notes," *American Canoeist,* December 1887:224.

Lake Boats" are characterized by one-piece decks with pie-piece-shaped deck caps; rectangular stem posts with an angled front; two pairs of scribe ribs at bow and stern, chamfered at the bottom board; rib spaces of six to seven inches; board seats (Spanish cedar or mahogany); and square gunwales.

A guideboat attributed to Rushton at the Adirondack Museum (accession 71.39.1) has features consistent with this early period. For instance, it has board seats (Rushton began to use caned seats in 1891) and the brass plate of his New York City agent, Henry C. Squires. There are two pairs of scribe ribs at bow and stern whose bottom ends are chamfered. This is the hallmark of guideboats built by Frederick W. Rice of Saranac Lake, but has not been observed in the guideboats of any other builder.

Hurst, who worked for Martin in Saranac Lake before joining Rushton, would have known Rice, and the construction details of his boats. He worked for Rushton for this brief period from 1888–1890, when he left to form a partnership with Myron Nickerson.

### Field Notes (1888 to 1890)

**Stem posts:** Narrow.

**Stems:** Tumblehome (Saranac profile). Stem foot is a horizontal rectangle.

**Decks:** One piece, let into the gunwales. Spanish cedar or mahogany.

**Deck caps:** Pie-piece-shaped at bow and stern; rounded inboard edge.

**Ribs:** No reverse-curved ribs; rib feet ends are beveled and do not extend all the way across the bottom board.

**Hull:** Number of strakes each side: 7; feather-lap construction.

**Gunwales:** Square edged.

**Seats:** Spanish cedar or mahogany boards.

**Oarlock straps:** Scroll pattern.

## The Period from 1891 to 1902

In the spring of 1890, Hurst and Myron Nickerson left Rushton's employ to form a boatbuilding partnership. In the following year, Rushton hired Saranac Lake boatbuilder Alric Moody to oversee the building of guideboats. From 1891 until 1902, Rushton guideboats were mainly characterized by one-piece decks with pie-piece-shaped deck caps; a differently shaped stem post; rib spaces of four or seven inches depending on the model; caned seats and a "cane back for the stern seat, and extra cane back and straps which may be used on either of the other seats."[10]

Significantly, the first pair of ribs under the bow and stern decks were half-round, steam-bent, red elm scribe ribs. The other builder using similar steam-bent scribe ribs was W. A. Martin of Saranac Lake. As a former Martin employee, Moody introduced this rib type and placement to Rushton guideboats. As of 1901, the gunwales were D-shaped, that is, a rounded top and bottom along the outside edge.

### Field Notes (1891 to 1902)

**Stem posts:** Narrow.

**Stems:** Tumblehome (Saranac profile). The stem feet are horizontal rectangles.

**Decks:** One piece, let into the gunwales; arced at bow and stern.

**Deck caps:** Pie-piece-shaped with a rounded inboard edge.

10 J. H. Rushton, *Catalogue, Canoes, Pleasure & Hunting Boats*, Watertown, NY: Hungerford & Coates, 1893:18.

**Figure 2-297** (Top Left) The stem post is narrow and rectangular, with length about 2¼ inches, width about ⅜ inch, height about ½ inch. The front end is angled with some wear. The back end is vertical; the top is flat. (Top Right) The deck is one piece, let into the gunwales. The inboard edge of the deck slightly overhangs the carlin at the bow and stern. (Bottom Left) One pair of half-round, steam-bent, red elm scribe ribs and one pair of footed ribs under the bow deck. Ribs are not reverse curved. The scribe ribs are the same under the stern deck, but there are no footed ribs. (Bottom Right) Center seat and backrest.

**Ribs:** No reverse-curved ribs. One pair of half-round, steam-bent, red elm scribe ribs and one pair of footed ribs under the bow deck. One pair of half-round, steam-bent, red elm scribe ribs under the stern deck and one pair of footed ribs under, or just inboard of the stern deck. Rib feet ends are beveled and do not extend all the way across the bottom board.

**Hull:** Number of strakes each side: 7; feather-lap construction.

**Gunwales:** Extend to stem fronts.

**Seats:** Caned.

## The Period from 1903 to 1916

In 1903 significant changes were made that continued until the closing of the shop in 1916. "Decks were strips about ¼-inch wide, blind nailed to follow the gunwale line, joints grooved with an instrument of steel about pencil size and sharpened to make a V-shaped shallow groove."[11] Coamings were added, as were tapered center cover boards that butt to the stem post. These were used by Rushton in his earlier canoes and used routinely on guideboats built by the Brown's Tract builders. Decorative deck beams

11 Manley, 1968:167.

FIGURE 2-298 (Left) A strip-built deck with the distinctive shallow V-grooves between each strip. The center cover board is tapered at the stem end and butts to the stem post. The coaming is narrow. The stem band and cap are missing. (Right) Decorative deck beam beneath the deck; a single pair of half-round, steam-bent, red elm scribe ribs beneath the deck. The stem-foot end is a horizontal rectangle. The center cover board has been removed.

FIGURE 2-299 Some Rushton yoke cleats have short arms of almost equal length. The arm toward the bow is slightly longer.

with mirrored ogees were also added.

Brass stem bands run from the bottom board, over the stem post, and extend onto the cover board, forming a stem-post cap. The first pair of ribs under the bow and stern decks, like the 1891–1902 design, are half-round, steam-bent, red elm scribe ribs. The ribs are spaced four inches apart. The metal shoes, protecting the bottom-board/garboard overlap are brass rather than iron. The gunwales remained D-shaped; this is the most common of the three Rushton guideboat designs.

In 1903, and only for that year, there was an option to order a guideboat with all ribs made from half-round, steam-bent red elm, spaced three inches apart.

## Field Notes (1903 to 1916)

**Stem post and stem band:** The stem post is narrow and sloping, and the continuous brass stem band, extending from the bottom board to the center cover board, serves as a stem-post cap.

**Stems:** Tumblehome (Saranac profile). The shape of the stem foot is a horizontal rectangle.

**Decks:** Strip-built with V-grooves between strips. The strips follow the line of the gunwales.

**Center cover board:** Tapered at the stem and butts to the stem post.

**Deck beams:** Decorative mirrored ogee.

**Coamings:** Narrow, often secured with round-head brass screws.

**Ribs:** No reverse-curved ribs. One pair of half-round, steam-bent, red elm scribe ribs and two pairs of footed ribs under the bow and stern decks. Rib feet ends are beveled and do not extend all the way across the bottom board.

**Hull:** Number of strakes each side: 7; feather-lap construction.

**Gunwales:** Extend to stem fronts; rounded D-shape.

**Seats:** Caned.

**Shoes:** Brass, 2 or 3.

**Oarlock straps:** Scroll pattern.

FIGURE 2-300 The stem post and stem band of Rushton guideboats built from 1903 to 1916. The gunwales are D-shaped. (Top Left) The brass stem band is continuous from the bottom board along the stem front and over the narrow sloping stem post to end on the center cover board. (Top Right) The stem band forms a protective stem post cap and is secured to the deck by two screws. The stem post width is about ½ inch; its thickness is about ¼ inch. (Right) The Saranac stem profile.

**FIGURE 2-301** Mitchell Sabattis. (Courtesy of Adirondack Museum)

## MITCHELL SABATTIS (ATTRIBUTED)

**Date of birth:** Circa 1824
**Date of death:** April 17, 1906
**Location:** Long Lake, Hamilton County
**Active:** Late 1860s to 1870
**Estimate of guideboats built:** Unknown
**Number reviewed:** 1 (attributed)
**Builder's plate:** Not used
**Adirondack Museum accession:** 82.132.1

### Biographical Sketch

Mitchell Sabattis was one of the best-known woodsmen and guides of his era. The name Sabattis may be a contraction of the French name Saint Jean Baptiste. His year of birth has been variously cited between 1801 and 1825. His gravestone in the Long Lake Cemetery records his year of birth as 1824.

His place of birth is believed to be Parishville, St. Lawrence County. In 1900 J. Dyneley Prince wrote:

> During a recent visit to Long Lake Village, Hamilton County, I called upon Mr. Mitchell Sabattis of the Abenaki tribe. . . . My informant's father, the late Peter Sabattis, dead fifty years ago, but still remembered familiarly as Captain Peter, was a native of St. Francis, P.Q. [Province of Quebec], the ancient reserve of the remnant of the Abenakis in Canada. Peter Sabattis and his Abenaki wife removed to the Mohawk Community at St. Regis Falls [*sic*] late in the last century, where Mitchell was born about ninety years ago.[1]

Sabattis first came to Long Lake with his father at the age of eight.[2] In 1844 he married Elizabeth Dornburgh (1827–1901) from the Mohawk Valley. They had thirteen children. Three of the boys, Charles,

1 J. Dyneley Prince, "Some Forgotten Indian Place-Names in the Adirondacks," *Journal of American Folk-Lore,* April–June 1900:124.
2 William L. Wessels, *Adirondack Profiles,* Lake George, NY: Adirondack Resorts Press, 1961:84.

**FIGURE 2-302** Mitchell Sabattis gravestone (1824–1906), Long Lake Cemetery.

Isaac, and Harry, followed in their father's footsteps and became woodsmen and guides. Charles and Isaac served in the Union Army during the Civil War. In Long Lake, Isaac and one of his brothers both reportedly built the "celebrated Adirondack boats in the winter."[3] County supervisors' reports for 1885 and 1888 list only Isaac as a boatbuilder.[4]

As Alfred Donaldson wrote in his *History of the Adirondacks*:

> Nothing of greater historical interest attaches to Long Lake than the fact that the Adirondack guide-boat was evolved there. Its progenitors were Mitchell Sabattis and one of the Palmers who saw the need of devising something sturdier and swifter than the canoe. Their joint product must have been put in use as early as 1842, for that was the date of Dr. Todd's second visit [to Long Lake], in recounting which he says "We procured a little [boat], such a one as a man can carry on his head through the woods, from river to river, and from lake to lake."
>
> It differed in one important respect, however, from the guide-boat of today. It had a square stern, but the disadvantages of this feature became apparent and soon disappeared. This modification, and many a less conspicuous refinement, was tooled into the craft by the patient, cunning hands of Caleb Chase of Newcomb.[5]

There is no description of the boat Todd saw in Long Lake, other than that it was little, relatively light, and had a square stern. Furthermore, in 1842 Sabattis may have been as young as eighteen years old, and Ransom and Cyrus Palmer had not yet been born.

By the 1870s, the Sabattis home provided rooms and supplies for about sixteen guests. As well as guiding for many prominent visitors, Sabattis was a leader in the Long Lake Wesleyan Church. A mountain and a settlement, also known as Long Lake West, on the Mohawk & Malone Railroad have been named after him. In 1886 and again in 1900, he suffered a stroke, becoming severely disabled after the second one. He died in Long Lake on April 17, 1906.

As mentioned, Mitchell's son Isaac was listed as boatbuilder in 1885 and 1888, as well as guide, farmer, and town assessor in the various proceedings of the county supervisors from 1885 to at least 1902.[6] In 1905 he was listed as a State Game Protector.[7]

Many Adirondack guides, not considered to be boatbuilders, built a guideboat or two to suit their needs. The guideboat attributed to Mitchell Sabattis at the Adirondack Museum may fall into this category. The museum files state that this boat (accession 82.132.1) was built by "a Sabattis." There is no confirmation that it was Mitchell Sabattis who built it. It is more likely that was Mitchell's son Isaac, a documented boatbuilder. In a 1958 interview with Kenneth Durant, Willard Sutton, then aged ninety-three, stated that Mitchell Sabattis "did not build

3 L. E. Chittenden, "The Story of Mitchell Sabattis," *Personal Reminiscences*, New York: Richmond, Croscup, 1893:157.
4 *Hamilton County Supervisors' Reports*, 1886:4, 1889:8.
5 Donaldson, 1921, II:79.
6 *Hamilton County Supervisors' Reports*, 1886–1902.
7 Aber and King, 1965:224.

boats."[8] This is despite the fact that he has been given credit by different authors for the origin, alone or with others, of the guideboat.

There is one source, however, that lends credence to the possibility that Mitchell Sabattis did build a guideboat. A letter dated February 16, 1918, from Henry S. Harper, the publisher and a local camp owner on Long Lake, to Donaldson offers the following:

> Yesterday afternoon at a meeting of the Adirondack Association, I asked one of our trustees, Professor Ernest T. Carter, who used to go to Long Lake as a boy, if he remembered Mitchell Sabattis. He said he remembered him very well and that he still had and used a guide boat which Mitchell Sabattis made. He also had a tomahawk which belonged to Captain Peter and was given to him by Mitchell Sabattis.[9]

## Guideboat Characteristics

The guideboat at the museum is short: 14 feet 2 inches long and 37 inches wide, a size appropriate for a guide's own use. The straight bow deck and the arced stern deck indicate an early boat from the late 1860s to the early 1870s.

8 Willard Sutton, *Interview with Kenneth Durant, 1958*, Durant Collection.
9 Henry S. Harper, *Letter to Alfred L. Donaldson, February 16, 1918*, Adirondack Research Room, Saranac Lake Free Library, Donaldson Collection.

**FIGURE 2-303** The boat attributed to Sabattis at the Adirondack Museum. (Top) The stem post wide, high with a large rounded notch at its front and a smaller, rounded notch at its rear. Its front is chamfered, and the top is slightly rounded. It is similar to those of G. W. Smith and Charles Hamner. (Bottom) The yoke cleat.

## Field Notes

**Stems:** Width from the rabbet line to the leading stem edge; upper stem (just under gunwale) about 2½ inches; lower stem (greatest width) 3½ inches.

**Ribs:** One pair of reverse-curved scribe ribs and one pair of reverse-curved footed ribs under both bow and stern decks.

**Hull:** Number of strakes on each side: 9; feather-lap construction. Length, 14 feet 2 inches; bottom board length is 12 feet 7 inches (greatest width 8 inches); beam 36¾ inches. Rib spaces on center 6 inches. Weight 58 pounds.

**Gunwales:** Do not reach stem front, bevel follows the chamfer line.

**FIGURE 2-304** Decks and deck caps. (Left) Bow deck: straight, one piece, flush with the carlin, let into the gunwales. Deck cap is pie-piece-shaped with a beveled inboard edge. (Right) Stern deck: arced, one piece, let into the gunwales. Deck cap is also pie-piece-shaped with a beveled inboard edge.

**Figure 2-305** An undated photograph of Harry Sabattis in a guideboat that may have been built by his father, Mitchell. The design of the yoke-cleat is similar to that of the boat at the Adirondack Museum. Note the typical cross-handed position of the oars. (Courtesy of Long Lake Historical Society)

## HERBERT L. AND WRIGHT SALISBURY

**Date of birth:** Unknown
**Date of death:** Unknown
**Active:** Early 1880s–1894
**Location:** Long Lake, Hamilton County (early 1880s, 1887–1889); Saranac Lake, Franklin County (1890–1894)
**Estimate of guideboats built:** Unknown, possibly more than 20
**Number reviewed:** 3
**Builder's plate:** 1
**Adirondack Museum accession:** 63.165.1

### Biographical Sketch

Little is known about the Salisbury brothers and their guideboat-building activities. According to Syracuse, New York, city directories, Herbert Salisbury was a pattern maker.[1] His brother Wright appears to have been his assistant in the construction of boats, as well as his companion on stays in the Adirondacks to improve his poor health, most likely due to tuberculosis. The Salisbury brothers were in Long Lake in 1882. From 1883 until 1886 Herbert was in Syracuse and then back again in Long Lake from 1887 to 1889, as noted in the history of the local Wesleyan church: "At a meeting held March 30, 1889, it was resolved that H. L. Salisbury be Chorister and Orello E. Boyden and Isaac Sabattis assistants with power to invite anyone to assist in singing or playing that they think best."[2] (All three were local boatbuilders.) An undated billhead from the early 1890s of Charles H. Marsha, "Builder of Adirondack Boats" includes the mention that he was the successor to "H. L. Salisbury & Bro."[3]

Although chronically ill, Salisbury built guideboats in Saranac Lake from 1890 to 1894. His brother Wright is listed in the 1902–1903 *Adirondack Directory,* as a taxidermist in Saranac Lake. In subsequent directories (1908, 1910) he is listed as a gardener with a greenhouse at 17 Balsam Street, within a block of

1 John Gardner, "Appendix C, The Guide-Boat Drawings", in Durant, 1980:203–204.
2 Long Lake Wesleyan Church, *Long Lake Wesleyan Church History,* https://longlakewesleyan.wordpress.com/history-of-llwc/, 2013.
3 C. H. Marsha, Billhead, circa early 1890s, Adirondack Museum.

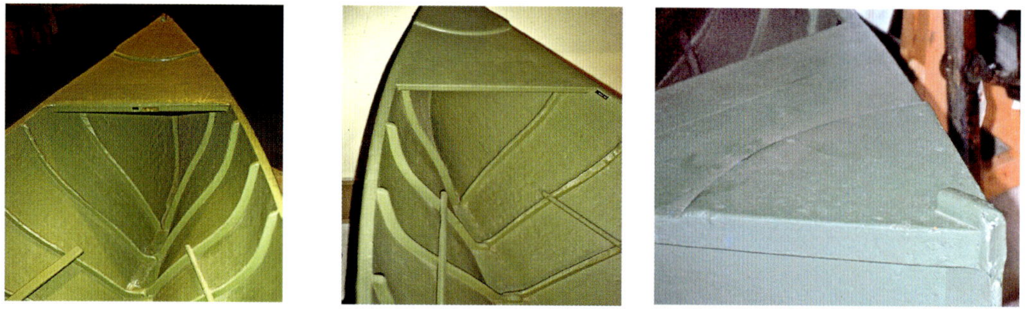

**FIGURE 2-306** (Left) Bow: straight deck and a pie-piece-shaped deck cap, one pair of reverse-curved scribe ribs beneath the deck and a pair of reverse-curved footed ribs inboard of the deck. (Center) Stern: straight deck and the same type and placement of rib pairs as the bow. (Right) The stem post is wide with a rounded top and a vertical front and back. Narrowing of the stem begins at the lower gunwale edge.

Theodore Hanmer.[4] From the *Watertown Daily Times* in 1940, Willard Hanmer, on the occasion of his father Theodore's eightieth birthday, commented:

> Four boat shops were working full time [in Saranac Lake] when [Theodore] Hanmer came here in 1890. Will Martin, Fred Rice, Herb Salisbury and Chet Peck had orders to fill the year around, for the country was just then filling up and transportation was needed.[5]

In an interview with Adirondack Museum director Robert Bruce Inverarity in 1961, Hanmer again stated:

> I know there was a number of different ones [guideboat builders]. There was one by the name of [Chester W.] Peck that used to build a boat; and this fellow Salisbury was one. I told you my father worked for him. He was originally a pattern-maker that came up here and built boats, though not too many. He wasn't able to do much work anyway. I think he was a sick man when he came up here.[6]

## Guideboat Characteristics

The Adirondack Museum has in its collection a boat (accession: 63.165.1) built by Herbert Salisbury for Colonel Franklin Brandreth of Brandreth Park. Named *Cub*, it was built in 1882. Brandreth had four children and apparently requested Salisbury to build a particularly stable craft so that they could fly fish safely. The *Cub* is a large boat, 17 feet 3 inches long, 49 inches wide, 16 inches deep, weighing 92 pounds. The *Cub*'s straight decks are typical of guideboats built before the early 1880s. The reverse-curved ribs and the wide stem post identify the boat as having been built in the Long Lake style.

The *Cub* is noted for its size and stability, characteristics also found in some of Wallace Emerson's boats. In 1906, Emerson, who had worked many summers at Brandreth Park since 1891, was asked by Colonel Brandreth to build other boats like *Cub*. Although similar, the *Cub* and these Emerson boats have several differences in construction. *Cub's* decks are straight, Emerson's decks are arced; *Cub's* decks are let into the gunwales, Emerson's decks are mitered. The *Cub*'s rib feet are rounded, whereas Emerson's rib feet are beveled. Neither builder included yoke cleats on their wide-beamed boats, since they were not intended to be carried.

Fox Brandreth Conner, son of Major General Fox Conner and Virginia Brandreth, noted:

4 *Adirondack Directory*, 1902:79, 1908, 1910.
5 *Watertown Daily Times*, 1940.
6 Inverarity, 1961.

**Figure 2-307** Rib feet are rounded and do not extend all the way across the bottom board.

**Figure 2-308** (Left) One of two guideboats with keelsons attached to the flat, elliptical bottom boards, at Mystic Seaport Museum. The one builder's plate reads: "H. L. Salisbury & Bro., Long Lake, N.Y." (Center) The brass-capped stem post is narrow and sloped. The center cover board has beveled edges and surrounds the stem post. (Right) An arced, two-piece deck, center cover board, sloping stem post, with a brass stem-post cap, and smooth-lapstrake hull. One boat has nine strakes, the other, eleven. The ribs are natural crook; yoke cleats are not present.

> Reuben Cary worked as superintendent and lived on the Brandreth land for many years. He built guideboats there in the winter, and built several models; square stern, regular double end, and a lap strake double end that I have seen. His double end boats were narrow and inclined to be cranky. Wallace Emerson came to Brandreth as a young man and worked there on and off. My Grandfather, Col. Franklin Brandreth, was very fond of him, and I believe was dissatisfied with Reuben's boats, and he started buying boats from Wallace. He was supposed to have suggested the wider boat for fishing. Wallace must have developed the design.[7]

It is possible that Wallace Emerson based his design on the lines of Salisbury's *Cub*, well known to Emerson as it had remained in the Brandreth boathouse from the time of its construction. Franklin B. Brandreth was interviewed at the Adirondack Museum on August 27, 1985. He said:

> The guideboat *Cub* was not only designed by Salisbury but it was also built by him. It was built in this manner so that the extra wide beam would make it more stable. Also, that the wider boat was more suitable for fishing.[8]

Kenneth Durant has suggested that the *Cub* and Emerson's wide-beamed guideboats should more properly be referred to as Brandreth Lake fishing boats.

Two short (14 feet 4 inches) boats, one with a Salisbury & Brother builder's plate, are in the collection of Mystic Seaport Museum in Mystic, Connecticut (accessions 74.460 and 74.461).

7 Fox B. Conner, *Letter to Kenneth Durant, September 6, 1962*, Durant Collection.
8 Franklin B. Brandreth, *Interview, August 27, 1985*, Adirondack Museum.

## GEORGE WASHINGTON SMITH

**Date of birth:** October 2, 1866 (Agawam, Massachusetts)
**Date of death:** August 11, 1926 (Long Lake, Hamilton County)
**Active:** 1888–1926
**Location:** Long Lake
**Estimate of guideboats built:** More than 100
**Number reviewed:** 16
**Builder's plate:** 6
**Adirondack Museum accessions:** 60.37.1, 66.248.1, 70.141.1

**FIGURE 2-309** Smith builder's plate on the bow deck.

**FIGURE 2-310** George Washington Smith.

### Biographical Sketch

George Washington Smith and his brother Abijah (Bige) were raised in Agawam, Massachusetts. Smith is said to have come to Saranac Lake around 1884, where he learned carpentry and boatbuilding from W. A. Martin. By 1888 he had moved to Long Lake and set up a boat shop at the Deerland end of the lake.[1] However, Hale Palmer claims it was his grandfather, Cyrus, who taught George Smith how to build guideboats.[2]

The 1890 federal census listed Smith as a twenty-six-year-old carpenter, not an unusual listing for a boatbuilder. In the county supervisors' reports for 1897, 1898, and 1900, his occupation was given as "boat builder." He is also listed as "boat builder" in the federal census for 1900 and 1910, and the 1905 New York State Census in Hamilton County.[3]

A privately printed Long Lake camp

1 Vincent Engels, *Adirondack Fishing in the 1930s: A Lost Paradise*, Syracuse, NY: Syracuse University Press, 1978:132.
2 Durant, 1980:114.
3 *Hamilton County Supervisors' Reports*, 1897, 1898, 1900; federal census, 1890, 1900, 1910; New York State Census, 1905.

history by owner Catherine C. Trowbridge recalls her favorite guideboats, *Big Cedar* and *Little Cedar*:

> The two guideboats had been specially ordered to be made during the winter of '07–'08. Grandpa had asked George Smith, one of the best boat builders in the Adirondacks, to build these two guideboats for him. The *Big Cedar* was exceptionally wide with a firm seat, made for grandma. Smith's shop was up the hill from the Grove House.[4]

Smith's home and boat shop were located in the area of Long Lake known as the Grove Community (named Deerland in 1903) situated at the bottom of the hill from the turn to Blue Mountain Lake on the road to Forked Lake. He was respected as a builder, not only of guideboats, but also of the first gasoline launch, *Evelyn,* on Long Lake (used as a mail boat), and the steamboat, *Iris II,* the last steamboat to run on Long Lake.[5]

In 1888, George's brother Bige came to Long Lake for a visit and remained as gardener and caretaker for the Grove House, which had opened the previous year. In 1890, he borrowed a boat from George in order to guide New York City watchmaker and inventor Henry Abbott, eventually becoming his full-time guide and life-long friend.

A story about George W. Smith and the Long Lake steamboat was told by Henry Abbott to author Vincent Engels:

> On every pleasant summer's day the steamboats on Raquette and Blue Mountain lakes carried many of these one-time passengers. "The fact that Raquette and Blue Mountain had such boats had something to do with the wish of the Long Lakers to have one too" said Mr. Abbott. George Smith, the master guide-boat maker, was commissioned to build the steamboat. . . . George Smith's boats were second to none in beauty, stability, and lightness, yet so durable that many are in use today, this half century after their maker's death and ninety years after he set up his own boat shop at Deerland. It took some persuasion to coax George Smith to give up the guide-boats for a year and turn to building a steamboat, but Mr. Harper had the gift of words and it was done. George built the boat with the help of his brother-in-law Sam Smith in time for the start of a new summer season.[6]

Over the years from 1914 to 1932, Henry Abbott wrote nineteen annual accounts of his and Bige's adventures and observations in and around Long Lake, titled *Birch Bark Books.* The cover of each year's account was a photograph of birchbark. Abbott sent them to friends at Christmas time.[7] Today these limited editions, reportedly fewer than one hundred printed annually, are collector's items.

Smith was a mentor to Blue Mountain Lake/Raquette Lake guideboat builder John Blanchard. John's son Paul said: "George Smith gave John Blanchard a set of his patterns at the end of his apprenticeship in [the] 1890s."[8]

George W. Smith died on August 11, 1926, crushed when a chain gave away that was holding up a large gasoline launch he was working under.

## Guideboat Characteristics

A Smith guideboat can be identified by his characteristic stem post and the first ribs under the bow deck that are

4 Catherine C. Trowbridge, comp. and ed., *Durand Camp*, Tucson, Arizona: Private printing, 1975:70.
5 Frances Seaman, "Recall When the *Iris* Towed Thousands of Boom Logs Down Long Lake . . .," *Tupper Lake Free Press and Herald*, 1952.
6 Engels, 1978:132, 134.
7 Engels, 1978:129.
8 Durant, *Letter to Louis Little, 1959*, Durant Collection.

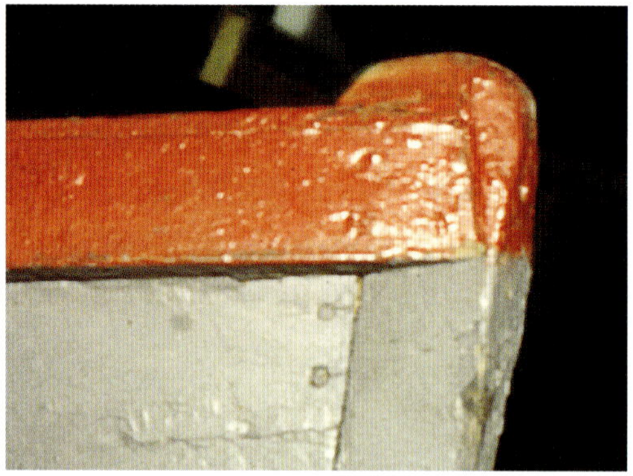
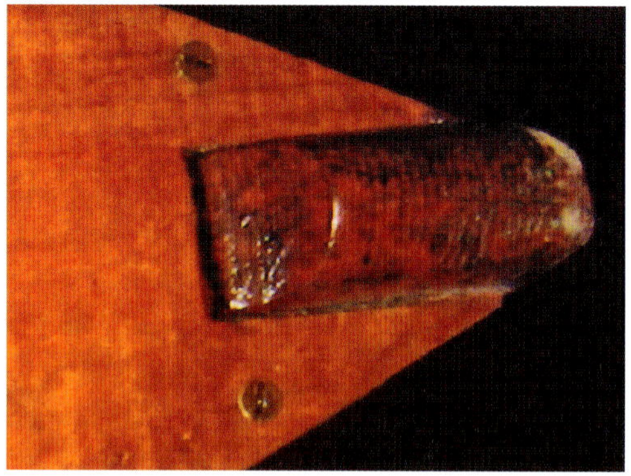

**Figure 2-311** (Left) The stem post is wide, with a length of 2 to 2½ inches, width about 1 inch, and height about ½ inch. The front has chamfered sides, and the top is rounded. The narrowing of the stem begins about 1½ inches below the gunwale. (Center) The back of the stem post is a rounded indentation. (Right) The chamfering of the sides of the stem.

footed and pointed at their upper ends.

Unlike any other Long Lake builder, Smith placed his two- or three-piece decks between the gunwales. His guideboats have deep arced decks. In some, the rib feet extend onto the garboard, an unusual rib construction. At least one guideboat built by John Blanchard has rib feet that extend onto the garboard. The rounded notches of the yoke cleat have flat tops. Smith often used a shield-shaped deck cap. His stems were typical of the Long Lake profile, and the stem feet are bull-nosed with a rounded top edge. Some of his guideboats were wider toward the bow, referred to as cod-headed.

**Figure 2-312** (Left) Rib design and placement. Beneath the bow deck one pair of reverse-curved footed ribs. The rib ends are pointed at the top. No ribs are under the stern deck. Rarely, one pair of scribe ribs and one pair of footed ribs under the bow deck have pointed upper ends. (Right) Scribe rib with a pointed upper end (deck is removed).

## Field Notes

**Stems:** Straight leading edge (Long Lake profile). Width, measured from the rabbet line to the leading edge of the stem: upper (below gunwale), about 1¼ to 2 inches; lower (greatest width), about 2¼ to 3 inches. Beginning of stem narrowing is 1½ to 2 inches below the gunwale. Stem-foot end is bull-nosed.

**Decks:** Two-piece (most common) or three-piece, set between the gunwales. Deep arced deck that slightly overhangs the carlins. One boat reviewed has decks mitered into the gunwales.

**Hull:** Number of strakes each side: 8, rarely 9; feather-lap construction. Beam may be wider towards the bow, (cod-headed).

**Gunwales:** Do not extend to the front edge of the stem. May have two beads along the lower edge. Carlins may also be beaded.

FIGURE 2-313 (Top) A deep arced, two-piece deck, with the pieces placed between the gunwales. A shield-shaped deck cap. Usually there is a shield-shaped cap at the bow and a pie-piece-shaped cap at the stern. (Top Center) A three-piece deck, set between the gunwales, with a shield-shaped deck cap. (Top Right) A three-piece stern deck with a pie-piece-shaped deck cap.

FIGURE 2-314 (Left) Long Lake profile: A plumb, straight, narrow stem. (Right) Bull-nosed stem foot.

FIGURE 2-315 (Left) Four of the guideboats reviewed have rib feet that extend beyond the bottom board and overlap onto the garboard. Only one other builder, John Blanchard, is known to have done this. (Right) Yoke cleat with flat tops of the rounded notch.

## WILLIAM VASSAR

**Date of birth:** 1866 (Au Sable Forks, Essex County)
**Date of death:** 1952 (Bloomingdale, Essex County)
**Active:** Late 1890s ~ mid-1920s
**Location:** Bloomingdale
**Estimate of guideboats built:** More than 100
**Number reviewed:** 28
**Builder's plate:** 17
**Adirondack Museum accession:** 2005.058.1

FIGURE 2-316 William Vassar.

## WILLIAM VASSAR, JR.

**Date of birth:** 1891 (Black Brook, Clinton County)
**Date of death:** 1937
**Active:** About 1910–1920s

FIGURE 2-317 Builder's plate for William Vassar, and for Wm. Vassar & Son, used after 1910. The plates are located on the bow deck or carlin.

## Biographical Sketch

According to his grandson Everett Merritt Brown, William Vassar came to Bloomingdale from Au Sable Forks in the early 1890s. He married Julia Fortune and they had a son, William Jr., born in Black Brook, Clinton County, in 1891, and a daughter, Jessie Jane. William Vassar was "quiet and good natured" and was respected in the Bloomingdale and Paul Smiths communities as a carpenter, guideboat builder, mechanic (including repairing pocket and railroad watches), and inventor. At Paul Smiths, he would "go from camp to camp" repairing boats and mechanical items.[1]

Vassar apparently learned boatbuilding in the late 1890s from William McCaffrey, a fellow Bloomingdale guideboat builder. For a brief period, Vassar and McCaffrey shared a building known locally as "the boat shop." Passersby on Main Street might see one to three guideboats for sale on the veranda.[2]

Vassar is listed in the *Adirondack Directory* for 1902–1903 and 1906 as a boatbuilder.[3] According to his grandson, he continued to build boats until the mid-1920s. His son, William, joined him in about 1910.[4] William Jr. was also listed as a boatbuilder in the New York State Census at the time of his marriage to Mary Martin in 1916.[5] He died in 1937 while a private in the Army Medical Corps.

**FIGURE 2-318** William Vassar at the Paul Smith's railroad station, circa 1910. (Courtesy of Everett M. Brown)

**FIGURE 2-319** An example of William Vassar's carpentry skills. An octagonal inlaid game table he made as a gift to his grandson. The use of contrasting colors of wood is similar to some of his guideboat deck designs. (Courtesy of Everett M. Brown)

1 Everett Merritt Brown, *Personal communication*, August 1, 1992.
2 Brown, 1992.
3 *Adirondack Directory*, 1902:169, 1906:154.
4 Brown, 1992.
5 New York State Census, 1915.

## Guideboat Characteristics

Vassar and McCaffrey both used a pair of upward-pointed scribe ribs at bow and stern that do not extend to the gunwales. The scribe ribs at the stern have a ledge to support the stern-seat cleats. The upper ends of the scribe ribs in Vassar boats end on the sixth strake, while McCaffrey's end on the fifth. Their stem posts differ significantly: Vassar's are narrow and semicircular; McCaffrey's are narrow and rectangular with a concave slope at the inboard end.

The Vassar guideboat patterns were destroyed in a fire. The only tool surviving is a gauge made by Vassar that was used to fashion the yoke. Most, if not all, Vassar guideboats were varnished. It is said that he placed the "boat number under the third rib" of each of his guideboats; none have been found, however.

The Vassars built one guideboat whose hull is made of alternating dark and light strakes.[6] The author is aware of three such guideboats; one built by Theodore Hanmer, one by Willard Hanmer, and one by William Vassar and his son.

The shortest boat of guideboat construction seen by the author was built by Wm. Vassar & Son. It is only 8 feet 11 inches in length.

They also built canoes of guideboat construction—as did Theodore and Willard Hanmer, Albert Billings, George & Bliss, and Myron Nickerson.

FIGURE 2-320 Stem posts. (Left) A narrow, semicircular stem post. Length about 21/4 inches, width about 1/4 inch, and height (highest point of arc) about ¾ inch. (Right) A stem post with a brass cap.

6 Paul F. Jamieson, *Letter to Kenneth Durant,* November 15, 1965, Durant Collection.

## Field Notes

**Hull:** Number of strakes on each side: 7. One 15½-foot guideboat was seen with 8; feather-lap construction.

**Gunwales:** Extend to stem fronts.

**Heel Plates:** One piece, with lateral upper ends cut off at an angle (similar to McCaffrey's).

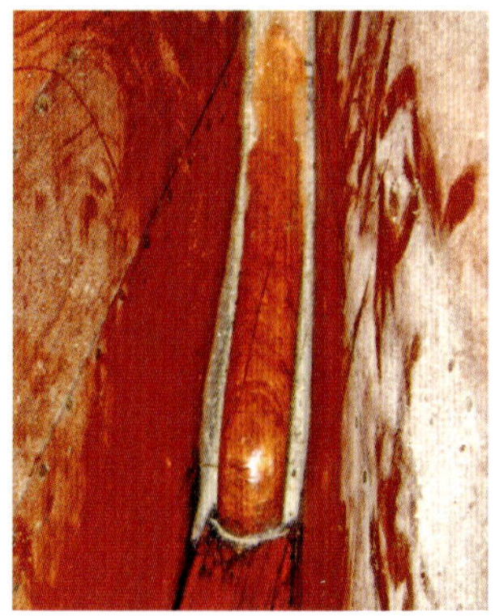

FIGURE 2-321 Stem profile, and stem foot. (Left) A similar stem profile was also used by the two other Bloomingdale builders, William McCaffrey and E. G. Ricketson, and is referred to as the Bloomingdale profile. The horizontal width from rabbet line to stem front is, for the upper stem, about 2 inches and for the lower stem 4 ½ or more inches. (Bottom) The bull-nosed stem foot.

**Figure 2-322** Ribs. (Left) At the bow: one pair of scribe ribs under the deck. The pointed ends of these ribs reach the sixth strake. A three-piece deck is placed between the sheer strakes. (Right) At the stern, one pair of scribe ribs, pointed at their upper ends, and rising to the sixth strake. They have ledges to support the stern-seat cleats.

**Figure 2-323** Three different deck types. (Left) A one-piece deck with an unusual heart-shaped deck cap (most Vassar deck caps were pie-piece shaped). (Center) A two-piece deck placed between the sheer strakes with a pie-piece-shaped deck cap. (Right) A strip deck with a pie-piece-shaped deck cap. There is no center cover board or coaming. The pointed scribe rib ends on the sixth strake.

**Figure 2-324** A boat of guideboat construction, measuring 8 feet 11 inches in length, built by Wm. Vassar & Son.

**Figure 2-325** (*Above*) William Vassar, Jr., and his father with a so-called "zebra" guideboat. (Courtesy of Adirondack Research Room, Saranac Lake Free Library)

FIGURE 2-326 Allison W. Warner.

## ALLISON WOOD WARNER

**Date of birth:** July 15, 1975 (Odessa, Texas)
**Active:** 2003–
**Location:** Adirondack Museum, Blue Mountain Lake, and Lake Clear (Franklin County)
**Estimate of guideboats built:** 9
**Builder's plate:** Most

### Biographical Sketch

Growing up in West Texas, Allison Warner developed an early passion for the outdoors, spending time on the water, and racing wood canvas canoes and war canoes. After graduating from Washington and Lee University in Virginia, she spent a year working in Europe. Upon her return, she served as an SCA Americorps volunteer in the Adirondacks.

Warner was exposed to guideboats for the first time as a volunteer at a No-Octane Regatta event hosted by the Adirondack Museum. She first rowed a guideboat on Newcomb Lake while on a restoration project at Camp Santanoni and was inspired to build one. The boat's owner, craftsman Michael Frenette, agreed to teach Warner how to restore guideboats over the next winter. The experience introduced her to Michael's brother Rob, a professional guideboat builder and restorer, under whom she would restore guideboats for several years. With Rob's support, Warner was hired as Educator/Demonstrator for the boatbuilder in Residence Program at the Adirondack Museum, where she began building boats during the summer of 2003. In 2012 Warner joined the mathematics department of North Country Community College as a full-time faculty member. During the summer she continues to demonstrate and build boats at the

Adirondack Museum, and she divides the remainder of the year between boatbuilding and teaching college math courses.

Since 2003, Warner has built nine guideboats; five were built at the museum, while the remaining boats were for clients. In 2011, she began building and restoring boats out of her own shop, Adirondack Wooden Boats, in Lake Clear.

## Guideboat Characteristics

Warner reproduces guideboats built by past builders. Where some present-day builders have one design they have settled upon, she instead builds several different models. Working in the museum's Boat Building, she is surrounded by a variety of guideboat designs and styles that serve as inspiration. Thus far, Warner has built boats patterned after those of Frederick W. Rice, John Blanchard, Warren Cole, and the Parsons Brothers, representing all three regional styles.

To date, the boats that Warner has built are not exact replicas, but often include a combination of design elements that she finds appealing. Her favorite builders are Parsons and Blanchard, and one can see Blanchard's influence in the details of her seats, oars, and paddles. After finishing her first Parsons boat, while demonstrating during the summer of 2017, she began designing her own guideboat hull. It has turned out "to be most influenced aesthetically by the Brown's Tract region, with a forward-raking stem."[1]

FIGURE 2-327 Allison Warner carving a stem rabbet as the Boatbuilder in Residence at the Adirondack Museum. (Courtesy of Nancy Battaglia)

1 Allison W. Warner, *Personal communication*, 2017–2018.

## ANSEL C. WILDER

**Figure 2-328** Wilder builder's plate, located on the center cover board.

**Date of birth:** 1849

**Date of death:** 1906 (Watson, Lewis County, Beaches Bridge Cemetery)

**Active:** 1890s–early 1900s

**Location:** Petries Corners, Lewis County

**Estimate of guideboats built:** More than 20

**Number reviewed:** 1

**Builder's plate:** 1

### Biographical Sketch

Ansel Wilder was married to Ella Bickford. They had one son, Jesse H., born in 1873. The *Gazetteer and Business Directory of Lewis County* for 1872–1873 lists Wilder as a carpenter and farmer.[1] A later directory for 1895–1896 lists: "Wilder Ansel, w[wife] Ella (Bickford), p o Petries Corners, r 15, carpenter, boat builder and farmer , 61[acres], 3 cows, 1 horse."[2] The similarities between Wilder's guideboats and those of Dwight Grant of nearby Boonville and Seeber & Parsons of Old Forge suggest that he began building boats sometime after 1890.

### Guideboat Characteristics

The author has examined one Wilder guideboat with its builder's plate and is aware of two others. The hulls of all three boats were built using the modified-bevel method first used by Grant in 1886 and by Seeber & Parsons after 1890.

Wilder's stem post with its brass stem-post cap (thin, with three holes; two for screws and one limber hole) and the shape of his stem foot are all similar to those of Seeber & Parsons.

Wilder's two-piece decks are let into the gunwales. They have a center cover board butting to the stem post, and a wide coaming. This design was initiated by Grant in 1882 and later used by Seeber & Parsons in 1890. Wilder's outward-raked stems are also similar to those of Seeber & Parsons.

Wilder guideboats have some features

1 Hamilton Child, *Lewis County Directory, 1872–1873.*
2 William Adams, comp., *Business Directory of Lewis County, N.Y.,1895–96*, Lowville, NY: 1895:533.

 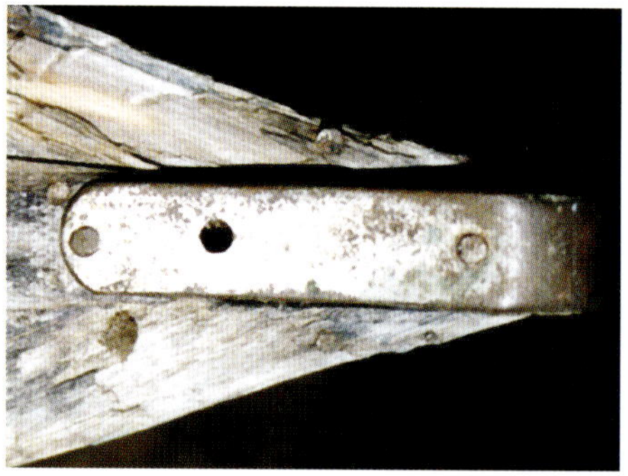 

FIGURE 2-329 (Left) The junction of the stem post and tapered center cover board that butts to it. The stem post is wide and sloping. The gunwale is beaded along its upper and lower edge. (Center) The stem post with a thin brass cap. The cap is fastened with two screws, one on either side of a limber hole—similar to Seeber & Parsons guideboats. (Right) The flattened, semicircular stem foot, typical of the Brown's Tract builders.

that differentiate them from the other Brown's Tract builders. His ribs are not reverse curved, while those of Grant, Seeber, and Parsons are. There are two beads along his gunwales, one along the top edge and one along the bottom. The design, number, and placement of his scribe ribs under the decks at bow and stern are similar to those of Grant.

## Field Notes

**Decks:** Two-piece, let into the gunwales. Bow and stern have deep arcs.

**Center cover board**: Tapered, end butts to the stem post.

**Coamings:** Wide at center, tapered at the ends.

**Gunwales:** Do not extend to stem front; one bead along the upper and another the lower gunwale edge.

**Heel plates:** Three-piece, with rounded lateral borders.

FIGURE 2-330 (Left) A two-piece Wilder deck, similar to those of Grant. (Center) The outward rake of the stem (Brown's Tract profile) is similar to Seeber & Parsons after 1891 and Grant after 1894. (Right) No reverse-curved ribs, and no ribs pointed at their lower ends, unlike Parsons. Wilder guideboats have two pairs of scribe ribs under the bow and stern decks.

**Figure 2-331** Christopher Woodward in his shop. (Courtesy of Joseph Rector)

## CHRISTOPHER H. WOODWARD

**Date of birth:** November 17, 1957 (Kittery, Maine)
**Active:** 1987–
**Location:** Saranac Lake, Franklin County
**Estimate of guideboats built:** 18
**Builder's plate:** Used

**Figure 2-332** Woodward builder's plate. (Courtesy of Woodward Boat Shop)

### Biographical Sketch

Christopher H. Woodward is the son of Edwin C. and Ruth Weston Woodward. His father was a naval officer who after retirement earned a degree in forestry at Paul Smith's College and then taught there from 1958 to 1978. The Woodward family lived at White Pine Camp, the 1926 Summer White House for President Calvin Coolidge. In 1991 Chris married Catherine Largess of Jamestown, Rhode Island. They have two children, Patrick and Gabriel.

Woodward was introduced early to wooden boats that were often in need of maintenance and repair. In his teens he had a wood and canvas canoe but preferred rowing to paddling. After rowing a friend's guideboat and seeing them on display at the Adirondack Museum, he became determined to build one. In 1980–1981 he completed the inaugural class in traditional guideboat building through the Adirondack Guideboat Apprenticeship Program, offered by the North Country Community College of Saranac Lake, and taught by master builders Carl Hathaway and Ralph Morrow.

From 1980 to 1987, Chris worked at various jobs, including for two boatbuilding companies building modern wooden runabouts and composite boats. During the winters he worked part time for Hathaway, cutting and storing ice at a camp where Carl was caretaker. In the spring of 1987, he went to work full time with Hathaway in his boat shop in Saranac Lake, and that winter (1987–1988), assisted him with the last guideboat class. During this period he built his first guideboat. In 1991, he bought the Hathaway shop, now known as the Woodward Boat Shop.[1]

Woodward works mostly with the tools that came with the shop, many of which were used by Willard Hanmer, the original owner, who built it in 1930. The shop is the only building and repair shop for traditional guideboats that has been in continuous operation since then, through three generations. In 2010, it was placed on the Register of Very Special Places by Traditional Arts of Upstate New York (TAUNY) in recognition of its historical value to the local community and regional culture.[2]

Woodward offers presentations on the history of the guideboat and its early builders. He has contributed an introduction to its history and construction on his website.[3]

**Figure 2-333** Some of the sixty-five guideboats at the 50th Annual Hanmer Memorial Race and guideboat regatta in 2012. (Courtesy of Joseph J. Spadaro, Jr.)

For several years Chris helped organize the Willard J. Hanmer Memorial Race, a popular summer event on Lake Flower in Saranac Lake. Together with local guideboat enthusiast, Christopher W. Covert, Jr., owner of Guide Boat Realty, in 2012 they put on the most successful race and regatta in decades in celebration of the race's fiftieth anniversary. Sixty-five guideboats participated.

1 Christopher Woodward, *Personal communication*, 2012.
2 Register of Very Special Places, TAUNY, 2010.
3 Adirondack Guideboats, www.guideboats.com., 2009.

## Guideboat Characteristics

Bloomingdale style stems.

Gunwales, seats, and cleats are cherry.

Decks are 7-piece, crowned, with shield-shaped, western red cedar deck caps.

One pair of scribe ribs at both bow and stern, under the decks. The stern scribe rib has a ledge to support the aft end of the stern-seat cleat.

Stem post is narrow and rectangular. At the stern, it may have a brass stem-post cap.

Stem foot is bull-nosed and is stamped with the number built to date and year the boat was completed.

**Figure 2-334** Woodward Boat Shop. It has served as a boat shop for three generations of builders: Willard Hanmer, Carl Hathaway, and currently Christopher Woodward. It is the oldest active guideboat-building shop in the Adirondacks. (Courtesy of Woodward Boat Shop)

**Figure 2-335** The stem foot is bull-nosed, with the number of guideboats built to date (7) and the year (1997). (Courtesy of Woodward Boat Shop)

**Figure 2-336** (Above) A typical crowned (slightly arched) seven-piece deck with a shield-shaped deck cap. (Right) The rectangular stem post is high and narrow. (Courtesy of Woodward Boat Shop)

**FIGURE 2-337** A 16-foot Woodward guideboat. There are eight strakes. The planking is feather-beveled, white pine or cedar. (Courtesy of Woodward Boat Shop)

## GUIDEBOAT

# Deck Designs and Placements

THESE SIX TWO-PART drawings illustrate the various guideboat deck designs, components, placements, and support structures. They are not to scale. They are cutaway views split down the centerline. The lower drawing of each shows the deck, deck support structure, scribe ribs, ribs underneath the deck, stem post, stem foot, and how the deck is placed relative to the gunwale and sheer strake. The right side of the lower drawing shows how the gunwale is shaped for the deck placement. The upper drawing is a cross-section showing the left half of the deck from a straight-on perspective. At the left side is the detail of the deck placement. The double-ended arrows show the relationship between the two views. The arrows and dotted line in the lower drawing correspond with the arrows in the upper drawing.

## One-piece deck with a pie-piece-shaped deck cap

This is the simplest of the decks. The deck is a single piece that extends from gunwale to gunwale. This deck is mitered, or beveled, into the gunwales. Both the deck and the gunwales are beveled so that the deck sits flush in the gunwales. The gunwales are covered and there is no apparent seam on the edge. The deck cap surrounds the stem post and overrides the deck. It has an arced inboard edge and straight sides that resemble a slice of pie. The deck support is made up of a forward deck beam that supports the deck and the inboard edge of the deck cap. A carlin (the curved deck beam) supports the inboard edge of the deck. The deck is cut flush with the carlin. This is a Long Lake style boat, with a wide stem post that has a concave front and rounded over top. The stem foot is bullnosed. There is one pair of scribe ribs and the ribs are reverse curved. The planking lap is a feathered bevel.

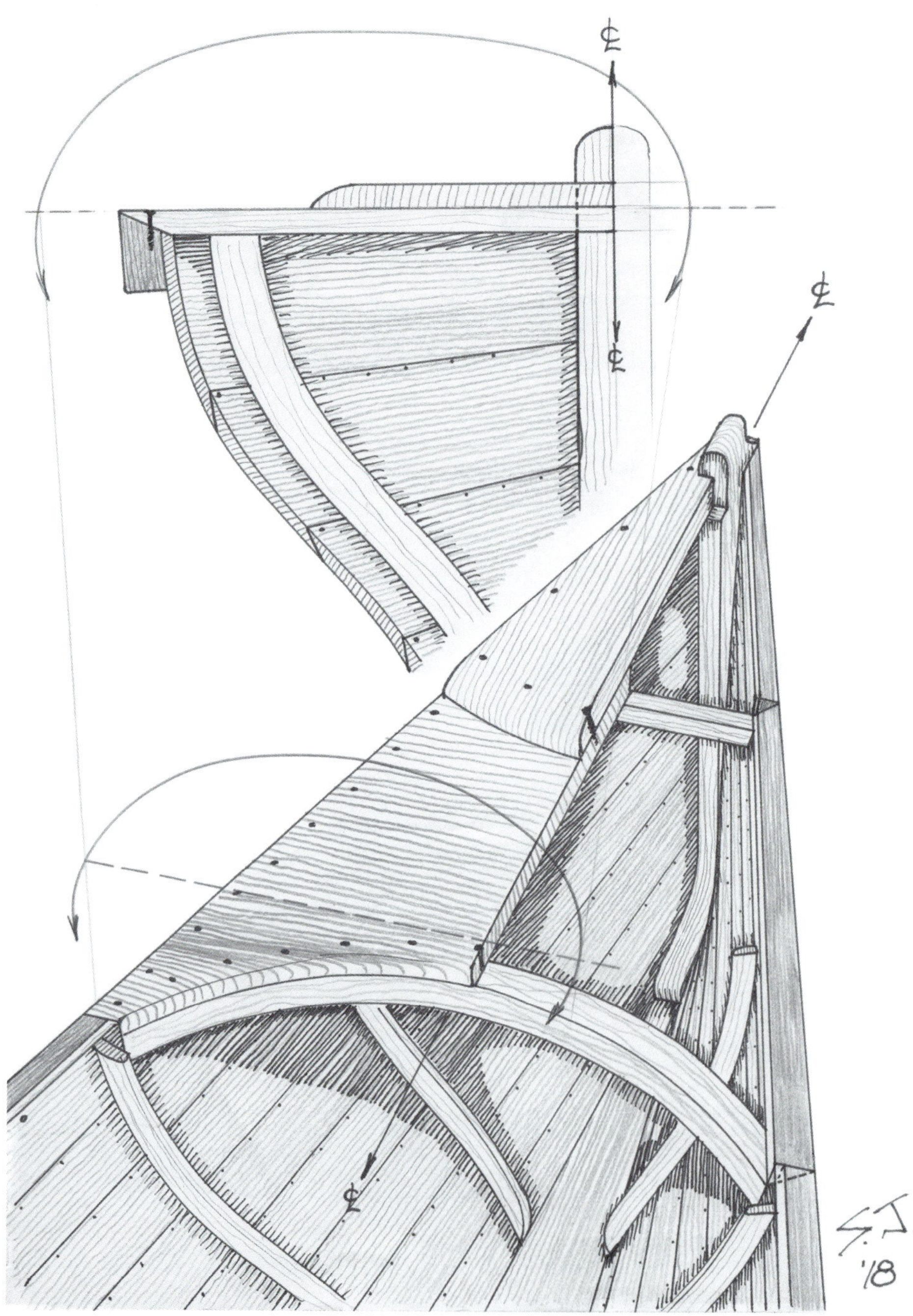

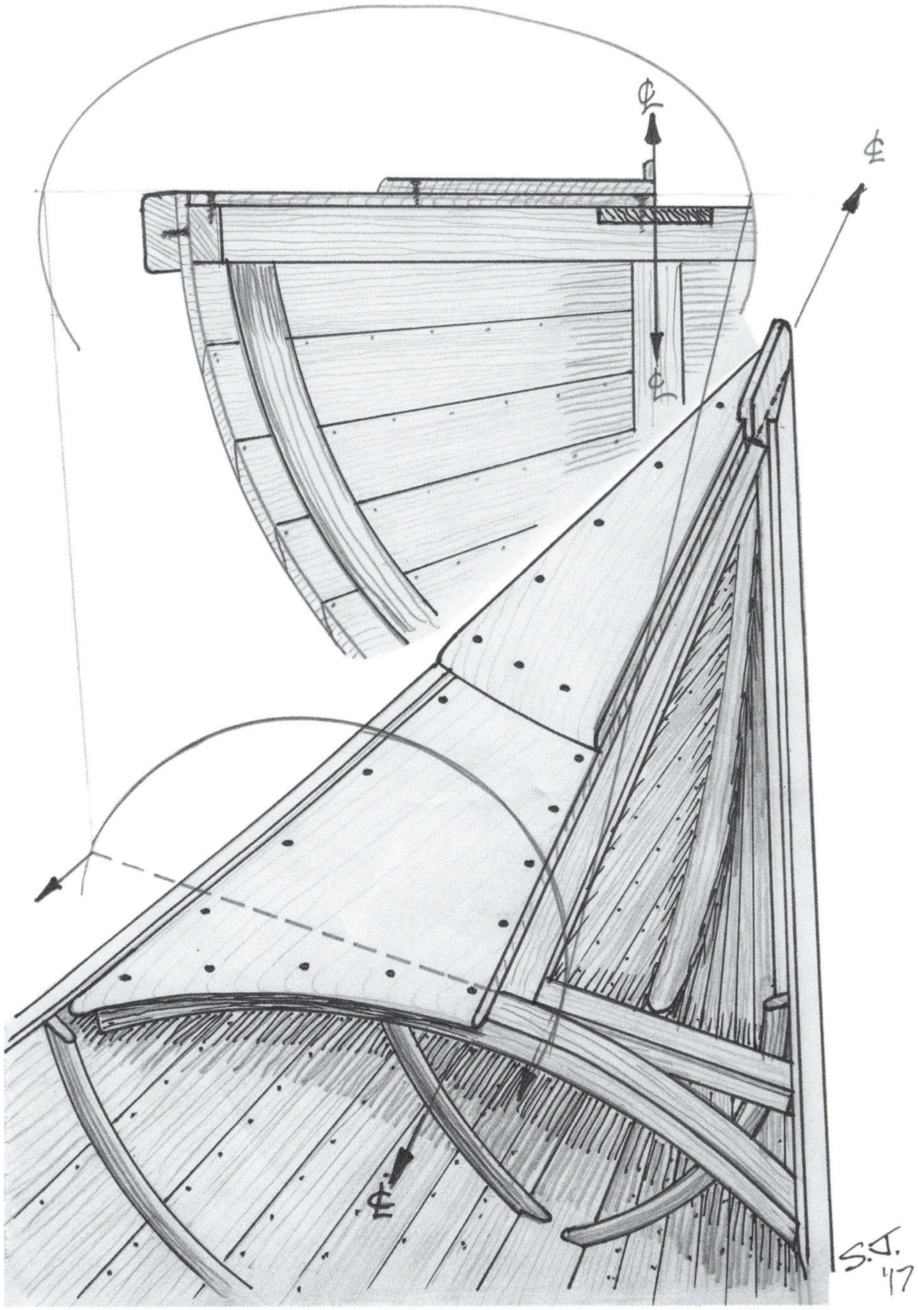

## Two-piece deck with a pie-piece-shaped deck cap

This deck is made up of two pieces that run fore and aft, and butt together at the centerline. The deck is set between the sheer strakes. The outboard edges butt against the sheer strakes, sitting flush with them and the gunwales. The gunwales and the sheer strakes are not covered, and the deck seams are all visible. The deck cap is a pie-piece shape, surrounding the stem post. The deck support structure is made up of a deck beam and carlin that supports the inboard edge of the deck, and pieces that run alongside the sheer strake to support the outboard edges. A fore and aft center deck support is attached to the stem, and the other end is let into the deck beam. This supports the center edges of the deck. The deck overhangs the carlin. This is a Saranac style boat with a long, narrow rectangular stem post. The stem foot is rounded and pointed. The ribs are not reverse curved, and there is one pair of scribe ribs. The planking lap is a feathered bevel.

## Two-piece deck with a shield-shaped deck cap

This deck is made up of two pieces that run fore and aft and butt together at the centerline. The deck is set between the gunwales. The sheer strakes are cut away so that the outboard edges butt to the gunwales and are flush with them. The sheer strakes are covered, but the gunwales are not. The deck seams are all visible. The deck cap is not a smooth arc, but is a mirrored ogee, resulting with a small protrusion at the center, resembling a shield shape. The cap surrounds the stem post and overrides the deck. The deck support structure is made up of a forward deck beam that supports the forward edge of the deck and the inboard edge of the deck cap. The inboard edge of the deck is supported by a carlin. The deck overhangs the carlin. A center deck support, attached to the carlin and deck beam, runs fore and aft and supports the center edges of the deck. Attached to the sheer strake are pieces that support the outboard edge. This is a Long Lake style boat with a short, wide stem post with a concave back and rounded top. The stem foot is a horizontal rectangle. The ribs are reverse curved and there are no scribe ribs. The planking lap is a feathered bevel.

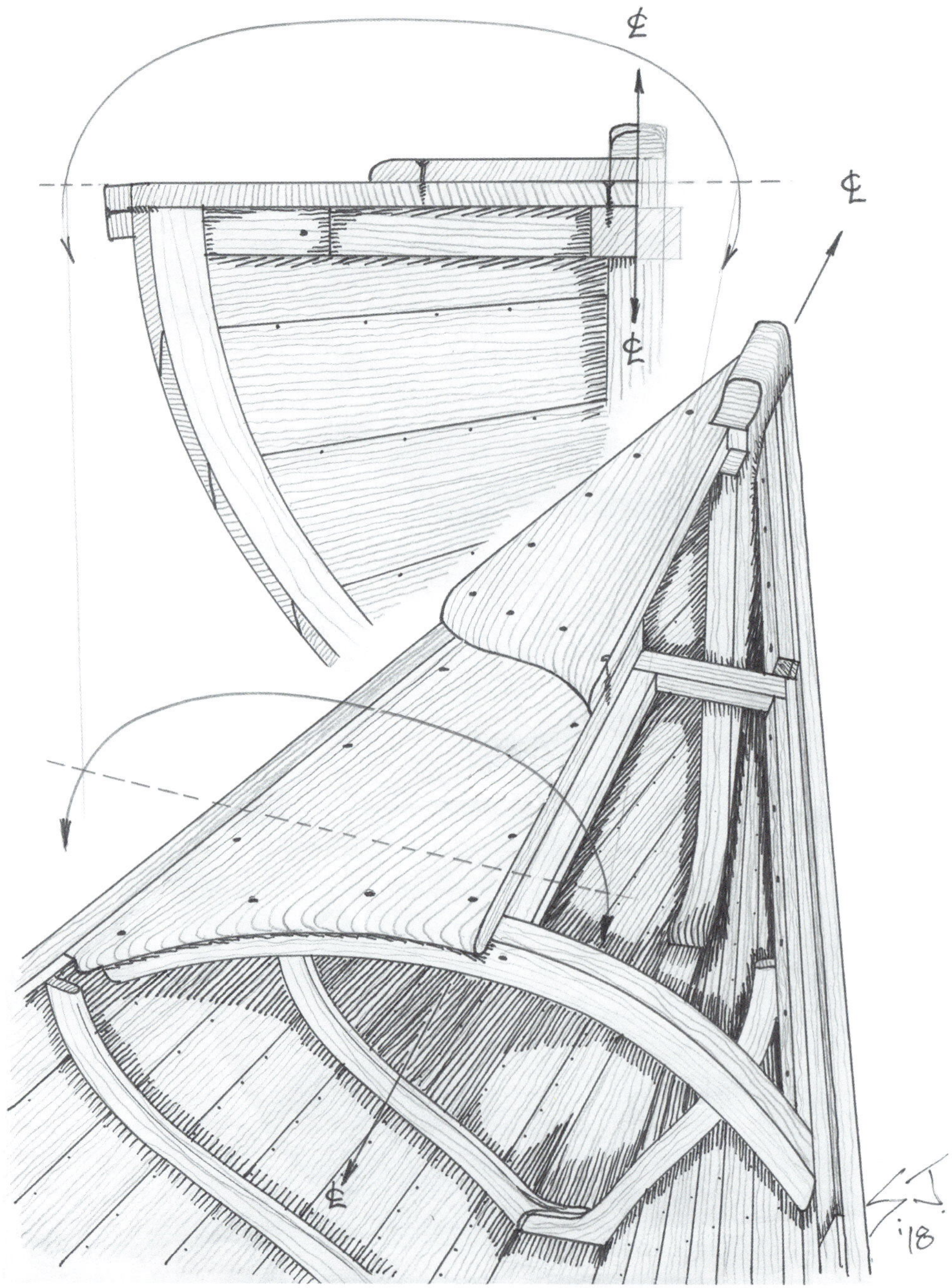

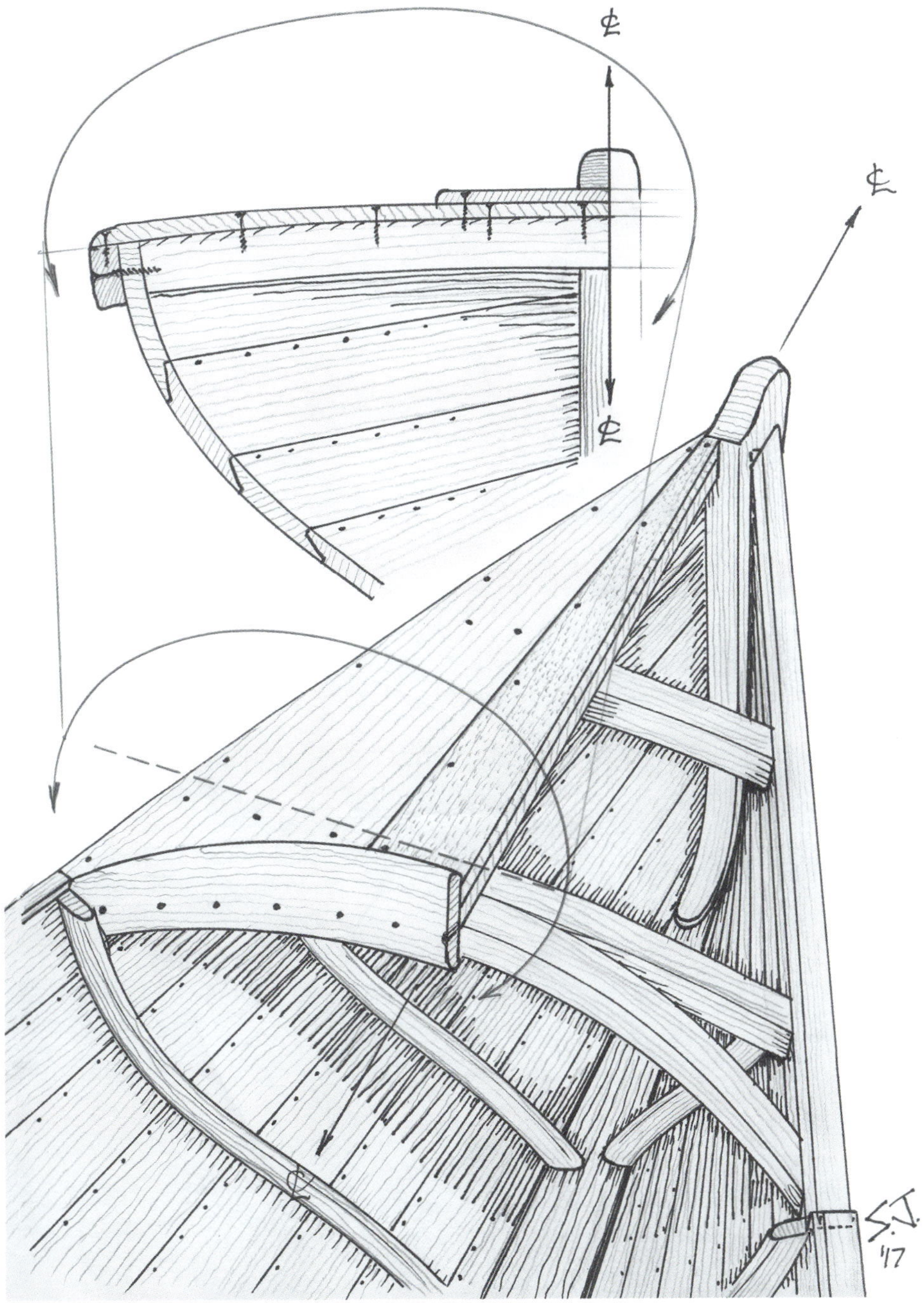


## Two-piece deck with a center cover board

This deck is made up of two pieces that run fore and aft, and butt together at the centerline. The deck is let into the gunwale. The gunwale and sheer strake are cut out so that the deck fits into the gunwale and is flush with it. The gunwale is covered and the deck edge is visible only from the side view. A center cover board covers the center deck seam, and butts to the stem post. The deck support structure is made up of a forward deck beam that supports the middle of the deck, and a deck beam and attached carlin that support the inboard of the deck. Attached to the facing edge of the carlin and deck is a wide coaming. This is a Brown's Tract style boat, with a wide, sloping stem post, and a flat, circular stem foot. There is a pair of scribe ribs, and the ribs are reverse curved. The planking lap is a modified bevel (Grant lap).

## Five-piece deck

This deck is made up of five pieces of alternating light and dark woods, butting together, with a slight V-groove between them. The outer pieces are set between the sheer strakes and are flush with the strakes and the gunwales. The strakes and the gunwales are not covered. An oval handhold is cut through the deck and deck beam. A pie-piece-shaped deck cap surrounds the stem post and overrides the deck. The deck support structure is made up of a forward deck beam, a middle deck beam, and an oversized deck beam that supports the inboard edges of the deck pieces. This is a Saranac style boat, with a short, narrow, rectangular stem post. The stem foot is bull-nosed, or rounded over. The ribs are not reverse curved and there are no scribe ribs. The planking lap is a feathered bevel.

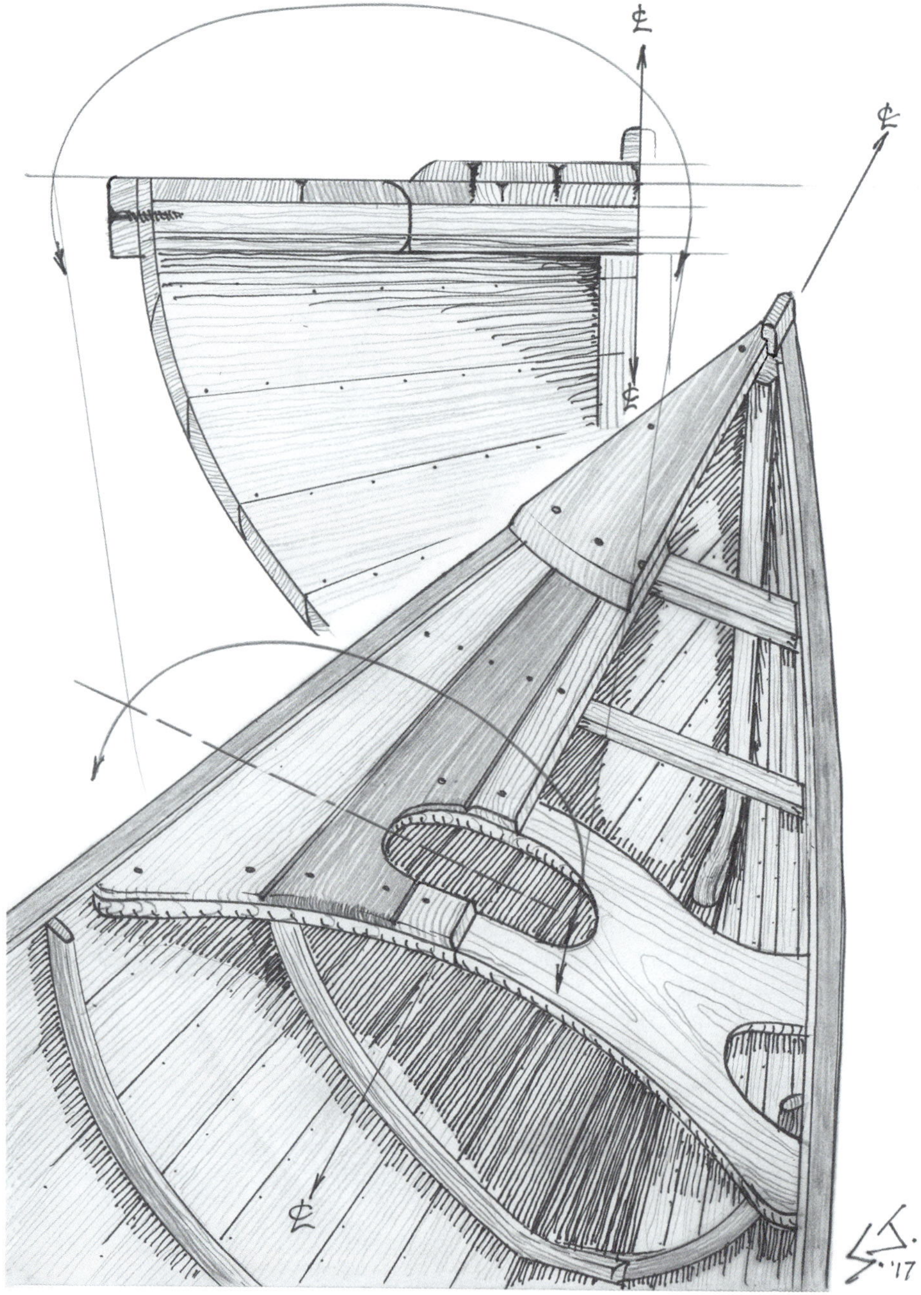

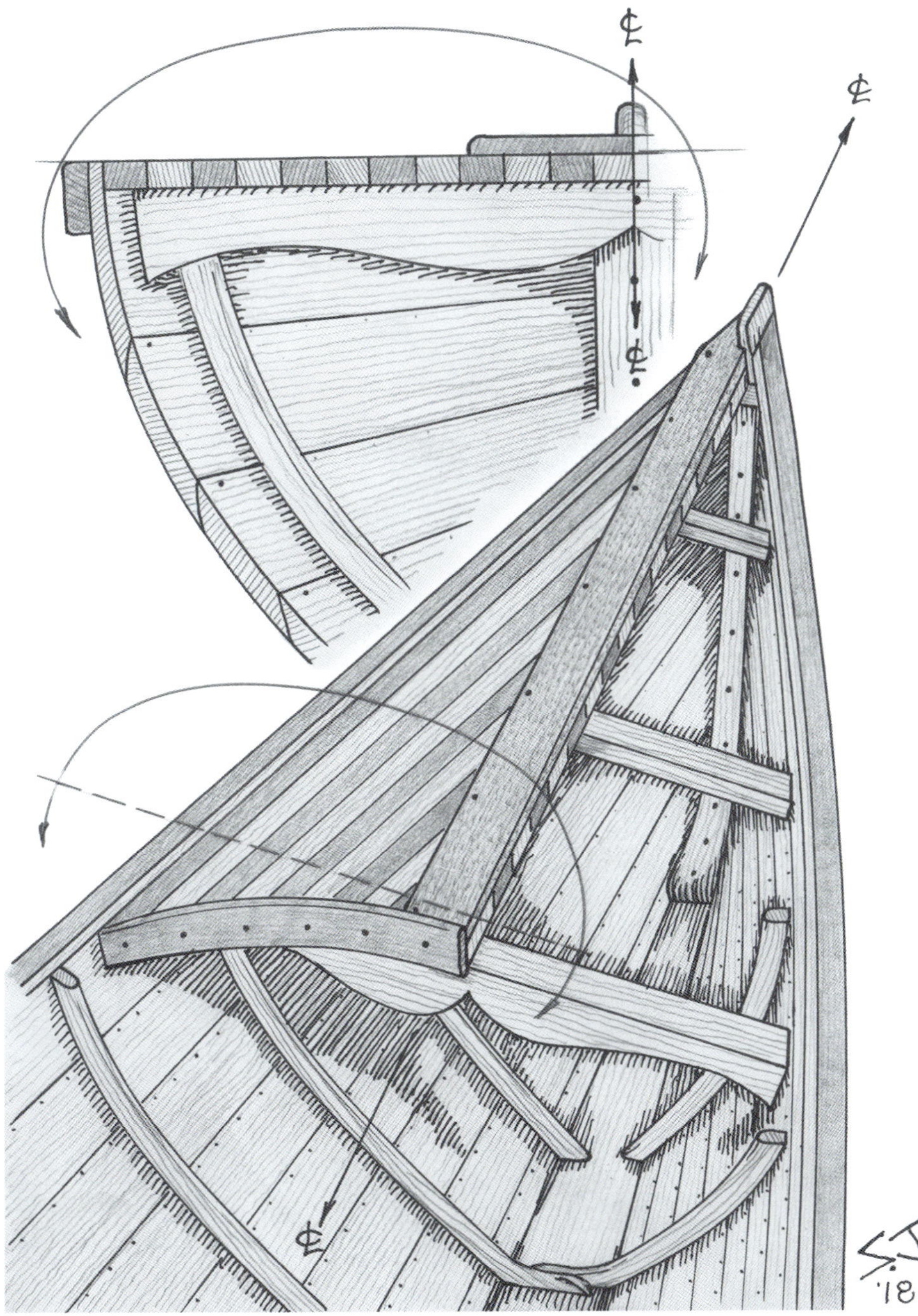


## Strip-deck

This is a multipiece deck made up of strips of alternating light and dark woods. The strips are parallel with the gunwale, and with each other, and are edge-nailed together. They are set between the sheer strakes and meet at the centerline. A center cover board that surrounds the stem post covers the center seam. The gunwales and sheer strakes are not covered. The deck support structure is made up of a forward deck beam, a middle deck beam, and a decorative deck beam that supports the inboard edges of the deck pieces. The decorative deck beam is a mirrored ogee. A narrow coaming is attached to the facing edge of the deck. There is no carlin. The stem is two-piece, as evidenced by the screw heads in the stem face. This is a Saranac style boat with a short, narrow, rectangular stem post. The deck beam is decorative, with a mirrored ogee. The stem foot is a horizontal rectangle. The ribs are not reverse curved, and there is one pair of scribe ribs. The planking lap is a feathered-edge bevel.

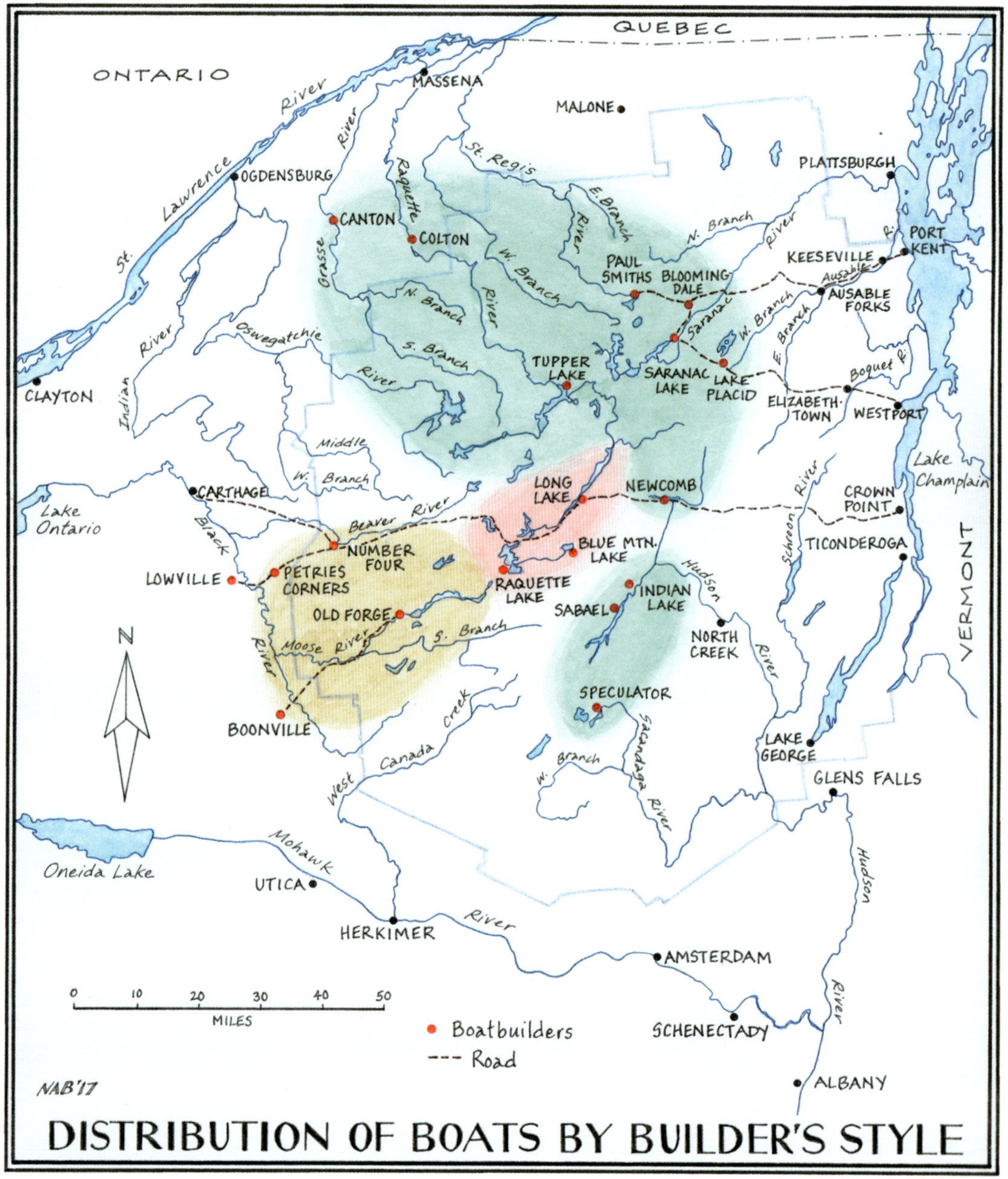


Saranac Style

(Bloomingdale Style)

Long Lake Style

Brown's Tract Style

# 3

## GUIDEBOAT IDENTIFICATION

# Who Built That Boat?

*by Stephen Sulavik and Christopher Woodward*

SOME YEARS AGO, the author purchased an old guideboat with no builder's plate. Discussions with several people knowledgeable about such matters yielded no further information about the builder. This, it turns out, is a common experience.

Fortunately, there are regional differences in construction that indicate where in the Adirondacks the builder of a particular guideboat was probably working. The shape of the stem profile, for example, will indicate whether the boat is of Saranac Lake, Long Lake, or Brown's Tract origin. There are also similarities that identify lineages of builders—from father to son, for example, or from a boatbuilder to a workman in his shop who then strikes out on his own. Finally, and most important, the construction of these boats makes it reasonable to assume that each builder has incorporated unique structural characteristics—a "signature"—by which he can be identified.

In the early stages of his search, the author was completely unaware as to which parts of the boat would turn out to be important in identifying its builder. Eventually, by examining a great many boats and boat parts, a procedure—a protocol—was devised for narrowing down the identity of the builder. Photographs were taken of as many parts of each guideboat as possible and proved to be critical for this work. Particular attention was given to boats with a builder's plate, or other compelling builder provenance, in an effort to find unique characteristics not present in other builders' boats. The accounts of more than fifty traditional guideboat builders and their boats are in Part 2 of this book. What follows here is a protocol for identifying a particular builder based on this information.

A few cautions should be borne in mind. Not all the boats of a particular builder are likely to be identical. As the Guideboat Characteristics for a few builders in Part 2 point out, certain aspects of their boats changed over time. Keep in mind that some guides or carpenters may have built only one or two boats, sometimes incorporating features similar to a known builder. These builders remain unknown.

Another factor to consider is that the stem post, one of the key identifying features of a guideboat, is subject to wear. There may no longer be evidence, for instance, of a concave indentation, or it may be angled when originally it was vertical. The stem post at the stern usually gets the most wear, so the bow stem post is probably a better indicator of its original shape. How to determine which is the bow of a double-ended boat in which both ends appear the same can be problematic. Usually, the bow deck is the larger of the two. If both decks appear to be the same size, the seat placement determines which end is the bow. The bow seat and cleats are farther from the deck than the stern seat is, usually by one or more ribs, as determined by the screw holes in the ribs if the seat and cleats are missing. A third way to determine the bow is to examine which way the scarph joints runs in each strake. The outer scarph will run past the inner scarph from bow to stern, so that the joint points to the stern.

## Protocol for Identifying a Guideboat's Builder

**Builder's Plates**

**Stems**

- Stem profile
- Stem thickness under the gunwales
- Stem post shape
- Stem foot

**Decks**

- Number of deck pieces
- Deck inboard-edge shape
- Deck placement
- Deck cap shape
- Center cover board
- Coamings
- Decorative deck beams

**Ribs**

- Reverse-curved ribs
- Scribe ribs
- Stern seat cleat ledge
- Rib feet

**Hull**

- Number of strakes on each side
- Planking lap method

**Other Components**

- Carlins
- Gunwales
- Seat cleats
- Seats
- Seat backrests
- Yoke cleats
- Carry yoke
- Oars
- Paddle
- Hardware
- Oarlock straps (socket plates)
- Stem bands

## Regional Stem Profiles

The stems of a guideboat are the upright pieces of natural crook forming the bow and stern of the boat. They are attached to each end of the bottom board and rise above the height of the decks. They are rabbeted to receive the ends of the hull planking. Usually one solid piece, they are sometimes made from two pieces, an inner and an outer stem.

Four distinctive stem profiles are widely recognized: Bloomingdale, Saranac, Long Lake, and Brown's Tract. Bloomingdale boats are considered to be a subset of the Saranac style.

FIGURE 3-1 Regional stem profiles. The three guideboat stems on the left are tumblehome to varying degrees, that is, the upper portion of the stems incline inward. (Left to Right) **Bloomingdale stem:** A wide stem at the waterline, with pronounced tumblehome. **Saranac stem:** A curvilinear leading edge, with moderate tumblehome. **Long Lake stem:** Narrow, with a nearly straight and plumb leading edge. **Brown's Tract stem:** Narrow with an outward rake.

### Stem thickness under the gunwales

The stem thickness where the gunwales attach is the primary indicator in determining whether a boat was built in the Saranac style (northern region), the Long Lake style (central region), or the Brown's Tract style (southern region).

Stems are approximately 1-inch thick at the rabbet line and are tapered toward the leading edge, where they are approximately ⅜-inch thick. In Saranac style boats the stems are tapered the full length, from the stem post to the bottom. Where the gunwales attach to the stem, the stem is tapered from full thickness at the rabbet line to thin at the leading edge. In Long Lake- and Brown's Tract-style boats, the taper starts below the gunwales and continues to the bottom. But where the gunwales attach to the stem, the stem is the full thickness from the rabbet line to the leading edge. The stem profile, either straight and plumb or raked forward, and the shape of the stem post will further determine whether the boat was built in the Long Lake or the Brown's Tract style.

## Dimensions of stems and stem posts as clues to the builder

The stem and stem post are described by their height, width, and thickness (akin to board measurement).

### Stem dimensions

Only stem thickness is described here. The stem thickness can be:

**Thick:** Refers to the stem underneath the gunwales. Full thickness.

**Thin:** Refers to the stem underneath the gunwales. Tapered to thin at the stem leading edge.

### Stem post dimensions

The stem post length is relative to the width of the stem:

**Long:** Refers to the length of the stem post relative to the width of the stem. It spans the full width of the stem, from its leading edge all the way to its inner face, hidden behind the planking.

**Short:** Refers to the length of the stem post relative to the width of the stem. It extends only to the rabbet line.

The stem post height is the distance above the deck cap or cover board:

**High:** Refers to the height of the stem post above the deck cap or cover board. It is ¾ inch or higher.

**Low:** Refers to the height of the stem post above the deck cap or cover board. It is ½ inch or lower.

The stem post width is relative to the thickness of the stem:

**Wide:** Refers to the stem post above the decks. Wide is the full thickness of the stem.

**Narrow:** Refers to the stem post above the decks. Narrow is the thickness of the stem leading edge.

FIGURE 3-2 (Left) Thick: Full thickness where the gunwales join the stem. Long Lake style. (Center) Tapered thin: Stem is tapered to the thickness of the stem band. Saranac style. (Right) Thick: Sloped with a metal cover band. Brown's Tract style.

| | | |
|---|---|---|
| *William M. Alden* | 1870s–1880s | Newcomb |
| *Leonard Anderson* | 1902–1925 | Tupper Lake |
| *Albert Henry Billings* | early 1880s–1903 | Lake Placid |
| *John F. Buyce* | 1889–1940s | Speculator |
| *Caleb Judson Chase* | 1850s–1908 | Newcomb |
| *Edmund Judson Chase* | 1911~1923 | Newcomb |
| *James Fletcher Cameron* | 1984– | Upper St. Regis |
| *Raleigh Raymond Fish* | late 1960s–early 1970s | Indian Lake |
| *Robert W. Frenette* | 1983– | Tupper Lake |
| *George & Bliss* | 1904–1927 | Lake Placid |
| *Frederick D. Graves* | early 1870s–1893 | South Boston, MA |
| *Theodore Salter Hanmer* | 1898–1945 | Saranac Lake |
| *Willard J. Hanmer* | 1927–1962 | Saranac Lake |
| *Edward Harvey* | 1910s–1930s | Colton |
| *Carl George Hathaway* | 1963–1991 | Saranac Lake |
| *Hurst & Nickerson* | 1890–1895 | Canton |
| *Isaac Abraham Hurst* | 1890–1910 | Canton |
| *William Bartlett Kerst* | 1895–early 1940s | Indian Lake |
| *Fuat Latif* | 1985– | Vermontville |
| *William McCaffrey* | mid-1880s–1903 | Bloomingdale |
| *William McLenathen* | 1851~1875 | Saranac Lake |
| *William Allen Martin* | 1865–mid-1890s | Saranac Lake |
| *Henry Kilburn Martin* | mid-1890s~1915 | Saranac Lake |
| *Adirondack Boat Building Company* | 1885–1909 | Saranac Lake |
| *Alric B. Moody* | 1880s–early 1900s | Tupper Lake |
| *Ralph R. Morrow* | 1970–2007 | Saranac Lake |
| *Myron Augustus Nickerson* | 1890–1907 | Canton |
| *Frederick William Rice* | 1874–1903 | Saranac Lake |
| *Frederick Marsh Rice* | 1905–1931 | Saranac Lake |
| *Elbridge Gerry Ricketson* | late 1870s–mid-1890s | Bloomingdale |
| *John Henry Rushton* | 1888–1916 | Canton |
| *William Vassar* | late 1890s–mid-1920s | Bloomingdale |
| *Christopher H. Woodward* | 1987– | Saranac Lake |

## Saranac Style Builders

The Saranac style region includes Essex, Franklin, and St. Lawrence counties of the northern Adirondacks. It encompasses Saranac Lake, Bloomingdale, Paul Smiths, Lake Placid, Newcomb, Tupper Lake, Colton, and Canton. Saranac style boats are characterized by a tapered stem where the gunwales are attached, resulting in a narrow stem post. There are no reverse-curved ribs. The boats tend to be narrower than Long Lake boats. The seats and backrests are plain, while the decks may be ornate. Usually the hulls have seven strakes rather than eight. The stem profile has more curvature and tumblehome than the Long Lake profile. The few builders in the Indian Lake and Lake Pleasant area of Hamilton County also built in the Saranac style.

## BUILDER'S PLATES

Albert Billings

George & Bliss

John Buyce

Raleigh Fish

Robert Frenette

Fuat Latif

Theodore Hanmer

Willard Hanmer

Carl Hathaway

Isaac Hurst

Hurst & Nickerson

Ralph Morrow

William A. Martin

H. K. Martin

Adirondack Boat Building Co.

Myron Nickerson

J. H. Rushton

## STEMS

### Stem profile

Saranac profile:

*All*, except:

Bloomingdale profile: (See under **Bloomingdale Style Builders**)

Stem width at the waterline (greatest width) is more than 5 inches.

*James Cameron*
*William McCaffrey*
*E. G. Ricketson*
*William Vassar*
*Christopher Woodward*

Long Lake profile:

*William Kerst*

Brown's Tract profile:

*Fuat Latif*

### One-piece

*All*

### Two-piece (inner and outer)

*George & Bliss*
*Hurst & Nickerson*
*Isaac Hurst*
*William Kerst*
*Myron Nickerson*

### Stem thickness under the gunwales

Tapered to thin at the stem leading edge:

*All*, except:

Full thickness:

*Robert Frenette*
*Ralph Morrow*

### Stem post shape

Narrow:

*All*

Wide:

*Robert Frenette*
*Willard Hanmer*
*Carl Hathaway*

Stem post is not present:

*Leonard Anderson*
*William Kerst*

Long, concave back, vertical front:

*Leonard Anderson*

*Albert Billings*

Long, low, concave back, vertical front:

*Theodore Hanmer*

Long, low, concave back, angled front:

*William A. Martin*

*H. K. Martin*

Long, low, ridged on top, vertical back, angled front:

*William Alden*
*Caleb Chase*
*Edmund Chase*

Long, rectangle, vertical back and front:

*Adirondack Boat Building Co.*
*John Buyce*
*William Kerst*

*Edward Harvey*

Long, vertical back, angled front:

*Alric Moody*

*J. H. Rushton*

Long, angled back, vertical front:

*Willard Hanmer*

*Ralph Morrow*

Long, concave back and front, flat top:

*Willard Hanmer*
*Frederick W. Rice*
*Frederick M. Rice*

*William A. Martin*

Long, rounded back, concave front:

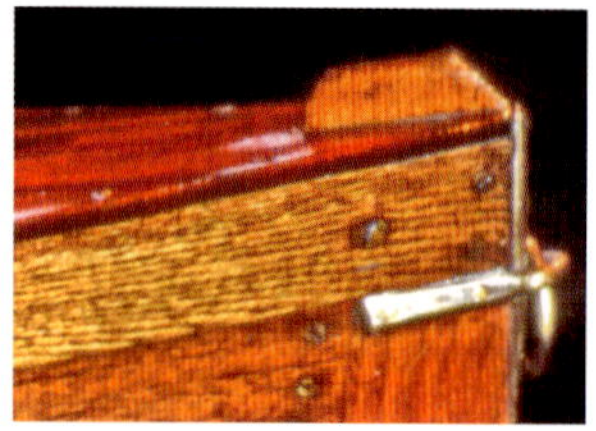

*J. H. Rushton*

Short, high, rounded, vertical back and front:

*Carl Hathaway*

*Myron Nickerson*
*John Buyce (no photograph)*

Short, rectangle, vertical back and front:

*George & Bliss*

Short, concave back, angled front:

*Hurst & Nickerson*

Short, high, angled back and front:

*Isaac Hurst*

Low, sloping, brass-capped:

*Fuat Latif*

*J. H. Rushton*

*Isaac Hurst*

Low, sloping, no cap:

*Frederick Graves*

High, rounded, sloped:

*Raleigh Fish*

Wide, tapered, rises to a point, sloping to the deck:

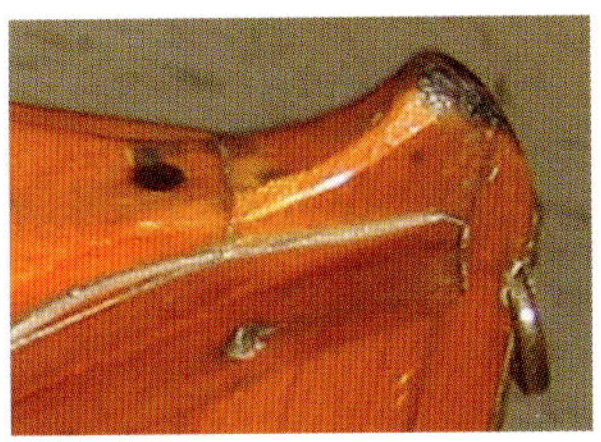

*Willard Hanmer*

*Carl Hathaway*

Full thickness stem with a wide, high, sloped stem post:

*Robert Frenette*

Full-thickness stem with a narrow stem post:

*Ralph Morrow*

**Stem foot**

Horizontal rectangle:

*Adirondack Boat Building Co.*
*Leonard Anderson*
*Albert Billings*
*John Buyce*
*George & Bliss*
*Raleigh Fish*
*Willard Hanmer*
*Isaac Hurst*
*William Kerst*
*William A. Martin*
*H. K. Martin*
*Myron Nickerson*
*Frederick W. Rice*
*Frederick M. Rice*
*J. H. Rushton*

Rounded over, bull-nosed:

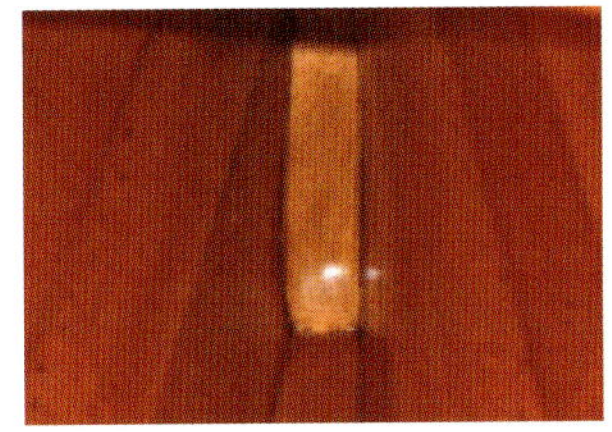

*Theodore Hanmer*
*Willard Hanmer*
*Edward Harvey*
*Carl Hathaway*

Pointed, ridged on top:

*Caleb Chase*
*Edmund Chase*

Sharply pointed, talon-like:

*Robert Frenette*

Rounded point, no ridge:

*William Alden*
*Caleb Chase*
*William Kerst*

# DECKS

## Number of deck pieces

One piece:

*William Alden*
*Leonard Anderson*
*Robert Frenette*
*Frederick Graves*
*Theodore Hanmer*
*Edward Harvey*
*William Kerst*
*John Buyce*
*William A. Martin*

One piece, plywood:

*Raleigh Fish*

Two pieces:

*Adirondack Boat Building Co.*
*Leonard Anderson*
*Caleb Chase*
*Edmund Chase*
*Fuat Latif*
*H. K. Martin*
*Alric Moody*
*Ralph Morrow*
*Frederick W. Rice*
*Frederick M. Rice*
*J. H. Rushton*

Five pieces with handhold:

*Carl Hathaway*

Six or more pieces, with handhold:

*Willard Hanmer*

Strip deck:

*Leonard Anderson*
*Albert Billings*
*George & Bliss*
*Theodore Hanmer*
*Willard Hanmer*
*Hurst & Nickerson*
*Isaac Hurst*
*Alric Moody*
*Ralph Morrow*
*Myron Nickerson*
*Frederick W. Rice*
*Frederick M. Rice*

Strip decks are V-grooved:

*Fuat Latif*
*Hurst & Nickerson*
*J. H. Rushton*

## Deck inboard-edge shape

Straight:

*Caleb Chase*
*Frederick Graves*
*Edward Harvey*
*John Buyce*

Arced:

*All*

Deep arc:

*Albert Billings*

*Edward Harvey*
*Hurst & Nickerson*
*Isaac Hurst*
*William A. Martin*
*H. K. Martin*
*Ralph Morrow*
*Myron Nickerson*
*J. H. Rushton*

**Deck placement** (See drawings, page 317)

Let into the gunwales:

*Adirondack Boat Building Co.*
*William Alden*
*Caleb Chase*
*Robert Frenette*
*Frederick Graves*
*Theodore Hanmer*
*Edward Harvey*
*William Kerst*
*William A. Martin*
*Ralph Morrow*
*Frederick W. Rice*
*Frederick M. Rice*
*J. H. Rushton*

Set between the gunwales:

*Caleb Chase*
*Edmund Chase*
*Robert Frenette*
*Theodore Hanmer*
*Willard Hanmer*
*William A. Martin*
*H. K. Martin*
*Myron Nickerson*
*Frederick W. Rice*
*Frederick M. Rice*

Mitered into the gunwales:

*William Kerst*

Set between the sheer strakes:

*Leonard Anderson*
*Albert Billings*
*George & Bliss*
*John Buyce*
*Robert Frenette*
*Carl Hathaway*
*H. K. Martin*
*Alric Moody*
*Ralph Morrow*
*J. H. Rushton*

**Deck cap shape**

Straight:

*Caleb Chase*

Pie-piece-shaped:

*Adirondack Boat Building Co.*
*Caleb Chase*
*Edmund Chase*
*Raleigh Fish*
*Robert Frenette*
*Frederick Graves*
*Theodore Hanmer*
*Carl Hathaway*
*William A. Martin*
*Frederick W. Rice*
*Frederick M. Rice*
*J. H. Rushton*

Shield-shaped:

*William Alden*

*Willard Hanmer*

Teardrop-shaped:

*Leonard Anderson*

Heart-shaped:

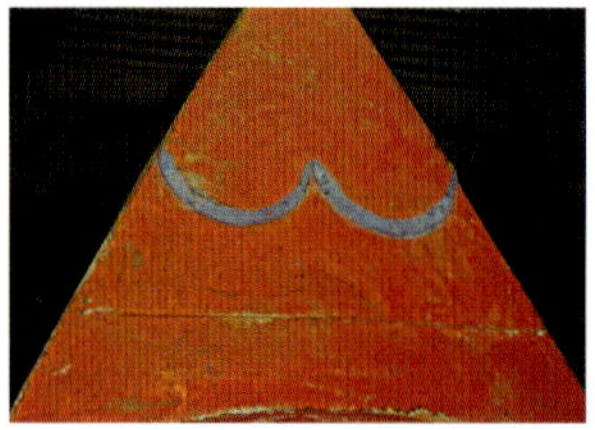

*Edward Harvey*

Diamond-shaped, with rounded points:

*John Buyce*

**Center cover board**

Surrounds the stem post:

*Leonard Anderson*
*Albert Billings*
*George & Bliss*
*Theodore Hanmer*
*Willard Hanmer*
*Hurst & Nickerson*
*Isaac Hurst*
*William A. Martin*
*H. K. Martin*
*Alric Moody*
*Ralph Morrow*
*Myron Nickerson*
*Frederick W. Rice*
*Frederick M. Rice*

Butts to the stem post:

*Fuat Latif*
*Willard Hanmer*
*Ralph Morrow*
*J. H. Rushton*

**Coamings**

Narrow, not tapered:

*Leonard Anderson*
*Albert Billings*
*George & Bliss*
*Hurst & Nickerson*
*Isaac Hurst*
*William A. Martin*
*H. K. Martin*
*Alric Moody*
*Ralph Morrow*
*Myron Nickerson*
*Frederick W. Rice*
*Frederick M. Rice*
*J. H. Rushton*

**Decorative deck beams**

Mirrored ogee:

*George & Bliss*

*J. H. Rushton*

Four concave arcs, three points:

*Myron Nickerson*

Three concave arcs, two points:

*H. K. Martin*

Nine to eleven circular scallops:

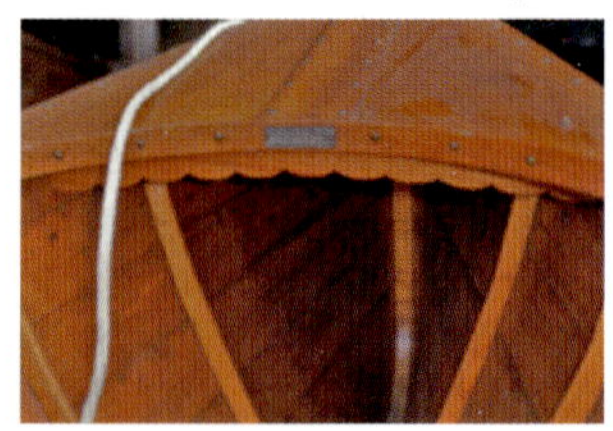

*Albert Billings*

## RIBS

**Reverse curved**

None, except:

Slight:

*William Alden*
*Caleb Chase*
*Edmund Chase*
*Raleigh Fish*
*William Kerst*

**Scribe ribs**

No Scribe Ribs:

*Adirondack Boat Building Co.*
*Leonard Anderson*
*Albert Billings*
*George & Bliss*
*John Buyce*
*Raleigh Fish*
*Frederick Graves*
*Willard Hanmer*
*Carl Hathaway*
*Myron Nickerson*

One pair at bow and stern:

*Edward Harvey*
*Hurst & Nickerson*
*William Kerst*
*Isaac Hurst*
*Myron Nickerson (rarely)*

Two pairs at bow and stern:

*Leonard Anderson*
*Theodore Hanmer*
*Alric Moody*
*J. H. Rushton*

Two pairs at bow and stern, chamfered at the bottom:

*Robert Frenette*
*Frederick W. Rice*
*Frederick M. Rice*

More than two pairs at bow and stern:

*Theodore Hanmer*

One pair steam-bent, half-round, red elm scribe ribs at bow and stern:

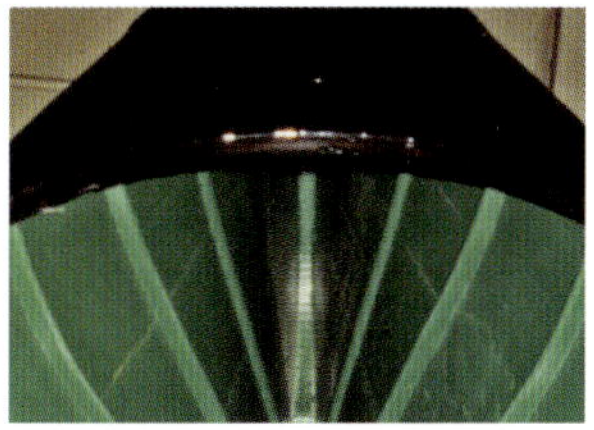

*William A. Martin*
*H. K. Martin*
*J. H. Rushton*

Stern seat cleat ledge

*William Alden*
*Caleb Chase*
*Edmund Chase*

One pair scribe ribs at bow, full length; one pair at stern, half length, with a stern seat cleat ledge:

*William Alden*
*Caleb Chase*

One pair scribe ribs at bow, full length; one pair at stern, full length, with a stern

seat cleat ledge:

*Caleb Chase*
*Edmund Chase*

**Rib feet**

Rounded and tapered:

*William Alden*
*Caleb Chase*
*Edmund Chase*
*Edward Harvey*
*William Kerst*

Beveled:

*All, except:*
*Raleigh Fish*

Cut square:

*Raleigh Fish*

Extend all the way across the bottom board:

*Albert Billings*
*George & Bliss*
*John Buyce*
*Frederick Graves*
*Edward Harvey*
*Carl Hathaway*
*Isaac Hurst*
*Ralph Morrow*
*Myron Nickerson*

Do not extend all the way across the bottom board:

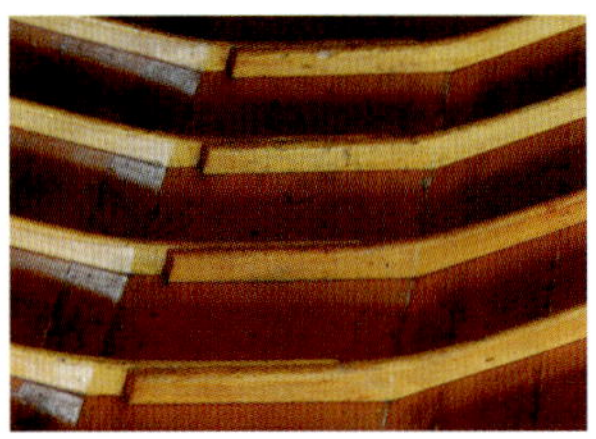

*William Alden*
*Leonard Anderson*
*Caleb Chase*
*Edmund Chase*
*Robert Frenette*
*Raleigh Fish*
*William Kerst*
*Theodore Hanmer*
*Willard Hanmer*
*Hurst & Nickerson*
*William A. Martin*
*Alric Moody*
*Frederick W. Rice*
*Frederick M. Rice*
*J. H. Rushton*

## HULL

### Number of strakes on each side

Less than seven:

*William Alden*
*Caleb Chase*
*Frederick Graves*

Seven:

*All, except:*
*Carl Hathaway*
*Ralph Morrow*

Seven or eight:

*William Alden*
*Albert Billings*
*Caleb Chase*
*Edmund Chase*
*George & Bliss*
*Raleigh Fish*
*Theodore Hanmer*
*Edward Harvey*
*Fuat Latif*
*Myron Nickerson*

Eight:

*Robert Frenette*
*William Kerst*
*Carl Hathaway*
*Ralph Morrow*

*More than eight:*
*William Alden*
*Caleb Chase*

### Planking lap method

Feather bevel:

*All, except:*

Modified bevel (Grant lap):

*Fuat Latif*

Heavy clapboard-lapstrake livery boats:

*John Buyce*

## OTHER COMPONENTS

### Gunwales

Beaded:

*Robert Frenette*
*Fuat Latif*

D-shaped:

*Hurst and Nickerson*
*Myron Nickerson*
*J. H. Rushton*
*Willard Hanmer*

### Seats

Board seats:

*John Buyce*
*Caleb Chase (early)*
*William Kerst*

### Yoke cleats

Wide, rectangular section spanning two ribs, where the yoke notch is located:

*Leonard Anderson*

Tips of the notch are sharply pointed:

*Hurst & Nickerson*
*Isaac Hurst*
*Myron Nickerson*

Short, spanning four ribs, arms are nearly equal in length:

*J. H. Rushton*

**Paddle**

Round grip with a diamond-shaped transition into the shaft, may be marked "C J C":

*Caleb Chase*

**Oarlock straps (socket plates)**

Short, six screws:

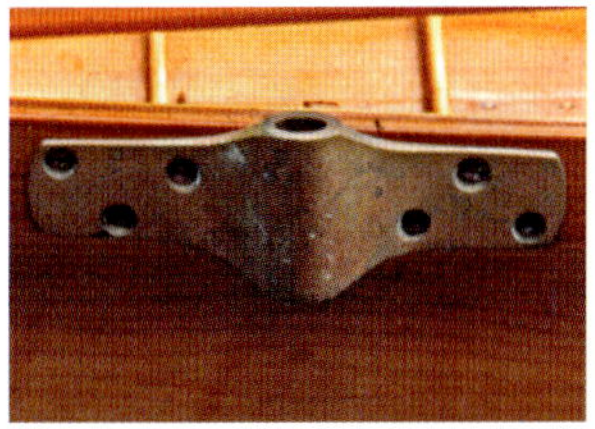

*Willard Hanmer*

Stem bands

No foot attached, aluminum or copper strips are used:

*Willard Hanmer*

**Shoes**

Wooden:

*Robert Frenette*
*Willard Hanmer*
*Carl Hathaway*
*Ralph Morrow*

## Bloomingdale Style Builders (A Subset of the Saranac Style Builders)

Bloomingdale is a small village, five miles north of Saranac Lake. In the 1850s and 1860s, it was the largest settlement in the region, on the stage route from Keeseville to Martin's and Paul Smith's hotels. The Bloomingdale builders are a subset of the Saranac builders. These boats are characterized by a wide stem forefoot at the waterline. This gives the stem a pronounced tumblehome. It is sometimes erroneously referred to as a ram bow such as that on ancient Greek triremes. This style bow gains almost a foot of waterline, resulting in the boat running faster and straighter. However, it takes a much larger share of the root stock to get the extra curvature.

| | |
|---|---|
| *James Fletcher Cameron* | 1982– |
| *William McCaffrey* | mid-1880s–1903 |
| *Elbridge Gerry Ricketson* | late 1870s–mid-1890s |
| *William Vassar* | late 1890s–mid-1920s |
| *Christopher H. Woodward* | 1987– |

### BUILDER'S PLATES

*James Cameron*

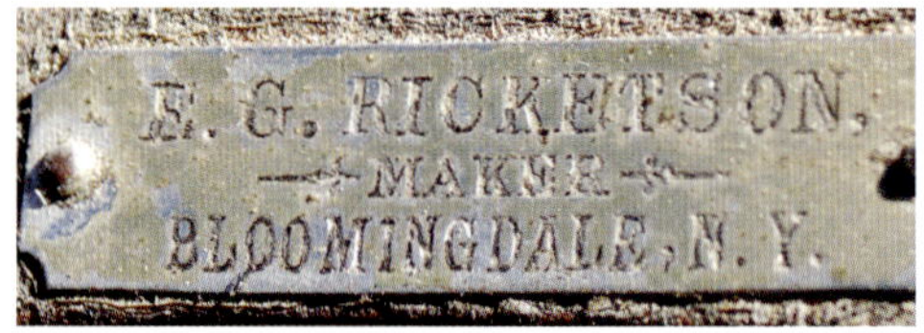


*E. G.Ricketson*

*William Vassar*

*William Vassar & Son*

*William McCaffrey*

*Christopher Woodward*

## STEMS

### Stem profile

Width of the lower stem at the waterline (greatest width) is more than 5 inches:

*All*

### Stem thickness under the gunwales

Tapered to the thickness of the stem leading edge (tapered thin):

*All*

### Stem post shape

Narrow:

*All*

Long, with a concave back and vertical front:

*William McCaffrey*

Long, with a concave back and angled front:

*E. G. Ricketson*

Long, semicircle:

*William Vassar*

Long, high semicircle, with brass cap:

*James Cameron*

Short, high, rectangle:

*Christopher Woodward*

### Stem foot shape

Arch:

*E. G. Ricketson*
*William McCaffrey*

Rounded over, bull-nosed:

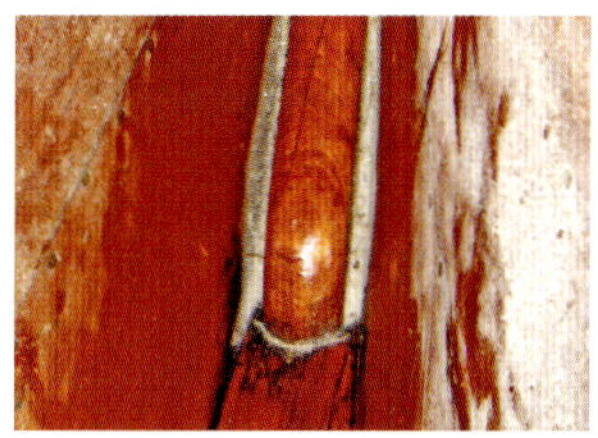

*James Cameron*
*William Vassar*
*Christopher Woodward*

Stem foot is numbered:

*Christopher Woodward*

## DECKS

### Number of deck pieces

One piece:

*E. G. Ricketson*
*William Vassar*

Two pieces, bow; one piece, stern:

*E. G. Ricketson*

Two pieces:

*William McCaffrey*
*E. G. Ricketson*
*William Vassar*

Seven pieces:

*Christopher Woodward*

More than seven pieces:

*James Cameron*

Strip:

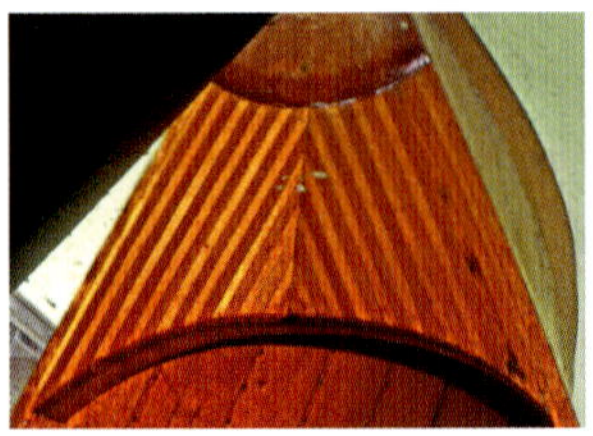

*William McCaffrey*
*E. G. Ricketson*
*William Vassar*
*James Cameron*

Strip, with decorative inlays:

*James Cameron*

**Deck inboard-edge shape**

Arced:

*All*

**Deck placement**

Let into the gunwales:

*William Vassar*

Set between sheer strakes:

*All*

**Deck cap shape**

Pie-piece:

*William McCaffrey*
*E. G. Ricketson*
*William Vassar*

Shield:

*Christopher Woodward*

Heart:

*William Vassar*

**Center cover board**

Surrounds the stem post:

*E. G. Ricketson*

Arrow:

*James Cameron*

**Coamings**

Wide, tapered to the ends:

*E. G. Ricketson*

**Decorative deck beams**

Saw-toothed, three points: (uncommon)

*E. G. Ricketson*

## RIBS

### Reverse curved

None, except:

Slight:

*William Vassar*

### Scribe ribs

No Scribe Ribs:

*James Cameron*
*Christopher Woodward*

One pair, bow and stern, ending on the fifth strake, tapered at the top:

*William McCaffrey*

One pair, bow and stern, ending on the sixth strake, tapered at the top:

*William Vassar*

One pair, bow and stern, full length:

*E. G. Ricketson*
*Christopher Woodward*

### Stern seat cleat ledge

*William McCaffrey*
*William Vassar*
*Christopher Woodward*

### Rib feet

Beveled:

*All*

Extend all the way across the bottom board:

*James Cameron*
*Christopher Woodward*

Do not extend all the way across the bottom board:

*William McCaffrey*
*E. G. Ricketson*
*William Vassar*

## HULL

### Number of strakes on each side

Seven:

*William McCaffrey*
*E. G. Ricketson*
*William Vassar*

Eight:

*James Cameron*
*Christopher Woodward*

### Planking lap method

Feather bevel:

*All*

### Reverse-Curved and Non-Reverse-Curved Ribs

The original Saranac boats built at Martin's had a small wine-glass shaped transom at the stern. This gave the stern considerable "flare" or reverse curve. The bows did not have this reverse curve, their shapes were fuller, that is straighter or even slightly rounded. The widest cross section of the boat was not in the middle or amidships, but about a third of the boat's length from the bow stem (cod-headed). The ribs transitioned from straight or rounded in the forward sections to reverse-curved in the after sections. When guideboats became double enders, Saranac builders apparently favored the rounder fuller shape both fore and aft, while the Long Lake builders went with reverse-curved ribs at bow and stern.

Why? Well, that is an unsettled matter. For one thing, the straighter non-reverse-curved ribbed boats of the Saranac builders were easier to build. The most common explanation is that the reverse-curved boat has a finer entry at the bow and stern (the part that is in the water) so that they will pierce the waves rather than ride over them. Long Lake, having a north/south aspect, and being long and narrow, gets big waves that are pushed by the prevalent north/south winds, and being able to drive through them instead of riding up over them was an advantage. The Long Lake boats also have a flatter rocker, which would accentuate this ease of rowing ten or more miles in a straight line through a head wind. However, this causes the boat to be slightly harder to turn. The Saranac boats have a pronounced rocker and a fuller entry, which makes them easier to turn. In the Saranac lakes, with their islands and twisting, interconnecting rivers, this turning ability was an advantage.

## Long Lake Style Builders

Long Lake boats are characterized by the full thickness of the stem where the gunwales are attached. The stems are then tapered beneath the gunwales often with decorative chamfering. The stem posts are wide. The boats have reverse-curved ribs resulting in a hollow entry at the waterline. The boats tend to be wider and flatter with less rocker, than the Saranac boats. While the decks are mostly plain, the seat backrests tend to be decorative. The hulls usually have eight strakes. The stem profile is straighter, with little or no tumblehome, approaching plumb.

| | |
|---|---|
| *Farrand Benedict Austin* | 1880s–1890s |
| *Merlin Edward Austin* | 1910–1930 |
| *Harold Merlin Austin, Sr.* | 1925–1955 |
| *Harold Merlin Austin, Jr.* | 1965–2015 |
| *Lewis Austin* | 1893–1900 |
| *John H. Blanchard* | 1898–1941 |
| *Fred C. Burns* | 1968–1983 |
| *Reuben Cary* | 1860s–1910 |
| *Warren William Cole* | 1892–1909 |
| *Wallace Franklin Emerson* | 1905–late 1930s |
| *Nathaniel S. Graves* | 1896–1912 |
| *Charles J. Hamner* | 1920s–mid-1950s |
| *Cyrus Hale Palmer* | 1860s–1874 |
| *Mitchell Sabattis (attributed)* | 1860s–early 1870s |
| *Herbert and Wright Salisbury* | 1880s–1889 |
| *George Washington Smith* | 1888–1926 |

### BUILDER'S PLATES

*Fred Burns*

*Warren Cole*

*George Smith*

*H. L. Salisbury & Bro. (no photograph)*

### STEMS

**Stem profile**

Long Lake profile:

*All*

**Stem thickness under the gunwales**

Full:

*All*

**Stem post shape**

Narrow:

*Reuben Cary*

Wide:

*All*

Low, truncated pyramid (beveled all four sides, flat top):

*Farrand Austin*

High, rectangle, beveled four sides, flat top:

*Harold Austin, Jr.*

High rectangle, vertical back and front, rounded top, barrel-shaped:

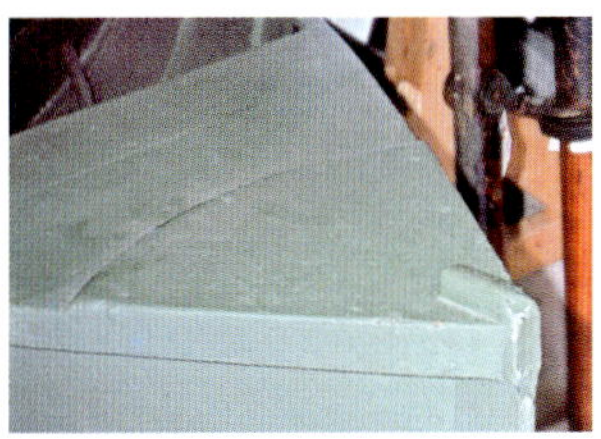

*Herbert Salisbury*

High, vertical back, concave front, barrel-shaped:

*Wallace Emerson*

*Fred Burns*

Concave back, barrel-shaped:

*Cyrus Palmer* (front has been repaired and reshaped)

Low, concave back and front, rounded top:

*Warren Cole*

Angled back, vertical front, rounded top:

*Nathaniel Graves*

Angled back, chamfered front, rounded top:

*Merlin Austin*

*Lewis Austin*

*John Blanchard*

Low, concave-angled back, concave front, chamfered sides, top edges rounded:

*Charles Hamner*

Tapered upward, concave back and front, chamfered front sides:

*Mitchell Sabattis (attributed)*

Concave back, chamfered front on three sides, rounded top:

*George Smith*

Low, sloped, metal-capped:

*Herbert Salisbury*

**Stem foot**

Ridged, pointed:

*Lewis Austin*

Horizontal rectangle:

*Reuben Cary*
*Wallace Emerson*
*Cyrus Palmer*

Rounded over, bull-nosed:

*John Blanchard*
*Reuben Cary*
*Warren Cole*
*Nathaniel Graves*
*Charles Hamner*
*George Smith*

Rounded:

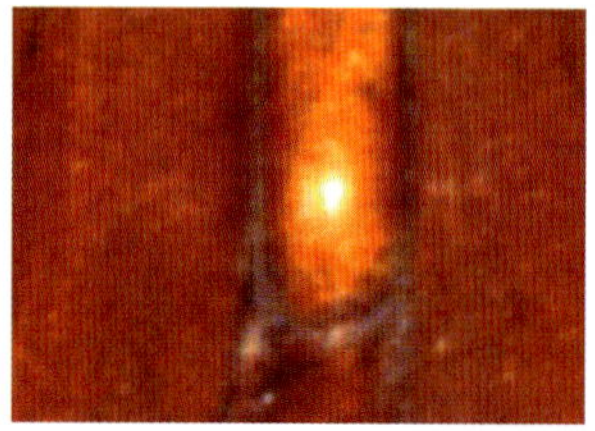

*Merlin Austin*

## DECKS

**Number of deck pieces**

One piece:

*All*, except:
*Harold Austin, Jr.*

Two pieces:

*Harold Austin, Jr.*
*Wallace Emerson*
*Charles Hamner*
*George Smith*

Three pieces:

*Harold Austin, Jr.*
*Fred Burns*
*Charles Hamner*
*George Smith*

Three pieces, crowned:

*Lewis Austin*

Four or more pieces:

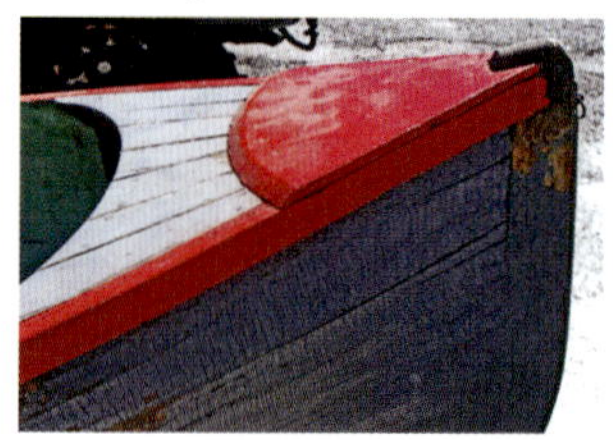

*Harold Austin, Jr.*
*Charles Hamner*

Nine to eleven pieces:

*Warren Cole*

**Deck inboard-edge shape**

Straight:

*Reuben Cary*
*Herbert Salisbury*

Straight bow deck, arced stern deck:

*Mitchell Sabattis (attributed)*

Arced bow, **C**-shaped stern deck:

*Merlin Austin*
*Warren Cole*

Arced:

*All*

Deep arc:

*George Smith*

**Deck placement** (Refer to drawings; page 317)

Let into the gunwales:

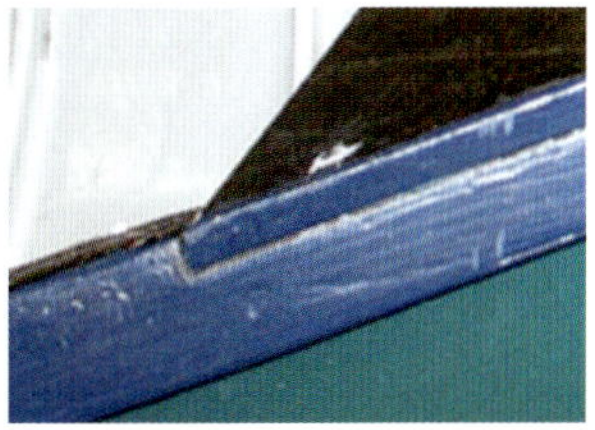

*Farrand Austin*
*Reuben Cary*
*Nathaniel Graves*
*Charles Hamner*
*Mitchell Sabattis (attributed)*
*Herbert Salisbury*

Mitered into the gunwales:

*Merlin Austin*
*Harold Austin, Jr.*
*John Blanchard*
*Fred Burns*
*Warren Cole*
*Wallace Emerson*
*Cyrus Palmer*

Set between the gunwales:

*George Smith*

Set between the sheer strakes:

*Warren Cole*
*Charles Hamner*

**Deck cap shape**

Pie-piece:

*Farrand Austin*
*Merlin Austin*
*John Blanchard*
*Reuben Cary*
*Warren Cole*
*Wallace Emerson*
*Charles Hamner*
*Mitchell Sabattis (attributed)*
*Herbert Salisbury*
*George Smith*

Three-piece pie-piece:

*Lewis Austin*

Shield:

*Harold Austin, Jr.*
*John Blanchard*
*Fred Burns*
*Wallace Emerson*
*Nathaniel Graves*
*Charles Hamner*
*Cyrus Palmer*
*George Smith*

Center cover board

*Herbert Salisbury*

Coamings

*None*

Decorative deck beams

*None*

## RIBS

**Reverse curved**

*All*

**Scribe ribs**

No Scribe Ribs:

*Cyrus Palmer*
*George Smith*

One pair at bow:

*Farrand Austin*
*Reuben Cary*

One pair at bow, pointed at top:

*George Smith*

One pair bow and stern:

*Merlin Austin*
*Harold Austin, Jr.*
*Warren Cole*
*Charles Hamner*
*Mitchell Sabattis (attributed)*
*Herbert Salisbury*

One pair bow and stern, pointed at bottom:

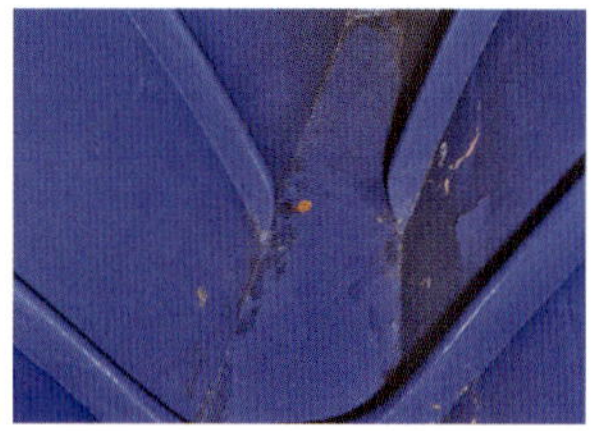

*Nathaniel Graves*
*John Blanchard*

One pair bow, two pairs stern:

*Lewis Austin*

Two pairs bow, one pair stern:

*Wallace Emerson*

**Stern seat cleat ledge**

*None*

**Rib feet**

Extend onto the garboard:

*George Smith*
*John Blanchard*

Beveled:

*All, except:*
*Herbert Salisbury*

Rounded:

*Herbert Salisbury*

Extend all the way across the bottom board

*Farrand Austin*
*John Blanchard*
*Fred Burns*
*Wallace Emerson*
*Nathaniel Graves*
*George Smith*

Do not extend all the way across the bottom board

*Reuben Cary*
*Warren Cole*
*Charles Hamner*
*Cyrus Palmer*
*Mitchell Sabattis (attributed)*
*Herbert Salisbury*

## HULL

**Number of strakes on each side**

Eight:

*All*

Nine:

*Cyrus Palmer*
*George Smith*

**Planking lap method**

Feather bevel:

*All*

**Boat's greatest width is ahead of midships (cod-headed)**

*Farrand Austin*
*Merlin Austin*
*John Blanchard*
*Reuben Cary*
*George Smith*

## OTHER COMPONENTS

### Carlins

Beaded:

*Merlin Austin*
*Nathaniel Graves*
*George Smith*

### Gunwales

Beaded:

One bead on lower edge:

*Harold Austin, Jr.*
*Charles Hamner*

Two beads on lower edge:

*Merlin Austin*
*George Smith*

Three beads on lower edge:

*Nathaniel Graves*

Two beads on upper edge, one bead on lower edge:

*Warren Cole*

### Seat backrests

Center seat backrest is attached with wooden rods:

*Farrand Austin*

Center and stern seat backrest top rail is three semicircles:

*Warren Cole*

Center and stern seat backrest top rail is a mirrored ogee:

*Wallace Emerson*

Center seat backrest top rail is a mirrored ogee with pointed shoulders:

*Charles Hamner*

Stern seat backrest top rail is semicircles with rounded shoulders:

*Charles Hamner*

### Yoke cleats

Tips of the notch are sharply pointed, sides are convex:

*Warren Cole*

Sides of notch are quarter-rounded:

*Charles Hamner*

Tips of notch are flattened, sides are convex:

*Wallace Emerson*

Tips of notch are flattened, sides are concave:

*George Smith*

## Brown's Tract Style Builders

Brown's Tract boats are characterized by narrow stems that are slightly tumblehome, plumb, or have a pronounced forward rake. These boats were patterned by H. D. Grant, Theodore Seeber, and Riley Parsons. They were mainly built in Boonville, Oneida County, and Old Forge, Herkimer County. They are all remarkably similar but with subtle differences, and it may be difficult to distinguish one builder from another.

| | | |
|---|---|---|
| *Oren Fenton* | 1900s–1920s | Number Four |
| *H. Dwight Grant* | 1880–1906 | Boonville |
| *Lewis L. Grant* | 1916–1934 | Boonville |
| *Seeber & Parsons* | 1890–1895 | Old Forge |
| *Parsons & Company* | 1896–1903 | Old Forge |
| *Parsons & Roberts* | 1903–1909 | Old Forge |
| *Parsons Brothers* | 1910–1945 | Old Forge |
| *Theodore Seeber* | 1896–1902 | Old Forge |
| *Old Forge Boat Company* | 1903–1909 | Old Forge |
| *Ansel Wilder* | 1880s–1900s | Petries Corners |

### BUILDER'S PLATES

*Parsons & Company*

*Seeber & Parsons*

*Parsons Brothers*

*Old Forge Boat Company*

*Parsons & Roberts*

*Ansel Wilder*

**Boat number and year stamped on stem foot**

*All*, except:
*Oren Fenton*
*Ansel Wilder*

Numbers run serially starting with 1 each year, from 1884 to 1906:
*H. Dwight Grant*

Numbers run serially starting with 1 each year, from 1916 to 1934:
*Lewis Grant*

Numbers run sequentially from 1 to about 60, no year:
*Seeber & Parsons*

Numbers run serially starting with 1 each year, from 1896 to 1902:
*Theodore Seeber*

Numbers run serially starting with 1 each year, from 1903 to 1909:
*Old Forge Boat Company*

Numbers run sequentially from 1 to about 50, from 1896 to 1902:
*Parsons & Company*

Numbers run sequentially from 1 to about 40, from 1902 to 1909:
*Parsons & Roberts*

Numbers run sequentially from 1 to about 125, from 1910 to 1924:
*Parsons Brothers*

Numbers run sequentially from 1 to about 25, from 1925 to 1927:
*Parsons Brothers*

Numbers run serially starting with 1 each year, from 1928 to 1945:
*Parsons Brothers*

## STEMS

**Stem profile**

Long Lake profile:

*H. Dwight Grant (1880–1890)*

Narrow, slight tumblehome, plumb, or outward rake:

*All*

**Stem thickness under the gunwales**

Full:
*All*

**Stem post shape**

Wide:
*All*

Rectangular, vertical back and front, barrel-shaped:

*H. Dwight Grant (1880–1888)*

Rounded top, sloping to the cover board:

*All*

Metal-capped:
*All*, except:
*Oren Fenton*

Thick, nickel-plated brass cap, let into the stem under the stem band.
One screw attaching the cap to the deck:

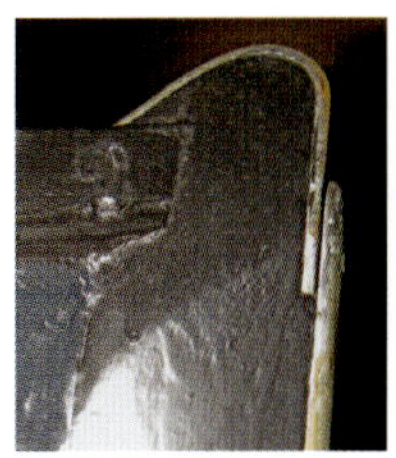

*H. Dwight Grant*
*Lewis Grant*

Thin metal cap, not let into the stem under the stem band.

Two screws attaching the cap to the deck:

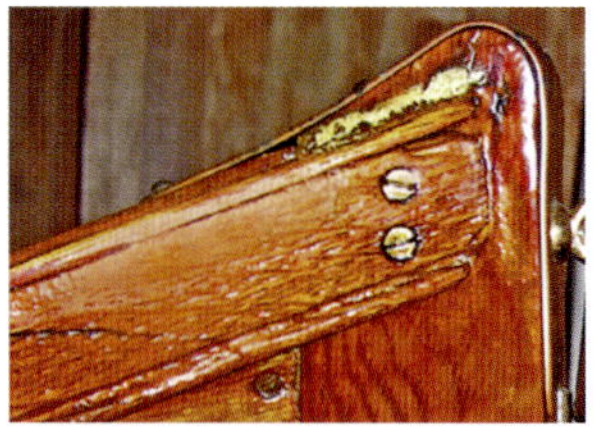

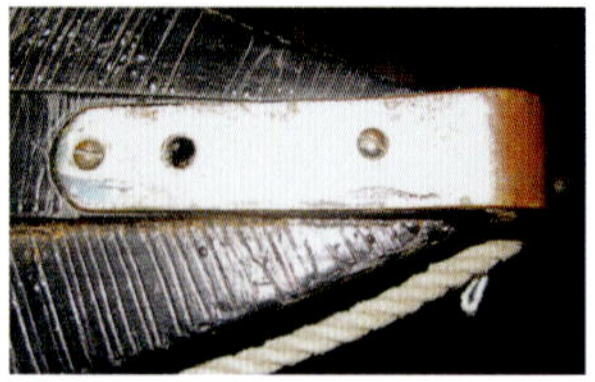

*Seeber & Parsons*
*Theodore Seeber*
*Parsons & Company*
*Old Forge Boat Company*
*Parsons & Roberts*
*Parsons Brothers*
*Ansel Wilder*

**Stem foot**

Low, flat, circular:

*All*

## DECKS

**Number of deck pieces**

One piece:

*H. Dwight Grant (1880–1881)*

Two pieces:

*All*

**Deck inboard-edge shape**

Straight:

*H. Dwight Grant (1880–1881)*

Deep arc, circular:

*All*

**Deck placement** (Refer to drawings; page 317)

Let into the gunwales:

*All*

**Deck cap shape**

Heart-shaped at bow, pie-piece-shaped at stern:

*H. Dwight Grant (1880–1881)*

**Center cover board**

Butts to the stem post:

*All*

Limber hole at center cover board and stem post juncture:

*All,* except:
*Oren Fenton*

**Coamings**

Wide, tapered to the ends:

*All*

**Decorative Deck Beams**

*None*

## RIBS

**Reverse curved**

*All,* except:

Ribs are not reverse curved

*Oren Fenton*
*Ansel Wilder*

**Scribe ribs**

No Scribe Ribs:

*Oren Fenton*

One pair, bow and stern:

*Theodore Seeber*
*Old Forge Boat Company*

Two pairs, bow and stern:

*H. Dwight Grant*
*Lewis Grant*
*Seeber & Parsons*
*Theodore Seeber*
*Ansel Wilder*

Three pairs, bow and stern, first two pairs are pointed at the bottom:

*Seeber & Parsons*
*Parsons & Company*
*Parsons & Roberts*
*Parsons Brothers*

Stern seat cleat ledge

*None*

### Rib feet

Beveled:

*All*

Extend all the way across the bottom board:

*All,* except:
*Oren Fenton*

## HULL

### Number of strakes on each side

Eight:

*All*

### Planking lap method

Modified bevel:

*All*

Tacked from outside only:

*Oren Fenton*

## OTHER COMPONENTS

### Gunwales

Gunwales are not beaded:

*Oren Fenton*

Gunwales are beaded:

*All,* except:
*Oren Fenton*

One bead on lower edge:

*All,* except:
*Oren Fenton*
*Ansel Wilder*

Two beads, one on upper edge, one on lower edge:

*Ansel Wilder*

### Seat Cleats

Cleats are molded:

*All*

### Seats

Seats are half-lapped, with molded shoulders:

*All,* except:
*Oren Fenton*
*Ansel Wilder*

### Seat Backrests

Four-piece frames:

*H. Dwight Grant (1880–1889)*

Two-piece steam-bent frame:

*All,* except:

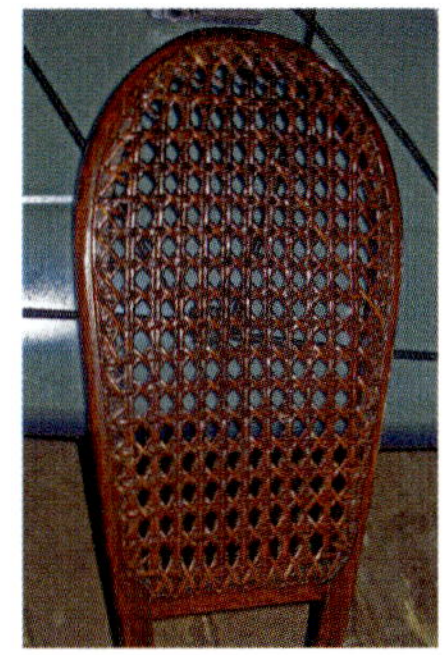

*Oren Fenton*
*Ansel Wilder*

### Yoke cleats

Numbers and dates stamped on the back side:

*All,* except:
*Oren Fenton*
*Seeber & Parsons*
*Ansel Wilder*

Number only:

*Seeber & Parsons*

# APPENDIX A

## The H. D. Grant Catalogue, circa 1890

### "The Famous Adirondack Guide Boats"

HERE REPRINTED for the first time, is the expanded version of H. Dwight Grant's original catalogue published in 1890. This is the only known surviving copy. It is a variant of the one that Kenneth Durant included in *Guide-Boat Days and Ways* (1963), his anthology of historical accounts of the Adirondack guideboat. This revised edition, produced by the same job printer in Boonville, likely succeeded the original printing shortly after 1890. It includes three additional pages that note prices and describe what "grades and styles of finish and trimmings" were available.

Durant declared the catalogue to contain:

> . . . a unique description of boat-building by a master-builder. Seldom has any craftsman left such a detailed record of his work. Though he mentions in passing the distinctive feature of the Grant model, the "improved bevelled lap," and states his preference for pine over cedar, what he wrote will serve, with only minor variations for an account of the essential features of all guide-boats: smooth lap-strake on knees of natural crook rising from an elliptical flat bottom-board. Beyond advertising his own product, Grant's concern was to declare the superiority of guide-boat construction, for its special uses, over all other forms. Insistently searching for ease on the carries, the old guide was later to decrease some of the dimensions given here, with consequent reduction in weight.[1]

Together the catalogue and Grant's "Price List" for 1900, which follows, are a window into what the boat shop offered. (Grant's use of the term rivets on page three refers to clinch tacks.) In distributing such printed items, Grant was the exception among guideboat builders. Like J. H. Rushton, a consummate marketer who produced annual catalogues, Grant considered himself a "manufacturer." As Durant noted, the Boonville builder had "the advantage of yearly production in a well-organized shop with experienced workmen." This is reflected in the shop's final tally: 378 guideboats by 1934, the year Dwight's son Lewis built his last Grant model boat.

—E.C.

1 Durant, 1963:217.

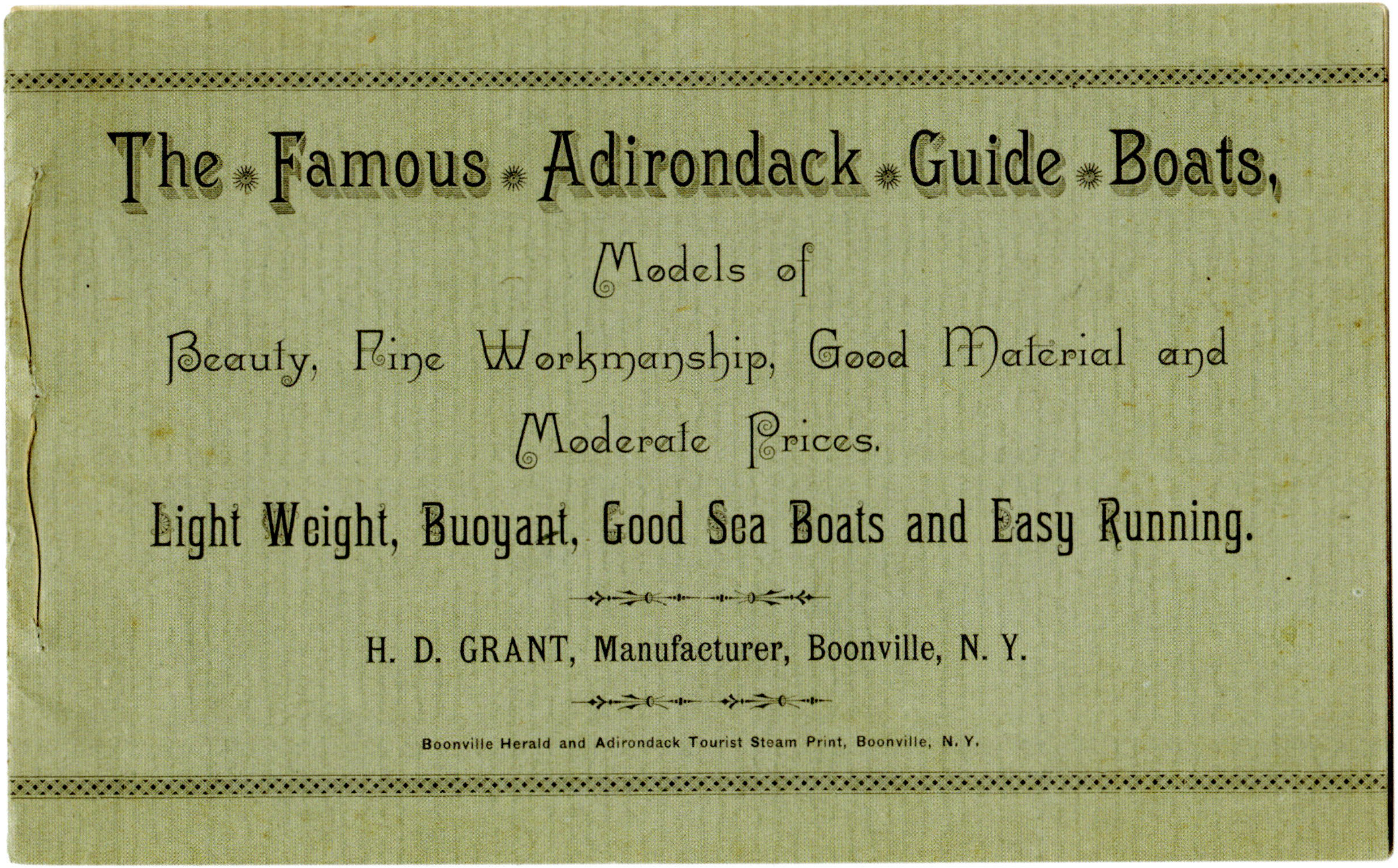

The Famous Adirondack Guide Boats,

Models of

Beauty, Fine Workmanship, Good Material and

Moderate Prices.

Light Weight, Buoyant, Good Sea Boats and Easy Running.

H. D. GRANT, Manufacturer, Boonville, N. Y.

Boonville Herald and Adirondack Tourist Steam Print, Boonville, N. Y.

THIRTY YEARS of experience has demonstrated to the Adirondack Guide that no other boat manufactured can begin to compete with them for durability, speed, lightness, capacity and ability to ride through rough water in safety.

## Mode of Construction.

First, a bottom board of one-half inch pine, from 6 to 9 inches wide in the middle, tapered to five-eighths inch to each end. To this is fastened the bow and stern stems and knees, 5 inches apart through the body of the boat with screws running through from the bottom board into each. The stems and knees are made from natural crooks of spruce roots, a strong and durable timber, the grain of the timber running with the model of the knee, knees five-sixteenth by three-fourth inches, rounded on inside edge. This constitutes the frame-work of the boat and of itself will convince any thinking person that it will always retain its original shape.

No steamed and bent knees in this boat to be kept from spreading by seats fastened to each side of the boat.

This frame-work is then placed and fastened to an adjustable stock which firmly holds it in place and gives the desired rake to the bottom. The top of the stems are fastened to an adjustable stanchion reaching down from floor overhead.

A light batt is then fastened to the upper end of each stem, running along on the outside of the knees on each side of the frame, the butt being fastened to each knee at the proper heighth to give the top of the boat the desired rake and hold the knees in place until the siding is put on.

The bottom board having been bevelled to the model of each knee the first round of siding is then put on by being fastened to the knees and bottom board with screws one and one-fourth inches apart and two screws in each round into all of the knees and four screws where it is fastened to the stem. The siding is made from knotless Adirondack pine, sawed across the grain or toward the heart of the tree, a light and hardy timber that is unequalled by any other for this purpose.

White cedar, the only other timber used by boat-builders, is spongy, leathery and puffy when thoroughly wet thereby destroying the symmetry of the boat. The bottom round on light boats is one-fourth inch thick and each succeeding round is gradually thinned to three-sixteenths of an inch on top of last round. The siding is made to fit the model of the knee from solid timber, not warped nor sprung on but made to fit and fastened with screws, thereby giving it wonderful strength for the amount of material used.

Each round of siding lays two and one-half inches surface in width and are joined to each other by an improved bevelled lap three-fourths of an inch in width and cut by a tool made for the purpose, and cutting all places alike thereby fitting as perfect as the bark to a tree. The joints are leaded with best Brooklyn lead, thinned with spar composition, and then riveted on each edge of lap inside and out with copper rivets three fourths of an inch apart, making a perfectly smooth and water-tight joint. In the Adirondacks these boats are termed double enders, being built exactly alike at each end, except the bow being one inch deeper than the stern to throw off the heavy swells from rough water.

Wales are made of straight-grained spruce or oak ; deck circles of red elm backed by natural

3

Grant's use of the term rivets (above) refers to clinch tacks.

crooks of spruce roots for carlin and decked with pine, oak or walnut. All of my first-class boats are furnished with three cane seats and one cane back rest for stern seat. The frames are made to fit the boat and are strung with heavy binding cane. Oars and paddles are of soft maple and boat yoke of cedar.

The bottom board is protected by two shoes of five-eighth inch band iron put on with screws and counter-sunk at each end under a solid brass nickel-plated stem band, reaching from bottom to top of stem. The row-locks consist of two pins and four straps and sockets fastened firmly to the wales of the boat with screws, allowing the use of two pairs of oars at the same time. Brass-lined foot braces are fitted for each oarsman to prevent chafing the boat.

Finally, as a clincher, I will say that in the Adirondacks where thousands of boats are used and men who use them know what a good boat is, and have to have such to stand the racket, that for every one of the bent kneed, lap streak or clinker built boats found in use by the guides, I will find one hundred in use by them made by this method.

# Prices.

My prices are regulated by the grade and style of finish and trimmings used after the boat or hull is taken from the stocks and are designated by figures.

## No. 1.

Sixteen feet long, thirty-six inches wide inside, twelve and one-half inches deep in centre, twenty-three inches deep at bow and twenty-two at stern, put together with brass screws, highly finished in natural wood and varnished with three coats of best spar varnish; wales, oak or spruce; decks, black walnut or oak; brass nickel-plated Adirondack row-locks, stem bands and stem caps, three cane seats, two cane back rests, one pair soft maple oars, one paddle, one boat yoke. Price at shop.............................................................................$75.00.

For longer boats, all grades, add $4.00 for each additional foot; for shorter boats, deduct $3.00 for each foot taken off.

5

## No. 2.

Same as No. 1, except wooden seats and back rest in place of cane ....................$67.00

## No. 3.

Same as No. 1, except steel screws in place of brass, and being finished in any desirable color instead of natural wood....................................................... $65.00

## No. 4.

Same as No. 3, except wooden seats instead of cane, malleable iron row-locks. .........$55.00

Weight of light boats with fittings will be about as follows:

| | | | |
|---|---|---|---|
| 16 feet long | 70 pounds | 13 feet long | 60 pounds |
| 15 " | 65 " | 12 " | 57 " |
| 14 " | 62 " | | |

Heavier weights made to order.

# Oars.

Oars, soft maple, straight blade, 8 and 8 ft. 2 in., painted or varnished, $3.00 per pair.
" " " " 7½ " 7 " 10 " " " $2.50 "

Oars, spoon, for Adirondack lock, 8 ft., copper tipped, painted or varnished, $4.00 per pair.

5½ foot paddle, varnished or painted, each. $2.00.

Boat yoke, varnished or painted, each, $1.50.

Cane seats and back rest, each, $2.00.

Adirondack row-locks, two pins, four straps, screws and rivets, malleable iron, $1.50
" " plain brass steel pins, " " " " .............. 3.00
" " nickel-plated brass steel pins, four straps, screws and rivets ..... 4.00

# Stem Bands.

Polished brass, $1.00 per pair.
Nickel-plated brass, $1.25 per pair.

# Stem Caps.

Nickel-plated brass, 50 cents per pair.

7

# Adirondack Guide Boats.

## H. D. GRANT, BUILDER,

BOONVILLE, N. Y.

1900

## Price List, F. O. B.

| LENGTH. | NATURAL FINISH. | | PAINTED. | |
|---|---|---|---|---|
| | BOARD SEATS. | CANE SEATS. | BOARD SEATS. | CANE SEATS. |
| 19½ ft. | $88 00 | $ .... | $80 00 | $..... |
| 17½ ft. | 80 00 | 86 00 | 72 00 | 78 00 |
| 16½ ft. | 76 00 | 82 00 | 68 00 | 74 00 |
| 16 ft. | 74 00 | 80 00 | 66 00 | 72 00 |
| 15½ ft. | 72 50 | 78 50 | 64 50 | 70 50 |
| 15 ft. | 71 00 | 77 00 | 63 00 | 69 00 |
| 14½ ft. | 69 50 | 75 50 | 61 50 | 67 50 |
| 14 ft. | 68 00 | 74 00 | 60 00 | 66 00 |
| 13½ ft | 66 50 | 72 50 | 58 50 | 64 50 |
| 13 ft. | 65 00 | 71 00 | 57 00 | 63 00 |
| 12½ ft. | 63 50 | 69 50 | 55 50 | 61 50 |
| 12 ft. | 62 00 | 68 00 | 54 00 | 60 00 |

All boats furnished with nickel trimmings, one pair oars, one paddle and carrying yoke.

| | |
|---|---|
| Paddles, | $1.75 |
| Oars, first quality, per pair, | 3.25 |
| Cane Seats and Back Rests, each, | 2.00 |
| Middle Cane Back Rests, each, | 3.00 |
| Boat Chairs, (cane seat and back) | 3.00 |
| Rowlocks, (nickel plate) per set, | 3.50 |
| Rowlocks, (malleable iron) per set, | 1.40 |
| Carrying Yokes, | 1.75 |
| Bottom Racks, (Oak or Elm)— | 4.00 |
| Crating Boats, | 2.50 |

# APPENDIX B

## Adirondack Guideboats in Public Collections

### New York

| | |
|---|---|
| Adirondack Museum, Blue Mountain Lake | 79 |
| Antique Boat Museum, Clayton | 5 |
| Essex County Historical Society, Elizabethtown | 3 |
| Franklin County Historical and Museum Society, Malone | 1 |
| Lake Placid/North Elba Historical Society, Lake Placid | 1 |
| New York State Museum, Albany | 6 |
| Town of Webb Historical Association, Old Forge | 4 |

### Other New York Public Collections

| | |
|---|---|
| Adirondack Medical Center, Saranac Lake | 1 |
| New York State Department of Environmental Conservation, Ray Brook, Saranac Inn | 2 |
| Northern Forest Institute, SUNY/ESF, Newcomb | 3 |
| Paul Smith's College, Paul Smiths | 2 |
| Sagamore Institute, Raquette Lake | 1 |
| Saranac Lake Free Library, Saranac Lake | 2 |

### Connecticut

| | |
|---|---|
| Mystic Seaport Museum, Mystic | 8 |

### District of Columbia

| | |
|---|---|
| National Museum of American History, Washington (Entered the collection in 1876; not located at present) | 1 |

### Maine

| | |
|---|---|
| Penobscot Marine Museum, Searsport | 1 |

### Vermont

| | |
|---|---|
| American Museum of Fly Fishing, Manchester | 1 |
| Shelburne Museum, Shelburne | 2 |

### Virginia

| | |
|---|---|
| Mariners' Museum, Newport News | 2 |
| TOTAL | 125 |

—E. C. and C. W.

# APPENDIX C

## Common and Scientific Names of Woods Used in Adirondack Guideboats

Ash, white *(Fraxinus americana)* Gunwales, seats, oars
Basswood; Linden *(Tilia americana)* Yokes, floorboards
Birch, white *(Betula papyrifera)* (Bark canoes)
Cedar, northern white; Arborvitae *(Thuja occidentalis)* Bottom boards, planking, yokes, decks
Cedar, western red *(Thuja plicata)* Bottom boards, sheer planks, decks
Cedar, Spanish *(Cedrela ororata)* Sheer planks, decks, seats
Cherry, black *(Prunus serotina)* Gunwales, seats, cleats, oars, paddles
Cypress *(Taxodium distichum)* Bottom boards
Elm, red; slippery *(Ulmus pubescens)* Scribe ribs, floor boards
Mahogany, Honduran *(Swietenia macrophylla)* Sheer planks, decks
Maple, hard; sugar; white* *(Acer saccharum)* Oars, paddles
Maple, soft; red *(Acer rubrum)* Oars, paddles
Oak, white *(Quercus alba)* Gunwales, decks, seats, cleats, floor boards, shoes
Pine, eastern white *(Pinus strobus)* Bottom board, planking, decks
Spruce, red *(Picea rubens)* Ribs, stems, gunwales oars, paddles
Spruce, black *(Picea mariana)* Ribs, stems, gunwales, oars, paddles
Larch, eastern; Tamarack; Hackmatack *(Larix laricina)* Ribs, stems
Walnut, black *(Juglans nigra)* Gunwales, decks, seats, cleats
Walnut, white; Butternut *(Juglans cinerea)* Gunwales, decks, seats, cleats

* E. G. Ricketson offered "white maple oars" in an 1889 railway guide advertisement; see his Biographical Sketch.

—C. W.

# SELECTED BIBLIOGRAPHY

THIS BIBLIOGRAPHY IS arranged by general categories and is comprised of selected items reviewed in the course of research for this book. Included are reference works, Adirondack regional books, boats and boatbuilding titles, guidebooks, government publications, newspapers, and manuscript collections. Not included are periodical articles and infrequently cited items as well as personal communications such as interviews and letters. For a listing of all citations in this book, consult the endnotes in Part 1 and footnotes in Part 2.

—C. W.

## Reference


Adams, William, comp. *Business Directory of Lewis County, N.Y., 1895–96.* Lowville, NY: William Adams, 1895.

*Adirondack Directory for 1902–03.* Saranac Lake, NY: Jos. Mannix and Geo. H. Foy, 1902.

*Adirondack Directory: Saranac Lake and Vicinity.* Saranac Lake, NY: MacDonald and Foy, 1906, 1908, and 1910.

Beers, Daniel G. *Franklin County Atlas.* Philadelphia: D. G. Beers, 1876.

*Boston Almanac and Business Directory.* Boston: Sampson, Davenport, 1879–1893.

*Boston City Directory:* Publisher unknown, 1860.

Boyd, Andrew, comp. *New York State Business Directory, 1776–1876.* Syracuse, NY: A. Boyd, 1876.

Child, Hamilton, comp. *Gazetteer and Business Directory of Lewis County, 1872–1873.* Syracuse, NY: Journal Office, 1872.

Damrell & Moore and Geo. Coolidge, eds. *Boston Almanac.* Boston: Brown & Taggard, 1861.

De Kerchove, René. *International Maritime Dictionary.* Princeton: D. Van Nostrand, 1948.

French, J. H. *Map of Essex County, N.Y.* Philadelphia: E. A. Balch, 1858.

*General and Business Directory of Lowville...Boonville... for 1888–89.* Lyons, NY: Globe Directory, 1888.

McEwen, W. A. and A. H. Lewis. *Encyclopedia of Nautical Knowledge.* Centreville, MD: Cornell Maritime Press, 1953.

*New Century Atlas, Herkimer County.* Philadelphia: Century Map Publishing, 1906.

*New York State Business Directory.* Albany, NY: Adams, Sampson, 1864.

*New York State Business Directory.* Boston: Sampson, Davenport, 1867,1874.

## Adirondack Regional Books

Abbott, Henry. *Birch Bark Books of Henry Abbott.* Harrison, NY: Harbor Hill Books, 1980.

Aber, Ted and Stella King. *History of Hamilton County.* Lake Pleasant, NY: Great Wilderness Books, 1965.

Ackerman, David, H. *Placid Lake: A Centennial History, 1893–1993.* Lake Placid, NY: Shore Owners' Association of Lake Placid, 1993.

Allerton, R. G. *Brook Trout Fishing . . . Oquossoc Angling Association.* New York: R. G. Allerton,1869.

Beetle, David. *Up Old Forge Way.* Utica, NY: Utica *Observer-Dispatch*, 1948.

*Biographical Review, Leading Citizens of Essex and Clinton Counties, New York.* Boston: Biographical Review Publishing, 1896.

Boardman, William H. *The Lovers of the Woods.* New York: McClure, Phillips, 1901.

Brandreth, Paul [pseud.]. *Trails of Enchantment.* New York: G. Howard Watt, 1930.

Brown, Henry A. L. and Richard A. Walton. *John Brown's Tract: Lost Adirondack Empire.* Canaan, NH: Phoenix Publishing, 1988.

Brumley, Charles. *Guides of the Adirondacks, A History.* Utica, NY: North Country Books, 1994.

Cadbury, Warder H. "Introduction." In *Adventures in the Wilderness* by William H. H. Murray, 1869. Syracuse, NY: Syracuse University Press, 1970.

———. "Introduction." In *Long Lake* by John Todd, 1845. Harrison, NY: Harbor Hill Books, 1983.

Cadbury, Warder H. and Henry F. Marsh. *Arthur Fitzwilliam Tait, Artist in the Adirondacks.* Newark, DE: University of Delaware Press, 1986.

Chittenden, L. E. *Personal Reminiscences.* New York: Richmond, Croscup, 1893.

Clark, Raymond C. *A View of Westport, N.Y., on Lake Champlain: 1902–1972.* Elizabethtown, NY: Denton Publications, 1972.

Collins, Geraldine. *The Brighton Story.* Lakemont, NY: North Country Books, 1977.

Cunningham, John L. *Three Years with the Adirondack Regiment.* Norwood, MA: Private printing, 1920.

De Sormo, Maitland C. *Summers on the Saranacs.* Utica, NY: North Country Books, 1980.

Donaldson, Alfred L. *A History of the Adirondacks.* 2 vols. New York: Century, 1921.

Emerson, Ralph Waldo. "The Adirondacs." In *May-Day and Other Pieces.* Boston: Ticknor and Fields, 1867.

Engels, Vincent. *Adirondack Fishing in the 1930s: A Lost Paradise.* Syracuse, NY: Syracuse University Press, 1978.

Fennessy, Lana. *The History of Newcomb.* Newcomb, NY: Private printing, 1977.

Foster, Jeanne Robert. *Adirondack Portraits: A Piece of Time.* Noel Riedinger-Johnson, ed. Syracuse, NY: Syracuse University Press, 1986.

Gerster, Arpad G. *Notes Collected in the Adirondacks, 1895 & 1896.* Sidney S. Whelan, Jr., ed. Blue Mountain Lake, NY: Adirondack Museum, 2005.

Grady, Joseph F. *The Adirondacks: Fulton Chain–Big Moose Region, The Story of a Wilderness.* Little Falls, NY: Journal & Courier, 1933.

Guild, J. F. *Westport on Lake Champlain.* Dedham, MA: circa 1885–early 1890s.

Hammond, S. H. *Hills, Lakes, and Forest Streams; or, a Tramp in the Chateaugay Woods.* New York: J. C. Derby, 1854.

———. *Wild Northern Scenes; or, Sporting Adventures with the Rifle and the Rod.* New York: Derby & Jackson, 1857.

Headley, Joel T. *The Adirondack; or Life, in the Woods.* New York: Charles Scribner, 1849.

Hochschild, Harold K. *Township 34.* New York: Private printing, 1952.

McMartin, Barbara. *To the Lake of the Skies: The Benedicts in the Adirondacks.* Canada Lake, NY: Lake View Press, 1996.

Masters, Raymond D. *The Huntington Wildlife Forest.* Utica, NY: North Country Books, 1993.

Murray, Amelia M. *Letters from the United States, Cuba, and Canada.* New York: G. P. Putnam, 1856.

Murray, William H. H. *Adventures in the Wilderness; or, Camp-Life in the Adirondacks.* Boston: Fields, Osgood, 1869.

Northrup, A. Judd. *Camps and Tramps in the Adirondacks.* Syracuse, NY: Davis, Bardeen, 1880.

Pierce, Henry B. and Samuel W. Durant. *History of St. Lawrence County, N.Y.* Philadelphia: L. H. Everts, 1878.

Pilcher, Edith. *Up the Lake Road.* Keene Valley, NY: Adirondack Mountain Reserve, 1987.

———. *The Constables: First Family of the Adirondacks.* Utica, NY: North Country Books, 1992.

Plunz, Richard, ed. *Two Adirondack Hamlets in History: Keene and Keene Valley.* Fleischmanns, NY: Purple Mountain Press, 1999.

Potter, Orlando B., III and Donald B. Potter. *Brandreth: A History of Brandreth Park, 1851–2010.* Bennington, VT: Two Loon Media, 2011.

Reben, Martha. *The Healing Woods.* New York: Crowell, 1952.

Roth, Richard P. *The Adirondack Guide (1820–1919): Hewing Out an American Occupation.* PhD diss. Syracuse University, 1990.

*Saranac & Raquette Journal.* Brooklyn: S. and R. Topographical Society, 1865.

Schlett, James. *A Not Too Greatly Changed Eden: The Story of the Philosophers' Camp in the Adirondacks.* Ithaca, NY: Cornell University Press, 2015.

Seaver, Frederick J. *Historical Sketches of Franklin County.* Albany, NY: J. B. Lyon, 1918.

Shaw, George and Robert. *Tahawus, Newcomb, & Long Lake, 1842–1900.* Howard I. Becker, ed. Rexford, NY: Private printing, 1955.

Simmons, Louis J. *Mostly Spruce and Hemlock.* Tupper Lake, NY: n.p., 1976.

Smith, H. Perry, ed. *History of Essex County.* Syracuse, NY: D. Mason, 1885.

Stewart, Gustav L., III. *Hewitt Lake and the Sage Family.* Fitchburg, MA: Private printing,1979.

Street, Alfred B. *Woods and Waters; or, The Saranacs and Racket.* New York: M. Doolady, 1860.

Sulavik, Stephen B. *Adirondack: Of Indians and Mountains.* Fleischmanns, NY: Adirondack Museum/Purple Mountain Press, 2005.

Swinney, H. J. *The New York State Firearms Trade, Vol. I.* Tom Rowe, comp. Rochester, NY: Rowe Publications, 2003.

Sylvester, Nathaniel B. *Historical Sketches of Northern New York.* Troy, NY: William H. Young, 1877.

Tatham, David. *Winslow Homer in the Adirondacks.* Syracuse, NY: Syracuse University Press, 1996.

Timm, Ruth. *Raquette Lake: A Time to Remember.* Utica, NY: North Country Books, 1989.

Todd, John. *Long Lake.* Pittsfield, MA: E. P. Little, 1845.

Tolles, Bryant F., Jr. *Resort Hotels of the Adirondacks, The Architecture of a Summer Paradise, 1850–1950.* Lebanon, NH: University Press of New England, 2003.

Trowbridge, Catherine C., comp. and ed. *Durand Camp.* Tucson, AZ: Private printing, 1975.

Van Dyke, Henry. *Little Rivers.* New York: Charles Scribner's Sons, 1895.

Wessels, William L. *Adirondack Profiles.* Lake George, NY: Adirondack Resorts Press, 1961.

White, William Chapman. *Adirondack Country.* Boston: Little, Brown, 1954.

## Boats and Boatbuilding Titles

Adney, Edwin Tappan and Howard I. Chapelle. *The Bark Canoes and Skin Boats of North America.* Washington, DC: Smithsonian Institution Press, 1964.

Bond, Hallie E. *Boats and Boating in the Adirondacks.* Syracuse, NY: Adirondack Museum/Syracuse University Press, 1995.

Brandreth, Franklin B. *Wallace Franklin Emerson, November 1874–October 1953.* Profile sent to author, 1994.

Bray, Maynard, Benjamin A. G. Fuller, and Peter T. Vermilya. *Mystic Seaport Museum Watercraft.* Mystic, CT: Mystic Seaport Museum, 2001.

Brown, Ken. *The Invention of the Board Canoe: The Peterborough Stories from Their Sources.* Peterborough, Ontario: Canadian Canoe Museum, 2001.

Chapelle, Howard I. *American Small Sailing Craft.* New York: W. W. Norton, 1951.

Crowley, William. *Rushton's Rowboats and Canoes: The 1903 Catalog in Perspective.* Camden, ME: Adirondack Museum/International Marine, 1983.

Durant, Kenneth, comp. and ed. *Guide-Boat Days and Ways.* Blue Mountain Lake, NY: Adirondack Museum, 1963.

Durant, Kenneth and Helen. *The Adirondack Guide-Boat.* Camden, ME: Adirondack Museum/International Marine, 1980.

Gardner, John. *The Dory Book.* Mystic, CT: Mystic Seaport Museum, 1987.

———. *Building Classic Small Craft, Commemorative Edition.* Camden, ME: International Marine, 1997.

MacKenzie, Mary. *Albert H. Billings.* Unpublished biography. July 30, 1988.

Manley, Atwood. *Rushton and His Times in American Canoeing.* Syracuse, NY: Adirondack Museum/Syracuse University Press, 1968.

Smith, Mason. "Tests of Integrity: The Boats of a Hundred Years." In *The Adirondack League Club: 1890–1990.* Edward Comstock, Jr., ed. Old Forge, NY: Adirondack League Club, 1990.

Steever, Andrew B. *Oars for Pleasure Rowing: Their Design and Use.* Mystic, CT: Mystic Seaport Museum, 1993.

Stephenson, Gerald F. *John Stephenson and the Famous "Peterborough" Canoes.* Peterborough, Ontario: Peterborough Historical Society, 1987.

## Trade Catalogues

*Boat, Canoe and Yacht Hardware.* Catalogue No. 15., Utica, NY: M. E. Blasier Manufacturing Co., 1907.

Grant, H. Dwight. *The Famous Adirondack Guide Boats.* Boonville, NY: Boonville Herald, circa 1890.

Joyner, F. & Son. *Practical Light Boat and Canoe Builders, Catalogue and Price List for 1885.* Glens Falls, NY: West Bros., 1885.

Rice, Fred M. *Builder of Adirondack Row Boats.* Saranac Lake, NY: Adirondack Enterprise Press, circa 1920s.

Rushton, John Henry. Annual catalogues. Canton, NY: Various publishers, 1888–1916.

## Guidebooks

Bryant, F. H. *Nooks in the North.* New York: New York News, 1887.

Delaware & Hudson. *In the Adirondacks: Illustrated Railway Guide of the Delaware & Hudson and Chateaugay Railroads.* Plattsburgh, NY: Telegram Printing House, 1889.

Farrar, Charles A. J. *From Lake to Lake; or a Trip across Country: A Narrative of the Wilds of Maine.* Boston: Lee & Shepard, 1887.

Hallock, Charles. "Sporting Boats and Canoes." In *Sportsman's Gazetteer and General Guide.* New York: Forest and Stream, 1877.

Richards, T. Addison. *Appleton's Illustrated Hand-Book of American Travel.* New York: D. Appleton, 1857.

Sears, E. S. *Faxon's Illustrated Hand–Book of Summer Travel.* Boston: Charles A. Faxon, 1875.

Stoddard, Seneca Ray. *The Adirondacks: Illustrated.* Albany and Glens Falls, NY: Various publishers, 1874–1886.

Wallace, E. R. *Descriptive Guide to the Adirondacks.* In *The Modern Babes in the Wood* by H. Perry Smith. Hartford, CT: Columbian Book Co., 1872.

———. *Descriptive Guide to the Adirondacks.* New York and Syracuse: Various publishers, 1876–1900.

## Government Publications

Colvin, Verplanck. *Seventh Annual Report of the Topographical Survey of the Adirondack Region of New York to the Year 1879.* Albany, NY: Weed, Parsons, 1880.

Essex County. *Proceedings of the Board of Supervisors of the County of Essex.* Various publishers, 1884–1894.

Goode, G. Brown. *Philadelphia Centennial Exposition, 1876: Catalogue of the Collection.* Washington, DC: Government Printing Office, 1879, Paper 14.

———. "The Fisheries and Fish Culture of the United States of America." In *International Fishery Exhibition, Berlin, 1880.* United States National Museum, Washington, DC: Government Printing Office, 1880, Paper 21, Bulletin 18.

Hamilton County. *Proceedings of the Board of Supervisors of the County of Hamilton.* Various publishers: 1883–1903.

New York State. *Fourteenth Report of the Commissioners of Fisheries.* Albany, NY: Weed, Parsons, 1886.

———. *Annual Report of the Forest Commission of the State of New York for 1891.* Albany, NY: James B. Lyon, 1892.

———. *Annual Report of the Forest Commission of the State of New York for 1893.* 2 vols. Albany, NY: James B. Lyon, 1894.

*New York State Registry of Guides.* Albany, NY: Conservation Department, 1927, 1942.

Strough, A.B. "Forest, Fish, and Game Exhibit." In *New York at the Louisiana Purchase Exposition, St. Louis, 1904.* Delancey M. Ellis, comp. Albany, NY: James B. Lyon, 1907.

## Newspapers

| | |
|---|---|
| *Adirondack Arrow* (Old Forge) | 1942 |
| *Adirondack Daily Enterprise* (Saranac Lake) | 1957–1958, 1966 |
| *Adirondack News* (Newcomb) | 1895 |
| *Adirondack News* (St. Regis Falls) | 1896 |
| *Boonville Herald* | 1880s–1910, 1960 |
| *Elizabethtown Post* | 1885 |
| *Essex County Republican* (Keeseville) | 1892 |
| *Hamilton County News* (Lake Pleasant) | 1982 |
| *Lake Placid News* | 2001 |
| *Morning Herald* (Gloversville) | 1939 |
| *New York Evening Post* | 1880 |
| *New York Times* | 1858 |
| *New-York Tribune* | 1850 |
| *Port Henry Herald* | 1877 |
| *St. Lawrence Plaindealer* (Canton) | 1890 |
| *Saturday Globe* (Utica) | 1904 |
| *Spirit of the Times* (New York) | 1840, 1849 |
| *Syracuse Post-Standard* | 1944 |

| | |
|---|---|
| *Ticonderoga Sentinel* | 1917 |
| *Tupper Lake Free Press* | 1980 |
| *Tupper Lake Free Press and Herald* | 1952 |
| *Warrensburg–Lake George News* | 1962 |
| *Watertown Daily Times* | 1940, 1963, 2004 |
| *Wilkes' Spirit of the Times* (New York) | 1867 |

## Manuscript-Related Collections

Adirondack Museum (now the Adirondack Experience)
  Boatbuilders' Files
  Kenneth and Helen Durant Collection (*The Adirondack Guide-Boat*)
  John Gardner-Kenneth Durant Collection
  Atwood Manley Papers
  Frederick W. Rice Papers
  Stephen B. Sulavik Papers
Adirondack Research Room, Saranac Lake Free Library
  Alfred L. Donaldson Collection
  Frederick W. and Frederick M. Rice Papers
Edward Comstock, Jr. Collection
Lake Placid Public Library
  Mary MacKenzie Papers
Town of Webb Historical Association
  Boatbuilders' Files

# CREDITS AND PERMISSIONS

All photos not otherwise credited are by Stephen B. Sulavik and used by permission.

Photographs and images from The Adirondack Experience (formerly The Adirondack Museum), used by permission.

Photographs from Christopher Woodward, ©2018, used by permission.

Maps of the boatbuilding regions by Nancy Bernstein.

Deck Drawings by Spencer Jenkins.

Boat drawings by Sam F. Manning.

*The Adirondack Guide*, Winslow Homer, 1894. Photograph ©2018 Museum of Fine Arts, Boston, MA Watercolor over graphite pencil on paper. Used by permission.

*An Anxious Moment*, Arthur Fitzwilliam Tait, Photograph ©2018, Michele and Donald D'Amour Museum of Fine Arts, Springfield, MA. Used by permission.

*The Blue Boat*, Winslow Homer, 1892. Photograph ©2018 Museum of Fine Arts, Boston, MA. Watercolor over graphite pencil on paper. Used by permission.

*Boy Fishing*, Winslow Homer, 1892. Photograph ©2018 San Antonio Museum of Art, San Antonio, TX. Watercolor on paper. Used by permission.

*The Painter Eliphalet Terry Fishing from a Boat*, Winslow Homer, 1874. Photograph ©2018 The Century Association, New York, NY. Watercolor on paper, gift of the artist, 1876.

*The Trapper*, Winslow Homer, 1870. Photograph ©2018, Colby College Museum of Art, Waterville, ME. Oil on canvas. Used by permission.

# INDEX